FRENCH VERB PIVOTS

UNLOCKING FRENCH GRAMMAR

FOR BEGINNER TO PRE-INTERMEDIATE LEARNERS

SENTENCE BUILDERS

A lexicogrammar approach

 THE LANGUAGE GYM

Adapted, Created, and Edited by:

Aurélie Lethuilier, Jérôme Nogues & Nadim Cham,

 THE LANGUAGE GYM

About the authors

Nadim Cham has taught for the last five years in England and internationally, both in state and independent schools. He has been teaching for the last two years in Cairo, in a British International School, in which he has obtained outstanding results with his students at iGCSE level using EPI. He thoroughly enjoys collaborating with other practitioners as well as creating and sharing resources which apply the EPI pedagogy developed in this book. Nadim enjoys sports, discovering new technology, international food, and spending time with his family, as well collaborating on fantastic projects such as this book and many others, which contribute to improving the way languages are taught around the world.

Aurélie Lethuilier has taught for 23 years and has been at her current school for 21 years (17 years as Curriculum Leader for Modern Languages). She is very passionate about teaching and learning and loves creating resources that will get the best out of students. She has been using and testing the EPI approach for a few years now and has successfully implemented it amongst her dedicated team of amazing teachers, without whom this journey would not have been possible.

Jérôme Nogues has taught for over 20 years in London and in Shropshire and state and independent schools. He is an EPI enthusiast, Head of Languages and Digital Learning in a small Prep school near Shrewsbury. He has a passion for education technology and its use in and out of the classroom to enhance teaching and learning. He regularly leads CPD sessions for fellow teachers to develop their IT skills face to face or online. When he is not busy working on wonderful projects like this one with amazing people, he enjoys spending time with his family and hitting the road or the trail to chill.

THE LANGUAGE GYM

About the authors (ORIGINAL EDITION)

Gianfranco Conti taught for 25 years at schools in Italy, the UK and in Kuala Lumpur, Malaysia. He has also been a university lecturer, holds a Master's degree in Applied Linguistics and a PhD in metacognitive strategies as applied to second language writing. He is now an author, a popular independent educational consultant and a professional development provider. He has written around 2,000 resources for the TES website, who awarded him the Best Resources Contributor in 2015. He has co-authored the best-selling and influential books for world languages teachers, "The Language Teacher Toolkit", "Breaking the sound barrier: Teaching learners how to listen", in which he puts forth his Listening As Modelling methodology and "Memory: what every language teacher should know". Last but not least, Gianfranco has created the instructional approach known as E.P.I. (Extensive Processing Instruction).

Dylan Viñales has taught for 17 years, in schools in Bath, Beijing and Kuala Lumpur in state, independent and international settings. He lives in Kuala Lumpur. He is fluent in five languages, and gets by in several more. Dylan is, besides a teacher, a professional development provider, specialising in E.P.I., metacognition, teaching languages through music (especially ukulele) and cognitive science. In the last five years, together with Dr Conti, he has driven the implementation of E.P.I. in one of the top international schools in the world: Garden International School. Dylan authors an influential blog on modern language pedagogy in which he supports the teaching of languages through E.P.I.

Esmeralda Salgado has taught for 22 years in schools in Bromley, Chatham and Ely, in both state and independent schools. She is an Advanced Skills Teacher and currently works at King's Ely, as Head of Modern Foreign Languages and Digital Learning Lead. Esmeralda is passionate about the use of digital technology to enhance the learning of languages, as well as using project based learning, all underpinned by E.P.I instruction. Esmeralda also authors her own influential pedagogical blog where she shares resources and reflects on her own practice supported by E.P.I and provides professional development workshops as a language consultant. Finally, Esmeralda is a Silver Winner of the Pearson National Teaching Awards 2022, under the category of Teacher of the Year in a secondary school.

 THE LANGUAGE GYM

Dedication

For Catrina

-Gianfranco

For Ariella & Leonard

-Dylan

For Horatio

-Aurélie

For Inaya

-Nadim

For Luc

-Jérôme

Acknowledgements

Creating a book is a time-consuming yet rewarding endeavour.

Our sincere gratitude to Nicolas Asse Drouet, Laure & Celeste Vaubourg, Lorène, Benjamin, & Victoria Carver, Ken & Adélaïde Herve-Sorreau, and Sabine Sadjian for your help in the recording of the listening audio files: your energy, enthusiasm and passion are clear in every recording and are the reason why the listening sections are such a successful and engaging resource, according to the many students who have been alpha and beta testing the book.

Thanks to Flaticon.com and Mockofun.com for providing access to a limitless library of engaging icons, clipart and images which we have used to make this book more user-friendly than any other Sentence Builders predecessor, with a view to be as engaging as possible for students.

Additionally, our gratitude to the MFL Twitterati for their ongoing support of E.P.I. and the Sentence Builders book series. In particular a shoutout to our team of incredible educators who helped in checking all the units: Darren Lester, Tom Ball, Sabine Sadjian, Joanna Asse Drouet, Sally Solomon, Corinne Lapworth, Lorène Carver, Adélaïde Herve Sorreau, Yusuf Amejee, Laure Vaubourg and Pauline Livreau. It is thanks to your time, patience, professionalism and detailed feedback that we have been able to produce such a refined and highly accurate product.

Merci à tous et à toutes,

Gianfranco, Dylan, Aurélie, Jérôme & Nadim

Introduction

Who is it for?

The French Verb Pivots book is aimed at learners in the **A1-B1 proficiency range**. It was conceived both for classroom and independent use, whatever the method, setting or course, as it offers ample opportunities for practice through a wide range of activities designed to appeal to learners with a variety of cognitive styles and learning preferences.

It can be used to **introduce** the target verbs and associated grammar and lexicogrammar patterns to **absolute beginners**. It can also be useful if you teach **lower-to-intermediate learners** (years 9 to 11 in the U.K.) in order to consolidate, expand and deepen their mastery of those verbs and patterns. The latter learners, in my experience, are often able to master verb formation, but lack **depth of knowledge**, i.e. knowledge of verb **collocations** (which lexis the verbs partner with) and **colligations** (the rules which bind the verbs with what comes before and after them in a sentence).

Why this book?

Based on the premise that second language instruction should be first and foremost about **empowering learners with the ability to convey meaning in the real world** and not to learn grammar for grammar's sake, the book sets out to teach **lexicogrammar** (or pattern grammar), i.e.: the grammar glueing together the **sentence patterns** (or syntactic schemata) that we make use of in order to fulfil **a communicative purpose** (e.g. describing a person; comparing and contrasting people; making arrangements for an evening out; describing one's daily activities, etc.).

I conceived and created this book because **I felt the current trends in modern language teaching were too concerned with the teaching of isolated grammar rules as totally divorced from a communicative context.** Also, I have always found that textbooks, even when used in synergy with their associated workbooks, provide insufficient *multimodal* practice. This is a major shortcoming of traditional grammar instruction at large, as **research shows clearly that the learning of L2 grammar structures must be multimodal for them to be effectively learnt**. Multimodality is one of the most innovative features of this book: the target sentence patterns and morphemes are learnt **across all four language skills**, including speaking and listening, which are usually the most neglected skills.

Why is the book called "French Verb Pivots"?

Verbs constitute the core of every sentence we utter and write. In other words, they are **the 'pivots' around which each sentence patterns develops**. Each verb one selects, as well as the social context and the purpose one selects it for, **constrains the range of lexical and grammatical choices we can make in producing a sentence**. So, for instance, using the verb *vouloir* to express what one wants to do will require the use of *vouloir + infinitive + noun* (e.g. je veux jouer au foot).

This book aims at teaching how to use the most useful and frequent French verbs in everyday communication in terms of how to:

- **manipulate them effectively** (inflectional morphology, e.g. how to conjugate the verbs in the present)
- **deal with the linguistic choices they trigger** (pattern grammar, i.e.: the constructions associated with each verb)
- **master the rules which bind words together** within a given syntactic pattern (colligations, i.e.: how each word affects the next; for instance how determiners or adjectives agree in gender and number with nouns)

As it is clear from (1), (2) and (3) above, exploring how a verb works also **entails learning a lot of other grammar and lexicogrammar rules which emerge organically from the communicative context at hand.** For instance, teaching the verb *aller* will lead to learning articled prepositions (e.g. je vais/il va/nous allons/etc. **au** ciné), possessives (e.g. avec **mon/mes/son/ses**/etc. parents/amis/frères/etc.) and even how to form a final clause (e.g. je vais au centre commercial **pour acheter un nouvel ordinateur**).

What's in the book?

The French book includes 9 macro-units, each focusing on a different verb or verb set in the present tense. The verbs are: *Avoir, Être, Aller, Faire, Aimer, Jouer, Mettre, Prendre* and *Modal Verbs*. Each macro-unit centres on a key verb and explores and drills in, through a wide range of engaging and enjoyable **multimodal** tasks, all the possible patterns associated with it deemed to be learnable at this level of proficiency. Every macro-unit includes a variety of sub-units for a total of 62 sub-units. For instance, the unit on *'Avoir'* is broken down into the following sub-units:

1. **Avoir + un/une + noun** (What animals I have)
2. **Avoir + un/une + noun + adjective** (What animal I have and its colour)
3. **Avoir (all persons) + noun + relative clause** (What animal one has)
4. **Avoir + noun** (How one feels)
5. **Avoir + classroom objects + adjective** (What school items one has)
6. **Avoir + clothing item + adjective** (What clothes one has)
7. **Avoir + number + plural nouns + adjectives** (How many things one has)
8. **Avoir + number + ans** (Telling one's age)

Each macro-unit **ends with a games unit that brings all the content of that unit together** and consolidates it through written and oral retrieval-practice tasks.

How does the book work?

Each macro-unit starts 'small' with the target verb being learnt within very basic sentence patterns and in the first person only. As each unit progresses **the target verbs are modelled in sentence patterns which gradually increase in length and complexity.** In order to enhance transferability of learning and lexical depth, each verb is also practised with a variety of lexical sets. For instance, the verb *Avoir* is practised with animals, classroom objects, clothes, emotional and physical states, age, etc.

Task-essentialness is pervasive: each unit contains a plethora of tasks which elicit the application of the target grammar structure multiple times.

Recycling is carefully engineered to allow for repeated receptive and productive processing of the target language items within the same units and across the whole book. As mentioned above, each new unit builds on the previous one in a 'what I know + 1" fashion, so that the stem of a new sentence builder was covered in the previous sub-unit. Also, every macro-unit ends with a massive recap of everything covered thus far.

Subconscious learning through input flood and repeated processing works in synergy with explicit learning in the way of (1) awareness-raising boxes at the beginning of each sub-unit, (2) tasks focusing the students' attention on the target features and (3) metacognitive activities eliciting self-reflection and self-evaluation.

Traditional grammar and lexicogrammar intersect throughout the whole book, as, in order for the learners to be able to become creative with each sentence pattern, they must also master the manipulation of the changeable items in each sentence such as verbs, adjectives, pronouns determiners, etc. **The teaching of grammar arises organically from the need to enhance the generative power of each target sentence pattern** – this is a major innovation of this book.

The book is very mindful of cognitive load. Hence, each instructional sequence gradually increases the cognitive challenge, with receptive activities in the initial section of each sub-unit paving the way for the productive ones located at the end and **with each task priming the next**. It goes without saying that the repeated processing and the constant recycling also makes it easier for the content to become effortlessly entrenched.

How can one supplement this book to enhance its impact?

Please note that this book is best used in synergy with language-gym.com and sentencebuilders.com. Both websites feature self-marking games and activities based on its content.

 **THE LANGUAGE GYM**

TABLE OF CONTENTS

 THE LANGUAGE GYM

THE LANGUAGE GYM

THE LANGUAGE GYM

UNIT 1 – AVOIR

J'	ai
Tu	as
Il / Elle / On	a
Nous	avons
Vous	avez
Ils / Elles	ont

POSSESSION

J'ai **un** crayon

STATES

J'ai **froid**

AGE

J'ai **trois ans**

Avoir *To have* – FIRST PERSON			
Masculine nouns			
J'ai *I have*	**un** *a*	**cheval** *horse* **chat** *cat* **chien** *dog* **oiseau** *bird* **perroquet** *parrot* **poisson** *fish*	**qui s'appelle Rémy** *that is called Rémy*
Feminine nouns			
J'ai *I have*	**une** *a*	**araignée** *spider* **chèvre** *goat* **gerbille** *gerbil* **poule** *hen* **tortue** *turtle* **vache** *cow*	**qui s'appelle Marie** *that is called Marie*

LANGUAGE AWARENESS - NOUNS IN FRENCH

The verb ***avoir*** (to have) is used in a similar way to English: to describe possession.

It is important to know that in French, every noun (object/thing) is either **masculine** or **feminine**. The indefinite article "a" is translated as either *un* or *une* depending on the gender of the noun.

Un poisson *a fish* is a masculine noun, but we only know it thanks to *un*

Une vache *a cow* is a feminine noun, but we only know it thanks to *une*

Tip: Recognising when a noun is **masculine** or **feminine** in French is not an exact science. Nevertheless, a study by McGill University has shown that 80% ending in **'-e'** are **feminine**.

1. Match

Un oiseau	A cat
Une souris	A bird
Un poisson	A mouse
Une vache	A fish
Une chèvre	A cow
Une tortue	A dog
Un cheval	A spider
Un chien	A goat
Un chat	A horse
Une araignée	A turtle

2. Listen and complete with the missing indefinite article (*un/une*)

a. J'ai ___ chien qui s'appelle Raoul

b. J'ai ___ chèvre qui s'appelle Caramel

c. J'ai ___ chat qui s'appelle Félix

d. J'ai ___ poule qui s'appelle Amélie

e. J'ai ___ poisson qui s'appelle Oscar

f. J'ai ___ vache qui s'appelle Marguerite

g. J'ai ___ gerbille qui s'appelle Théa

3. Break the flow

a. J'aiunevacheetunperroquet

b. J'aiunchienetunetortue

c. J'aiunpoissonetunchat

d. J'aiunearaignéeetunchien

e. J'aiunchatetunepoule

f. J'aiunpoissonetunoiseau

g. J'aiunchienetunevache

h. J'aiunechèvreetunegerbille

4. Spot and correct the errors

a. J'ai une cheval qui s'appelle Raoul

b. J'ai une chien qui s'appelle Patrice

c. J'ai un tortue qui s'appelle Anna

d. J'ai une perroquet qui s'appelle Alex

e. J'ai une poisson qui s'appelle Némo

f. J'ai un chèvre qui s'appelle Lise

g. J'ai une gerbille qui s'appelle Paula

h. J'ai une chat qui s'appelle Latte

5. Listen and complete the table following the same pattern in the example

	Subject & Verb	Indefinite Article	Noun
e.g.	*J'ai*	*une*	*vache*
a.			
b.			
c.			
d.			
e.			
f.			

THE LANGUAGE GYM

3

6. Guess the missing words, then listen to check if you got them correct

a. J'ai u__ c__ __ __ __ __

b. J'ai u__ c__ __ __ __

c. J'ai u__ __ a__ __ __ __ __ __ __

d. J'ai u__ __ t__ __ __ __ __

e. J'ai u__ c__ __ __

f. J'ai u__ __ v__ __ __ __

g. J'ai u__ __ p__ __ __ __

h. J'ai u__ p__ __ __ __ __ __ __ __

7. Complete with 'a', 'e', 'i' or 'o'

a. J'ai un chev__l et un perr__quet

b. J'ai une t__rtue et un chi__n

c. J'ai une v__che et un l__pin

d. J'ai un ch__t et un oise__u

e. J'ai un perr__quet et un ch__en

f. J'ai une chèvr__ et une ar__ignée

g. J'ai une p__ule , un ch__t et un __iseau

h. J'ai une araigné__, une s__uris et une vach__

8. Guided translation

a. *I have a dog and a cat*   J'_____ u__ c_____ et u__ c_____

b. *I have a parrot and a fish*   J'_____ u__ p_____ et u__ p_____

c. *I have a horse and a gerbil*   J'_____ u__ c_____ et u___ g_____

d. *I have a spider and a goat*   J'_____ u__ a_____ et u__ c_____

e. *I have a cat, a dog and a bird*   J'_____ u__ c_____ , u__ c_____ et u__ o_____

f. *I have a turtle, a spider and a cat* J'_____ u__ t_____ , u__ a_____ et u__ c_____

g. *I have a gerbil and a horse*   J'_____ u___ g_____ et u__ c_____

9. Translate into French, then listen and check your answers

a. I have a dog called Philippe and a parrot called Antoine

b. I have a cat called Max and a dog called Julien

c. I have a cow called Sylvie and a goat called Nicole

d. I have a rabbit called Mario and a cat called Luigi

e. I have a parrot called Dylan and a gerbil called Daniella

f. I have a turtle called Marina and a bird called Véro

g. I have a horse called Francis and a dog called Rex

h. I have a gerbil called Lola and a spider called Claire

THE LANGUAGE GYM

J'ai *I have*	**un** *a*	**canard** *duck* **chat** *cat* **cheval** *horse* **chien** *dog* **lapin** *rabbit* **oiseau** *bird* **poisson** *fish*	**bleu** *blue* **blanc** *white* **gris** *grey* **noir** *black* **vert** *green* **violet** *purple*	**qui s'appelle**	**Marc**
		These colours stay the same in masculine & feminine	**jaune** *yellow* **marron** *brown* **orange** *orange* **rose** *pink* **rouge** *red*		**Marjorie**
	une *a*	**araignée** *spider* **chèvre** *goat* **gerbille** *gerbil* **poule** *hen* **tortue** *turtle* **vache** *cow*	**bleue** *blue* **blanche** *white* **grise** *grey* **noire** *black* **verte** *green* **violette** *purple*		

LANGUAGE AWARENESS – ADJECTIVAL AGREEMENT (GENDER)

As mentioned in the last section, in French all nouns are either **masculine** or **feminine.**

- **Un** poisson or **une** vache

When a noun is feminine, the adjective that follows usually needs to change its ending. **"E"** is usually the **feminine** ending:

- **Un** oiseau noir   *A black bird*
- **Une** tortue noir**e**   *A black turtle*

With a slight exception for 'blanc' which becomes blan**che** and 'violet' which becomes viole**tte**

This notion is called **gender agreement.**

Adjectives already ending in an **"e"**, like *jaune, orange, rose, rouge + marron,* **do not** change their ending:

- **Un** canard jaune**,** rose et orang**e**   *A yellow, pink and orange duck*
- **Une** poule rouge et marron   *A red and brown hen*

Adjectives in French are placed after the noun!

Je suis <u>un</u> lapin <u>blanc</u>

Ssssais-tu que tout le livre est en <u>noir</u> et <u>blanc</u>?

C'est vrai…

1. Match

Une gerbille grise	An orange bird
Une poule rouge	A brown rabbit
Un oiseau orange	A red hen
Un poisson rouge	A grey gerbil
Une vache blanche	A red fish
Une chèvre noire	A grey cat
Une araignée jaune	A white cow
Un cheval noir	A black goat
Un chien blanc	A yellow spider
Une tortue verte	A green turtle
Un lapin marron	A black horse
Un chat gris	A white dog

2. Select the correct adjective

	Masculine Adjective	Feminine Adjective
Un oiseau	bleu	bleue
Une vache	violet	violette
Un poisson	noir	noire
Un chien	blanc	blanche
Une poule	noir	noire
Une chèvre	gris	grise
Un lapin	blanc	blanche
Une gerbille	noir	noire
Un cheval	gris	grise
Une araignée	vert	verte

3. Faulty translation: fix the English

a. Une gerbille jaune   *A blue gerbil*

b. Un poisson bleu   *A blue cat*

c. Un lapin marron   *A red rabbit*

d. Une chèvre blanche   *A green goat*

e. Un chat blanc   *A white dog*

f. Une tortue verte   *A brown turtle*

g. Un canard gris   *A green duck*

h. Une araignée noire   *A black cat*

i. Une poule rouge   *A pink hen*

4. Likely or Unlikely: write L or U depending on whether you are likely to find animals of that colour

a. J'ai un poisson bleu et vert

b. J'ai un chat blanc et noir

c. J'ai un cheval rose et orange

d. J'ai une araignée noire

e. J'ai un pingouin blanc et noir

f. J'ai une gerbille bleue

g. J'ai une chèvre rouge

h. J'ai une tortue bleue

i. J'ai un oiseau vert

5. Listen and complete the gaps with *un* or *une*

a. J'ai _____ chat marron

b. J'ai _____ lapin blanc

c. J'ai _____ gerbille marron

d. J'ai _____ tortue verte

e. J'ai _____ poisson rouge et bleu

f. J'ai _____ poule blanche

g. J'ai _____ oiseau bleu et blanc

6. Translate into English

a. J'ai un poisson rouge et bleu

b. J'ai une tortue verte

c. J'ai une gerbille blanche

d. J'ai un lapin blanc et noir

e. J'ai une araignée bleue

f. J'ai un oiseau jaune et vert

g. J'ai une chèvre grise

h. J'ai un cheval blanc et marron

THE LANGUAGE GYM

7. Spot and correct the mistakes

a. J'ai une gerbille blanc

b. J'ai un chèvre rouge

c. J'ai une araignée vert

d. J'ai un poule rouge

e. J'ai une poisson bleu

f. J'ai un chat blanc et noire

g. J'ai une oiseau jaune

h. J'ai un poisson rosé

i. J'ai un pingouin blanche et noir

8. Listen and cross out the wrong words

a. J'ai un **chien/chienne** noir

b. J'ai **un/une** oiseau bleu

c. J'ai **un/une** souris verte

d. J'ai un pingouin **blanc/blanche** et **noir/noire**

e. J'ai **un/une** chèvre marron

f. J'ai une gerbille **blanc/blanche**

g. J'ai **un/une** tortue bleue

h. J'ai une araignée **vert/verte**

i. J'ai un cheval **gris/grise**

9. Insert *un* or *une* as appropriate

a. J'ai _____ poule blanche

b. J'ai _____ poisson rouge

c. J'ai _____ oiseau vert et bleu

d. J'ai _____ chat blanc

e. J'ai _____ gerbille marron

f. J'ai _____ araignée noire

g. J'ai _____ chèvre blanche

h. J'ai _____ chat orange

10. Missing letter challenge

a. J'ai un cheval noi__ qui s'appelle Laurel

b. J'ai un oiseau ros__ qui s'appelle David

c. J'ai une gerbille orang__ qui s'appelle Laura

d. J'ai un chien blan__ qui s'appelle Alphonse

e. J'ai une tortue vert__ qui s'appelle Lily

f. J'ai un chat jaun__ qui s'appelle Robert

g. J'ai un canard ver__ qui s'appelle Donald

11. Slalom listening: follow the speaker from top to bottom and connect the boxes accordingly. You'll need to listen till the end to complete each one as the word order is different in French :)

e.g. Je m'appelle Céleste. J'ai un chien marron et une tortue.

e.g. Céleste	a - Anne	b - Marius	c - Esmeralda	d - Benjamin
My name is Céleste.	My name is Anne.	My name is Marius.	My name is Esmeralda.	My name is Benjamin.
I have a yellow	**I have a brown**	I have a black	I have a white	I have an orange
cat and a	parrot and a	**dog**	gerbil and a	horse and a
pink	**and a**	black	yellow	blue
penguin	bird	**turtle**	cow	fish

12. Guided translation

a. J'__ __ u __ oiseau n__ __ __ __

I have a black bird

b. J'__ __ u __ perroquet b__ __ __ __

I have a blue parrot

c. J'__ __ u __ chat bla__ __ __ ...

I have a white cat...

d. ...q__ i s'__ppe__ __ __ Miaou

...that is called Miaou

e. J'__ __ u __ pingouin noir et b__ __ __ __

I have a black and blue penguin

f. J'__ __ u __ __ tortue verte

I have a green turtle

g. J'__ __ u __ __ chèvre m__ __ __ __ __

I have a brown goat

	Verb	Indefinite article	Noun	Adjective
a.	J'ai			
b.	J'ai			
c.	J'ai			
d.	J'ai			
e.	J'ai			
f.	J'ai			
g.	J'ai			
h.	J'ai			

14. Tangled translation: translate into French

a. *I have* un *dog* qui s'appelle Raphaël

b. J'ai *a cat* qui s'appelle Marie

c. J'ai *a bird* vert et *white*

d. J'ai *a* gerbille *black*

e. *I have* une araignée *green* qui *is called* Sophie

f. J'ai un oiseau *blue and* jaune

g. J'ai *a* poisson *orange that* s'appelle Dory

h. J'ai *two* animaux: *a* araignée et *a* cheval

i. J'ai un *rabbit* blanc et *a* chèvre *brown*

15. Translate into French, then listen to check your answers

a. I have a green turtle

b. I have a yellow bird

c. I have a black dog

d. I have a red and yellow fish

e. I have a white duck

f. I have a cow that is called Lola

g. I have a black horse that is called Martin

h. I have a blue spider that is called Sisi

16. Reflection: now make some notes, in your own words, about what you have learnt so far

I use "un" for...

I use "une" for...

I add an "e" to the adjective ending to make it...

Adjectives like "orange", "rouge" and "marron"...

I have also learnt...

1.3 ALL PERSONS OF AVOIR + UN/UNE + NOUN + RELATIVE CLAUSE
(SAYING WHAT ANIMAL ONE HAS)

				Masculine nouns		
J'ai	*I have*			ami	*friend*	
Tu as	*You have*			cheval	*horse*	
Il a	*He has*			chat	*cat*	
Elle a	*She has*	un *a*		chien	*dog*	qui s'appelle Léo
On a	*One has*			perroquet	*parrot*	
				oiseau	*bird*	
Nous avons	*We have*			poisson	*fish*	
				Feminine nouns		
Vous avez	*You guys/girls have*			amie	*friend*	
				araignée	*spider*	
Ils ont	*They have*	une *a*		chèvre	*goat*	qui s'appelle Marie
				gerbille	*gerbil*	
Elles ont	*They have (f)*			poule	*hen*	
				souris	*mouse*	
				tortue	*turtle*	

LANGUAGE AWARENESS

CONJUGATING *AVOIR*

The verb *avoir* (to have) has different forms (or **conjugations**) depending on whom we are talking about.

e.g. *J'ai* means "I have" whereas *tu as* means "you have". This is different from English where you only have two options: "have" or "has".

ILS & ELLES

These are **masculine** and **feminine subject pronouns.** They are used if talking about a group made up **entirely** of boys or girls. For example:

• **Elles ont un chien**
They (group of girls) have a dog

If the group is masculine or mixed then we use the masculine subject pronouns: *ils*

• **Ils ont un perroquet**
They (group of boys or mixed group) have a parrot

SUBJECT PRONOUNS

'*Je*, tu, il, elle, on, nous, vous, ils, elles*' are called **subject pronouns**.

* We use **J'** in front of a word starting by a vowel: a, e, i, o, u **and** y.

ON & NOUS

Nous is a **plural** pronoun: this is the *we* you use mostly in **written** form, or when you want to be **more formal**.

On is a more informal *we*, used predominantly in **speech** or **casual** writing (in emails to your friends for example). This is also a **singular** pronoun which is followed by the same form of the verb as singular il or elle.

e.g. Nous **avons** une poule rouge

On **a** un oiseau et une tortue.

> Vous avez un animal?

> On a un poisson rouge

1. Match

Tu as	You guys have
Vous avez	I have
Il a	We have
Elles ont	You have
J'ai	They (f) have
Nous avons	He has

2. One of three

	1	2	3
J'	avons	ai	ont
Mon frère	a	ai	ont
Ils	ai	avez	ont
Vous	ai	avez	as
Il	avons	ont	a
Nous	avons	ai	a
Elles	a	ont	avons
Tu	as	avez	ont

3. Translate into English

a. J'ai une tortue verte

b. Tu as un chien?

c. Nous avons un chat blanc

d. Vous avez un cheval?

e. Ils ont une souris blanche

f. Elles ont une araignée?

g. Elle a un perroquet

h. Tu as quels animaux?

i. Nous avons un canard et un lapin

4. Faulty translation: fix the English translation

a. Nous avons un cheval	They have a horse
b. Tu as une gerbille	He has a gerbil
c. Elle a une tortue	They have a turtle
d. Il a une souris	I have a mouse
e. Tu as une araignée?	Do I have a spider?
f. J'ai un canard	We have a duck
g. Elles ont un chien	I have a dog
h. Vous avez un animal?	Do we have an animal?
i. Ils ont un chat et un chien	You have a cat and a dog

5. Listen and complete

a. Nous a__ons un chat

b. Elles o__t un lapin

c. Vous __vez une tortue?

d. J' a__ un chat

e. Tu __s une souris?

f. Mes parents on__ un chat noir

g. Mon ami __ une araignée

h. Tu a__ un animal?

i. Elles n'on__ pas d'animaux

j. J'_i un chien blanc, Lily

6. Spot and correct the mistakes in French

a. Nous avions une tortue	We have a turtle
b. J'avez un lapin	I have a rabbit
c. Elles on un chat noir	They (f) have a black cat
d. Tu a un chien?	Do you have a dog?
e. Ils avez une gerbille	They (m) have a gerbil
f. Il n'ai pas d'animaux	He doesn't have animals
g. Tu ont quel animal?	What animal do you have?
h. Mon ami avez un cheval	My friend has a horse
i. On ont un poisson bleu	One has a blue fish

THE LANGUAGE GYM

7. Find the French translation and write it next to the English prompts

a. We have a dog c. You have a duck e. They (m) have a rabbit g. They (f) have a bird

b. I have a cat d. He has a fish f. You guys have a horse h. We have a spider

v	a	g	e	n	i	n	t	u	a	s	u	n	c	a	n	a	r	d	o	p	e
j'	s	u	i	r	n	i	p	a	l	n	u	t	n	o	s	l	i	a	m	e	t
a	o	w	n	j	a	v	e	r	t	v	a	l	j	e	a	n	c	o	s	e	t
i	d	k	o	e	l	l	e	s	o	n	t	u	n	o	i	s	e	a	u	o	l
u	m	t	y	c	h	a	i	r	s	a	t	e	m	t	y	t	a	b	l	e	s
n	o	u	s	a	v	o	n	s	u	n	c	h	i	e	n	t	f	o	r	e	t
c	e	e	s	u	o	h	e	h	t	n	o	s	s	i	o	p	n	u	a	l	i
h	e	s	t	i	n	y	i	d	r	e	a	m	a	d	r	e	a	m	m	a	s
a	d	e	é	n	g	i	a	r	a	e	n	u	s	n	o	v	a	s	u	o	n
t	r	e	h	t	o	n	a	y	a	d	r	e	h	t	o	n	a	e	r	o	m
y	a	d	e	n	v	o	u	s	a	v	e	z	u	n	c	h	e	v	a	l	o

8. Put the correct pronouns *j'*, *tu*, *il/elle*, *nous*, *vous*, *ils/elles* in the brackets

a. (_____) avons un chien

b. (_____) a une souris

c. (_____) avez un poisson à la maison?

d. (_____) ai une araignée

e. (_____) as un cheval?

f. (_____) a un animal à la maison?

g. (_____) ont une poule et un chat?

Remember:

J'	I
Tu	*You*
Il/Elle	*He/She*
Nous	*We*
Vous	*You guys*
Ils/Elles	*They*

9. Provide the correct form of *AVOIR*

a. J'__ __

b. Tu __ __

c. Elle __

d. Nous __ __ __ __ __

e. Vous __ __ __ __

f. Ils __ __ __

10. Dictation: complete with the missing forms of *AVOIR*

a. J'__ __ un perroquet qui s'appelle Patrice

b. Nous __ __ __ __ __ une tortue qui s'appelle Lola

c. Elles __ __ __ un chien qui s'appelle Bill

d. On __ une souris qui s'appelle Susie

e. Ils __ __ __ un cheval?

f. Tu __ __ une chèvre?

g. Il __ un chien et un chat à la maison

h. Vous __ __ __ __ un oiseau bleu et jaune

i. Mon ami __ un pingouin qui s'appelle Nils

11. Translate into French

a. He has a white cat

b. I have a black horse

c. You have a yellow fish

d. He has a green mouse

e. She has a blue spider

f. We have a brown goat

g. They (f) have a white gerbil

h. We have a black and white rabbit

i. Do you guys have an animal?

 THE LANGUAGE GYM

1.4 AVOIR + NOUN *(SAYING HOW ONE FEELS)*

J'ai	Real meaning		Literal Translation
Tu as	**chaud**	*hot*	*to have heat*
Il a Elle a On a Mon frère (brother) a	**froid**	*cold*	*to have cold*
	faim	*hungry*	*to have hunger*
Ma sœur (sister) a	**peur**	*scared*	*to have fear*
Nous avons	**soif**	*thirsty*	*to have thirst*
Vous avez	**sommeil**	*sleepy*	*to have sleep*
Ils ont Elles ont	**mal à la tête** *a headache* **mal à l'estomac** *a stomachache* **mal aux dents** *a toothache*		*to have 'pain of head'* *to have 'pain of stomach'* *to have 'pain of teeth'*

Author's note: *J'ai mal à la tête / à l'estomac / aux dents* actually means *"I have"* a headache / a stomachache / a toothache, as opposed to the other expressions above (*chaud* / *froid* / faim…) which translate into English as *"I am…"*

LANGUAGE AWARENESS

AVOIR OU NE PAS AVOIR? TO "BE" OR NOT TO "BE"?

The expressions above are very useful, idiomatic and commonly used. They all take the verb *avoir* in French, but they nearly all translate in English as "to be".

• **J'ai faim**	*I **am** hungry*	literally:	*I have hunger*
• **Tu as froid?**	***Are** you cold?*	literally:	*Do you have cold?*
• **Mon chien a soif**	*My dog **is** thirsty*	literally:	*My dog has thirst*
• **Nous avons peur**	*We **are** scared*	literally:	*We have fear*
• **Elles ont sommeil**	*They **are** sleepy*	literally:	*They have dream*

Suis-je un vrai pingouin?

Oui, pourquoi?

Parce que j'ai froid!

THE LANGUAGE GYM

1. Match

J'ai peur	I am cold
J'ai faim	I am thirsty
Nous avons froid	I am hungry
J'ai soif	We are cold
Nous avons soif	We are hungry
J'ai froid	I am sleepy
Nous avons peur	We are thirsty
J'ai chaud	I am hot
J'ai sommeil	We are scared
Nous avons faim	I am scared

2. Cross out the wrong verb

e.g. **Ma mère a/~~ai~~ faim**   *My mother is hungry*

a. J'ai/avons soif   *I am thirsty*

b. Nous a/avons sommeil   *We are sleepy*

c. Tu as/ont froid?   *Are you cold?*

d. Il ai/a peur   *He is scared*

e. Mes parents sommes/ont chaud   *My parents are hot*

f. Vous as/avez sommeil?   *Are you guys sleepy?*

g. On avez/a faim   *We are hungry*

3. Missing letter challenge

a. Nous avon__ peur

b. Ils n'on__ pas soif

c. Vous av__z faim?

d. Je n'__i pas peur

e. Tu a__ froid?

f. Mes parents o__t chaud

g. J'a__ peur des araignées

h. Tu __s sommeil?

i. Elles n'o__t pas froid

4. Faulty translation: fix the English translation

a. Vous avez soif?   *Are you hungry?*

b. J'ai peur   *He is scared*

c. David a chaud   *David is cold*

d. Marie a froid   *Marie is sleepy*

e. Tu as faim?   *Are you guys hungry?*

f. Nous avons sommeil   *We are hot*

g. Je n'ai pas chaud   *I am not sleepy*

h. Vous avez froid?   *Are they cold?*

i. Elles ont faim?   *Are they scared?*

5. Multiple choice: select which one you hear, then translate the sentence into English

a. Nous avons **faim / peur / soif**

b. J'ai **sommeil / chaud / froid**

c. Vous avez **froid / peur / faim?**

d. Marie a **froid / peur / chaud**

e. Nous avons **froid / chaud / sommeil**

f. Mes grands-parents ont **chaud / sommeil / froid**

g. Ma tante a **sommeil / faim / peur**

h. Elle a **chaud / soif / peur?**

THE LANGUAGE GYM

13

6. Gapped translation: listen and complete the translation

a. My aunt Véronique is very _____ of cats

b. Today we are very _____

c. My friends are always very _____

d. My dad is often _____

e. I am sometimes _____ at school

f. We are _____ today

g. Are you guys _____?

7. Spot and correct the mistakes

a. Nous avons pure

b. J'ai faime

c. Elles on soif

d. Tu as frod?

e. Vouse avez chaud

f. David n'as pas sommeil

g. Tu avez faim?

8. Complete with the missing forms of *AVOIR*

a. J' __ __ peur des araignées

b. Nous __ __ __ __ __ faim aujourd'hui

c. Ils __ __ __ froid

d. Mon frère __ chaud

e. Tu __ __ sommeil?

f. Nous __ __ __ __ __ faim

g. Elle __ sommeil

h. Elles __ __ __ peur *du noir (of the dark)*

i. J' __ __ chaud

9. Guided translation

a. J'__ __ p __ __ __ __
I am scared

b. Nous a __ __ __ __ __ f __ __ __ __
We are hungry

c. Il __ c __ __ __ __ __
He is hot

d. Elles o __ __ s __ __ __ __ __ __ __
They (f) are sleepy

e. Vous a __ __ __ s __ __ __ __?
Are you guys thirsty?

f. Tu a __ f __ __ __ __ __
You are cold

10. Translate into French, then listen to check your answers

a. I am hungry

b. Luc is thirsty

c. We are scared

d. They (f) are hot

e. You are sleepy

f. I am cold

g. They (m) are thirsty

h. We are hungry

THE LANGUAGE GYM

11. Match

J'ai mal à la tête	*I have a toothache*
J'ai mal à l'estomac	*I have a headache*
J'ai mal aux dents	*I have a stomachache*
J'ai froid	*I am thirsty*
J'ai chaud	*I am hungry*
J'ai peur	*I am cold*
J'ai faim	*I am scared*
J'ai soif	*I am hot*

12. Cross out the wrong verb

e.g. Ma mère **a/ai** mal à la tête
My mother has a headache

a. J'**ai/avons** mal à l'estomac
I have a stomachache

b. Aujourd'hui il **a/avez** mal aux dents
Today he has a toothache

c. Tu **ont/as** mal à la tête?
Do you have a headache?

d. On **ai/a** mal à l'estomac
We have a stomachache

e. Mes parents **avons/ont** mal aux dents
My parents have a toothache

13. Missing letter challenge

a. Nous avon__ mal à la tête

b. Tu n'a__ pas mal aux dents

c. Vous av__z mal à l'estomac?

d. Nous n'av__ns pas mal à la tête

e. Tu __s mal à la tête?

f. Mon ami __ mal aux dents

g. J'__i mal à la tête

h. Ils __nt mal aux dents

i. Elles n'o__t pas mal à l'estomac

14. Faulty translation: fix the French translation

a. *Are you hungry?*	Vous avez mal aux dents?
b. *He is scared*	Il a mal à la tête
c. *Gian is cold*	Gian a faim
d. *Lise has a headache*	Lise à mal à l'estomac
e. *Do you have a toothache?*	Tu as mal à la tête?
f. *We have a headache*	Nous avons mal aux dents
g. *He is sleepy*	Il a chaud
h. *Are you guys hot?*	Vous avez faim?
i. *We have a headache*	Ils ont mal à la tête

15. Translate into French

a. My mother is cold and she has a stomachache

b. I am sleepy and I have a headache

c. My parents have a headache and they are hot

d. Marie is hot and she has a headache

e. We have a toothache

f. My sister has a stomachache and she is cold

g. My father is hot and he has a headache

16. Listen and translate into English

a.

b.

c.

d.

e.

f.

g.

h.

1.5 AVOIR + INDEFINITE ARTICLE + CLASSROOM OBJECTS + ADJECTIVE
(SAYING WHAT SCHOOL ITEMS ONE HAS)

J'ai	un cahier	an exercise book		
	un cartable	a schoolbag	bleu	blue
Tu as	un crayon	a pencil	blanc	white
	un feutre	a felt tip	noir	black
Il a	un livre	a book	vert	green
Elle a	un stylo	a pen		
On a			jaune	yellow
Mon frère (brother) a	These colours stay the same in masculine & feminine forms		orange	orange
Ma sœur (sister) a			rouge	red
			rose	pink
Nous avons				
	une gomme	a rubber	bleue	blue
Vous avez	une paire de ciseaux	a pair of scissors	blanche	white
	une règle	a ruler	noire	black
Ils ont	une trousse	a pencil case	verte	green
Elles ont				

LANGUAGE AWARENESS

ADJECTIVAL GENDER AGREEMENT IN FRENCH

All nouns in French are either masculine or feminine (generally ending in -e).

- **Un stylo**   • **Une gomme**

When we want to describe a noun (such as colours), we must use an **adjective**.

Gender Agreement means that if a noun is masculine, the adjective describing it must be in the masculine form too. Similarly, if a noun is feminine its adjective must be in the feminine form too:

HOW DO WE MAKE ADJECTIVES AGREE?

As a rule of thumb, to make an adjective agree with a feminine word, add an **-e** to the end of the adjective.

- • J'ai **un stylo** bleu   • J'ai **une gomme** bleue

There are, however, exceptions! For colours, **blanc** becomes blan**che** and **violet** becomes **violette**

- • J'ai **un** crayon **blanc**   • J'ai **une** trousse **blanche**

Furthermore, as we have seen earlier, adjectives already ending in an **"e"**, like *jaune, orange, rose, rouge + marron,* __do not__ change their ending:

- • J'ai **un** cahier **orange**   • J'ai **une** règle **orange**

- • J'ai **un** feutre **jaune**   • J'ai **une** paire de ciseaux **jaune**

Où gardes-tu tes crayons?

Quoi?

Dans ma « trourse »

Trourse = combo of 'une trousse' & 'un ours'(bear)

THE LANGUAGE GYM

1. Complete with the missing verb

a. J'_____ une trousse marron

b. Il _____ un stylo rouge

c. Nous _____ une règle blanche

d. Tu _____ une paire de ciseaux?

e. Vous _____ quoi dans votre cartable?

f. On _____ un livre blanc et noir

g. Elles _____ un crayon bleu

2. Spot and correct the grammar mistakes: then listen and check your answers

a. J'ai un gomme jaune

b. Nous avons une règle blanc

c. Ils ont un trousse noire

d. Elle a une livre orange

e. J'ai un crayone rose

f. Mon frère a un cartable verte

g. Elles ont un rose cahier

3. Guess the sentences

a. J'_ _ u_ _ g_ _ _ _ b_ _ _ _ _ _

b. E_ _ _ a u_ s_ _ _ _ n_ _ _

c. I_ a u_ _ t_ _ _ _ _ _ _ j_ _ _ _

d. V_ _ _ a_ _ _ u_ f_ _ _ _ _ r_ _ _ _?

e. N_ _ _, i_ a u_ c_ _ _ _ _ _ _ _ _ _ v_ _ _

f. T_ a_ u_ s_ _ _ _ o_ _ _ _ _?

g. E_ _ _ _ o_ _ u_ _ r_ _ _ b_ _ _ _ _ _

4. Translate into French, then listen and check your answers

a. We have a white rubber

b. I have a white schoolbag

c. She has a red pencil case

d. They (f) have a pink pair of scissors

e. He has a red pen

f. Do you have a green exercise book?

g. We have a white and blue schoolbag

h. Do you guys have an orange exercise book?

THE LANGUAGE GYM

1.6 AVOIR + INDEFINITE ARTICLE + CLOTHING ITEM + ADJECTIVE
(SAYING WHAT CLOTHES ONE HAS)

J'ai	un chapeau	*a hat*	blanc	white
	un costume	*a suit*	bleu	blue
Tu as	un manteau	*a coat*	gris	grey
	un pull	*a pullover*	noir	black
Il a	un t-shirt	*a t-shirt*	vert	green
Elle a	un uniforme	*a uniform*		
On a				

 These colours stay the same in masculine & feminine

	jaune	*yellow*	marron	*brown*
Mon frère (brother) a				
Ma sœur (sister) a	orange	*orange*	rose	*rose*

Nous avons	une casquette	*a cap*	blanche	white
	une chemise	*a shirt*	bleue	blue
Vous avez	une cravate	*a tie*	grise	grey
	une jupe	*a skirt*	noire	black
Ils ont	une robe	*a dress*	verte	green
Elles ont	une veste	*a jacket*		
Mes parents ont				

---

1. Translate into English

a. J'ai un t-shirt rouge

b. Il a un manteau noir

c. Nous avons une casquette bleue

d. Elles ont une chemise jaune

e. Tu as une robe orange?

f. Nous avons une cravate verte

g. Vous avez un uniforme noir?

2. Complete with *j', tu, elle, on, nous, vous, elles* as appropriate

a. _____ a une jupe rouge (f)

b. _____ avons un uniforme vert et blanc

c. _____ ont une robe noire (f)

d. _____ as une jupe bleue?

e. _____ ai une cravate verte

f. _____ avez un chapeau jaune?

g. _____ a une robe rose (We)

3. Correct the errors, then listen to check

a. Nous avons un jaune uniforme

b. J'ai une cravate noir

c. Ma mère a une rouge robe

d. Tu as un jupe bleue?

e. Nous avons une veste vert

f. Vous avez une chapeau blanc?

g. On a une chemise gris

4. Translate into French

a. I have a white tie

b. She has a black and white hat

c. We have a green dress

d. They (m) have an orange cap

e. Do you have a grey and black coat?

f. He has a white and red t-shirt

g. Do you guys have a green and white uniform?

1.7 AVOIR + NUMBER + PLURAL NOUNS + ADJECTIVES
(SAYING HOW MANY THINGS ONE HAS)

J'ai Tu as Il a Elle a On a Mon frère a Ma sœur a Nous avons	**des** *some* **deux** *2* **trois** *3* **quatre** *4* **cinq** *5* **six** *6* **sept** *7* **huit** *8* **neuf** *9* **dix** *10*	**chats** *cats* **chevaux** *horses* **poissons** *fish*		**blancs** *white* **bleus** *blue* **noirs** *black* **verts** *green*		
		cartables *school bags* **crayons** *pencils* **stylos** *pens*				
		jeans *jeans* **pantalons** *trousers* **t-shirts** *t-shirts*				

These colours stay the same in masculine & feminine plural	**jaunes** *yellow* · **oranges** *orange* — **marron*** *brown* · **roses** *rose*

Vous avez Ils ont Elles ont Mes parents ont	**des** *some* **deux** *2* **trois** *3* **quatre** *4* **cinq** *5* **six** *6* **sept** *7* **huit** *8* **neuf** *9* **dix** *10*	**araignées** *spiders* **gerbilles** *gerbils* **poules** *hens* **chèvres** *goats* **tortues** *turtles*		**blanches** *white* **bleues** *blue* **noires** *black* **vertes** *green*	
		gommes *rubbers* **trousses** *pencil cases* **règles** *rulers*			
		chaussures *shoes* **chemises** *shirts* **pulls** *pullovers* **cravates** *ties* **bottes** *boots*			

LANGUAGE AWARENESS

NUMBER AGREEMENT: MAKING NOUNS & ADJECTIVES PLURAL

In French, like in English, when we talk about more than one item, we need to make the noun plural.

To make a noun plural, we just add **-s**

- J'ai **une** araignée
- J'ai **deux** araignée**s**

- J'ai **une** trousse
- J'ai **sept** crayon**s**

Ajouter un 's' c'est sssuper facile

C'est sûr, c'est sensationnel.

* The spelling remains the same even in the plural

LANGUAGE AWARENESS

Number agreement: adjectives must also become plural!

To make an adjective plural and make it agree with the noun, we follow the same rules as per nouns (add an **-s**)

· J'ai **un** stylo bleu.

becomes:

· J'ai **trois** stylo**s** bleu**s**

This means that adjectives must **agree in gender** (masculine / feminine) **and number** (singular / plural) with the nouns they describe.

MAKING A WORD IN AL PLURAL

If a word ends in **al**, such as **cheval** when we make it plural, we take off the **l** and add **-ux**.

• J'ai un chev**al**

•J'ai trois cheva**ux**

> Il fait si froid que même moi je porte un manteau.

> Tu exagères!

---

1. Faulty translation: fix the English translation

a. Nous avons deux oiseaux jaunes — *They have two yellow birds*

b. Ils ont un pantalon marron — *They have some brown boots*

c. Il a deux trousses rouges — *He has two red pencils*

d. J'ai deux araignées noires — *I have two black snakes*

e. Elles ont des poules blanches — *They have some white cats*

f. Vous avez deux poissons verts — *You guys have some red fish*

g. Elle a des règles blanches — *She has some white rubbers*

h. J'ai neuf cravates rouges — *We have eight red shirts*

2. Find the spelling mistakes, listen and verify.

a. J'ai de chemises bleues

b. Elle a cinq crayons noires

c. Nous avons trois gommes blancs

d. Ils ont set poulet marron

e. Vous avez trois robs roses

f. J'ai des chaussures noirs

g. Mon frère a des bottes gris

h. Il a des crayons blanches

i. Tu as deux chèvres noir

3. Complete with the correct option

jaunes	noires	bleus	blanches	roses	blanches	noirs	rouges	jaunes	marron

a. J'ai des bottes _____   *I have some black boots*

b. Nous avons six poissons _____   *We have six blue fish*

c. Il a des cartables _____   *He has some black schoolbags*

d. Elles ont deux poules _____   *They have two white hens*

e. Vous avez deux jeans _____   *You guys have two pink jeans*

f. Il a deux perroquets _____   *He has two yellow parrots*

g. Elle a trois crayons _____   *She has three brown pencils*

h. Nous avons cinq t-shirts _____   *We have five yellow t-shirts*

i. J'ai deux jupes _____   *I have two red skirts*

j. Elle a trois cravates _____   *She has three white ties*

---

4. Listen and translate into English 🔊

a.

b.

c.

d.

e.

f.

g.

h.

---

5. Missing letters challenge

a. De__ t-shirt__ blanc__

b. D__s cray__ns noir__

c. __es tortu__s vert__s

d. D__s poisso__s ble__s

e. De__ poule__s marr__n

f. __es t-shi__ts ro__es

g. D__s bo__tes noi__es

h. __es ju__es bleu__s

---

6. Tangled translation into French

a. *We have* deux *hens* blanches

b. He *has* cinq t-shirts *blue*

c. J'ai *two* araignées *black*

d. Mon frère *has* deux *schoolbags* bleus

e. J'ai *some* chemises *yellow*

f. Mes parents *have* deux chiens *black*

g. Elle a *ten* feutres *green*

h. Tu as des *trousers white*?

---

7. Anagrams

e.g. Deux crayons **uajens** = **Deux crayons jaunes**

a. Des **serftue** noirs

b. Cinq poissons **ulbes**

c. Des **seshscuaur** blanches

d. **eDs** tortues **reesvt**

e. Huit **oeplus labhnesc**

f. **ueDx** cartables **osers**

g. Des **pnaosnlta rroman**

THE LANGUAGE GYM

8. Slalom translation: use one item from each row of the table to translate each sentence

J'ai	Nous avons	Elle a	Ils ont	Tu as	Il a
quatre	trois	deux	six	neuf	huit
feutres	t-shirts	chemises	chiens	poissons	poules
roses	blanches	noirs	bleus	jaunes	vertes

a. I have two blue fish

b. We have three black dogs

c. She has six white hens

d. They (m) have four green shirts

e. You have eight yellow t-shirts

f. He has nine pink felt tips

9. Complete with the missing words

a. Des gommes __ __ __ __ __ __   *Some blue rubbers*

b. __ __ __ robes roses   *Some pink dresses*

c. Trois poissons __ __ __ __ __   *Three green fish*

d. Des __ __ __ __ __ __ __ __ __ noires   *Some black shoes*

e. Six feutres __ __ __ __ __ __   *Six red felt tips*

f. Dix t-shirts __ __ __ __ __ __   *Ten white t-shirts*

g. Des __ __ __ __ __ __ marron   *Some brown hens*

h. Deux oiseaux __ __ __ __ __ __   *Two yellow birds*

i. Des __ __ __ __ __ bleus   *Some blue jeans*

10. Complete the grid

English	Français
Shoes	
Pencils	
	Jaunes
	Roses
Hens	
Trousers	
	Chemises
Fish	
Parrots	

11. Guided translation

a. N_____ a_____ d_____ j____ n_____   *We have two pairs of black jeans*

b. I_____ o____ t_____ c_____ b_____   *They have three white dogs*

c. E_____ a s_____ r_____ r_____   *She has six red dresses*

d. N_____ a_____ d_____ p_____ b_____   *We have some blue fish*

e. J'____ c_____ a_____ n_____   *I have five black spiders*

f. O___ a q_____ c_____ v_____   *We (One) has four green pencils*

g. V_____ a_____ d_____ s_____ j_____   *You guys have ten yellow pens*

h. T__ a_ d_____ c_____ b_____   *You have two blue schoolbags*

THE LANGUAGE GYM

12. Change the phrases from singular to plural

Singular	Plural
Un t-shirt vert	*Des t-shirts verts*
Un chien blanc	
Un crayon marron	
Un poisson bleu	
Une casquette noire	
Une chèvre blanche	
Une chaussure jaune	
Un cartable rose	
Une cravate jaune	
Une robe rouge	
Une araignée noire	
Un oiseau violet	

13. Translate into French

a. I have two blue fish

b. We have some white t-shirts

c. They (f) have six yellow shirts

d. He has two pink schoolbags

e. You guys have three black spiders

f. My brother has six green turtles

g. Do you have ten red caps?

h. My parents have two brown dogs

i. She has four white goats

j. They (m) have eight or nine yellow ties

 THE LANGUAGE GYM

1.8 AVOIR + NUMBER + ANS *(TELLING ONE'S AGE)*

Saying your age

J'ai	un	*1*	an
Tu as			
	deux	*2*	
Il a	trois	*3*	
Elle a	quatre	*4*	
On a	cinq	*5*	
Mon frère a	six	*6*	
Ma sœur a	sept	*7*	
	huit	*8*	
Nous avons	neuf	*9*	ans
	dix	*10*	
Vous avez	onze	*11*	
	douze	*12*	
	treize	*13*	
	quatorze	*14*	
Ils ont	quinze	*15*	
Elles ont	etc.		
Mes parents ont			

1. Translate into English

a. Nous avons quinze ans

b. Il a quatre ans

c. Vous avez quel âge?

d. Elles ont douze ans

e. J'ai onze ans

f. Il a treize ans

g. Ils ont quel âge?

h. Elle a sept ans

i. Tu as quel âge?

j. Nous avons quatorze ans

LANGUAGE AWARENESS

TELLING ONE'S AGE IN FRENCH

In French, to tell one's age we use the verb *avoir* (to have) as opposed to using *être* (to be) like we do in English. Therefore, in French we are literally saying "I have 12 years [old]" when we say *j'ai 12 ans.*

To ask the question 'How old are you?', we can use **Tu as quel âge?** or **Quel âge as-tu?** When using the latter, if you ask the question 'How old is he/she?', we can say **Il/Elle a quel âge?** or **Quel âge a-*t*-il/elle?**

Quel âge a-t-il?

Il a trois ans

2. Complete the verbs below

a. Nous __ __ __ __ douze ans *We are 12*

b. J'__ __ cinq ans *I am 5*

c. Ils __ __ __ quinze ans *They are 15*

d. Tu __ __ quel âge? *How old are you?*

e. Mon frère _ onze ans *My brother is 11*

f. Elles __ __ __ huit ans *They are 8*

g. Il __ vingt ans *He is 20*

h. Vous __ __ __ __ seize ans *We are 16*

i. Il __ quel âge? *How old is he?*

j. Tu __ __ dix-huit ans? *Are you 18?*

3. Listen: Choose one in three

a.	**Nous avons**	douze ans	onze ans	trois ans
b.	**Tu as**	deux ans	quinze ans	cinq ans
c.	**J'ai**	quatre ans	treize ans	six ans
d.	**Vous avez**	six ans	sept ans	seize ans
e.	**Elle a**	quatorze ans	neuf ans	un an
f.	**Ils ont**	dix ans	huit ans	dix-sept ans

4. Find the French translation and write it next to the English prompts

a. I am 15   b. We are 12   c. She is 6   d. We are 15   e. He is 9   f. You guys are 3   g. You are 5

j'	a	i	q	u	i	n	z	e	a	n	s	e	l	o	s	e	l	c	e	v	a
x	l	e	s	p	i	g	e	o	n	s	e	s	l	o	n	r	e	v	e	i	l
u	a	n	o	u	s	a	v	o	n	s	d	o	u	z	e	a	n	s	e	n	i
s	u	r	s	o	n	b	a	l	c	o	n	p	o	u	r	a	t	t	i	r	e
n	i	l	a	n	e	u	f	a	n	s	s	n	a	x	i	s	a	e	l	l	e
v	o	u	s	a	v	e	z	t	r	o	i	s	a	n	s	o	m	s	e	l	r
p	x	u	e	i	v	u	d	t	e	m	e	l	l	e	e	t	n	a	h	c	e
a	o	i	s	e	t	u	a	s	c	i	n	q	a	n	s	t	p	u	i	s	j
i	b	s	e	l	t	e	s	p	m	a	h	c	s	e	l	s	r	u	o	c	r
a	p	p	e	l	l	e	r	o	b	i	n	d	e	s	b	o	i	s	j	e	a
m	n	o	s	n	a	e	z	n	i	u	q	s	n	o	v	a	s	u	o	n	p

5. Guided translation

a. N_____ a_____ q_____ a_____   *We are 15*

b. J'___ t_____ a_____   *I am 13*

c. E_____ a q_____ a_____   *She is 14*

d. I____ o____ t_____ a_____   *They are 3*

e. T___ a__ d_____ a_____?   *Are you 18?*

f. I__ n'__ p___ d____ a_____   *He isn't 10*

g. N_____ a_____ n____ a_____   *We are 9*

h. E_____ o____ d____ a_____   *They are 17*

6. Translate into French

a. She is fifteen

b. I am thirteen

c. We are twelve

d. How old are you?

e. You guys are eighteen

f. She is not fourteen

g. How old is he?

h. I am not eighteen

ENGLISH 1	FRENCH 1	ENGLISH 2	FRENCH 2
I have a turtle that is called Manon.	J'ai une tortue qui s'appelle Manon	My goat is thirsty.	
I have a gerbil that is called Rosie.	J'ai une gerbille qui s'appelle Rosie.	I have a red hen that is called Suzanne.	
They (m) have a horse, a dog and a duck.	Ils ont un cheval, un chien et un canard.	We have a white and brown dog who is four.	
She has a white shirt and a pink dress.	Elle a une chemise blanche et une robe rose	Do you have a green pen?	
We have a black cap and two red ties.	Nous avons une casquette noire et deux cravates rouges	I have a stomachache and I am sleepy.	
You have six red dresses and two pairs of jeans.	Tu as six robes rouges et deux jeans.	My black horse has a toothache.	
I am hungry and thirsty.	J'ai faim et soif.	Do you have two orange books?	
My cat is sleepy.	Mon chat a sommeil	They (f) have a white rubber.	

INSTRUCTIONS - You are **PARTNER A.** Work in pairs. Each of you has two sets of sentences - one set has already been translated for you. You will ask your partner to translate these. The other set of sentences have not been translated. Your partner will ask you to translate these.

HOW TO PLAY - Partner A starts by reading out his/her/their first sentence <u>in English</u>. Partner B must translate. Partner A must check the answer and award the following points: **3 points** = perfect, **2 points** = 1 mistake, **1 point** = mistakes but the verb is accurate. If they cannot translate correctly, Partner A will read out the sentence so that Partner B can learn what the correct translation is.

Then Partner B reads out his/her/their first sentence, and so on.

OBJECTIVE - Try to win more points than your partner by translating correctly as many sentences as possible.

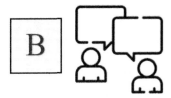

ORAL PING PONG

AVOIR

ENGLISH 1	FRENCH 1	ENGLISH 2	FRENCH 2
I have a turtle that is called Manon.		My goat is thirsty.	Ma chèvre a soif
I have a gerbil that is called Rosie.		I have a red hen that is called Suzanne.	J'ai une poule rouge qui s'appelle Suzanne.
They (m) have a horse, a dog and a duck.		We have a white and brown dog who is four.	Nous avons un chien blanc et marron qui a quatre ans.
She has a white shirt and a pink dress.		Do you have a green pen?	Tu as un stylo vert?
We have a black cap and two red ties.		I have a stomachache and I am sleepy.	J'ai mal à l'estomac et j'ai sommeil
You have six red dresses and two pairs of jeans.		My black horse has a toothache.	Mon cheval noir a mal aux dents
I am hungry and thirsty.		Do you have two orange books?	Tu as deux livres oranges?
My cat is sleepy.		They (f) have a white rubber.	Elles ont une gomme blanche

INSTRUCTIONS - You are **PARTNER B.** Work in pairs. Each of you has two sets of sentences - one set has already been translated for you. You will ask your partner to translate these. The other set of sentences have not been translated. Your partner will ask you to translate these.

HOW TO PLAY - Partner A starts by reading out his/her/their first sentence in English. Partner B must translate. Partner A must check the answer and award the following points: **3 points** = perfect, **2 points** = 1 mistake, **1 point** = mistakes but the verb is accurate. If they cannot translate correctly, Partner A will read out the sentence so that Partner B can learn what the correct translation is.
Then Partner B reads out his/her/their first sentence, and so on.

OBJECTIVE - Try to win more points than your partner by translating correctly as many sentences as possible.

AVOIR

No Snakes No Ladders

DÉPART	1 I am 13 years old	2 I have a green duck	3 We have two blue shirts	4 Do you guys have a dog?	5 I have a black schoolbag	6 He has a toothache	7 I have a red hen
15 We are scared and hungry	14 We are scared and hungry	13 Are you thirsty?	12 They have two green pens	11 He has a red ruler	10 They (f) have a pink skirt	9 We are 12 years old	8 My blue duck is 2 years old
16 She has a blue parrot	17 Do you have a spider?	18 We have ten yellow birds	19 She has ten dresses	20 I am sleepy and cold	21 They are hot	22 Are you hot?	23 She is scared
ARRIVÉE	30 We are scared and cold	29 My dog is hungry	28 They have ten red hats	27 I have two black spiders	26 They have a blue shirt	25 Are you thirsty?	24 My parrot is scared

15 My dog, that is called Patrick, is scared

No Snakes No Ladders

AVOIR

1 DÉPART J'ai treize ans	**2** J'ai un canard vert	**3** Nous avons deux chemises bleues	**4** Vous avez un chien?	**5** J'ai un cartable noir	**6** Il a mal aux dents	**7** J'ai une poule rouge
14 Nous avons peur et faim	**13** Tu as soif?	**12** Ils ont deux stylos verts	**11** Il a une règle rouge	**10** Elles ont une chemise rose	**9** Nous avons douze ans	**8** Mon canard bleu a deux ans
15 Mon chien, qui s'appelle Patrick, a peur	**18** Nous avons dix oiseaux jaunes	**19** Elle a dix robes	**20** J'ai sommeil et froid	**21** Ils ont chaud	**22** Tu as chaud?	**23** Elle a peur
16 Elle a un perroquet bleu	**17** Tu as une araignée?	**28** Ils ont dix chapeaux rouges	**27** J'ai deux araignées noires	**26** Elles ont une chemise bleue	**25** Tu as soif?	**24** Mon perroquet a peur
ARRIVÉE	**30** Nous avons peur et froid	**29** Mon chien a faim				

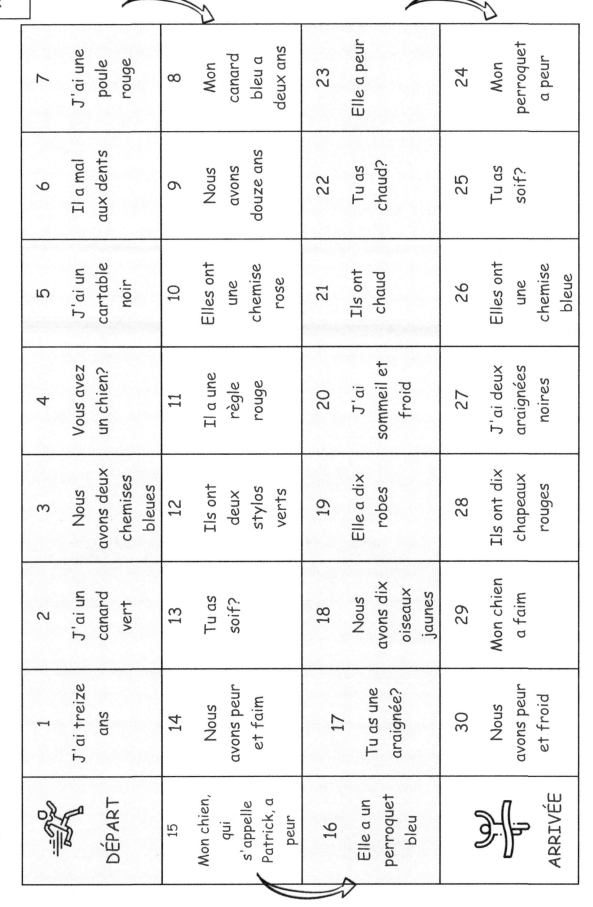

PYRAMID TRANSLATION

Unit 1 - Avoir

Translate each part of the pyramid out loud with your partner, then write it into the spaces provided below.

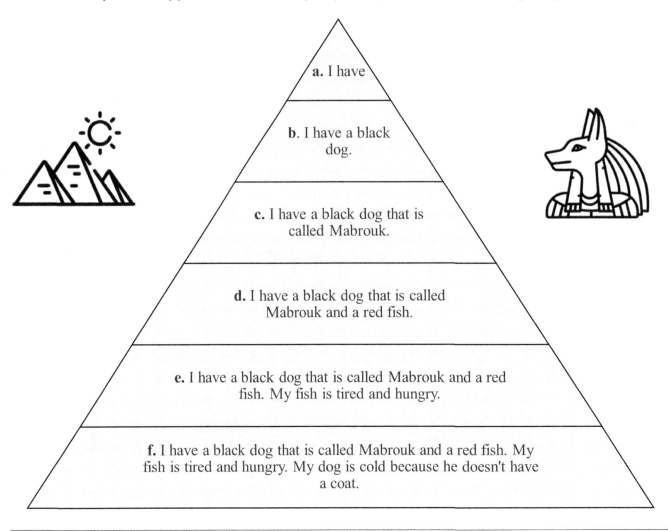

a. I have

b. I have a black dog.

c. I have a black dog that is called Mabrouk.

d. I have a black dog that is called Mabrouk and a red fish.

e. I have a black dog that is called Mabrouk and a red fish. My fish is tired and hungry.

f. I have a black dog that is called Mabrouk and a red fish. My fish is tired and hungry. My dog is cold because he doesn't have a coat.

Write your translation here

SOLUTION: J'ai un chien noir qui s'appelle Mabrouk et un poisson rouge. Mon poisson est fatigué et il a faim. Mon chien a froid car il n'a pas de manteau.

THE LANGUAGE GYM

UNIT 2 – ÊTRE

Je	suis
Tu	es
Il / Elle / On	est
Nous	sommes
Vous	êtes
Ils / Elles	sont

PHYSICAL DESCRIPTIONS

Je suis **grande**

Je suis **petit**

CHARACTER DESCRIPTIONS

Je suis **drôle**

HA HA!

COUNTRY & NATIONALITY

Je suis **de France**

Je suis **espagnol**

2.1 ÊTRE + ADJECTIVE
(DESCRIBING PEOPLE'S PERSONALITY AND APPEARANCE)

Masculine					
Verb		**Physical description**		**Character description**	
Je suis	*I am*	**beau**	*handsome*	**amusant**	*fun*
		fort	*strong*	**drôle**	*funny*
Tu es	*You are*	**grand**	*tall*	**énervant**	*annoying*
		gros	*fat*	**ennuyeux**	*boring*
Il est	*He is*	**jeune**	*young*	**intelligent**	*intelligent*
Mon frère est	*My brother is*	**mince**	*slim*	**malin**	*clever*
Mon père est	*My father is*	**musclé**	*muscular*	**méchant**	*mean*
Mon papa est	*My dad is*	**petit**	*small*	**paresseux**	*lazy*
		vieux	*old*	**sympa**	*nice*
				travailleur	*hard-working*

Feminine					
Verb		**Physical description**		**Character description**	
Je suis	*I am*	**belle**	*beautiful*	**amusante**	
		forte	*strong*	**drôle**	
Tu es	*You are*	**grande**	*tall*	**énervante**	
		grosse	*fat*	**ennuyeuse**	
Elle est	*She is*	**jeune**	*young*	**intelligente**	
Ma sœur est	*My sister is*	**mince**	*slim*	**maline**	
Ma mère est	*My mother is*	**musclée**	*muscular*	**méchante**	
Ma maman est	*My mum is*	**petite**	*small*	**paresseuse**	
		vieille	*old*	**sympa**	
				travailleuse	

LANGUAGE AWARENESS

ÊTRE – TO BE

This unit will look into how and when we use the verb
être. The first three parts which we will practise in this
sub-unit are ***suis/es/est***

One of its main uses is for describing people and things in
terms of **physical appearance** and **personality/character**.

- **Je suis grand**   *I **am** tall (m)*
- **Je suis musclée**   *I **am** muscular (f)*
- **Ma sœur est intelligente** *My sister **is** clever (f)*
- **Mon prof est amusant** *My teacher **is** fun (m)*

Je suis un paresseux
paresseux

Tu es un patient
patient

Merci

THE LANGUAGE GYM

1. Match

Je suis grand	I am nice
Elle est amusante	He is mean
Je suis sympa	You are beautiful
Tu es belle	I am muscular
Il est méchant	I am tall
Je suis musclé	You are hard-working
Je suis forte	She is slim
Tu es gros	She is fun
Elle est mince	I am strong
Tu es travailleuse	You are lazy
Tu es paresseux	You are fat

2. Complete the box

Masculine	Feminine
Je suis grand	
	Je suis travailleuse
	Tu es grosse
Il est paresseux	
Je suis petit	
	Elle est méchante
	Elle est sympa
Tu es beau	

3. Faulty translation: fix the English translation

a. Je suis mince — *He is slim*

b. Il est méchant — *He is tall*

c. Tu es ennuyeux — *You are tall*

d. Elle est belle — *She is funny*

e. Je suis petit et musclé — *I am fun and muscular*

f. Je suis sympa et amusant — *He is strong and fun*

g. Tu es beau et fort — *He is short and weak*

h. Je suis paresseux — *I am hard-working*

4. Dictation: listen and complete the words

a. J _ s _ _ _ g _ _ _ — *I am fat*

b. I _ e _ _ m _ _ _ _ — *He is slim*

c. T _ e _ f _ _ _ _ — *You are strong (f)*

d. E _ _ _ e _ _ d _ _ _ _ — *She is funny*

e. J _ s _ _ _ g _ _ _ _ _ — *I am tall (f)*

f. I _ e _ _ m _ _ _ _ — *He is clever*

g. T _ e _ g _ _ _ _ — *You are tall (m)*

h. I _ e _ _ b _ _ _ — *He is handsome*

5. Tangled translation: translate to French, then listen & check

a. *I am* grande *and* mince

b. *He is* paresseux et *mean*

c. Elle est *short* et *annoying*

d. *You are small and* ennuyeux

e. Elle est *small*, mais *very* sympa

f. Ma *mother* est *very* travailleuse

g. Je suis musclé *and handsome*

h. *She is* grande et *slim*

6. Guided translation

a. M___ s_____ e__ g_____ et m_____
My sister is big and clever

b. M___ m_____ e__ b_____ et t_____
My mum is beautiful and hard-working

c. M___ a_____ e__ m_____ m____ t__ p_____
My friend (m) is muscular but very small

d. M___ p_____ e__ p_____ et a_____
My dad is short and fun

e. M__ f_____ e__ i_____ m_____ é_____
My brother is intelligent but annoying

7. Slalom translation: use one item from each row of the table to translate each sentence

Ma sœur	Je	Ma mère	Mon frère	Mon ami	Tu
suis	est	est	est	es	est
grand	énervante	musclé	malin	belle	méchant
mais amusante	mais méchant	mais malin	et grand	et petite	et sympa

a. *My friend is mean but clever*

b. *My sister is annoying but fun*

c. *You are muscular and tall*

d. *My mother is beautiful and short*

e. *I am tall and nice*

f. *My brother is clever but mean*

8. Slalom listening: listen and then use one item per row to create a sentence

Ma sœur	Je	Ma mère	Mon frère aîné	Mon ami	Tu	Ma sœur aînée
suis	est	est	est	est	est	es
travailleuse,	sympa	musclée	malin,	belle,	méchant,	travailleur,
grand	petit	grande	belle	et petite,	et petite,	beau,
mais amusante	mais méchant	mais maline	et paresseux	et maline	et drôle	et maline

a.

b.

c.

d.

e.

f.

g.

2.2 ALL PERSONS OF ÊTRE + INTENSIFIER + SINGULAR NOUN + ADJECTIVE
(DESCRIBING PEOPLE)

Subject	Intensifiers	Physical adjectives		Personality adjectives	
		Masculine			
Je suis **Tu es**	**assez** *quite* **trop** *too* **très** *very* **un peu** *a bit*	**beau** **fort** **grand** **gros** **jeune** **mince** **petit** **vieux**	*beau* *strong* *tall* *fat* *young* *slim* *short/small* *old*	**amusant** **bavard** **drôle** **énervant** **ennuyeux** **joyeux** **malin** **paresseux** **réservé** **sympa** **travailleur**	*fun* *talkative* *funny* *annoying* *boring* *joyful* *clever* *lazy* *reserved* *nice* *hard-working*
Il est **Mon grand-père est** **Mon frère est** **Mon frère aîné est** **Mon frère cadet est** **Mon père est** **Mon oncle Pierre est**					
		Feminine			
Elle est **Ma grand-mère est** **Ma sœur est** **Ma sœur aînée est** **Ma sœur cadette est** **Ma mère est** **Ma tante Martine est**		**belle** **forte** **grande** **grosse** **jeune** **mince** **petite** **vieille**		**amusante** **bavarde** **drôle** **énervante** **ennuyeuse** **joyeuse** **maline** **paresseuse** **réservée** **sympa** **travailleuse**	

LANGUAGE AWARENESS

WHAT ARE INTENSIFIERS?

Intensifiers are **adverbs** such as *too, very, quite* and *a bit*. They are used to intensify the meaning of other words such as adjectives and verbs. In French, the most frequently used **intensifiers** are:

- **assez** — *quite, enough*
- **trop** — *too*
- **très** — *very*
- **un peu** — *a bit*

Just as in English, **intensifiers** go before **adjectives**.

- Mon père est **assez** grand — *My father is quite tall*
- Ma maman est **très** maline — *My mum is very clever*
- Ma sœur est **un peu** paresseuse — *My sister is a bit lazy*
- Mon frère est **trop** bavard — *My brother is too chatty*

Mon oncle Gian est assez grand et très fort. Il est très bavard et amusant.

HA! HA!

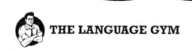

1. Gapped translation: complete the translation

a. Ma mère est assez grande et belle   *My mother is _____ tall and beautiful*

b. Mon père est un peu gros et malin   *My father is _____ fat and clever*

c. Mon frère est trop paresseux   *My brother is _____ lazy*

d. Mon frère aîné n'est pas très musclé   *My older brother is not very _____*

e. Mon grand-père maternel est très vieux   *My maternal grandfather is very _____*

f. Ma grand-mère n'est pas très joyeuse   *My grandmother is not _____ joyful*

g. Mon oncle Philippe est trop bavard   *My uncle Philippe is too _____*

h. Ma tante Claire est très réservée   *My aunt Claire is very _____*

2. Listen and arrange the words in the correct order: then translate into English

a. mère Ma bavarde assez est

b. maternelle grand-mère Ma très est joyeuse

c. travailleur père Mon trop est

d. paresseux est un Mon peu grand-père

e. frère Mon intelligent cadet très est

f. Ma musclée Marie tante assez est

g. est Ma sœur grosse un peu

h. ne très Je pas suis grand

3. Tangled translation: translate into French

a. Mon **grandfather** maternel **is very** vieux

b. **My** tante Claudie est **quite talkative**

c. Mon **father** est très **tall** et **muscular**

d. **My** sœur **younger** est **a bit lazy**

e. Ma mère est **very reserved** et timide

f. Mon grand-père paternel **is too** bavard

g. Mon chat est **very fat** et paresseux

4. Broken translation: complete with the missing letters

a. Tr__ __ sy__ __ __   *Very nice*

b. As_____ b_____   *Quite handsome*

c. U__ p__ __ pares__ __ __ __ __   *A bit lazy (f)*

d. Pa__ tr__ __ gr__ __ __ __   *Not very tall (f)*

e. Tr__ __ m__ __ __   *Too clever (m)*

f. __ __ __ __ z ennuyeux   *Quite boring*

g. __n p__ __ gr__ __ __ __   *A bit fat (f)*

h. As__ __ __ pe__ __ __ __   *Quite short (f)*

5. Listen and translate into French

a. My aunt is very tall

b. My brother is too talkative

c. My sister is quite lazy

d. My grandfather is very old

e. My grandmother is very reserved

f. I am a bit fat but muscular

g. My mother is very joyful

h. My dog is very strong

6. Find the French translation and write it next to the English prompts

i	l	i	s	e	d	e	e	l	l	e	b	z	e	s	s	a
u	n	p	e	u	g	r	a	n	d	e	u	n	a	n	c	h
n	é	o	u	i	t	r	è	s	p	e	t	i	t	t	r	a
p	t	e	n	e	t	i	t	e	p	z	e	s	s	a	i	s
e	u	n	p	e	u	m	i	n	c	e	i	c	h	s	o	s
u	a	u	m	o	a	x	u	e	i	v	u	e	p	n	u	e
p	i	e	a	f	n	l	d	x	q	i	o	h	c	a	v	r
e	t	j	r	e	s	l	u	n	p	e	u	b	e	a	u	s
t	u	s	c	d	t	r	è	s	g	r	a	n	d	e	a	a
i	n	è	h	d	l	i	e	i	u	a	f	a	a	s	s	n
t	e	r	a	n	a	v	f	o	i	s	a	s	s	e	t	s
e	f	t	t	r	o	p	f	o	r	t	m	s	r	r	i	o
t	r	o	p	g	r	a	n	d	d	i	t	e	u	d	o	n

a. Very tall (f)

b. A bit handsome

c. A bit short (f)

d. Too strong (m)

e. Too tall (m)

f. Quite short (f)

g. A bit tall (f)

h. A bit old (m)

i. Very young

j. Very short (m)

k. Quite beautiful

l. A bit slim

7. Staircase translation: translate each sentence from memory and then listen to check

a.	My mother is	very tall.				
b.	My father is	quite short	and slim.			
c.	My brother is	very handsome,	but a bit fat.	He is very lazy!		
d.	My sister is	quite slim	and muscular.	She is very intelligent	and hard-working.	
e.	My grandfather is	very old,	but quite strong.	He is very joyful	and fun	but too talkative.

a. _____

b. _____

c. _____

d. _____

e. _____

THE LANGUAGE GYM

2.3 PRONOUN/NOUN + *ÊTRE* + SINGULAR/PLURAL NOUN + ADJECTIVE
(DESCRIBING PEOPLE)

Masculine					
Je	*I*	**suis**	*am*	**amusant**	*fun*
				énervant	*annoying*
Tu	*You*	**es**	*are*	**fort**	*strong*
				grand	*tall*
Il	*He*			**jeune**	*young*
				méchant	*mean*
Mon frère	*My brother*	**est**	*is*	**mince**	*slim*
				petit	*small*
Mon père	*My father*			**travailleur**	*hard-working*
				vieux	*old*
Nous	*We*	**sommes**	*are*	**ennuyeux**	*boring*
Mon père et moi	*My father and I*			**gros**	*fat*
Vous	*You guys*	**êtes**	*are*	**intelligents**	*intelligent*
				jeunes	*young*
Ils	*They*			**joyeux**	*joyful*
				malins	*clever*
Mes frères	*My brothers*	**sont**	*are*	**paresseux**	*lazy*
				réservés	*reserved*
Mes parents	*My parents*			**sympas**	*nice*
Feminine					
Je	*I*	**suis**	*am*	**amusante**	*fun*
				énervante	*annoying*
				forte	*strong*
Tu	*You*	**es**	*are*	**grande**	*tall*
				jeune	*young*
				méchante	*mean*
Elle	*She*			**mince**	*slim*
Ma sœur	*My sister*	**est**	*is*	**petite**	*small*
Ma mère	*My mother*			**travailleuse**	*hard-working*
				vieille	*old*
Nous	*We*	**sommes**	*are*	**ennuyeuses**	*boring*
Ma mère et moi	*My mother and I*			**grosses**	*fat*
Vous	*You girls*	**êtes**	*are*	**intelligentes**	*intelligent*
				jeunes	*young*
				joyeuses	*joyful*
Elles	*They*			**malines**	*clever*
Mes sœurs	*My sisters*	**sont**	*are*	**paresseuses**	*lazy*
				réservées	*reserved*
Mes tantes	*My aunts*			**sympas**	*nice*

THE LANGUAGE GYM

LANGUAGE AWARENESS
ADJECTIVAL AGREEMENT – GENDER & PLURALS

As we mentioned in the previous unit, in French the adjective (describing word) must agree with the noun it describes:

• Mon frère est *amusant* (*My brother is fun*).

Amusant is masculine and singular as it agrees with *frère*

Masculine Singular

• Mes frères sont amusant**s** (*My brothers are fun*).

Amusants is masculine and plural as it agrees with *frères*.

Masculine Plural

• Ma sœur est énervant**e** (*My sister is annoying*).

Énervante is feminine and singular as it agrees with *sœur*.

Feminine Singular

• Mes sœur**s** sont énervant**es** (*My sisters are annoying*).

Énervantes is feminine and plural as it agrees with *sœurs*.

Feminine Plural

ADJECTIVAL AGREEMENT: GENDER – RECAP

In general, to make an adjective feminine, you need to add an **-e** at the end, including adjectives ending in **-é**:

• Mon père est **grand** et **réservé**
  My father is tall and reserved
• Ma mère est **grande** et **réservée**
  My mother is tall and reserved

If an adjective *already* ends with **-e**, it stays the same for the masculine and feminine forms:

• Mon frère est **mince**
  My brother is slim
• Ma sœur est **mince**
  My sister is slim

ADJECTIVES ENDING IN "EUX" or "EUR"

If an adjective ends in **-eux** (*ennuyeux*) or in **-eur** (*travailleur*) it becomes **-euse** in the feminine form:

• Mon père est **travailleur**
  My father is hard-working
• Ma mère est **travailleuse**
  My mother is hard-working
• Mon frère est **paresseux**
  My brother is lazy
• Ma sœur est **paresseuse**
  My sister is lazy
• Mon oncle est **ennuyeux**
  My uncle is boring
• Ma tante est **ennuyeuse**
  My aunt is boring

 **THE LANGUAGE GYM**

MAKING ADJECTIVES PLURAL:

To make them plural:

... we just add **-S**

• Mes parents sont grand**S**   • Mes sœurs sont grande**S**

... **but** we **do not add anything** to the masculine if it already ends in **-S** or **-X**

• Mes éléphants sont **gris**   • Mes frères sont **paresseux**

... *however* we add **-X** at the end of **beau**

• Les chiens sont beau**X**

Adjective	Masculine singular	Feminine singular	Masculine plural	Feminine plural
grand	Mon père est **grand**	Ma mère est **grande**	Mes parents sont **grands**	Mes tantes sont **grandes**
gris	Mon chat est **gris**	Ma souris est **grise**	Mes éléphants sont **gris**	Mes chèvres sont **grises**
paresseux	Mon frère est **paresseux**	Ma sœur est **paresseuse**	Mes oncles sont **paresseux**	Mes tantes sont **paresseuses**
beau	Mon père est **beau**	Ma mère est **belle**	Mes frères sont **beaux**	Mes sœurs sont **belles**

Il n'oublie rien!

Mes parents sont gris et très grands, mais moi je suis très petit.

Pourquoi je suis grise?

---

1. Listening dictation 🔊

a. J___ s_____ b_____   f. M___ p_____ e___ t___ r_____

b. I___ e_____ g_____   g. M___ f_____ e___ g_____

c. I___ s___ p_____   h. N____ s_____ m_____

d. N___ s_____ s_____   i. E____ e___ t___ p_____

e. E___ e___ m_____   j. M____ p_____ s_____ t____

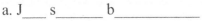

2. Complete the table

Français	English
ennuyeux	
	fun
	nice
	clever
énervant	
mince	
	hard-working
vieux	
	muscular
jeune	

3. Complete with the endings *-e*, *-es*, *-eur*, *-eux* or *-euse*, then listen and check

a. Ma sœur est trop paress__ __ __ __

b. Mon père est travaill__ __ __

c. Mes parents sont assez jeun__ __

d. Mon frère aîné est minc__

e. Mes tantes sont très énervant__ __

f. Ma grand-mère maternelle est très réservé__

g. Mes grands-parents sont très vi__ __ __

h. Mon amie Laurence est très fort__

i. Mes sœurs sont assez gross__ __

j. Ma prof de maths est très intelligent__

4. Correct the mistakes:

a. Ma mère est très petit

b. Mes parents sont assez vieilles

c. Mes frères sont très belles

d. Ma tante est très bavard

e. Mes oncles sont très travailleur

f. Mes grands-parents sont très amusante

g. Mes amies sont très simpas

h. Mon ami Marc est très énervantes

i. Mes cousines sont très junes

j. Mon pingouin est très forte

5. Gapped translation: complete the translation

a. Je suis très g__ __ __ __   *I'm very tall (m)*

b. Nous sommes assez p__ __ __ __ __ __   *We're quite short (f)*

c. Ils sont tr__ __é__ __ __ __ __ __ __   *They are too annoying (m)*

d. Vous êtes très f__ __ __ __   *You guys are very strong*

e. Je suis trop t__ __ __ __ __ __ __ __ __ __ __   *I'm too hard-working (f)*

f. Elle est très b__ __ __ __   *She is very beautiful*

g. Mes grands-parents sont v__ __ __ __   *My grandparents are old*

h. Mon frère est as__ __ __ s__ __ __ __   *My brother is quite nice*

REVISION QUICKIE: FAMILY; PRESENT OF ÊTRE; ADJECTIVES; AGREEMENT; POSSESSIVES

1. Faulty translation: fix the English translation

a. Je suis très réservé   *I am quite tall*

b. Nous sommes un peu gros   *We are very fat*

c. Ils sont trop bavards   *They are too lazy*

d. Vous êtes très paresseux   *They are very lazy*

e. Vous êtes assez minces   *We are quite short*

f. Je suis un peu ennuyeuse   *She is a bit boring*

g. Elles sont très sympas   *They are very clever*

2. Each French sentence contains TWO mistakes: spot and correct them

a. Ma mère es grandes
    My mother is tall

b. Mon sœurs sont petit
    My sisters are short

c. Je ne sommes pas paresseu
    I am not lazy

d. Tu est très travailleux
    You are very hard-working

e. Elles êtes inteligent
    They are intelligent

f. Mon ami Marc sont assez amusant
    My friend Marc is a bit funny

3. Sentence Puzzle

a. Ma très est grande, mère mince assez et un timide peu

    My mother is very tall, quite slim and a bit shy

b. père Mon assez est petit, beau très et un paresseux peu

    My father is quite small, very handsome and a bit lazy

c. Mes amusants sont frères bavards, très et sympas

    My brothers are talkative, friendly and very funny

d. méchant Mon Laurent ami musclé, très est mais est très et énervant il

    My friend Laurent is very muscular, but he is very mean and annoying

4. Complete with the missing letters

a. Mes parents so_ _   tr_ _ _   travaill_ _ _ _

b. Ma mère est as_ _ _ _   gra_ _ _ _

c. Mes frères s_ _ _ _   très pares_ _ _ _ _

d. Je ne s_ _ _ _ pas m_ _ _ _ _

e. Tu e_ t_ _ _ _ f_ _ _ _ _

f. Vous êtes t_ _ p ré_ _ _ _ _ _ _

g. Ma sœur e_ _ _ a_ _ _ _ _ amusante

h. Mon oncle e_ _ _ très bava_ _ _ _ et amusa_ _ _

5. Translate into French

a. My dog is quite strong and a bit fat

b. My mother is tall, slim and quite muscular

c. My father is quite handsome and fun

d. You are very intelligent and hard-working

e. You guys are very young and lazy

f. She is very funny, talkative and nice

g. My uncle Pascal is quite shy and reserved

Je suis *I am*		**affectueux/euse** *affectionate*			**moi** *I, me*	
Tu es *You are*		**amusant/e** *fun*			**toi** *you*	
Il/Elle est *He/She is*		**bavard/e** *talkative*			**lui/elle** *him/her*	
		beau *handsome*			**nous** *us*	
Mon amie Anne est		**belle** *beautiful*			**vous** *you*	
My friend Anne is		**bête** *stupid*			**eux/elles** *them*	
Mon ami Pascal est		**bruyant/e** *noisy*				
My friend Pascal is		**calme** *calm*			**ma grand-mère**	
	plus *more*	**drôle** *funny*			**mon grand-père**	
Mon frère est		**ennuyeux/euse** *boring*			**mes grands-mères**	
My brother is		**faible** *weak*			**mes grands-pères**	
Ma sœur est		**fort/e** *strong*			**mon amie Anne**	
My sister is		**grand/e** *tall*			**mon ami Laurent**	
	moins *less*	**gros/grosse** *fat*		**que/qu'** *than*	**mes amies**	
Ma mère est		**intelligent/e** *intelligent*			**mes amis**	
My mother is		**jeune** *young*				
Ma maman est		**malin/e** *clever*			**ma sœur**	
My mum is		**méchant/e** *mean*			**mon frère**	
Mon père est	**aussi** *as*	**mince** *slim*			**mes sœurs**	
My father is		**paresseux/euse** *lazy*			**mes frères**	
Mon papa est		**petit/e** *short*				
My dad is		**sérieux/euse** *serious*			**ma mère**	
		sportif/ive *sporty*			**mon père**	
Ma tante est		**sympa** *kind*			**mes parents**	
My aunt is		**têtu/e** *stubborn*			**ma tante**	
Mon oncle est		**travailleur/euse** *hard-working*			**mon oncle**	
My uncle is		**vieux/vieille** *old*			**mes tantes**	
					mes oncles	

THE LANGUAGE GYM

2.4 ÊTRE + COMPARATIVES *(COMPARING PEOPLE)*

Part 2 - PLURAL

Nous sommes *We are* **Vous êtes** *You guys/girls are* **Ils/Elles sont** *They are* **Mes grands-mères sont** *My grandmothers are* **Mes grands-pères sont** *My grandfathers are* **Mes amis/amies sont** *My friends are* **Mes sœurs sont** *My sisters are* **Mes frères sont** *My brothers are* **Mes parents sont** *My parents are* **Mes tantes et oncles sont** *My aunts & uncles are*	**plus** *more* **moins** *less* **aussi** *as*	**affectueux/euses** *affectionate* **amusants/es** *fun* **bavards/es** *talkative* **beaux** *handsome* **belles** *beautiful* **bêtes** *stupid* **bruyants/es** *noisy* **calmes** *calm* **drôles** *funny* **ennuyeux/euses** *boring* **faibles** *weak* **forts/es** *strong* **grands/es** *tall* **gros/grosses** *fat* **intelligents/es** *intelligent* **jeunes** *young* **malins/malines** *clever* **méchants/es** *mean* **minces** *slim* **paresseux/euses** *lazy* **petits/es** *short* **sérieux/euses** *serious* **sportifs/sportives** *sporty* **sympas** *kind* **têtus/es** *stubborn* **travailleurs/euses** *hard-working* **vieux/vieilles** *old*	**que/qu'** *than*	**moi** *I, me* **toi** *you* **lui/elle** *him/her* **nous** *us* **vous** *you* **eux/elles** *them* **ma grand-mère** **mon grand-père** **mes grands-mères** **mes grands-pères** **mon amie <u>Anne</u>** **mon ami <u>Laurent</u>** **mes amies** **mes amis** **ma sœur** **mon frère** **mes sœurs** **mes frères** **ma mère** **mon père** **mes parents** **ma tante** **mon oncle** **mes tantes** **mes oncles**

1. Match English and French

plus ennuyeuse que	*less clever than*
plus têtu que	*less noisy than*
moins maline que	*as strong as*
aussi réservée que	*as tall as*
moins bruyant que	*as stupid as*
aussi bête que	*more boring than*
aussi fort que	*shorter than*
plus petite que	*more stubborn than*
aussi grand que	*as reserved as*

2. Sentence Puzzle

a. Ma est petite sœur plus moi que

b. Mes sont frères moi grands plus que

c. tantes Mes sont parents aussi que strictes mes

d. Mes sont amis eux moins musclés qu'

e. amies Mes moins sont minces que moi

f. Je que aussi beau lui suis

g. aussi mes sont oncles drôles parents que Mes

h. Mon plus moi est meilleur ami bavard que

3. Complete with the missing words

a. Ma mère est plus grande _____ mon père   *My mother is taller than my father*

b. Ma mère est _____ bavarde que moi   *My mother is less talkative than me*

c. Mon _____ est plus petit que _____ père   *My grandfather is shorter than my father*

d. Mes cousins sont _____ paresseux que _____   *My cousins are lazier than us*

e. Mon chien _____ plus _____ que mon _____   *My dog is noisier than my cat*

f. Ma tante est _____ belle que _____ mère   *My aunt is less beautiful than my mother*

g. Mon _____ est plus _____ que moi   *My brother is more stubborn than me*

h. Mes parents _____ plus _____ que mes oncles   *My parents are shorter than my uncles*

4. Word detectives: work out what the hidden sentences are and then translate them into English

a. M__ m__ r__ e___ __ p__ __ __ p__t__ __ __ q__ __ m__ __ g__ __ __ __ __ - p__ __ __

b. J__ s__ __ __ a__ __ __ __ t__ __ __ q__ m__ __ f__ __ __ e

c. M__ t__ __ __ __ e__ __ p__ __ __ p__ __ s__ __ __ __ __ q__ m__ o__ __ __ e

d. M__ __ p__ __ __ nts s__ __ __ p__ __ __ gr __ __ __ __ __ q__ __ m__ __

e. M__ __ f__ __ __ e e__ __ a__ __ __ __ f__ __ t q__ __ m__ __

f. M__ g__ __ __ __ -m__ __ e__ __ a__ __ __ __ ba__a__ __ __ q__ m__ __ p__ __ __

THE LANGUAGE GYM

5. Tangled translation into French

a. *My* frères sont *as* grands et *handsome* que *I*

b. Mes *friends* sont *more* musclés et plus *strong than* moi

c. *My* père est *less* têtu et strict *than my mother*

d. Mes grands-parents *are* aussi généreux *as my parents*

e. Ma *mother* est aussi *talkative* que *my grandmother*

f. Ma *sister* aînée est *more hard-working* que moi

g. Mon chat *is* moins *strong* que *my dog*

h. *My* frère aîné est *more lazy* que mon *brother* cadet

6. Complete with suitable words

a. Ma mère est _____ grande _____ moi

b. _____ père _____ plus jeune que mon oncle

c. Mes parents _____ aussi grands que _____ grands-parents

d. _____ frère _____ plus sportif que moi

e. Mon chien est _____ bruyant _____ mon canard

f. Mes grands-parents _____ aussi affectueux ____ mes parents

g. Ma sœur est _____ jolie que _____ tortue

h. Mon oncle n'_____ pas aussi fort _____ mon père

7. Word translation

a. Less

b. Stubborn (m)

c. Young

d. More

e. Kind (sg)

f. Than

g. Old (f) (sg)

h. Strong (m) (sg)

8. Guided translation

a. J__ s__ __ __ m__ __ __ __ g__ __ __ __ q__ __ l__ __

I am less tall than him

b. E__ __ __ __ s__ __ p__ __ f__ __ __ __ __ q__ __ m__ __

They (f) are stronger than me

c. M__ __ g__ __ __ __ -p__ __ __ e__ __ t__ __ __ b__ __ __ __ __

My grandfather is too talkative

d. M__ __ f__ __ __ e__ __ p__ __ __ j__ __ __ __ q__ __ m__ __

My brother is younger than me

9. English to French translation

a. My sisters are taller than you

b. You guys (f) are stronger than us

c. They are as beautiful as us

d. My brother is shorter than me

e. She is lazier than me

f. My friend Julie is more fun than me

2.5 ALL PERSONS OF ÊTRE + ADJECTIVE
(SAYING WHAT NATIONALITY ONE IS)

Masculine					
SUBJECT PRONOUN		**VERB**		**ADJECTIVE**	
Je	*I*	**suis**	*am*	**allemand**	*German*
Tu	*You*	**es**	*are*	**américain**	*American (USA)*
				anglais	*English*
				écossais	*Scottish*
Il	*He*			**espagnol**	*Spanish*
Mon frère	*My brother*	**est**	*is*	**français**	*French*
Mon père	*My father*			**gallois**	*Welsh*
				italien	*Italian*
				suisse	*Swiss*
Nous	*We*	**sommes**	*are*	**allemands**	
Mon père et moi	*My father and I*			**américains**	
Vous	*You guys*	**êtes**	*are*	**anglais**	
				écossais	
Ils	*They*			**espagnols**	
Mes frères	*My brothers*	**sont**	*are*	**français**	
Mes parents	*My parents*			**gallois**	
				italiens	
				suisses	
Feminine					
SUBJECT PRONOUN		**VERB**		**ADJECTIVE**	
Je	*I*	**suis**	*am*	**allemande**	
				américaine	
Tu	*You*	**es**	*are*	**anglaise**	
				écossaise	
Elle	*She*			**espagnole**	
Ma sœur	*My sister*	**est**	*is*	**française**	
Ma mère	*My mother*			**galloise**	
				italienne	
				suisse	
Nous	*We*	**sommes**	*are*	**allemandes**	
Ma mère et moi	*My mother and I*			**américaines**	
Vous	*You girls*	**êtes**	*are*	**anglaises**	
				écossaises	
Elles	*They*			**espagnoles**	
Mes sœurs	*My sisters*	**sont**	*are*	**françaises**	
				galloises	
				italiennes	
				suisses	

THE LANGUAGE GYM

47

LANGUAGE AWARENESS: ÊTRE – NATIONALITY IN FRENCH

In French, we use the verb **être** to talk about nationality.

To change adjectives into feminine, add 'e'

If an adjective describing a nationality ends in a *consonant* you need to add an -**e** to describe a female person.

- Mon père est **français** *(French)*
- Ma tante est **française**

To speak about a group of people, as seen previously we just add -**s** to make the plural form:

- Mes parents **sont italiens** *(Italian)*
- Mes tantes sont **italiennes**

Adjectives ending in a 'en'

If nationality adjectives end in 'en' then we just add -**ne** to make the feminine form:

- Mon père est **italien**
- Ma mère est **italienne**

To speak about a group of people, as seen previously we just add -**s** to make the plural form:

- Mes parents sont italien**s**
- Mes tantes sont **italiennes**

Adjectives ending in an 's'

If nationality adjectives end in 's' then **we do not need** to add -**s** to make the plural form:

- Mon père est **gallois**
- Mes parents sont **gallois**

Adjectives ending in a 'e'

If a nationality adjective ends in -*e* (*suisse*) we **do not add anything** to make the feminine form:

- Philippe est **suisse**   *Phillippe is Swiss*

- Claudine est **suisse**   *Claudine is Swiss*

We just add -**s** to make the plural form:

- Philippe et Claudine sont suisse**s**

Quelle coïncidence!

Mon père est **français** et je suis **français**, mais mes amis sont **anglais**

Ma mère est **française** et je suis **française**, mais mes amies sont **anglaises**

In French, nationality adjectives do not have a capital letter unless used as a noun!

- Je suis **écossais**

- Je connais un **Écossais**

- Je suis **français**

- Je connais un **Français**

1. Match

espagnol	*German (masculine/singular)*
anglaise	*American (singular)*
français	*French (masculine/singular)*
anglais	*American (plural)*
française	*English (feminine/singular)*
italiens	*Italian (masculine/plural)*
américains	*French (feminine/singular)*
américain	*Spanish (masculine/singular)*
allemand	*English (masculine/singular)*

Salut! Je suis allemande

Nous sommes allemands

Ouaf! (Woof)

2. Sentence Puzzle: arrange the words in the correct order and then translate them into English

a. allemand père est Mon

b. Mon gallois ami est

c. anglais oncle est Mon

d. parents anglais sont Mes

e. suisse grand-mère Ma est

f. frère moi sommes et écossais Mon

g. tantes sont Mes italiennes

3. Complete and then listen to check

a. Ma mère est français__

b. Mes parents sont gallo__ __

c. Je suis alleman__

d. Madame Rossi est italien__ __

e. Mon père est américai__ et ma mère est anglais__

f. Mes grands-parents sont écossa__ __

g. Ma cousine Joanna est allemand__

h. Mes tantes sont français__ __

4. Each French sentence contains TWO mistakes: spot and correct them

a. Ma mère es allemand   *My mother is German*

b. Mon oncles sont suisse   *My uncles are Swiss*

c. Vous sommes galloises   *You girls are French*

d. Je es anglais   *I am English (f)*

e. Mes parents suis écossaise   *My parents are German*

f. Mon amie Lise es américain   *My friend Lise is American*

g. Nous sont écossais   *We are English*

h. Tu est italiens   *You are Italian*

5. Listen and circle the form of the adjective you hear

a. Elle est **allemand/allemande**

b. Ils sont **anglais/anglaise**

c. Elle est **écossais/écossaise**

d. Je suis **italien/italienne**

e. Ils sont **français/françaises**

f. Je suis **gallois/galloise**

g. Vous êtes **espagnols/espagnoles**

h. Elles sont **américains/américaines**

i. Nous sommes **italiens/italiennes**

j. Tu es **irlandais/irlandaise**

THE LANGUAGE GYM

6. Complete with the missing letters

a. Ma mère est a_ _ _ _ _ _ _   *German*

b. Mon père est e_ _ _ _ _ _ _   *Spanish*

c. Vous êtes a_ _ _ _ _ _ _ _   *English (f)*

d. Mes cousins sont a_ _ _ _ _ _ _ _ _   *American*

e. Tu es f_ _ _ _ _ _ _   *French (m)*

f. Mes frères sont a_ _ _ _ _ _ _ _   *German*

g. Mes parents sont s_ _ _ _ _ _   *Swiss*

h. Mes tantes sont i_ _ _ _ _ _ _ _ _   *Italian*

7. Dictation

a.

b.

c.

d.

e.

f.

g.

h.

i.

8. Word detectives: work out what the hidden sentences are and then translate them into English

a. M_ m_r_ e_ _ i_a_ _e_ _ _

b. M_ _ g_a_d -p_r_ _ _s s_ _ _ e_p_ _n_ _ _

c. V_ _s ê_ _s é_o_ _ _i_ _s

d. M_ _ o_c_ _ _ s_ _ _ f_a_ç_ _ _

e. M_ _ fr_ _ _ e_ m_i_s_ _ _ _ _ g_l_ _i_

f. M_ _ a_ _e e_ _ a_g_ _i_ _

g. M_ _ a_ _ Guillaume e_ _ s_ _ _ _ _

9. English to French translation

a. My grandparents are Welsh

b. My friends (f) are Spanish

c. My dad is Italian

d. My brothers and I are French

e. My aunts are Swiss

f. My parents are English

g. My aunt is German

THE LANGUAGE GYM

2.6 ALL PERSONS OF ÊTRE DE + PROPER NOUN *(SAYING WHERE ONE IS FROM)*

Je	*I*	**suis** *am*	**d'Allemagne**	*from Germany*
			d'Angleterre	*from England*
Tu	*You*	**es** *are*	**d'Écosse**	*from Scotland*
			d'Espagne	*from Spain*
Il / Elle	*He / She*	**est** *is*	**d'Irlande**	*from* Ireland
Mon frère	*My brother*		**d'Italie**	*from* Italy
Ma mère	*My mother*			
Nous	*We*	**sommes** *are*	**de Belgique**	*from Belgium*
Mon père et moi	*My father and I*		**de France**	*from France*
			de Suisse	*from Switzerland*
Vous	*You guys/girls*	**êtes** *are*	**des États-Unis**	*from the USA*
Ils	*They (guys)*	**sont** *are*	**du Canada**	*from Canada*
Elles	*They (girls)*		**du Maroc**	*from Morocco*
Mes frères et sœurs	*My siblings*		**du Pays de Galles**	*from Wales*
Mes parents	*My parents*			

1. Match English and French

Je suis d'Écosse	*They are from Germany*
Nous sommes d'Écosse	*She is from Italy*
Vous êtes d'Écosse	*We are from Spain*
Elles sont des États-Unis	*They are from Spain*
Tu es des États-Unis	*You guys are from Germany*
Vous êtes d'Allemagne	*You girls are from Scotland*
Ils sont d'Allemagne	*We are from Scotland*
Elle est d'Italie	*They are from the USA*
Nous sommes d'Italie	*You are from the USA*
Elles sont d'Espagne	*I am from Scotland*
Nous sommes d'Espagne	*We are from Italy*

LANGUAGE AWARENESS

COUNTRIES & NATIONALITIES

Like in English, you can also say where you are from by saying what your nationality is.

Be careful! **Nationalities** are always written in **lower case**. **Countries** are written with a **capital letter**, like in English.

- Je suis **de France**   *I am from **France***
- Je suis <u>f</u>rançais   *I am **French***

ÊTRE + DU/DE/D'/DES + COUNTRY

To say where you are from in French, we use the verb *être* (to be) + a preposition.

Je suis du/de/d'/des...*I am from*

The preposition changes according to the gender (masc/fem), the quantity or the spelling.

- masc -> **du** Canada   • fem -> **de** Belgique
- vowel -> **d'**Italie
- plural -> **des** États-Unis

THE LANGUAGE GYM

2. Each French sentence contains two mistakes: spot and correct

a. Mon amis êtes d'Espagne   *My friends are from Spain*

b. Mes oncle sont d'allemand   *My uncles are from Germany*

c. Vous es d'anglais   *You ladies are from England*

d. Mon parents êtes d'Espagne   *My parents are from Spain*

e. Mes grands-parents est d'italien   *My grandparents are from Italy*

f. Ma taunt Martine es de Belgique   *My aunt Martine is from Belgium*

g. Nos êtes de France   *We are from France*

h. Je est du Maroc   *You are from Morocco*

Je suis d'Allemagne, et toi?

Je suis du Canada. Enchantée.

3. Listen and translate

a. Je suis d'Angleterre

b. Ils sont de France

c. Nous sommes des États-Unis

d. Elle est d'Allemagne

e. Tu es d'Italie?

f. De quelle nationalité êtes-vous?

g. Il est de Belgique

h. Nous sommes d'Espagne

4. Tangled translation: translate into French

a. *My* parents *are* d'*England*

b. Mes *grandparents* sont *from France*

c. Vous *are* d'*Spain*

d. Mes *sisters* sont *from Germany*

e. *I am* de *Switzerland*

f. Nous *are from* Italie

g. *My* oncle *is* de Belgique

h. *My* ami est *from Morocco*

5. Guided translation

a. J__ s__ __ __ d'E__ __ __ __ __ __
   I am from Spain

b. M__ __ a__ __ e__ __ d__ F__ __ __ __ __
   My friend is from France

c. M__ __ p__ __ __ __ __ __ s__ __ __ d'É__ __ __ __ __
   My parents are from Scotland

d. M__ __ g__ __ __ __ __-__ __ __ __ e__ __ d'I__ __ __ __ __
   My grandfather is from Italy

e. M__ __ f__ __ __ __ __ e__ __ d'A__ __ __ __ __ __ __ __ __
   My brother is from England

f. M__ __ a__ __ __ __ s__ __ __ d__ C__ __ __ __ __ __
   My friends are from Canada

6. English to French translation

a. My sisters are from England. They are English.

b. My brother is from France. He is French.

c. I am from Spain. I am Spanish.

d. You are from Wales. You are Welsh.

e. They (f) are from France. They are (f) French.

THE LANGUAGE GYM

D'où *From where*	**es-tu?**	*are you?*
	est ton père?	*is your father?*
	est ta mère?	*is your mother?*
	êtes-vous?	*are you guys/girls?*
	sont tes grands-parents?	*are your grandparents?*
De quelle nationalité *Which nationality*	**es-tu?**	*are you?*
	est ton père/ta mère?	*is your father/mother?*
	êtes-vous?	*are you guys/girls?*
	sont tes amis?	*are your friends?*
Comment *What…*	**es-tu?**	*are you like?*
	est ton père?	*is your father like?*
	est ta mère?	*is your mother like?*
	êtes-vous?	*are you guys/girls like?*
	sont tes amis?	*are your friends like?*

LANGUAGE AWARENESS
QUESTION WORDS

Question words are used to make questions. In English "what?", "when?", "why?", "how?" and "why?" are all **question words**.

These are some of the most common **question words**:

• **Comment?**	*How?*
• **Quand?**	*When?*
• **D'où?**	*Where… from?*
• **De quelle nationalité?**	*Which nationality?*
• **Où?**	*Where?*
• **Pourquoi?**	*Why?*

ASKING QUESTIONS
WITH QUESTION WORDS

If you use question words like *Comment, Quand, Pourquoi etc…*you notice that you have to **invert the subject and the verb** (like in English) as well as **add a hyphen** (-) between them. You must also add a **question mark** at the end.

• *Comment* **es-tu?** (What are you like?)
• *Quand* **est-il** à la maison**?**
(When is he at home?)
• *D'où* **êtes-vous?** (Where are you from?)
• *De quelle nationalité* **est-elle?**
(Which nationality is she?)

1. Match

De quelle nationalité êtes-vous?	*Where are you from?*
D'où êtes-vous?	*Where are they from?*
Comment sont tes amis?	*What are you like?*
Comment sont-ils?	*Which nationality are you?*
De quelle nationalité sont tes parents?	*Which nationality are you guys/girls?*
Comment es-tu?	*What are they like?*
Comment est-il?	*Where are you guys from?*
D'où sont-ils?	*What are your friends like?*
D'où es-tu?	*Where are your friends from?*
D'où sont tes amis?	*Which nationality are your parents?*
De quelle nationalité es-tu?	*What is he like?*

2. Translate into French

a. You are

b. I am

c. She is

d. We are

e. They are

f. You guys are

g. Which nationality?

h. Where from?

i. What are you like?

j. She is Spanish

k. I am English

l. We are from England

m. Where are you from?

n. Which nationality are you?

o. Which nationality are you guys?

3. Listen and complete the table following the same pattern in the example

	Question Word	Verb	Translation
e.g.	*D'où*	*es-tu?*	*Where are you from?*
a.			
b.			
c.			
d.			
e.			
f.			

4. Match each question to its answer

De quelle nationalité êtes-vous?	Nous sommes d'Espagne
D'où êtes-vous?	Ils sont grands
Comment sont tes amis?	Je suis malin
Comment sont-ils?	Ils sont de Suisse
De quelle nationalité sont tes parents?	Il est intelligent
Comment es-tu?	Je suis du Pays de Galles
Comment est-il?	Nous sommes français
D'où sont-ils?	Mes amis sont du Maroc
D'où es-tu?	Je suis écossais
D'où sont tes amis?	Mes amis sont sympas
De quelle nationalité es-tu?	Mes parents sont allemands

5. Spot the mistake in each sentence and correct it

a. De comment es-tu?
   Which nationality are you?

b. De quand es-tu?
   What are you like?

c. De pourquoi es-tu?
   Where are you from?

d. Comment nationalité sont-elles?
   Which nationality are they (f)?

e. D'où nationalité est-elle?
   Which nationality is she?

f. D'où sont-elles?
   Where are you guys from?

g. Comment êtes-ils?
   What are they like?

h. De quelle nationalité es ils?
   Which nationality are they (m)?

6. Sentence Puzzle: arrange the words in correct order and translate them into English

a. es Comment -tu?

b. nationalité -tu quelle De es?

c. où es D' -tu?

d. quelle De -vous nationalité êtes?

e. -ils sont Comment?

f. -ils nationalité De quelle sont?

g. est Comment -il?

h. Comment -ils sont?

8. English to French translation

a. My parents are from Spain. They are Spanish.

b. My cousin Hans is from Germany. He is German.

c. I am from Switzerland. I am Swiss.

d. They (m) are from Wales. They (m) are Welsh.

e. My uncle is from Italy. He is Italian.

7. Guided translation

a. D'___ ê_____ - v____?
   Where are you from?

b. D_ q_____ n_____ _____ s____ - i__?
   Which nationality are they?

c. D'___ s____ - e_____?
   Where are they (f) from?

d. C_____ e__ - t_?
   What are you like?

e. C_____ s____ - e___ ___?
   What are they (f) like?

f. D_ q_____ n_____ _____ ê____ - v___?
   Which nationality are you guys?

g. D'___ e__ t__ o_____?
   Where is your uncle from?

THE LANGUAGE GYM

ORAL PING PONG

ÊTRE

ENGLISH 1	FRENCH 1	ENGLISH 2	FRENCH 2
My sister is tall, muscular and strong, but annoying.	Ma sœur est grande, musclée et forte, mais énervante.	My father is short, hansdome and fun, but quite lazy.	
My older brother is fifteen years old and is handsome, but he is a bit lazy.	Mon frère aîné a quinze ans et il est beau, mais il est un peu paresseux.	My best friend Laurent is Swiss. He is as fun as me.	
My parents are quite hard-working and fun, but my brothers and I are very lazy.	Mes parents sont assez travailleurs et amusants, mais mes frères et moi sommes très paresseux.	My grandparents are very affectionate and more talkative than my parents.	
You are more boring (f) than my best friend Anne.	Tu es plus ennuyeuse que ma meilleure amie Anne.	My older sister is sportier than my brother.	
My grandmother is more talkative than my grandfather.	Ma grand-mère est plus bavarde que mon grand-père.	I have a friend who is Italian. He is very shy, but very intelligent and fun.	
My sisters are calmer than me, but I am more hard-working.	Mes sœurs sont plus calmes que moi, mais je suis plus travailleur/travailleuse	My girlfriends are less noisy than me.	
My brother and I are English, but my parents are French.	Mon frère et moi sommes anglais, mais mes parents sont français.	My uncle is French. He is more serious than my father.	
I have friends who are Italian and Spanish. I am Scottish.	J'ai des amis qui sont italiens et espagnols. Je suis écossais/écossaise.	My brothers and I are French, but my mother is English and my father is Welsh.	

INSTRUCTIONS - You are **PARTNER A.** Work in pairs. Each of you has two sets of sentences - one set has already been translated for you. You will ask your partner to translate these. The other set of sentences have not been translated. Your partner will ask you to translate these.

HOW TO PLAY - Partner A starts by reading out his/her/their first sentence in English. Partner B must translate. Partner A must check the answer and award the following points: **3 points** = perfect, **2 points** = 1 mistake, **1 point** = mistakes but the verb is accurate. If they cannot translate correctly, Partner A will read out the sentence so that Partner B can learn what the correct translation is.

Then Partner B reads out his/her/their first sentence, and so on.

OBJECTIVE - Try to win more points than your partner by translating correctly as many sentences as possible.

 **THE LANGUAGE GYM**

ORAL PING PONG

ÊTRE

ENGLISH 1	FRENCH 1	ENGLISH 2	FRENCH 2
My sister is tall, muscular and strong, but annoying.		My father is short, handsome, and fun, but quite lazy.	Mon père est petit, beau et amusant, mais assez paresseux.
My older brother is fifteen years old and is handsome, but he is a bit lazy.		My best friend Laurent is Swiss. He is as fun as me.	Mon meilleur ami Laurent est suisse. Il est aussi amusant que moi.
My parents are quite hard-working and fun, but my brothers and I are very lazy.		My grandparents are very affectionate and more talkative than my parents.	Mes grands-parents sont très affectueux et plus bavards que mes parents.
You are more boring (f) than my best friend Anne.		My older sister is sportier than my brother.	Ma sœur aînée est plus sportive que mon frère.
My grandmother is more talkative than my grandfather.		I have a friend who is Italian. He is very shy, but very intelligent and fun.	J'ai un ami qui est italien. Il est très timide, mais très intelligent et amusant.
My sisters are calmer than me, but I am more hard-working.		My girlfriends are less noisy than me.	Mes amies sont moins bruyantes que moi.
My brother and I are English, but my parents are French.		My uncle is French. He is more serious than my father.	Mon oncle est français. Il est plus sérieux que mon père.
I have friends who are Italian and Spanish. I am Scottish.		My brothers and I are French, but my mother is English and my father is Welsh.	Mes frères et moi sommes français, mais ma mère est anglaise et mon père est gallois.

INSTRUCTIONS - You are **PARTNER B.** Work in pairs. Each of you has two sets of sentences - one set has already been translated for you. You will ask your partner to translate these. The other set of sentences have not been translated. Your partner will ask you to translate these.

HOW TO PLAY - Partner A starts by reading out his/her/their first sentence <u>in English</u>. Partner B must translate. Partner A must check the answer and award the following points: **3 points** = perfect, **2 points** = 1 mistake, **1 point** = mistakes but the verb is accurate. If they cannot translate correctly, Partner A will read out the sentence so that Partner B can learn what the correct translation is.

Then Partner B reads out his/her/their first sentence, and so on.

OBJECTIVE - Try to win more points than your partner by translating correctly as many sentences as possible.

ÊTRE

No Snakes No Ladders

7 My sister is more fun than my mum	**6** What is your sister like?	**5** What are you like?	**4** Which nationality is your father?	**3** Where are you from?	**2** We are from Italy	**1** I am from France, I am French
8 My best friend (m) is Italian	**9** My uncle is more talkative than my dad	**10** My father is less lazy than my sister	**11** I am 12 years old and I am from Spain	**12** My friends (f) are Welsh	**13** My older brothers are quite muscular	**14** I have a friend that is Swiss
23 My sister has a Moroccan friend	**22** I have six English friends	**21** My mother is more talkative than my father	**20** We are from Scotland.	**19** I have a Spanish dog	**18** My French friends are fun	**17** My sister is less lazy than my brother
24 My aunt is less serious than my sister	**25** My brothers and I are French	**26** Which nationality is your friend Anne?	**27** Where are you guys/girls from?	**28** My sister has a Belgian bird	**29** My parents are quite intelligent	**30** My friend is lazier than me
					15 My cat is French. He is 2 years old	**16** My brother has a friend that is annoying
					DÉPART	ARRIVÉE

No Snakes No Ladders

		7 Ma sœur est plus amusante que ma maman	**6** Comment est ta sœur?	**5** Comment es-tu?	**4** De quelle nationalité est ton père?	**3** D'où es-tu?	**2** Nous sommes d'Italie	**1** Je suis de France, je suis français(e).
		8 Mon meilleur ami est italien	**9** Mon oncle est plus bavard que mon papa	**10** Mon père est moins paresseux que ma sœur	**11** J'ai douze ans et je suis d'Espagne	**12** Mes amies sont galloises	**13** Mes frères aînés sont assez musclés	**14** J'ai un(e) ami(e) suisse
		23 Ma sœur a une amie marocaine	**22** J'ai six ami(e)s anglais(es)	**21** Ma mère est plus bavarde que mon père	**20** Nous sommes d'Écosse	**19** J'ai un chien espagnol	**18** Mes amis français sont amusants	**17** Ma sœur est moins paresseuse que mon frère
		24 Ma tante est moins sérieuse que ma sœur	**25** Mes frères et moi sommes français	**26** De quelle nationalité est ton amie Anne?	**27** D'où êtes-vous?	**28** Ma sœur a un oiseau belge	**29** Mes parents sont assez intelligents	**30** Mon amie est plus paresseuse que moi

DÉPART

15 Mon chat est français. Il a deux ans

16 Mon frère a un ami qui est énervant

ARRIVÉE

PYRAMID TRANSLATION

Unit 2 - Être

Translate each part of the pyramid out loud with your partner, then write it into the spaces provided below.

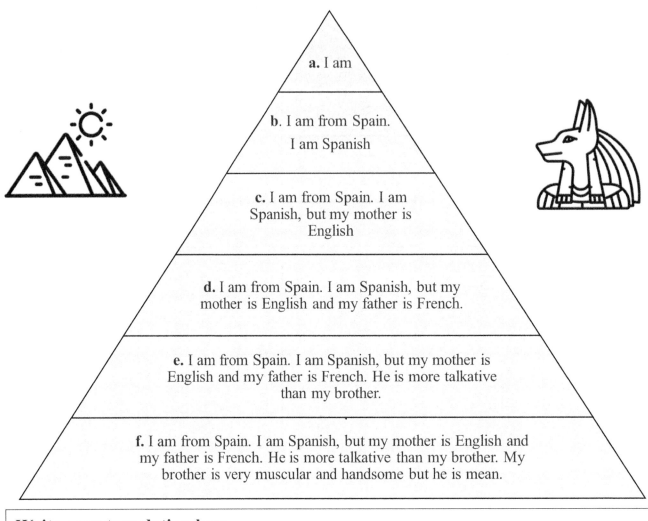

a. I am

b. I am from Spain.
I am Spanish

c. I am from Spain. I am
Spanish, but my mother is
English

d. I am from Spain. I am Spanish, but my
mother is English and my father is French.

e. I am from Spain. I am Spanish, but my mother is
English and my father is French. He is more talkative
than my brother.

f. I am from Spain. I am Spanish, but my mother is English and
my father is French. He is more talkative than my brother. My
brother is very muscular and handsome but he is mean.

Write your translation here

SOLUTION: Je suis d'Espagne. Je suis espagnol/e, mais ma mère est anglaise et mon père est français. Il est plus bavard que mon frère. Mon frère est très musclé et beau, mais il est méchant.

THE LANGUAGE GYM

2.8 AUJOURD'HUI + ÊTRE + FIRST THREE PERSONS OF ÊTRE + ADJECTIVE
(ASKING AND SAYING HOW ONE FEELS)

FEELINGS/MOOD - SINGULAR				
First person – I – masculine & feminine				
Je m'appelle Luc.	**Aujourd'hui** *Today*	**je suis** *I am*	**en colère** *angry* **énergique** *energetic* **énervé** *irritated* **fatigué** *tired* **joyeux** *joyful* **pressé** *in a hurry*	**calme** *calm* **de mauvaise humeur** *in a bad mood* **malade** *ill* **nerveux** *nervous* **préoccupé** *worried* **triste** *sad*
Je m'appelle Marie.			**en colère** **énergique** **énervée** **fatiguée** **joyeuse** **pressée**	**calme** **de mauvaise humeur** **malade** **nerveuse** **préoccupée** **triste**
Second person – you – masculine & feminine				
Bonjour Laurent,	**comment ça va aujourd'hui?** *how are you today?*		**Tu es énervé?** *Are you irritated?* **Tu es joyeux?** *Are you joyful?*	
Bonjour Aline,			**Tu es énervée?** *Are you irritated?* **Tu es joyeuse?** *Are you joyful?*	
Third person – he/she– masculine & feminine				
Pascal	**est**		**fatigué** *tired* **nerveux** *nervous*	**malade** *ill* **préoccupé** *worried*
Hélène	**est**		**fatiguée** *tired* **nerveuse** *nervous*	**malade** *ill* **préoccupée** *worried*
Mon frère aîné	**est**		**pressé** *in a hurry* **calme** *calm*	**en colère** *irritated* **énervé** *angry*
Ma sœur cadette	**est**		**pressée** *in a hurry* **calme** *calm*	**en colère** *irritated* **énervée** *angry*

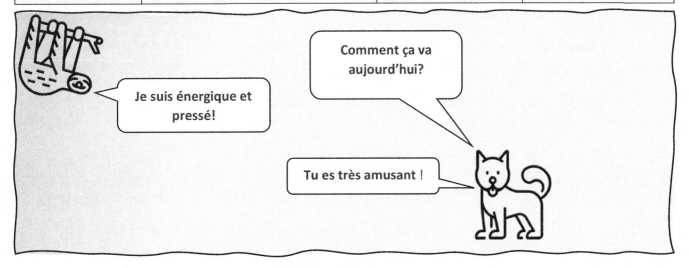

Je suis énergique et pressé!

Comment ça va aujourd'hui?

Tu es très amusant !

THE LANGUAGE GYM

1. Faulty translation: fix the English

a. Il est malade — *I am ill*

b. Il est triste — *I am sad*

c. Tu es préoccupé — *You are ill*

d. Il est énergique — *He is angry*

e. Je suis de mauvaise humeur — *I am bored*

f. Elle est en colère — *She is happy*

g. Je suis pressé — *I am tired*

2. Listen and write the words 🔊

a. aeCml   _ _ _ _ _ _

b. yeJoxu   _ _ _ _ _ _

c. ssPrée   _ _ _ _ _ _

d. coEnrelè   _ _ _ _ _ _ _ _ _

e. lMaeda   _ _ _ _ _ _

f. étguiFa   _ _ _ _ _ _ _

g. reNuexv   _ _ _ _ _ _ _

3. Split words

ste	ade	yeux
ervée	tigué	veuse
mes	pée	lère

a. Je suis fa_____

b. Il est jo_____

c. Tu es én_____

d. Tu es mal_____?

e. Je suis ner_____

f. Elle est préoccu_____

g. Tu es tri_____?

h. Je suis en co_____

i. On est cal_____(pl)

4. Complete with the missing word

malade	joyeux	nerveuse	préoccupé	triste
en colère	Comment	Je suis	calme	fatiguée

a. _____ fatigué — *I am tired (m)*

b. _____ ça va? — *How are you?*

c. Mon père est très _____ — *My father is very worried*

d. Ma mère est _____ — *My mother is tired*

e. Tu es _____? — *Are you joyful?*

f. Je suis très _____ — *I am very ill*

g. Elle est très _____ — *She is very angry*

h. Pourquoi es-tu aussi _____? — *Why are you so sad?*

i. Je ne suis pas _____ — *I am not nervous*

j. Ma petite amie est _____ — *My girlfriend is calm*

5. Spot the spelling mistake and rewrite the whole sentence correctly

e.g. Je suis fattigué   <u>*Je suis fatigué*</u>

a. Elle est nervouse _____

b. Tu es joieuse? _____

c. Je ne suis pas malard _____

d. Il est trist _____

e. Tu es presé? _____

f. Je suis préocupé _____

g. Elle est en calère _____

6. Listen, complete and translate: 🔊

a. Je suis fatigu____

b. Je suis mala____

c. Ma __ère est en colè____

d. Philippe est nerv____

e. Je suis pre_____

f. Cyril est jo_____

g. Je su____ de mauvaise humeur

h. Je suis préoccu____

 THE LANGUAGE GYM

7. Missing letter challenge: complete the words and translate them into English

a. Aujourd'h_i je sui_ fatigué

b. Tu e_ tris_e?

c. Il n'e_t pas malad_

d. El_e est de ma_vaise hu_eur

e. J_ suis trè_ pr_ssée

f. Aujourd'hui _e suis très nerv_use

g. El_e es_ en co_ère

h. T_ es jo_eux?

i. Co_ment ç_ v_?

j. Je ne suis p_s éner_ique

8. Find the French translation and write it next to the English prompts

l	p	r	e	e	m	l	a	c	e	t	e	v	r	g	p	o	k	l	a	e	a	s	i
e	a	r	h	a	s	e	n	c	o	l	è	r	e	n	r	o	j	n	l	j	w	é	m
s	l	e	é	r	s	e	r	l	s	t	r	e	l	i	i	h	a	l	d	d	s	i	t
a	i	s	e	o	i	u	r	f	h	o	f	n	a	v	v	n	e	a	e	s	r	o	e
v	e	u	p	u	c	g	e	f	a	t	i	g	u	é	e	e	w	m	e	a	e	r	s
e	d	e	s	j	p	c	d	i	t	r	i	s	t	e	s	a	s	r	r	s	n	t	u
n	s	v	e	e	a	a	u	o	a	p	m	n	n	t	a	y	p	e	n	i	c	u	e
t	r	r	r	t	j	l	s	p	r	y	n	a	d	t	n	e	m	m	o	c	o	d	y
u	e	e	d	e	r	k	e	t	é	r	d	i	s	a	t	r	s	p	i	o	n	e	o
r	i	n	u	d	e	m	a	u	v	a	i	s	e	h	u	m	e	u	r	r	t	r	j

a. Calm

b. Angry

c. I am

d. Nervous (f)

e. In a hurry

f. Worried

g. Sad

h. She is

i. How

j. Tired (f)

k. Joyful (f)

l. In a bad mood

9. Translate into French

a. Today I am tired

b. How are you?

c. He is very worried

d. She is very energetic today

e. My mother is nervous

f. My mother is ill today

g. My friend (f) is in a bad mood today

h. My friend (f) is joyful today

i. I am joyful (m) today

j. My sister is in a bad mood

k. I am in a hurry

l. My friend (f) is ill

m. Are you ill?

n. My mother is sad

o. My father is nervous

p. My older brother is worried

2.9 LOCATIVE OR TIME ADVERBIAL + ÊTRE (PLURAL PERSONS) + ADJECTIVE
(SAYING HOW ONE FEELS)

	Masculine plural			
En classe de biologie *In the biology lesson* **Ce matin** *This morning* **Cet après-midi** *This afternoon* **Ce soir** *This evening* **Aujourd'hui** *Today* **Le matin** *In the morning* **L'après-midi** *In the afternoon* **Le soir** *In the evening*	**nous sommes** *we are* **vous êtes** *you guys are* **ils sont** *they are*	**assez** *quite* **très** *very* **toujours** *always* **trop** *too* **un peu** *a bit*	**en colère** *angry* **énergiques** *energetic* **fatigués** *tired* **joyeux** *joyful* **tristes** *sad*	**calmes** *calm* **de mauvaise humeur** *in a bad mood* **en forme** *fit* **malades** *ill* **nerveux** *nervous* **préoccupés** *worried*
	Feminine plural			
	nous sommes *we are* **vous êtes** *you girls are* **elles sont** *they are*	**assez** *quite* **très** *very* **toujours** *always* **trop** *too* **un peu** *a bit*	**en colère** *angry* **énergiques** *energetic* **fatiguées** *tired* **joyeuses** *joyful* **tristes** *sad*	**calmes** *calm* **de mauvaise humeur** *in a bad mood* **en forme** *fit* **malades** *ill* **nerveuses** *nervous* **préoccupées** *worried*

1. Break the flow

a. Lesoirvousêtesasseztristesetencolère

b. Cematinnoussommestrèsénergiquesetjoyeux.

c. Mesparentssontunpeupréoccupésetcalmes

d. Enclassedebiologieilssonttoujoursnerveux

e. Cetaprès-midimessœurssonttrèsmalades

f. Aujourd'huivousêtestropfatigués

2. One of two

a. Mes parents sont **nerveux/nerveuses**

b. Nous sommes très **préoccupé/ préoccupés**

c. Vous (f) êtes **joyeux/joyeuses**

d. Mes frères sont **calme/calmes**

e. Marie et Noémie sont **triste/tristes**

f. Mes professeurs sont trop **fatigué/fatigués**

3. Spot and correct the mistakes. There is at least one in each sentence

a. Ma mère es trop nerveuse

b. Mes parents sont très préoccupé

c. Mon meilleur ami sont toujours nerveux

d. Mon professeur de français est de mauvais humeur

e. Ma professeure de musique est toujours joyeux

f. Mes parents sommes trop en colère

g. Mes frère sont calmes aujourd'hui

h. Nous sommes un peu énergique

i. Ma mère est toujours tristes

j. Ce matine ma grand-mère est calme

k. Mon oncle sont un peu fatiguées

4. Listen, complete the words and then decide if the sentence is positive (P) or negative (N)

a. Nous sommes très n__rv__ux

b. Ils sont un peu __at__gu__ __

c. Vous êtes toujours c__l__ __ __

d. Elles sont assez tr__st__ __

e. Je suis trop pr__oc__ __p__ __

f. Tu es toujours é__er__ __ __ qu__

g. Elle est e__ c__lè__ __

h. Nous sommes toujours e__ fo __m__

Nous sommes en forme!

Je suis fatigué

5. Fill in the blanks with the correct conjugation of the verb *être*

a. Ce soir je __ __ __ __ __ très calme

b. Mon père __ __ __ en colère

c. Mes frères __ __ __ __ en forme

d. Cet après-midi, nous __ __ __ __ __ __ nerveux

e. Vous __ __ __ __ de mauvaise humeur

f. Ma petite amie __ __ __ un peu fatiguée

6. Complete with the missing words, choosing from the option in the table below

a. Nous sommes très _____   *We are very tired*

b. Ils sont toujours _____   *They are always fit*

c. Aujourd'hui je suis _____   *Today I am sad*

d. Ce matin ma mère est _____   *This morning my mother is ill*

e. _____ ça va aujourd'hui?   *How are you today?*

f. _____ sommes de mauvaise humeur   *We are in a bad mood*

g. Ma sœur _____ nerveuse   *My sister is nervous*

h. Ils _____ très calmes   *They are very calm*

i. Nous _____ préoccupées   *We are worried*

j. Vous êtes _____ en colère?   *You are a bit angry*

un peu	en forme
nous	sommes
sont	malade
comment	est
fatigués	triste

7. Translate into English

a. Cet après-midi je suis très fatiguée

b. Aujourd'hui ma mère est malade

c. Ce matin mon frère est un peu triste

d. Ce soir mes parents sont très préoccupés

e. Le matin mon frère est toujours en colère

f. Aujourd'hui mon professeur de biologie est calme

g. La professeure de mathématiques est toujours de mauvaise humeur

h. En classe de français je suis assez joyeux

i. Ce matin mon amie Carole est nerveuse

j. Nous sommes toujours en forme

8. Tangled translation into French

a. Ma mère *is* très *tired*

b. Mon père est *quite worried*

c. *My parents* sont un peu *nervous*

d. Mes sœurs *are quite* tristes

e. Nous sommes *a bit ill today*

f. Christelle *and* Thomas *are angry* ce matin

g. *How* ça va cet *afternoon*?

h. Je suis *very calm*

i. *My* cousins *are* toujours *in a bad mood*

9. Guided translation

a. E__ __ __ __   s__ __ __   j__ __ __ __ __ __ __
   They are joyful

b. V__ __ __   ê__ __ __   f__ __ __ __ __ __ __
   You guys are tired

c. N__ __ __   s__ __ __ __ __ __   c__ __ __ __ __
   We are calm

d. J__   s__ __ __   n__ __ __ __ __ __ __ __
   I am nervous (f)

e. M__ __   f__ __ __ __   e__ __   t__ __ __ __ __
   My brother is sad

10. Translate into French

a. My mother is very worried

b. My father is quite joyful today

c. My French teacher is always in a bad mood

d. I am a bit angry

e. Today we are very calm

f. My brother is always sad

g. My parents are very nervous today

h. My sisters are very joyful this evening

2.10 DETERMINER + SINGULAR & PLURAL NOUN
+ LOCATIVE PREPOSITION + DEFINITE ARTICLE + NOUN
(SAYING WHERE BUILDINGS ARE LOCATED IN RELATION TO OTHERS)

LOCATION: MY AREA

			Masculine places	
Ma maison *My house* **Mon école** *My school* **La maison de mon ami(e)** *My friend's house*	**est** *is* *located*	**à cinq minutes** *5 minutes away from* **à côté** *next to* **à droite** *on the right of* **à gauche** *on the left of* **à l'intérieur** *inside*	**de l'aéroport**	*the airport*
			du centre-ville	*the city centre*
			du centre commercial	*the shopping centre*
			du centre sportif	*the sports centre*
			du château	*the castle*
			du ciné	*the cinema*
			du magasin de vêtements	*the clothes shop*
			du musée	*the museum*
			du parc	*the park*
			du poste de police	*the police station*
			du restaurant	*the restaurant*
			du stade	*the stadium*
			du supermarché	*the supermarket*
			Feminine places	
Les magasins *The shops*	**sont** *are* *located*	**en face** *opposite* **loin** *far from* **près** *near*	**de la bibliothèque**	*the library*
			de la boucherie	*the butcher's*
			de la boulangerie	*the bakery*
			de l'école	*the school*
			de la mairie	*the town hall*
			de la pâtisserie	*the cake shop*
			de la rue piétonne	*the pedestrian street*
			de la piscine	*the swimming pool*
			de la plage	*the beach*
			de la salle de sport	*the gym*

LANGUAGE AWARENESS: ÊTRE FOR LOCATION

Masculine places: DE + LE = DU

In the sentence "far from the castle" the *de (from)* + *le (the)* becomes *du*

e.g. **Ma maison est loin du château**   *My house is far from the castle*

Feminine places: DE + LA

In the sentence "near the beach" the *de (from)* + *la (the)* **stay as they are.**

e.g. **Ma maison est près de la plage**   *My house is near the beach*

Singular Places starting by a vowel: DE + L'

In the sentence "opposite the airport" or "opposite the school" the *de (from)* + *le/la (the)* become **de l'**

e.g. **Ma maison est en face de l'aéroport**   *My house is opposite the airport*

Ma maison est en face de l'école   *My house is opposite the school*

 **THE LANGUAGE GYM**

1. Match

Le stade	*The town hall*
L'aéroport	*My school*
Le parc	*The restaurant*
Le restaurant	*The park*
La mairie	*The shops*
La plage	*My house*
Mon école	*The stadium*
Ma maison	*The airport*
Les magasins	*The beach*

2. Translate into English

a. La maison de mon ami est près du stade

b. La bibliothèque est à côté de la maison d'Alain

c. La boulangerie est à l'intérieur du centre commercial

d. Le poste de police est loin du centre-ville

e. La piscine est à droite de la salle de sport

f. La rue piétonne est à gauche du supermarché

g. Le château est à cinq minutes de la boucherie

h. La plage est en face du restaurant italien

i. Le cinéma est à côté de la pâtisserie

3. *Vrai* (true) ou *faux* (false). Write V for *vrai* or F for *faux* next to each statement below, based on the map:

Club de golf			Parc			
Boucherie	**La maison de Luc**	**Bibliothèque**	**Château**	**Boulangerie**	**Supermarché**	**Magasin de vêtements**
Rue Marcel Pagnol						
La maison de Véro	**Salle de sport**	**Bar**	**Restaurant indien**	**Restaurant chinois**	**Cinéma**	**Piscine**
Auchan	**Mairie**	**Restaurant italien**	**Jardin public**		**Parking**	

a. La maison de Luc est en face de la salle de sport

b. La piscine est à côté du cinéma

c. Le restaurant indien est loin du restaurant chinois

d. Le supermarché est à l'intérieur du parc

e. La boulangerie est à droite du château

f. Le cinéma est loin de la mairie, mais à côté de la maison de Véro

g. Auchan est près du parking

h. Le bar est à gauche du restaurant indien

i. La boucherie est à l'intérieur du club de golf

THE LANGUAGE GYM

4. Faulty translation: fix the English translation

a. Ma maison est à côté du parc | *My house is near the park*

b. Le poste de police est près du cinéma | *The police station is far from the cinema*

c. La piscine est à droite du jardin | *The swimming pool is behind the garden*

d. La maison est loin du magasin | *The house is near the shop*

e. L'aéroport est en face du supermarché | *The airport is close to the supermarket*

f. La salle de sport est proche du restaurant | *The gym is far from the restaurant*

g. Le musée est à cinq minutes du parking | *The museum is 6 minutes away from the parking*

h. Le bar est loin de l'école | *The bar is next to the school*

i. La boulangerie est devant la boucherie | *The bakery is behind the butcher's*

---

5. Listen and break the flow: draw a line between each word

a. Lepostedepoliceestenfacedelapiscine

b. Lamaisondemonamieestprèsduparc

c. Lemagasinestloindel'école

d. Mamaisonestàcinqminutesducentre-ville

e. Masalledesportestàcôtédelapâtisserie

f. Leparkingestàcôtéduchâteau

g. LamaisondeLaurentestenfaceduparc

h. Lerestaurantestàl'intérieurducentrecommercial

i. Lejardinestàvingtminutesdelaruepiétonne

---

6. Tangled translation: translate into French

a. Ma *house* est *near* de la *beach*

b. Le *police station* est *opposite* du *park*

c. Ma maison *is located* à *five* minutes de la *pedestrian street*

d. La maison *of my friend* est à côté du *stadium*

e. Les *shops* sont *inside* du *shopping centre*

f. *My school* est *near* du *restaurant* italien

g. Le *shop* de vêtements est *next to* la *swimming pool*

h. *The house* de mon ami *is* à droite *from the castle*

---

7. Gapped translation: complete the translation

a. Le _____ est _____ du musée

   The police station is opposite the museum

b. La maison _____ Patrice est près _____ restaurant

   Patrice's house is near the restaurant

c. Le jardin est ___ _____ ___ l'école

   The garden is in front of the school

d. Les magasins _____ _____ de la salle de sport

   The shops are far from the gym

e. Le restaurant est _____ _____ ma maison

   The restaurant is near my house

f. Le _____ de musique est ___ _____ ___ la plage

   The music shop is next to the beach

g. La piscine est ___ _____ ___ stade

   The swimming pool is inside the stadium

h. Ma maison est _____ du centre-_____

   My house is near the city centre

8. Listen, fill in the gaps and translate into English 🔊

a. Ma maison est _____ du parc

b. Le stade est _____ de l'école

c. La plage est _____ du cinéma

d. Le château est _____ du parc

e. La mairie est _____ du centre-ville

f. Le magasin de musique est _____ du centre commercial

g. La maison d'Aurélie est à _____ de la boulangerie

h. Le bar est _____ du musée

i. La bibliothèque est _____ de la maison de Nadim

9. Complete with the missing letters

a. L'aéroport e __ __ près d__ ma maison

b. La pâtisserie est à c__ __ __ de l__ piscine

c. Le restaurant est d__ __ __ __ __ __ le p__ __ __

d. L__ __ magasins s__ __ __ en face du centre commercial

e. La maison de Benjamin est à d__ __ __ __ __ du musée

L'eau est-elle mouillée ou sèche?

Les aventures de Tibou, le requin philosophe.

10. Translate into French

a. My house is far from the city centre

b. The shops are near the school

c. The library is opposite the supermarket

d. The restaurant is on the right of my house

e. The park is far from the stadium

f. The castle is five minutes away from the gym

g. The library is inside the shopping centre

h. The cake shop is near Laurent's house

i. The music shop is on the left of the clothes shop

THE LANGUAGE GYM

2.11 DETERMINER + NOUN + ÊTRE + LOCATIVE PREPOSITION + DEFINITE ARTICLE + NOUN
(SAYING WHERE THINGS ARE LOCATED IN THE HOUSE)

				Masculine nouns	
L'ordinateur	The computer				
La porte	The door		**à côté**		
La salle de bains	The bathroom		*next to*	**de l'étagère**	*the shelf*
La table de nuit	The bedside table		**à droite**	**du bureau**	*the desk*
Le chat	The cat	**est**	*on the right of*	**du four**	*the oven*
Le fauteuil	The armchair	*is*	**à gauche**	**du frigo**	*the fridge*
Le livre	The book	*located*	*on the left of*	**du lit**	*the bed*
Le miroir	The mirror		**à l'intérieur**	**du miroir**	*the mirror*
Le réveil	The alarm clock		*inside*	**du sol**	*the floor*
Le t-shirt	The t-shirt		**en face**		
			opposite	Feminine nouns	
			loin	**de l'armoire**	*the wardrobe*
Les chaussettes	The socks		*far from*	**de la chaise**	*the chair*
Les chaussures	The shoes	**sont**	**près**	**de la fenêtre**	*the window*
Les rideaux	The curtains	*are*	*near*	**de la porte**	*the door*
Les souris	The mice	*located*		**de la table**	*the table*
				de la télévision	*the TV*
				Masculine nouns	
La lampe	The lamp	**est**	**derrière** *behind*	**l'oreiller**	*the pillow*
Le panier	The basket	*is* *located*	**devant** *in front of*	**le mur**	*the wall*
				Feminine nouns	
Les jouets	The toys	**sont**	**sous** *under*	**l'affiche**	*the poster*
Les photos	The pictures	*are* *located*	**sur** *on*	**la couverture**	*the blanket*

LANGUAGE AWARENESS: ÊTRE FOR LOCATION 2

The prepositions **'Derrière'**, **'Devant'**, **'Sous'**, and **'Sur'** work slightly differently from the rule we saw before. **They are immediately followed by a noun**:

e.g. **Le livre est** *derrière* **la lampe**   *The book is behind the lamp*

e.g. **Les chaussettes sont** *sur* **l'oreiller**   *The socks are on the pillow*

1. Break the flow

a. Lelivreestdanslebureau

b. Lechatestsurlelit

c. Lemiroirestàdroitedel'armoire

d. L'ordinateurestenfacedel'étagère

e. Lelitestàgauchedelachaise

f. Lesrideauxsontdevantlafenêtre

2. Missing letter challenge: complete the words

a. L__ ch__t e__t su__ l__ l__t

b. __e liv__e es__ s__r l'ét__gère

c. L__ T-s__irt __st d__rri__re l__ ch__ise

d. __es ri__eaux son__ __rè__ d__ la fen__tre

e. L__ f__ut__uil __st à c__t__ de l__ p__rt__

f. Le__ sou__is so__t so__s l__ __rigo

3. Match

Sous	*Next to*
Sur	*Under*
À l'intérieur	*On the left*
Loin	*Inside*
À côté	*On the right*
À gauche	*On*
En face	*Behind*
À droite	*Near*
Près	*Far*
Derrière	*Opposite*

4. One of two

	1	2
Sous	*Under*	*On*
Sur	*On*	*Far*
Dans	*Outside*	*Inside*
Loin	*Far*	*Near*
Derrière	*Behind*	*Under*
À côté	*Near*	*Next to*
À gauche	*To the right*	*On the left*
À droite	*Next to*	*On the right*
Près	*Far*	*Near*
En face	*In*	*Opposite*

5. Translate into English

a. Le T-shirt est dans l'armoire

b. Le lit est derrière la porte

c. La cuisine est à gauche

d. Les chaussettes sont sur la chaise

e. Les chambres sont près de la salle de bains

f. Les livres sont sur le lit

g. La télévision est en face du fauteuil

h. Le miroir est dans la salle de bains

i. La table de nuit est à côté du lit

j. Le panier est loin de la porte

6. Listen and complete: true or false?

a. Le _____ est sous le lit

b. La télévision est en face du _____

c. L'_____ est à droite

d. La table de nuit est _____ du lit

e. Le _____ est près de la porte

f. La porte est _____ le fauteuil

g. Le chat est _____ l'armoire

h. La _____ est à droite de la télévision

i. La télévision est _____ le lit

LEFT   RIGHT

7. Complete with *du, de la, de l', le, la* or *l'*

a. L'armoire est à côté _____ lit

b. Le bureau est près _____ armoire

c. Le chat est sur _____ télévision

d. Mon T-shirt est dans _____ armoire

e. Les rideaux sont derrière _____ bureau

f. La porte est à droite _____ fenêtre

g. Les jouets sont devant _____ porte

h. Les photos sont à gauche _____ chaise

8. Listen and complete: likely or unlikely?

a. Le fauteuil est _____ l'ordinateur

b. La porte est _____ les rideaux

c. Le bureau est _____ la lampe

d. Les chaussures sont _____ le bureau

e. La télévision est _____ du lit

f. L'armoire est _____ la table de nuit

g. Le chat est _____ la porte

h. Le lit est à _____ du miroir

9. Faulty translation: fix the French translation

a. *The armchair is near the bed* — Le fauteuil est à côté du lit

b. *The wardrobe is behind the door* — L'armoire est près de la porte

c. *The desk is in front of the mirror* — Le bureau est en face du miroir

d. *The cat is on the desk* — Le chat est sous le bureau

e. *The television is on the right of the door* — La télévision est derrière la porte

f. *The curtains are opposite the television* — Les rideaux sont derrière la télévision

g. *The t-shirts are near the wardrobe* — Les T-shirts sont dans l'armoire

h. *The mice are under the bed* — Les souris sont dans le lit

THE LANGUAGE GYM

10. Tangled translation: translate into French

a. L'*computer* est *next* de la *window*

b. Le *armchair* est *opposite* du *bed*

c. La lampe *is on* la table *behind* la porte

d. Les photos *are under* la table *on the right* du frigo

e. Les *toys* sont *inside* de l'*wardrobe*

f. *The curtains* sont *in front of* la *window*

g. Le *book* de maths est *on* le *desk*

h. *The socks* sont *under* l'*pillow*

11. Guided translation

a. L __ p __ __ __ __ __   The door

b. L __ r __ __ __ __ __ __   The alarm clock

c. L __ p __ __ __ __ __   The basket

d. L __ l __ __ __ __   The lamp

e. E __ f __ __ __ __   Opposite

f. P __ __ __   Near

g. D __ __ __ __ __ __ __   Behind

h. D __ __ __ __ __   In front of

i. À c __ __ __ __   Next to

12. Gapped translation: complete the translation

a. Le _____ est _____ du miroir

   The basket is opposite the mirror

b. Les _____ sont _____ le lit

   The toys are under the bed

c. Les _____ sont _____ de l'armoire

   The mice are inside the wardrobe

d. Les _____ sont _____ de la porte

   The shoes are next to the door

13. Complete

a. À c_____ d___ m_____   *Next to the mirror*

b. D_____ l__ p_____   *Behind the door*

c. S_____ l__ l_____   *Under the bed*

d. S_____ l___ f_____   *On the armchair*

e. E__ f_____ d__ l__ t_____   *Opposite the TV*

f. D_____ l___ r_____   *Behind the curtains*

g. D_____ l'a_____   *Inside the wardrobe*

h. D_____ l__ p_____   *In front of the door*

i. S_____ l__ b_____   *Under the desk*

14. Translate into French

a. The wardrobe is next to the door

b. The TV is opposite the bed

c. The cat is on the desk

d. The bed is on the right of the door

e. The window is behind the curtains

f. The toys are in front of the bed

g. The dog is under the desk

h. The shoes are in the wardrobe

i. The armchair is next to the window

THE LANGUAGE GYM

74

ORAL PING PONG

ÊTRE

A

ENGLISH 1	FRENCH 1	ENGLISH 2	FRENCH 2
Today I am tired but joyful. My sister is sad.	Aujourd'hui je suis fatigué, mais joyeux. Ma sœur est triste.	I am angry and in a hurry.	
My mother is quite nervous and worried.	Ma mère est assez nerveuse et préoccupée.	In the morning my cat is always energetic.	
My parents are not nervous today.	Mes parents ne sont pas nerveux aujourd'hui.	Are you tired this evening?	
My brothers are tired and cold. They are ill.	Mes frères sont fatigués et ils ont froid. Ils sont malades.	My dad is worried and in a bad mood.	
My friend's house is next to the castle behind the park.	La maison de mon ami(e) est à côté du château derrière le parc	The cinema is opposite my house, that's why (*c'est pourquoi*) I am joyful.	
The socks are in the fridge that's why (*c'est pourquoi*) my mother is angry.	Les chaussettes sont dans le frigo c'est pourquoi ma mère est en colère	My grandmother is joyful that's why (*c'est pourquoi*) my father is calm.	
The pictures are on the wall opposite the bedside table.	Les photos sont sur le mur en face de la table de nuit.	We are thirsty and hungry that's why (*c'est pourquoi*) we have a stomachache	
I am joyful because (*car*) I am in the sports centre.	Je suis joyeux car je suis dans le centre sportif.	The dog is joyful that's why (*c'est pourquoi*) he is energetic.	

INSTRUCTIONS - You are **PARTNER A.** Work in pairs. Each of you has two sets of sentences - one set has already been translated for you. You will ask your partner to translate these. The other set of sentences have not been translated. Your partner will ask you to translate these.

HOW TO PLAY - Partner A starts by reading out his/her/their first sentence <u>in English</u>. Partner B must translate. Partner A must check the answer and award the following points: **3 points** = perfect, **2 points** = 1 mistake, **1 point** = mistakes but the verb is accurate. If they cannot translate correctly, Partner A will read out the sentence so that Partner B can learn what the correct translation is.

Then Partner B reads out his/her/their first sentence, and so on.

OBJECTIVE - Try to win more points than your partner by translating correctly as many sentences as possible.

 **THE LANGUAGE GYM**

ORAL PING PONG

ÊTRE

ENGLISH 1	FRENCH 1	ENGLISH 2	FRENCH 2
Today I am tired but joyful. My sister is sad.		I am angry and in a hurry.	Je suis en colère et pressé(e)
My mother is quite nervous and worried.		In the morning my cat is always energetic.	Le matin mon chat est toujours énergique.
My parents are not nervous today.		Are you tired this evening?	Es-tu fatigué ce soir?
My brothers are tired and cold. They are ill.		My dad is worried and in a bad mood.	Mon papa est préoccupé et de mauvaise humeur.
My friend's house is next to the castle behind the park.		The cinema is opposite my house, that's why (*c'est pourquoi*) I am joyful.	Le ciné est en face de ma maison c'est pourquoi je suis joyeux.
The socks are in the fridge that's why (*c'est pourquoi*) my mother is angry.		My grandmother is joyful that's why (*c'est pourquoi*) my father is calm.	Ma grand-mère est joyeuse c'est pourquoi mon père est calme.
The pictures are on the wall opposite the bedside table.		We are thirsty and hungry that's why (*c'est pourquoi*) we have a stomachache	Nous avons soif et faim c'est pourquoi nous avons mal à l'estomac
I am joyful because (*car*) I am in the sports centre.		The dog is joyful that's why (*c'est pourquoi*) he is energetic.	Le chien est joyeux c'est pourquoi il est énergique

INSTRUCTIONS - You are **PARTNER B.** Work in pairs. Each of you has two sets of sentences - one set has already been translated for you. You will ask your partner to translate these. The other set of sentences have not been translated. Your partner will ask you to translate these.

HOW TO PLAY - Partner A starts by reading out his/her/their first sentence <u>in English</u>. Partner B must translate. Partner A must check the answer and award the following points: **3 points** = perfect, **2 points** = 1 mistake, **1 point** = mistakes but the verb is accurate. If they cannot translate correctly, Partner A will read out the sentence so that Partner B can learn what the correct translation is.

Then Partner B reads out his/her/their first sentence, and so on.

OBJECTIVE - Try to win more points than your partner by translating correctly as many sentences as possible.

THE LANGUAGE GYM

76

ÊTRE

No Snakes No Ladders

	1	2	3	4	5	6	7
DÉPART	The mice are under the chair	I am joyful because I am near the park	My school is behind the museum	The shops are on the pedestrian street	My room is far from the bathroom	The t-shirt is on the bed	The cat is under the table
15	14	13	12	11	10	9	8
The cat is on the television	My sister is joyful because she is near the shops	Are you worried?	My mum is joyful because my brothers are fit	The shoes are under the bed	I am from Madrid. I am Spanish	The police station is on the right of the park	The television is opposite the armchair
16	17	18	19	20	21	22	23
The window is opposite the door	In the afternoon you are always in a bad mood	My friend's house is five minutes away from the restaurant	My house is near the beach	The books are near the bed	The mirror is on the right of the door	We are tired and hot	My cat is on the table
ARRIVÉE	30	29	28	27	26	25	24
	The sports centre is far from the pool	The Indian restaurant is inside the shopping centre	We are joyful	The beach is behind the restaurant	The castle is near the bakery	We are in a bad mood	The shops are behind the library

THE LANGUAGE GYM

77

No Snakes No Ladders

ÊTRE

DÉPART	**1** Les souris sont sous la chaise	**2** Je suis joyeux car je suis près du parc	**3** Mon école est derrière le musée	**4** Les magasins sont dans la rue piétonne	**5** Ma chambre est loin de la salle de bains	**6** Le T-shirt est sur le lit	**7** Le chat est sous la table
15 Le chat est sur la télévision	**14** Ma sœur est joyeuse car elle est près des magasins	**13** Es-tu préoccupé?	**12** Ma maman est joyeuse car mes frères sont en forme	**11** Les chaussures sont sous le lit	**10** Je suis de Madrid. Je suis espagnol	**9** Le poste de police est à droite du parc	**8** La télévision est en face du fauteuil
16 La fenêtre est en face de la porte	**17** L'après-midi tu es toujours de mauvaise humeur	**18** La maison de mon ami(e) est à cinq minutes du restaurant	**19** Ma maison est près de la plage	**20** Les livres sont près du lit	**21** Le miroir est à droite de la porte	**22** Nous sommes fatigués et nous avons chaud	**23** Mon chat est sur la table
ARRIVÉE	**30** Le centre sportif est loin de la piscine	**29** Le restaurant indien est à l'intérieur du centre commercial	**28** Nous sommes joyeux(ses)	**27** La plage est derrière le restaurant	**26** Le château est proche de la boulangerie	**25** Nous sommes de mauvaise humeur	**24** Les magasins sont derrière la bibliothèque

THE LANGUAGE GYM

PYRAMID TRANSLATION

ÊTRE

Translate each part of the pyramid out loud with your partner, then write it into the spaces provided below.

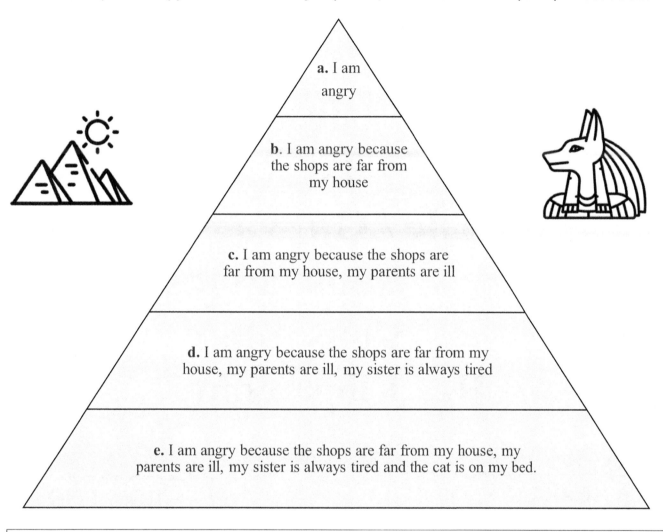

a. I am angry

b. I am angry because the shops are far from my house

c. I am angry because the shops are far from my house, my parents are ill

d. I am angry because the shops are far from my house, my parents are ill, my sister is always tired

e. I am angry because the shops are far from my house, my parents are ill, my sister is always tired and the cat is on my bed.

Write your translation here

THE LANGUAGE GYM

UNIT 3 – ALLER

Je	vais
Tu	vas
Il / Elle / On	va
Nous	allons
Vous	allez
Ils / Elles	vont

WHERE I GO

Je vais à la plage avec mon cheval

Salut!

WHAT I GO FOR

J'y vais **pour** nager

HOW I GO

J'y vais **en** voiture ou **à cheval**

Où vas-tu?

3.1 AUJOURD'HUI + ALLER + FIRST THREE PERSONS
(ASKING AND SAYING HOW I FEEL)

Comment vas-tu? *How are you?*					
				MASCULINE	**FEMININE**
Aujourd'hui *Today*	**je vais** *I am*	**super bien** *great*		**calme** *calm*	**calme** *calm*
		très bien *very well*	**parce que je suis** *because I am*	**détendu** *relaxed*	**détendue** *relaxed*
		bien *well*		**fatigué** *tired*	**fatiguée** *tired*
	je ne vais pas *I am not*	**comme ci comme ça** *so-so*		**heureux** *happy*	**heureuse** *happy*
			parce que je ne suis pas *because I am not*	**nerveux** *nervous*	**nerveuse** *nervous*
		mal *feeling bad*		**stressé** *stressed*	**stressée** *stressed*
		très mal *feeling awful*		**triste** *sad*	**triste** *sad*

Author's note : when asking how someone is feeling, we use the verb "**aller**" in French even though it means **to go**. When you say, "**Je vais bien**", it's like saying that "*everything is going well*".

1. Match

Je vais	*Calm*
Stressé	*Feeling bad*
Calme	*Sad*
Je ne vais pas	*Happy*
Triste	*Today*
Très bien	*I am*
Mal	*How are you?*
Détendu	*Very well*
Heureuse	*Stressed*
Comment vas-tu?	*Relaxed*
Aujourd'hui	*I am not*

2. Listen and complete with the missing word(s) 🔊

a. Aujourd'hui je vais _____ bien

b. parce que je _____ détendue

c. Aujourd'hui je ne _____ pas très bien

d. parce que je ___ suis _____ calme

e. Aujourd'hui je vais _____

f. parce que je suis _____

g. _____ je vais comme ci comme ça

h. _____ _____ je suis fatiguée

i. Aujourd'hui ___ vais _____ mal

j. parce que je suis _____

k. Je vais très mal parce que je suis _____

3. Faulty translation: fix the English translation

a. Aujourd'hui je ne vais pas bien   *Today I am well*

b. parce que je suis nerveuse   *because I am stressed*

c. Aujourd'hui je ne vais pas très bien   *Today I am not great*

d. parce que je suis fatigué   *because I am sad*

e. Aujourd'hui je vais super bien   *Today I am feeling awful*

f. parce que je ne suis pas stressée   *because I am stressed*

4. Tangled Translation: translate into French

a. *I am* super bien *because* je ne suis pas triste

b. Je vais *so-so* parce que je suis *tired (f)*

c. Je vais *feeling awful* parce que *I am not* détendu

d. *I am* très bien *today*

e. Aujourd'hui je vais *feeling bad* parce que je suis *nervous (m)*

f. *Today I am* bien *because I am* heureuse

5. Translate into English

a. Aujourd'hui je vais bien

b. parce que je suis heureuse

c. Aujourd'hui je ne vais pas bien

d. parce que je suis stressé

e. Aujourd'hui je vais mal

f. parce que je ne suis pas calme

g. Aujourd'hui je vais très bien

h. parce que je ne suis pas fatiguée

6. Break the flow

a. Aujourd'huijevaistrèsmalparcequejesuistriste

b. Jevaiscommecicommeçaparcequejesuisstressée

c. Aujourd'huijenevaispastrèsbien

d. Jevaissuperbienparcequejenesuispasfatigué

e. Commentvastu?

f. Aujourd'huijevaismalparcequejesuisnerveuse

g. Aujourd'huijevaistrèsbienparcequejesuisheureux

h. Aujourd'huijenevaispasbienparcequejesuisstressé

i. Aujourd'huijevaismalparcequejenesuispascalme

j. Jevaiscommecicommeçaparcequejesuisfatiguée

k. Jevaistrèsbienparcequejesuisheureuseetdétendue

l. Jevaissuperbienparcequejenesuispastriste

7. Listen and spot the missing words 🔊

a. Aujourd'hui je bien parce que je suis calme

b. Je ne vais très bien parce que je suis fatigué

c. Aujourd'hui je ne pas bien parce que je suis triste

d. Aujourd'hui je vais super bien parce que je suis

e. Je vais parce que je ne suis pas nerveuse

f. Aujourd'hui je vais comme ci comme ça je suis stressé

THE LANGUAGE GYM

8. One of two

		1	2
a.	**Comment vas-tu?**	*How are you?*	*Who are you?*
b.	**Aujourd'hui je vais bien**	*Today I am great*	*Today I am well*
c.	**Je vais super bien**	*I am very well*	*I am great*
d.	**Je suis détendu**	*I am relaxed (m)*	*I am relaxed (f)*
e.	**Je ne vais pas très bien**	*I am feeling bad*	*I am not very well*
f.	**Je suis heureux**	*I am happy (m)*	*I am happy (f)*
g.	**Je ne suis pas stressé**	*I am stressed*	*I am not stressed*
h.	**Aujourd'hui je vais mal**	*Today I am feeling awful*	*Today I am feeling bad*
i.	**Je suis triste et fatiguée**	*I am sad and tired (m)*	*I am sad and tired (f)*
j.	**Je suis calme et détendue**	*I am calm and relaxed (m)*	*I am calm and relaxed (f)*

9. Complete with a suitable word

a. Aujourd'hui je vais super b_____

b. parce que je suis c_____

c. Aujourd'hui je ne vais pas t____ bien

d. parce que je suis f_____

e. A_____ je vais bien

f. parce que je _____ heureuse

g. C_____ vas-tu?

h. Aujourd'hui je vais c_____ ci c_____ ça

i. parce que je suis t_____

10. Spot and correct the errors

a. Aujourd'hui je vas super bien

b. parce que je ne sui pas stressée

c. Aujourdhui je vais très bien

d. parce ke je suis heureuse

e. Aujourd'hui je vais male

f. parce que je ne pas suis calme

g. Aujourd'hui je vais ne pas bien

h. parce que je suis fatigue

11. Guided translation

a. A_____ j__ v____ t____ b_____   *Today I am very well*

b. A_____ j__ v____ t____ m____   *Today I am feeling awful*

c. J__ n__ v____ p___ b____ p____ q___ j__ s____ t_____   *I am not well because I am sad*

d. J__ v____ b____ p____ q___ j__ s___ h_____(m)   *I am well because I am happy*

e. A_____ j__ n__ s____ p____ s_____ (f)   *Today I am not stressed*

f. C_____ v___-t__?   *How are you?*

3.2 JE VAIS + PREPOSITION + PLACE + FREQUENCY ADVERB
(SAYING WHERE I GO AND HOW OFTEN)

NEGATIVE							
Je *I*	**ne** *don't*	**vais** *go*	**jamais** *never*		**chez** *to*	**Pierre**	*Pierre's house*
					à *to*	**Bruxelles** **Toulouse**	
			pas *not*		**au** *to the*	**centre comercial** **centre-ville** **ciné**	*shopping centre* *city centre* *cinema*
			presque jamais *hardly ever*		**à la** *to the*	**fête** **piscine**	*party* *swimming pool*
					à l' *to the*	**église** **hôtel**	*church* *hotel*
			nulle part			*nowhere*	

POSITIVE								
Je *I*	**vais** *go*	**de temps en temps** *from time to time* **parfois** *sometimes* **rarement** *rarely* **souvent** *often* **toujours** *always* **(presque) tous les jours** *(nearly) every day* **(presque) tous les week-ends** *(nearly) every weekend* **une fois par mois** *once a month* **une fois par semaine** *once a week*	**chez** *to*	**Marie**	*Marie's house*			
			à *to*	**Bruxelles** **Toulouse**				
			au *to the*	**collège** **gymnase** **parc** **stade** **supermarché**	*school* *gym* *park* *stadium* *supermarket*			
				restaurant	**chinois** **indien** **italien**	*Chinese* *Indian* *Italian*		
				magasin de *(...) shop*	**musique** **sport** **vêtements**	*music* *sport* *clothes*		
			à la *to the*	**plage** *beach*	**tous** *every*	**les lundis** **les mardis** **les mercredis** **les jeudis** **les vendredis** **les samedis** **les dimanches**	*Monday* *Tuesday* *Wednesday* *Thursday* *Friday* *Saturday* *Sunday*

LANGUAGE AWARENESS
DEFINITE ARTICLES: *LE & LA*

In English there is only one definite article, **"the"**. This is because English nouns are not assigned a gender. However, French nouns are **all** either **masculine** or **feminine** – this is known as their "gender". *Le* and *la* are **definite articles**. They both translate as **"the"** in English.

Masculine   –   **Le collège**   *The school*
Feminine   –   **La plage**   *The beach*

À + LA = À LA

À means **'to'** in English. The feminine form follows the same pattern as the English:

• Je vais **à la** plage   *I go **to the** beach*

À + LE = AU

In French when *à* comes into contact with *le* it mutates into *au*.

• Je vais *à + le* ciné   >>>>>> Je vais **au** ciné

    *I go **to the** cinema*

You must always say *au* when saying that you go to places that are masculine.

When *le* or *la* are followed by a noun that starts with a vowel or an "h", *le* and *la* become *l'*

Je vais **à l'**église *I go to church*

Je vais **à l'**hôtel *I go to the hotel*

NEGATIVES: *JAMAIS*

Jamais means never, and it is used as follows to form a sentence.

•Je **ne** vais **jamais** à la plage

I never go to the beach

Ne...jamais goes around the verb in French.

Je vais <u>à la</u> plage et <u>au</u> parc, mais je ne vais jamais <u>au</u> ciné.

1. Match

Fête	Swimming pool
Église	Party
Jamais	From time to time
Piscine	Church
Plage	Shop
De temps en temps	Beach
Magasin	Often
Stade	Never
Chez	Stadium
Souvent	Rarely
Rarement	To someone's house

2. Listen and complete with *chez, à, au, à la* or *à l'*

a. Je vais souvent _____ piscine

b. Je ne vais jamais _____ ciné

c. Je vais souvent _____ restaurant indien

d. Je vais tous les jours _____ Antoine

e. Je ne vais jamais _____ parc

f. Je ne vais pas souvent _____ hôtel

g. Je ne vais presque jamais _____ magasin de sport

h. Je vais une fois par mois _____ Toulouse

i. Je vais _____ fête de ma cousine

j. Je vais _____ église tous les dimanches

k. Je vais _____ stade tous les samedis

 **THE LANGUAGE GYM**

3. Faulty translation: fix the English translation

a. Je vais souvent à l'église — *I rarely go to church*

b. Je ne vais jamais au ciné — *I never go to the stadium*

c. Je vais rarement au magasin de sport — *I rarely go to the clothes shop*

d. Je ne vais jamais à Bruxelles — *I often go to Brussels*

e. Je vais souvent chez Marie — *I go to Marie's house from time to time*

f. Je vais au parc tous les dimanches — *I go to the park every Saturday*

g. Je vais de temps en temps à la plage — *I often go to the beach*

4. Complete with the missing letters

a. Je va__s au m__g__sin de sport

b. Je ne v__is j__mais au p__rc

c. Je __ais sou__ent ch__z Marie

d. Je vai__ de temp__ en temps à la pl__ge

e. Je vais à l'__glise tous les d__m__nches

f. Je n__ vais j__mais à la f__te

g. J__ vais au c__ntre-v__lle tous les samedis

h. Je vais une f__is par sem__ine au gymnas__

i. Je v__ __s une f__ __s par mois à Toulouse

5. Broken words

a. Je v_____ sou_____ à l'égl_____

b. Je ne vais ja_____ au p_____

c. Je v_____ chez Marie tous les _____medis

d. Je ne vais _____mais à la _____ge

e. Je vais une f_____ par ____maine à la pisc_____

f. Je vais rare_____ au restau_____ indien

g. Je ne vais ja_____ au gymn_____

h. Je vais tous les j_____ au cen_____ _____rcial

i. Je vais rarement au maga_____ de sp_____

6. Tangled Translation: translate into French

a. *I go to the* centre commercial *nearly* tous les week-ends

b. Je vais *to the* piscine *every day*

c. Je vais *to the* plage *every* les samedis

d. *I go to the* magasin de vêtements *every weekend*

e. Je vais *to the* église tous les *Sundays*

f. *I go to the* fête de mon *cousin*

7. Translate into English

a. Je vais souvent à Toulouse

b. Je ne vais jamais chez Pierre

c. Je vais tous les jours au parc

d. Je vais souvent au magasin de vêtements

e. Je ne vais jamais à Bruxelles

f. Je vais tous les jours au collège

g. Je ne vais jamais à la piscine

THE LANGUAGE GYM

86

8. Listen and translate into English 🔊

a. I go…

b. I never go…

c. I sometimes go…

d. I never go…

e. I go…

f. I go…

g. I never go…

h. I go…

9. Choose the correct option

a. Je vais tous les week-ends **à/à la/au** Toulouse

b. Je ne vais jamais **à/à la/au** gymnase

c. Je vais parfois **à/chez/au** Marie

d. Mon frère va souvent **à/à la/au** Bruxelles

e. Je vais **à/à la/au** fête de Pierre

f. Je vais une fois par semaine **à/à la/au** piscine

g. Je ne vais jamais **à/à la/chez** Michel

h. Je vais toujours **à/à la/au** centre commercial

i. Je vais tous les jours **à/à la/au** restaurant indien

10. Complete with *à, à la, au* or *chez* as appropriate

a. Je vais de temps en temps _____ plage

b. Je ne vais jamais _____ centre commercial

c. Le week-end je vais _____ piscine

d. Après le collège, je vais toujours _____ parc

e. Je vais rarement _____ Michel

f. Je vais _____ l'église tous les dimanches

g. Je ne vais jamais _____ Pierre

h. Je vais une fois par mois _____ Toulouse

11. Complete with an appropriate noun without repeating the same word twice

a. Je vais souvent au _____

b. Je vais rarement à la _____

c. Je vais au _____ tous les jours

d. Je ne vais jamais au _____

e. Je vais à la _____ tous les jours.

f. Quand vas-tu chez _____ ?

g. Je vais rarement à l'_____

h. Je vais chez _____ presque tous les jours

12. Translate into French

a. I go to the park every weekend

b. I go to Martine's house from time to time

c. I never go to the Italian restaurant

d. I go to the shopping centre once a week

e. I go to the beach sometimes with my friends

f. I go to the gym once a month

g. I go to the swimming pool every Monday

h. I rarely go to the stadium with my father

13. Complete with an appropriate word

a. Je vais à ___ piscine de temps en _____

b. Je vais _____ parc tous _____ jours

c. Je vais souvent _____ Michel

d. Je vais souvent ___ centre _____

e. Je vais au ___ gymnase tous _____ jours

f. Je vais ___ la plage de _____ en temps

g. Je vais _____ ciné une fois par _____

h. Je vais à _____ plage tous _____ dimanches

THE LANGUAGE GYM

3.3 FULL PRESENT CONJUGATION OF ALLER + PLACES + FREQUENCY ADVERB
(SAYING HOW OFTEN AND WHEN ONE GOES TO PLACES)

NEGATIVE						
Je *I*	**ne** *don't*	**vais** *go*		**chez** *to*	**Pierre** *Pierre's house* **mon ami** *my friend's house* **son ami** *his/her friend's house*	
Tu *You*	**ne** *don't*	**vas** *go*	**jamais** *never*	**à** *to*	**Bruxelles** **Toulouse**	
Il/Elle *He/She*	**ne** *doesn't*	**va** *go*	**pas** *not*	**au** *to the*	**centre comercial** *shopping centre* **centre-ville** *city centre* **ciné** *cinema*	
On *We*	**ne** *don't*	**va** *go*	**presque jamais** *hardly ever*	**à la** *to the*	**fête** *party* **piscine** *swimming pool*	
Nous *We*	**n'** *don't*	**allons** *go*		**à l'** *to the*	**église** *church* **hôtel** *hotel*	
Vous *You guys/girls*	**n'** *don't*	**allez** *go*				
Ils/Elles *They*	**ne** *don't*	**vont** *go*	**nulle part** *nowhere*			

POSITIVE							
				chez *to*	**Marie**		*Marie's house*
Je *I*	**vais** *go*	**de temps en temps** *from time to time*		**à** *to*	**Bruxelles** **Toulouse**		
		parfois *sometimes*					
Tu *You*	**vas** *go*	**rarement** *rarely*		**au** *to the*	**collège** *school* **gymnase** *gym* **parc** *park* **stade** *stadium* **supermarché** *supermarket*		
Il/Elle *He/She*	**va** *go*	**souvent** *often*					
On *We*	**va** *go*	**toujours** *always*			**restaurant**	**chinois** *Chinese* **indien** *Indian* **italien** *Italian*	
Nous *We*	**allons** *go*	**(presque) tous les jours** *(nearly) every day*			**magasin de** *(...) shop*	**musique** *music* **sport** *sport* **vêtements** *clothes*	
Vous *You guys/girls*	**allez** *go*	**(presque) tous les week-ends** *(nearly) every weekend*					
		une fois par mois *once a month*		**à la** *to the*	**plage** *beach*	**tous** *every*	**les lundis** *Monday* **les mardis** *Tuesday* **les mercredis** *Wednesday*
Ils/Elles *They*	**vont** *go*	**une fois par semaine** *once a week*					**les jeudis** *Thursday* **les vendredis** *Friday* **les week-ends** *weekend*

LANGUAGE AWARENESS
ADVERBS OF FREQUENCY

Some **adverbs of frequency** can go at the **start** or at the **end** of a sentence:

- **Je vais à la plage de temps en temps**
  I go to the beach from time to time
- **De temps en temps je vais à la plage**
  From time to time I go to the beach

Sometimes the adverbs work better at the **end** of the sentence:

- **Je vais à la plage une fois par mois**
  I go to the beach once a week

Adverbs of frequency like **parfois** and **souvent** must go after the verb

- **Je vais souvent à la plage**
  I often go to the beach

> Mon chien va très souvent au parc.

POSSESSIVES – *Le chien de Dylan*

French word order to explain possession is different from English. To say "Dylan's dog" we actually need to say "the dog of Dylan"

- **Le chien de Dylan**
  Dylan's dog
  Literally: *The dog of Dylan*

The same applies when saying what kind of shop you're going to!

- **Le magasin de musique**
  The music shop
  Literally: *The shop of music*

> Salut, je suis Lily. Je vais au parc presque tous les week-ends.

---

1. Match	
Nous allons	*I go*
Je vais	*You guys go*
Il/Elle va	*He/She goes*
Ils/Elles vont	*We go*
Vous allez	*You go*
Tu vas	*They go*

2. Select the correct form of *ALLER*

a. Aujourd'hui nous **vont/allez/allons** au ciné

b. Ils **allons/vont/vais** souvent à la piscine

c. Je ne **vas/vais/va** jamais au centre commercial

d. Elle **vas/va/vont** rarement à la plage

e. Où **vas/va/vais** -tu?

f. Où **allons/vais/allez** -vous?

g. Vous **allez/vais/va** au ciné tous les week-ends

h. Ils **vas/vais/vont** au gymnase l'après-midi

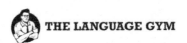
THE LANGUAGE GYM

3. Break the flow

a. Nousallonsàl'églisetouslessamedis

b. Jenevaisjamaisaucinéavecmesparents

c. Nousallonsaucentrecommercialdetempsentemps

d. Jevaissouventaumagasindesport

e. Oùallezvousleweek-end?

f. Monfrèrecadetvaaustadetouslesdimanches

g. Oùvastuaujourd'hui?

Tu y vas à cheval ou à pied?

Je ne sais pas... Je crois que j'y vais à pied

4. Complete with the missing letters

a. Nous n'all_ _ _ _ _ jam_ _ _ _ au ci_ _ _

b. Tu v_ _ à l'égl_ _ _ _ _ de temps _ _ temps

c. M_ mère v_ s_ _vent au sup_ _m_ _ché

d. M_s sœurs v_ _t au _tad_ to_ _ _ le_ d_ _ _ _ _ _ _ _ _ _

e. _ _ _ va_-tu le week-end?

f. _ _ _ a_ _ez-vous aujourd'_ _ _?

g. Je ne v_ _ _ _ nul_ _ _ par_

5. Partial dictation 🔊

a. Je ne _____ presque jamais à l'église

b. Ma sœur _____ parfois au gymnase

c. Mes parents _____ au centre-ville le week-end

d. Tu _____ au parc tous les jours?

e. Vous _____ parfois au ciné?

f. Mes amis ne _____ pas au stade

6. Sentence Puzzle

a. à n'allons la plage Nous jamais — *We never go to the beach*

b. à piscine tous Ils vont les jours la — *They go to the swimming pool every day*

c. week-end Où vas-tu le? — *Where do you go at the weekend?*

d. moi Paul et allons au gymnase souvent — *Paul and I often go to the gym*

e. parents centre au vont commercial Mes rarement — *My parents rarely go to the shopping centre*

f. dimanches au Vous allez stade tous les? — *Do you guys go to the stadium every Sunday?*

7. Spot the error

a. Je vais au plage.

b. Je vais à la église

c. Je vais à la gymnase

d. Nous allons à le parc

e. Il va à collège

f. Nous allons à la Sophie

g. Elle va à l' centre commercial

h. Ils vont au piscine

i. Je vais au fête

j. Elles vont à le restaurant indien

THE LANGUAGE GYM

8. One of two

		1	2
a.	**Nous allons à la plage**	They go to the beach	We go to the beach
b.	**Je vais souvent au gymnase**	We go to the gym often	I go to the gym often
c.	**Avec qui y vas-tu?**	Who are you going with?	Who are you guys going with?
d.	**Il y va de temps en temps**	He goes there from time to time	They go there from time to time
e.	**Il ne va jamais à l'église**	We never go to church	He never goes to church
f.	**Ils vont à la fête**	They are going to the party	You guys are going to the party
g.	**Nous n'y allons pas tous les samedis**	We don't go there every Saturday	We never go there every Saturday
h.	**J'y vais de temps en temps**	I go there from time to time	I go there every day
i.	**Où allez-vous?**	Where are you guys going?	Where are you going?
j.	**Nous n'allons jamais à Paris**	They never go to Paris	We never go to Paris

9. Complete with a suitable word

a. Je ne vais jamais à la p_____

b. Nous allons c_____ Nadim tous les jours

c. Ma mère v_____ au centre commercial

d. Aujourd'hui Jérôme et Marie v_____ à la plage

e. Mon père va au stade t_____ les samedis

f. Avec q_____ vas-tu au parc?

g. Mon frère v__ souvent au gymnase

h. Je vais au magasin de sport de temps en t_____

i. Mes parents vont au centre-v_____

10. Listen and translate into English 🔊

a. My mother…

b. My father…

c. My brother and I…

d. My friend…

e. Are you going…

f. We…

g. Are you guys going…

11. Faulty translation: fix the French translation

a. *They go to the beach every day* — Nous allons à la plage tous les jours

b. *They never go to church* — Ils ne vont jamais au centre commercial

c. *She rarely goes to the gym* — Je vais rarement au gymnase

d. *Eric and I go to the stadium from time to time* — Eric et moi allons souvent au stade

e. *Where are you guys going today?* — Où vas-tu aujourd'hui?

f. *You go to the park from time to time* — Il va au parc de temps en temps

g. *Who do you go to the party with?* — Avec qui vont-ils à la fête?

h. *My friends never go to Alice's house* — Mes amis vont toujours chez Alice

THE LANGUAGE GYM

12. Tangled translation: translate into French

a. *I go* souvent *to the* stade

b. Alexandre et moi allons *to the party* de Sandra

c. Avec *whom* vas-tu *to the swimming pool*?

d. Mes frères *go to the* gymnase *every day*

e. *Where* allez-vous?

f. *They go* rarement *to the* centre-ville

g. Mon frère *goes to the* ciné tous les *Sundays*

h. *Do you guys go* à la *beach* tous les jours?

i. *We* n' *go* jamais *to the* parc

13. Spot and correct the errors

a. Je vais à le stade tous les samedis

b. Je ne vais jamais au piscine

c. Ma mère va souvent à le centre comercial

d. Houda vas au parc maintenant

e. Mes frères ne va pas à la fête

f. Où va tes parents?

g. Nous n'allez nulle part

h. Mes sœurs va rarement au ciné

14. Complete with *vais, vas, va, allons, allez* or *vont* as suitable

a. Nous _____ au ciné tous les dimanches

b. Elle ne _____ jamais à la plage

c. Mon frère _____ au gymnase tous les jours

d. Alice et moi n'_____ pas à la fête

e. Mes sœurs _____ au centre commercial

f. Ma mère _____ parfois à la boulangerie

g. Il _____ au parc une fois par semaine

h. Où _____-vous aujourd'hui toi et ta mère?

i. Nawfel _____ souvent au parc d'attractions

j. Avec qui _____-tu à la piscine aujourd'hui?

k. Ma copine et moi _____ chez Claire

l. Nous n' _____ jamais à l'église

15. Guided translation

a. M___ p_____ v_____ s_____ a___ c_____ — *My parents often go to the cinema*

b. A_____ j__ v_____ __ l_ f_____ d__ Pierre — *Today I am going to Pierre's party*

c. N_____ n'_____ j_____ a__ s_____ — *We never go to the stadium*

d. E___ v___ p_____ a__ g_____ — *They sometimes go to the gym*

e. I__ v__ a__ c____ c_____ t____ l__ j_____ — *He goes to the shopping centre every day*

f. O__ v___-t__ a_____? — *Where are you (sg) going today?*

g. M___ f_____ et m__ a_____ à l__ p_____... — *My brother and I go to the pool...*

h. ...d__ t____ e_ t_____ — *...from time to time*

i. V____ a_____ à l__ f_____ d__ Solange? — *Are you guys going to Solange's party?*

j. I___ v____ r_____ à l__ p_____ — *They rarely go to the beach*

k. O__ v__ t__ s_____? — *Where is your sister going?*

 **THE LANGUAGE GYM**

92

3.4 TIME MARKER + PRESENT OF ALLER (FULL CONJUGATION) + PLACES
PRESENT OF ALLER + POUR + INFINITIVE + NOUN PHRASE
(SAYING WHERE ONE GOES ON DIFFERENT DAYS AND WHAT FOR)

Ce matin *This morning*	**je vais** *I go/am going*	**à** *to*	**Avignon** **Dieppe** **Paris**	
Cet après-midi *This afternoon*	**tu vas** *you go*	**chez** *to*	**Damien**	*Damien's house*
Ce soir *This evening*	**il/elle va** *he/she goes*	**au** *to the*	**centre-ville**	*city centre*
			centre comercial	*shopping centre*
			centre sportif	*sports centre*
Le mercredi *On Wednesdays*	**on va** *we go*		**ciné**	*cinema*
			gymnase	*gym*
Le vendredi *On Fridays*	**nous allons** *we go*		**magasin de musique / sport / vêtements**	
			parc	*park*
Le week-end *On weekends*	**vous allez** *you guys/girls go*		**stade**	*stadium*
			supermarché	*supermarket*
Tous les jours *Every day*	**ils/elles vont** *they go*	**à la** *to the*	**piscine**	*swimming pool*

		acheter *(to) buy*	**un CD**		**une robe**	*a dress*
			un tee-shirt	*a t-shirt*	**des baskets**	*trainers*
*J'y vais		**faire** *(to) do*	**les courses**	*the shopping*	**de la musculation** *weights*	
Tu y vas			**du jogging**	*jogging*	**de la natation** *swimming*	
Il/Elle y va		**faire** *(to) go*	**du lèche-vitrine**	*window shopping*		
			du tourisme	*sightseeing*		
			du vélo	*for a bike ride*		
On y va	**pour** *in order to*		**les magasins**	*shopping*		
			une promenade	*for a walk*		
Nous y allons		**jouer** *(to) play*	**à la PlayStation**	*the PlayStation*		
			au basket	*basketball*		
Vous y allez		**jouer** *(to) play*	**au foot**	*football*		
			de la guitare	*the guitar*		
Ils/Elles y vont		**regarder** *(to) watch*	**le match du PSG**	*the PSG match*		
			un concert	*a concert*		
			un film d'action	*an action film*		
			une comédie	*a comedy*		
		rendre visite à *(to) visit*	**mes grands-parents**	*my grandparents*		
			mes oncles et tantes	*my uncles and aunts*		

*Author's note: "**y**" is used to translate "*there*", i.e., J'**y** vais = I go *there* / I am going *there*

LANGUAGE AWARENESS: WHAT IS AN INFINITIVE?

An infinitive is a verb as we find it in the dictionary, before **conjugating** it. In English, infinitives have **"to"** in front of them. However, in French infinitives end in **-er/-ir/-re.**

This is why we talk about -er verbs, -ir verbs or -re verbs:

- **Acheter** = *to buy*
- **Finir** = *to finish*
- **Répondre**=*to answer*

THE VERB *ALLER* – I GO or I AM GOING?

Aller means "to go" in French and it can be translated in **two** different ways in English:

- **Normalement je vais au parc**   *I normally go to the park* **(describing a routine)**

We may also translate it as "I am going" when we are implying a future action of going.

- **Demain je vais au ciné**   *Tomorrow I am going to the cinema* **(future action)**

Où allez-vous?

On va au ciné pour regarder un film

Pop-corn!

ALLER ou FAIRE?

In English, we use the verb "to go" to talk about some sports and activities we do. For example, I go swimming/hiking/running. However, in French, we use the verb *faire* ("to do"):

- **Je vais au centre sportif pour faire de la natation.**
  *I am going to the sports centre in order **to go swimming (to do swimming)***

USE OF *POUR* – IN ORDER TO

Pour generally means "for", but when used with an infinitive it means "in order to" and we use it to express the purpose of doing something. We use *pour* after the verb *aller* to indicate the purpose of the action of "going" somewhere.

- Je vais au parc **pour** jouer au foot   *I go to the park (in order to) play football*

- Je vais au ciné **pour** regarder un film   *I am going to the cinema (in order to) watch a film*

In English, we can just translate the sentence as "I go to the park to play football", so it may be difficult to spot when to use *pour* before an infinitive in French. As a general rule, if we can say "in order to" in English, and the sentence makes sense, we will need *pour* in front of the infinitive in French!

1. Complete with the correct verb

a. Je vais au magasin de sport pour _____ un tee-shirt

b. Nous allons au stade pour _____ le match du PSG

c. Elles vont au ciné pour _____ un film d'action

d. Vous allez au parc pour _____ du vélo

e. Mes amis vont au gymnase pour _____ de la musculation

f. Je vais à Paris pour _____ _____ à mes grands-parents

g. Ma sœur va au parc pour _____ du jogging

h. Nous y allons pour _____ une promenade

2. Complete with a noun, then listen and check if you were right. Correct any that were different.

a. Acheter une r_____

b. Regarder une c_____

c. Faire les c_____

d. Aller au g_____

e. Rendre visite à mes p_____

f. Faire du t_____

g. Jouer au b_____

h. Faire du v_____

3. Sentence Puzzle

a. d'action J'y vais regarder pour film un — *I am going there to watch an action movie*

b. du au parc Nous allons pour vélo faire — *We go to the park to ride a bike*

c. tourisme Il va du pour à Avignon faire — *He goes to Avignon to go sightseeing*

d. cousine Ils vont à ma Paris à rendre visite pour — *They go to Paris to visit my cousin*

e. allez-vous Où week-end ce? — *Where are you guys going this weekend?*

f. supermarché Elle va faire au pour les courses — *She is going to the supermarket to do the shopping*

g. foot au y Nous allons pour jouer — *We go there to play football*

4. Break the flow

a. Ilsvontaumagasindesportpouracheterdesbaskets

b. Nousyallonspourfairedelamusculation

c. Oùallezvousceweek-end?

d. Ilvaaucinépourregarderunfilmromantique

e. MesparentsvontàParispourfairedutourisme

f. Mesfrèresyvontpourfaireduvélo

g. Jevaisaucentresportifpourfairedelanatation

h. NousallonschezPierrepourjouerdelaguitare

i. Ilsvontaucentrecommercialpourfairelesmagasins

j. Pourquoiallezvousausupermarchéaujourd'hui?

5. Match

Faire du vélo	To buy a dress
Faire les magasins	To go window shopping
Faire du tourisme	To play basketball
Faire du lèche-vitrine	To go swimming
Jouer au basket	To go for a walk
Regarder un match	To watch a film
Faire de la natation	To play the guitar
Regarder un film	To go sightseeing
Jouer de la guitare	To go shopping
Faire une promenade	To watch a match
Acheter une robe	To go for a bike ride

THE LANGUAGE GYM

6. Gapped sentences

a. Mes frères _____ au centre sportif pour _____ de la natation

My brothers go to the sports centre in order to go swimming

b. Je _____ au centre commercial pour _____ du lèche-vitrine

I go to the shopping centre in order to go window shopping

c. Ils _____ à Paris pour _____ _____ à leurs grands-parents

They go to Paris in order to visit their grandparents

d. Nous _____ au supermarché pour _____ des boissons

We go to the supermarket in order to buy some drinks

e. Elle _____ à Avignon pour _____ du tourisme

She goes to Avignon in order to go sightseeing

f. Nous _____ chez Isabelle pour _____ aux jeux vidéo

We go to Isabelle's in order to play videogames

g. Mon ami _____ au gymnase pour _____ de la musculation

My friend goes to the gym in order to do weights

h. Mes amis et moi _____ au parc pour _____ au foot

My friends and I go to the park in order to play football

7. Listen and translate into English

a. I am going to…

b. My sister…

c. We are going to…

d. I go to…

e. They go to…

f. I go to…

g. Are you going…

h. We are going to…

8. Guided translation

a. A_____ j__ v_____ a____ c_____ c_____. J'y v_____ p_____ f_____ d__ l_____-v_____ . *Today I am going to the shopping centre. I am going there in order to go window shopping.*

b. C___ m_____ m___ a_____ v__ a__ g_____ . I__ y v__ p___ f_____ d___ l___ m_____ . *This morning my friend is going to the gym. He is going there in order to do weights.*

c. C___ s_____ m____ a_____ et m____ a_____ a___ p_____ . N_____ y a_____ p_____ j_____ a__ b_____ . *This evening my friends and I are going to the park. We are going there in order to play basketball.*

d. A_____ j__ v_____ a__ c_____ . J'__ v____ p___ r_____ u___ c_____ *Today I am going to the cinema. I am going there in order to watch a comedy.*

e. A_____ m__ p_____ v_____ a_ g_____ . I___ y v____ p____ f____ d__ l__ n_____ . *Today my parents are going to the gym. They are going there in order to go swimming.*

THE LANGUAGE GYM

3.5 EN + NOUN + PRESENT OF ALLER + FREQUENCY ADVERB + À + NOUN + À/EN + TRANSPORT

(SAYING WHERE, WHEN, HOW OFTEN AND HOW ONE GOES TO DIFFERENT PLACES)

En *In*	**automne** *autumn* **été** *summer* **hiver** *winter* **janvier** *January* **février** **mars** **avril** **mai** **juin** **juillet** **août** **septembre** **octobre** **novembre** **décembre**	**je vais** *I go* **tu vas** *you go* **il/elle va** *he/she goes* **on va** *we go* **nous allons** *we go* **vous allez** *you guys/girls go* **ils/elles vont** *they go*	**de temps en temps** *from time to time* **généralement** *generally* **parfois** *sometimes* **rarement** *rarely* **souvent** *often* **(presque) toujours** *(nearly) always*	**à** *to*	**Caen** **Calais**	**Nantes** **Paris**	**à** *on/by*	**cheval** *horseback* **moto** *motorbike* **pied** *foot* **vélo** *bike*
				à la *to the*	**campagne** *countryside* **fête** *party* **piscine** *pool* **plage** *beach*			
				à l'	**étranger** *abroad*			
				au *to the*	**bord de la mer** *seafront* **bureau** *office* **Canada** **centre sportif** *sports centre* **centre-ville** *city centre* **ciné** *cinema* **collège** *school* **gymnase** *gym* **Maroc** *Morocco* **Pays de Galles** *Wales*		**en** *by*	**avion** *plane* **bateau** *boat* **bus** *bus* **car** *coach* **ferry** *ferry* **hélicoptère** *helicopter* **métro** *tube* **train** *train* **voiture** *car*
				aux *to the*	**Etats-Unis** *United States*			
Au *In*	**printemps** *spring*			**en** *to*	**Allemagne** *Germany* **Espagne** *Spain* **Pologne** *Poland* **Suisse** *Switzerland*			
				sur la *to the*	**place du marché** *market square*			

LANGUAGE AWARENESS: MEANS OF TRANSPORT

When we talk about means of transport, in French, we use the prepositions *en* and *à* while in English we use **"by"** or **"on"**.

• **Je vais au centre-ville en voiture**   *I go to the centre by car*   Literally: *I go to the centre in car*

• **Je vais à la plage à pied**   *I go to the beach on foot*   Literally: *I go to the beach to foot*

Only *à cheval, à moto, à pied* and *à vélo* take the proposition *à*. The vast majority of means of transport go with *en*.

> Tu vas à la fête en voiture?

> Non, je suis un chien. J'y vais à pied

1. Match

Généralement	*Often*
Rarement	*Sometimes*
Presque toujours	*In winter*
En été	*In spring*
En automne	*In autumn*
De temps en temps	*Always*
Toujours	*In July*
Au printemps	*From time to time*
Parfois	*Generally*
Souvent	*In summer*
En hiver	*Rarely*
En juillet	*Nearly always*

2. Translate into English

a. En hiver

b. En automne

c. Souvent

d. En juillet

e. En été

f. Généralement

g. Au printemps

h. Parfois

i. De temps en temps

j. En janvier

k. Toujours

l. Rarement

3. Listen and fill in the gaps with "à" or "en"

a. Je vais souvent au collège ____ pied

b. En hiver, nous allons en Allemagne ____ train

c. Ils vont à la fête ____ taxi

d. Il va toujours au gymnase ____ vélo

e. Où vont-ils ____ moto?

f. En été, nous allons en France ____ bateau

g. En août, elles vont à la campagne ____ cheval

4. Listen and complete the sentences

a. En été, je vais au collège en tr__ __n

b. Vous allez souvent au Maroc en __ __ion

c. Tu vas parfois au b__rd de la m__r à v__l__

d. En mars, il v__ à Paris en voit__r__

e. Où v__s-tu?

f. Je vais g__n__ralement à la pl__ge en bus

g. En automne, elle va au b__reau en m__tr__

5. Break the flow

a. EnétéjevaisgénéralementenItalieouenGrèceenavion

b. Enaoûtjevaisrarementàl'étranger

c. EnhiveràNoëljevaistoujoursenEspagne

d. AuprintempsjevaisdetempsentempsauxEtats-Unisenbateau

e. Enautomnejevaisparfoisàlacampagneàcheval

f. Enjuilletjevaistoujoursaubureauàpied

g. EnmarsjevaistoujoursenIrlandepourrendrevisiteàmamère

En été, je vais à la plage!

6. Broken words

a. N___ ___ ___ n'all___ ___ ___ jam___ ___ ___ a___ collè___ ___ à pi___ ___   *We never go to school on foot*

b. I___ v___ tou___ ___ ___ ___ au bur___ ___ ___ en b___   *He always goes to the office by bus*

c. D___ t___ ps e___ t___ ps ...   *From time to time...*

d. ... ils v___ ___ ___ à l'étran___ ___ ___ e___ avi___ ___   *...they go abroad by plane*

e. I___ ___ y v___ ___ t g___ n___ r___ l___ ment en ___ ___ ___ture   *Generally, they go there by car*

f. M___ ___ ___ ___rents vont t___ ___jours...   *My parents always go...*

g. ...ch___ ___ mes ___ ___ cles à p___ ___ ___ ___   *...to my uncles' house on foot*

h. Mon fr___re v___ au g___mn___se à v___lo   *My brother goes to the gym by bike*

i. Je v___ ___s à la ___ ___ ___pagne à che___ ___ ___   *I go to the countryside on horseback*

7. Faulty translation: fix the English translation

a. Je vais sur la place du marché à vélo   *I go to school by bike*

b. En juin, nous allons en Pologne en voiture   *In June, we go to Scotland by car*

c. Elles vont souvent au ciné en taxi   *She often goes to the cinema by taxi*

d. Nous n'allons jamais au centre-ville en bus   *We rarely go to the town centre by bus*

e. En été, nous allons toujours à la plage en taxi   *In summer, we never go to the beach by plane*

f. Mon père va rarement au bureau en train   *My mother rarely goes to the office by bus*

g. Au printemps, elle va toujours au collège à pied   *In spring, I always go to school on foot*

h. Comment vas-tu en Suisse? En voiture?   *How do you go to Sweden? By coach?*

8. Listen and spot the missing words

a. De temps temps nous allons en vacances à l'étranger

b. En août nous allons toujours Allemagne en avion

c. décembre, je vais généralement en Italie en train

d. Mes parents toujours en vacances en France en voiture

e. A Noël, nous allons toujours au Pays de Galles pour rendre visite mes grands-parents

f. Au printemps, nous allons parfois Canada en bateau

g. En juillet, nous allons temps en temps en vacances en Grèce en car

h. En été, parfois, je ne vais part

i. En hiver, ma famille ne nulle part en vacances

 **THE LANGUAGE GYM**

9. Sentence Puzzle

a. n'allons jamais En nous collège au vélo à hiver   *In winter we never go to school by bike*

b. parents vont Mes toujours au en bureau voiture   *My parents always go to the office by car*

c. à Mon sur la du marché frère va place pied   *My brother goes to the market square on foot*

d. à cheval nous allons été à la campagne En   *In summer we go to the coutryside on horseback*

e. toujours ils En vont la bus juillet plage à en   *In July they always go to the beach by bus*

f. allons Nous généralement Nantes à train en   *We generally go to Nantes by train*

g. Comment gymnase au vas-tu? À ou à vélo pied?   *How do you go to the gym? On foot or by bike?*

h. piscine Je jamais en vais ne à bus la   *I never go to the swimming pool by bus*

10. Translate into English

a. Nous allons généralement à la campagne en voiture

b. En été, ma mère va au bureau à pied

c. Je ne vais jamais au collège en métro

d. En juin, nous allons de temps en temps au club de polo à cheval

e. Je vais parfois à Paris en car

f. Nous allons de temps en temps à l'étranger en bus

g. En juillet, ils vont rarement à la piscine en voiture. Ils y vont souvent à pied.

h. Et vous? Comment allez-vous au collège? À pied ou à vélo?

11. Translate the following phrases into French

a. My parents	g. To the beach	m. He goes
b. We always go	h. On foot	n. By motorbike
c. Generally	i. To the party	o. By bus
d. From time to time	j. By coach	p. To the countryside
e. I never go	k. By car	q. She often goes
f. By bike	l. Abroad	r. They never go

12. Faulty translation: fix the French translation

a. In July, I generally go to the beach on foot — *En juillet, je vais parfois à la plage à pied*

b. In autumn, my parents go abroad by plane — *En automne, mes parents va à l'étranger en avion*

c. In spring, he sometimes goes to the pool by bus — *Au printemps, vous allez parfois à la piscine en bus*

d. In March, we go to the countryside by bike — *En mars, nous allons à la fête à vélo*

e. In winter, they always go to school by car — *En hiver, ils vont souvent au collège en car*

f. In August, I often go to Paris by train — *En juin, je vais rarement à Paris en train*

13. Guided translation

a. M___ p_____ n__ v_____ j_____ à P_____ — *My parents never go to Paris*

b. J__ v____ t_____ a__ g_____ à p_____ — *I always go to the gym on foot*

c. D__ t____ e__ t___ n____ a_____ a_ c_____ — *From time to time we go to school*

d. E___ v___ p_____ a__ p_____ à c_____ — *Sometimes she goes to the park on horseback*

e. G_____, n_____ a_____ en I_____ — *Generally, we go to Italy*

f. E__ h_____, j__ v____ a__ c_____ e__ b____ — *In winter I go to school by bus*

14. Translate the following sentences into French

a. I never go to England by coach. I always go there by plane.

b. We never go to the beach by coach.

c. In winter, we generally go to the beach by train.

d. In autumn, she never goes to school on foot. Generally, she goes there by car.

e. From time to time we go to the gym by bus.

f. We never go there by helicopter.

g. Sometimes my parents go to the town centre by bus, but generally they go there by car.

h. How do you go to the office usually? By car, by bus, by bike or on foot?

THE LANGUAGE GYM

Je *I*	**ne** *don't*	**vais** *go*	**nulle part** *nowhere*		
Tu *You*	**ne** *don't*	**vas** *go*			**à Paris**
Il / Elle *He / She*	**ne** *doesn't*	**va** *go(es)*	**pas** *not*		**en France**
					à la fête *to the party*
On *We*	**ne** *don't*	**va** *go*	**jamais** *never*		**à la piscine** *to the pool*
					à la plage *to the beach*
Nous *We*	**n'** *don't*	**allons** *go*			**chez Anne** *to Anne's house*
Vous *You guys/girls*	**n'** *don't*	**allez** *go*	**plus** *no longer*		**au centre commercial** *to the shopping centre*
Ils / Elles *They*	**ne** *don't*	**vont** *go*			**au ciné** *to the cinema*
Ni toi ni moi *Neither you nor I*		**n'allons** *(we) go*			**au collège** *to school*
Ni toi ni lui *Neither you nor he* **Ni toi ni elle** *Neither you nor she*		**n'allez** *(you guys/girls) go*			**au gymnase** *to the gym*
Ni lui ni elle *Neither he nor she* **Ni elle ni lui** *Neither she nor he*		**ne vont** *(they) go*			**au parc** *to the parc*
Personne *Nobody*		**ne va** *(he/she) goes*			**aux magasins** *to the shops*
Je ne vais	**ni** *neither*	**à la plage**	**ni** *nor*		**au ciné**
Je ne vais jamais *I never go*		**au gymnase**	**avec personne** *with anyone* **seul / seule** *alone*		

LANGUAGE AWARENESS
Using Negatives in French

To negate in French is to use **ne…pas** around the verb.
- Je **ne** vais **pas** au ciné   *I **don't** go to the cinema*

To say that you don't do anything **anymore**, or **no longer do** something you need to use **ne…plus**
- Je **ne** vais **plus** au ciné   *I **don't** go to the cinema **anymore** / I **no longer** go to the cinema*

To talk about what two people don't do, you use **ni + ni** (no need to use **pas** when using **ni…ni…**)
- **Ni** mon ami **ni** moi n'allons au ciné   *Neither my friend nor I go to the cinema*

To say that you **never** go somewhere with anyone, you need a double negative. **Personne** literally means "*nobody*"
- Je **ne** vais **jamais** au ciné avec **personne**   *I **never** go to the cinema with **anyone***   *(Lit. I never go with **nobody**)*
But to say that you **don't** go somewhere with anyone, you need to remove the "pas".
- Je **ne** vais au ciné avec **personne**   *I **don't** go to the cinema with **anyone***

SEUL

There are four forms of *seul* because it is a regular adjective:
- Je **ne** vais **jamais** au ciné **seul**   *I **never** go to the cinema **alone***   *(masculine singular)*
- Je **ne** vais **jamais** au ciné **seule**   *I **never** go to the cinema **alone***   *(feminine singular)*
- Nous **n'**allons **jamais** au ciné **seuls**   *We **never** go to the cinema **alone***   *(masc./mixed plural)*
- Nous **n'**allons **jamais** au ciné **seules**   *We **never** go to the cinema **alone***   *(feminine plural)*

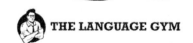 **THE LANGUAGE GYM**

1. Match

Personne	*Alone*
Ni toi ni moi	*With*
Ne…plus	*Never*
Nulle part	*Neither we nor them*
Ni nous ni eux	*Neither he nor I*
Avec	*Nowhere*
Jamais	*No longer*
Ni lui ni moi	*Neither you nor I*
Seul	*Nobody*

2. Missing letter challenge

a. Je ne vais jam__ __ __ au collège seule

b. Aujourd'hui je ne vais nu__ __ __ part

c. N__ toi n__ moi n'allons au centre commercial

d. Nous n'allons pl__ __ au gymnase

e. Dans ma famille, person__ __ ne va au stade

f. Mes frères ne vont pas au parc seul__

g. Mes parents v__ __ __ rarement au ciné

h. Nous all__ __ __ souvent au restaurant chinois

3. Listening, gapped translation

a. Je ne vais à la fête avec __ __ __ __ __ __ __ __   *I don't go to the party with anyone*

b. Ni toi __ __ moi n'allons au collège aujourd'hui   *Neither you nor I are going to school today*

c. Nous n'allons pas au gymnase __ __ __ __ __ __ (f)   *We don't go to the gym alone*

d. Aujourd'hui nous n'allons __ __ __ __ __ part   *Today we are not going anywhere*

e. Je ne vais __ __ __ __ __ __ au supermarché   *I never go to the supermarket*

f. Nous allons au centre commercial __ __ __ __ __ (m)   *We go to the shopping centre alone*

4. Faulty translation: fix the English translation

a. Nous n'allons en Angleterre avec personne   *We don't go to England any longer*

b. Elle va à la fête seule   *They are going to the party alone*

c. Je ne vais pas au collège sans ma mère   *She doesn't go to school without her mother*

d. Ni nous ni lui n'allons au stade   *Neither I nor he go to the gym*

e. Nous n'allons jamais au parc avec personne   *They never go to the beach with anyone*

f. Ils ne vont jamais à la piscine avec leurs parents   *He never goes to church with his parents*

5. Translate into English

a. Nous allons

b. Avec

c. Seule

d. Personne

e. Jamais

f. Ni…ni

g. Nulle part

h. Ils vont

i. Je vais

j. Église

k. Elle va

l. Ne…plus

6. Sentence Puzzle

a. au gymnase Il ne avec son frère va plus   *He doesn't go to the gym with his brother any longer*

b. toujours Je vais aux seul fêtes   *I always go to the parties alone*

c. n'allons la plage Ni toi à avec ni moi Éric   *Neither you nor I go to the beach with Éric*

d. Ce personne part soir ne nulle va   *This evening nobody is going anywhere*

e. Dans, ne va au stade personne ma famille   *Nobody in my family goes to the stadium*

7. Tangled translation: translate into French

a. **We never go** à Paris **with** nos parents

b. **They** ne **go** pas souvent au stade

c. Généralement, Alexandra **goes** au collège **alone**

d. Nous **never go** au parc **alone** (f)

e. Dans **my family** personne ne **goes** au **gym**

f. Je ne vais plus au club de **tennis** avec **my friends**

g. Mes frères **go to the sports centre alone**

h. Dans ma famille **nobody goes to church**

8. Listen and correct the errors

a. Nous n'allez jamais au collège seules

b. Je ne vais au ciné avec quelqu'un

c. Alexandra vais au gymnase seule

d. Mon père ne jamais va au marché avec ma mère

e. Ni mon frère ni ma sœur ne va au gymnase

f. Ce soir nous allons nulle part

g. Mes frères va toujours au collège seuls

h. Ni toi ni moi ne va au magasin de sport seuls

9. Guided translation

a. *We never go there*   N_ _ _ _ n'y a _ _ _ _ _ _ j_ _ _ _ _

b. *They always go*   I_ _ v_ _ _ _ t_ _ _ _ _ _ _ _

c. *Nobody goes*   P_ _ _ _ _ _ _ _ n_ v_

d. *She goes there alone*   Elle y v_ _ s_ _ _ _ _ _

e. *We (f) don't go there alone*   N_ _ _ _ n'y a _ _ _ _ _ _ p_ _ s_ _ _ _ _ _

f. *They don't go any more*   E_ _ _ _ _ n_ v_ _ _ _ p_ _ _

g. *I don't go anywhere*   J_ n_ v_ _ _ _ n_ _ _ _ _ p_ _ _

h. *You never go anywhere*   T_ _ n_ v_ _ _ j_ _ _ _ _ _ n_ _ _ _ p_ _ _

3.7 TIME MARKER + PRESENT OF ALLER + INFINITIVE + NOUN OR PREPOSITIONAL PHRASE + AVEC + POSSESSIVE + NOUN
(SAYING WHAT ONE IS GOING TO DO WHERE, WHEN AND WITH WHOM)

Aujourd'hui *Today*	**je vais** *I am going*	**manger un sandwich**	*(to) eat a sandwich*	
		acheter *(to) buy*	**des baskets**	*trainers*
			une robe	*a dress*
Ce matin *This morning*	**tu vas** *you are going*		**un tee-shirt**	*a t-shirt*
		faire une promenade	*(to) go for a walk*	
		faire les devoirs	*(to) do homework*	
Ce soir *This evening*	**il/elle va** *he/she is going*	**aller** *(to) go*	**au centre commercial**	*to the shopping centre*
			au collège	*to school*
			au supermarché	*to the supermarket*
			chez Marie	*to Marie's house*
Ce week-end *This weekend*	**on va** *we are going*	**jouer** *(to) play*	**à la PlayStation**	*on the PlayStation*
			au foot	*football*
		faire du vélo	*(to) ride a bike*	
		sortir avec ma famille	*(to) go out with my family*	
Cet après-midi *This afternoon*	**nous allons** *we are going*	**prendre un café**	*(to) have a coffee*	
		regarder *(to) watch*	**une série sur Netflix**	*a series on Netflix*
			un film d'action	*an action film*
Demain *Tomorrow*	**vous allez** *you guys/girls are going*			
Maintenant *Now*	**ils/elles vont** *they are going*	**rendre visite à mes grands-parents**	*(to) visit my grandparents*	

Avec qui? *With whom?*				
avec	**mon ami/e**	*my friend*	**mes amis**	*my friends*
	ton ami	*your friend*	**tes amis**	*your friends*
	son ami	*his/her friend*	**ses amis**	*his/her friends*
	nos amis	*our friends*	**vos amis**	*your (pl) friends*
			leurs amis	*their friends*

LANGUAGE AWARENESS: THE IMMEDIATE FUTURE

The immediate future is the easiest way to talk about the future in French. In English it is translated as "I am going to do something". It is a super handy and easy structure! It is formed following this pattern: **Present indicative of *ALLER* + *INFINITIVE VERB***

"Je vais jouer" literally translates to "I am going – **to** play".

Je vais	Jouer
I am going	to play
Present tense of ALLER	Infinitive verb

THE LANGUAGE GYM

105

POSSESSIVE ADJECTIVES

Possessive adjectives are used in order to say **with whom** someone is doing an activity.

• Je vais sortir avec **mes** amis	*I am going to go out with **my** friends*
• Mes amis vont sortir avec **tes** amis	*My friends are going to go out with **your** friends*
• Mon frère va sortir avec **ses** amis	*My brother is going to go out with **his** friends*
• Nous allons sortir avec **nos** amies	*We are going to go out with **our** friends*
• Vous allez sortir avec **vos** amies	*You guys are going to go out with **your** friends*

The **possessives agree with the <u>noun, not the speaker</u>!** We need to modify them to make them agree with the noun they refer to.

	Masculine (sg)	Masculine (pl)	Feminine (sg)	Feminine (pl)
my	mon	mes	ma	mes
your (sg)	ton	tes	ta	tes
his/her	son	ses	sa	ses
our	notre	nos	notre	nos
your (pl)	votre	vos	votre	vos
their	leur	leurs	leur	leurs

Je vais sortir **mon** chien	I am going to walk *my* dog
Il va prendre **ta** voiture	He is going to take *your* car
Tu vas prendre **ses** baskets	You are going to take *his / her* trainers
Nous allons faire **nos** devoirs	We are going to do *our* homework

If the noun is feminine and starting with a vowel, we use "mon/ton/son" instead of "ma/ta/sa"

Mon amie est gentille	*My* friend is nice
Ton armoire est grande	*Your* wardrobe is big

Les aventures de Pascal, le cheval lourd

INFINITIVES – RECAP

Infinitives are verbs as you find them in the dictionary before they are conjugated. The immediate future is one of several structures where you add on the infinitive at the end:

• Je vais **parler**   *I am going **to talk***

Another really useful infinitive structure is *j'aime* (I like):

• J'aime **parler**   *I like **to talk***

1. Match

Je vais	*Are you guys going to?*
Ma mère va	*I am going to*
Mes parents vont	*Are you going to?*
Nous allons	*My aunt is going to*
Ma sœur va	*We are going to*
Vas-tu?	*My brother is going to*
Mes amis vont	*My sister is going to*
Ma tante va	*My mother is going to*
Allez-vous?	*My parents are going to*
Mon frère va	*My friends are going to*

2. Match

Je vais rendre visite à mes amis	*I am going to go for a walk*
Je vais manger un sandwich	*Are you guys going to do the homework?*
Je vais faire une promenade	*I am going to visit my friends*
Nous allons regarder un film	*Are you going to go out with your friends?*
Allez-vous faire les devoirs?	*I am going to eat a sandwich*
Vas-tu sortir avec tes amis?	*We are going to watch a film*

3. Anagrams

a. rfaei ud éolv

b. llrea ua pesruémhcra

c. efira sle oiedvsr

d. rella zehc eiraM

e. arell ua necrte mmocecrail

f. fiera neu poendrmea

g. cthaeer uen cehimse

h. eacther nue orbe

i. regderar nue siére urs xfiNtel

j. etacher sde bkeasts

k. rdeeargr nu fmil d'aicton

l. rerend isveit à ems arpents

m. ngmaer nu ndsachwi

n. reeprnd nu féca

o. laler ua cgoèlle

4. Complete with a suitable verb

a. Aujourd'hui je vais _____ un tee-shirt neuf

b. Ce matin nous allons _____ aux échecs

c. Ce week-end nous allons _____ au ciné

d. Cet après-midi je vais _____ un sandwich

e. Aujourd'hui nous allons _____ du vélo au parc

f. Demain mes amis et moi allons _____ un film

g. Dimanche je vais _____ _____ à ma grand-mère

h. Ce matin nous allons _____ une promenade

i. Aujourd'hui mon père et moi allons _____ un café

5. Write the correct form of the verb *ALLER*

a. Mon frère _____ acheter un tee-shirt neuf au centre commercial

b. Mes frères et moi _____ rendre visite à nos grands-parents au Maroc

c. Ce matin mes parents _____ se promener au parc qui est dans la banlieue

d. Aujourd'hui mes amis et moi _____ jouer à la PlayStation

e. Mon meilleur ami _____ prendre un café

f. _____-tu sortir avec tes amis aujourd'hui?

g. _____-vous rendre visite à vos parents?

THE LANGUAGE GYM

6. Sentence Puzzle

a. sortir Je vais soir amis ce avec mes — *I am going to go out with my friends this evening*

b. mère au Ma demain va aller gymnase — *My mother is going to go to the gym tomorrow*

c. Mon va père acheter vert tee-shirt un — *My father is going to buy a green t-shirt*

d. sœur va regarder un Ma d'action film — *My sister is going to watch an action film*

e. Netflix Je vais regarder série une sur demain — *I am going to watch a series on Netflix tomorrow*

f. parents vont manger sandwich un Mes — *My parents are going to eat a sandwich*

7. Gapped dictation: listen, complete and translate into English

a. Je vais _____ ___ _____ avec mes amis ce _____

b. Mon _____ va aller au _____ avec son _____

c. Mes _____ vont _____ ___ _____ aujourd'hui

d. ____ - __ faire ____ _____ aujourd'hui?

e. _____ - vous _____ à la PlayStation ce _____ ?

f. Cet _____ - _____ nous allons _____ _____ à mes grands-parents

g. Aujourd'hui _____ _____ aller au ciné avec leurs parents

8. Tangled translation: translate into French

a. Je *am going to* regarder *an action film*

b. Mon *brother* ne *going* pas *to go* au centre commercial *this weekend*

c. Mes *parents* ne vont pas *to buy* de baskets

d. *My* grands-parents *are going to go for a walk* aujourd'hui

e. Je vais *to watch a* série sur Netflix *this evening*

f. *Tomorrow* je ne vais ni *to go out with* mes *friends neither* jouer au *football*.

g. Ni *my* mère *neither my* sœur *are going* manger un *sandwich*

h. *I am not going to* sortir *with my friends* ce soir

i. Mon *friend is not going to* aller au collège *today*

9. Translate into French

a. Tomorrow I am going to do my homework

b. My parents are going to watch a series on Netflix this weekend

c. My sister is going to go out with her friends to the shopping centre

d. Are you going to watch a film today?

e. My friends and I are going to buy trainers

f. My sister is going to play football and go to the supermarket

g. Neither my mum nor my dad are going to watch a film this morning

h. My friends are not going to play football this afternoon because they are ill

A		ORAL PING PONG	

ORAL PING PONG

ALLER

ENGLISH 1	FRENCH 1	ENGLISH 2	FRENCH 2
I never go to the cinema or to the shops with anyone.	Je ne vais jamais au ciné ou aux magasins avec personne.	Neither he nor she go either to the shopping centre or the gym alone.	
My mum goes to the shopping centre every weekend.	Ma maman va au centre commercial tous les week-ends.	Neither my mum nor my grandmother go to the park today.	
We often go to the gym in order to do weights.	Nous allons souvent au gymnase pour faire de la musculation.	This morning we are going to buy a t-shirt in the shops.	
My friends go to the park in order to go for a bike ride every Saturday.	Mes amis vont au parc pour faire du vélo tous les samedis.	In July I often go on holiday to Morocco, but I never go alone.	
Today my dad is going to Paris in order to visit his parents.	Aujourd'hui mon papa va à Paris pour rendre visite à ses parents.	My parents go to the gym in order to do weights every Thursday.	
My family and I often go on holidays to Greece by plane.	Ma famille et moi allons souvent en vacances en Grèce en avion.	My friend and I go to the shopping centre in order to go window shopping.	
Tomorrow my brothers are going to watch a Netflix series with their friends.	Demain mes frères vont regarder une série sur Netflix avec leurs amis.	I am going to ride a bike with my sister in the park today.	
We are going to visit our grandparents in Italy by car.	Nous allons rendre visite à nos grands-parents en Italie en voiture.	Neither my mum nor my sister go to the gym at the weekends.	

INSTRUCTIONS - You are **PARTNER A.** Work in pairs. Each of you has two sets of sentences - one set has already been translated for you. You will ask your partner to translate these. The other set of sentences have not been translated. Your partner will ask you to translate these.

HOW TO PLAY - Partner A starts by reading out his/her/their first sentence in English. Partner B must translate. Partner A must check the answer and award the following points: **3 points** = perfect, **2 points** = 1 mistake, **1 point** = mistakes but the verb is accurate. If they cannot translate correctly, Partner A will read out the sentence so that Partner B can learn what the correct translation is.

Then Partner B reads out his/her/their first sentence, and so on.

OBJECTIVE - Try to win more points than your partner by translating correctly as many sentences as possible.

 THE LANGUAGE GYM

ORAL PING PONG

ALLER

ENGLISH 1	FRENCH 1	ENGLISH 2	FRENCH 2
I never go to the cinema or to the shops with anyone.		Neither he nor she go either to the shopping centre or the gym alone.	Ni lui ni elle ne vont au centre commercial ou au gymnase seuls.
My mum goes to the shopping centre every weekend.		Neither my mum nor my grandmother go to the park today.	Ni ma maman ni ma grand-mère ne vont au parc aujourd'hui.
We often go to the gym in order to do weights.		This morning we are going to buy a t-shirt in the shops.	Ce matin nous allons acheter un tee-shirt dans les magasins.
My friends go to the park in order to go for a bike ride every Saturday.		In July I often go on holiday to Morocco, but I never go alone.	En juillet je vais souvent en vacances au Maroc mais je n'y vais jamais seul(e).
Today my dad is going to Paris in order to visit his parents.		My parents go to the gym in order to do weights every Thursday.	Mes parents vont au gymnase pour faire de la musculation tous les jeudis.
My family and I often go on holidays to Greece by plane.		My friend and I go to the shopping centre in order to go window shopping.	Mon ami et moi allons au centre commercial pour faire du lèche-vitrine.
Tomorrow my brothers are going to watch a Netflix series with their friends.		I am going to ride a bike with my sister in the park today.	Je vais faire du vélo avec ma sœur au parc aujourd'hui.
We are going to visit our grandparents in Italy by car.		Neither my mother nor my sister go to the gym at the weekends.	Ni ma mère ni ma sœur ne vont au gymnase le week-end.

INSTRUCTIONS - You are **PARTNER B.** Work in pairs. Each of you has two sets of sentences - one set has already been translated for you. You will ask your partner to translate these. The other set of sentences have not been translated. Your partner will ask you to translate these.

HOW TO PLAY - Partner A starts by reading out his/her/their first sentence in English. Partner B must translate. Partner A must check the answer and award the following points: **3 points** = perfect, **2 points** = 1 mistake, **1 point** = mistakes but the verb is accurate. If they cannot translate correctly, Partner A will read out the sentence so that Partner B can learn what the correct translation is.

Then Partner B reads out his/her/their first sentence, and so on.

OBJECTIVE - Try to win more points than your partner by translating correctly as many sentences as possible.

THE LANGUAGE GYM

110

No Snakes No Ladders

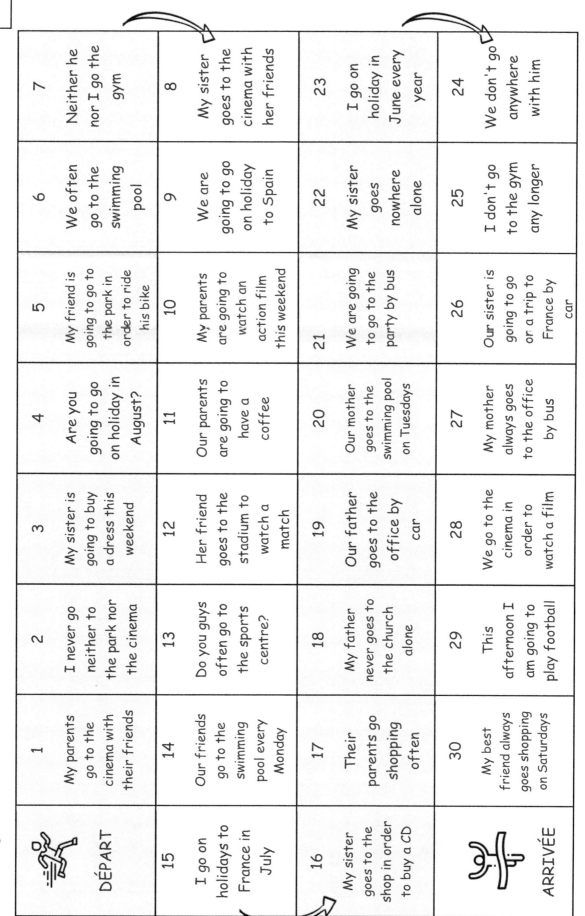

7 Neither he nor I go the gym	**6** We often go to the swimming pool	**5** My friend is going to go to the park in order to ride his bike	**4** Are you going to go on holiday in August?	**3** My sister is going to buy a dress this weekend	**2** I never go neither to the park nor the cinema	**1** My parents go to the cinema with their friends
8 My sister goes to the cinema with her friends	**9** We are going to go on holiday to Spain	**10** My parents are going to watch an action film this weekend	**11** Our parents are going to have a coffee	**12** Her friend goes to the stadium to watch a match	**13** Do you guys often go to the sports centre?	**14** Our friends go to the swimming pool every Monday
23 I go on holiday in June every year	**22** My sister goes nowhere alone	**21** We are going to go to the party by bus	**20** Our mother goes to the swimming pool on Tuesdays	**19** Our father goes to the office by car	**18** My father never goes to the church alone	**17** Their parents go shopping often
24 We don't go anywhere with him	**25** I don't go to the gym any longer	**26** Our sister is going to go or a trip to France by car	**27** My mother always goes to the office by bus	**28** We go to the cinema in order to watch a film	**29** This afternoon I am going to play football	**30** My best friend always goes shopping on Saturdays

(Left margin, bottom): **15** I go on holidays to France in July — **16** My sister goes to the shop in order to buy a CD — DÉPART — ARRIVÉE

 **THE LANGUAGE GYM**

111

No Snakes No Ladders

ALLER

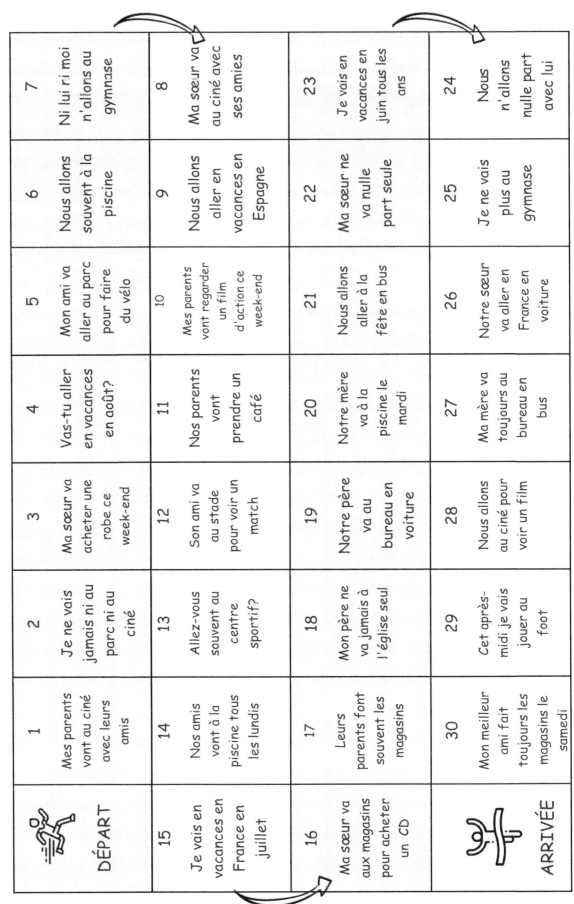

	7 Ni lui ri moi n'allons au gymnase	**6** Nous allons souvent à la piscine	**5** Mon ami va aller au parc pour faire du vélo	**4** Vas-tu aller en vacances en août?	**3** Ma sœur va acheter une robe ce week-end	**2** Je ne vais jamais ni au parc ni au ciné	**1** Mes parents vont au ciné avec leurs amis
	8 Ma sœur va au ciné avec ses amies	**9** Nous allons aller en vacances en Espagne	**10** Mes parents vont regarder un film d'action ce week-end	**11** Nos parents vont prendre un café	**12** Son ami va au stade pour voir un match	**13** Allez-vous souvent au centre sportif?	**14** Nos amis vont à la piscine tous les lundis
	23 Je vais en vacances en juin tous les ans	**22** Ma sœur ne va nulle part seule	**21** Nous allons aller à la fête en bus	**20** Notre mère va à la piscine le mardi	**19** Notre père va au bureau en voiture	**18** Mon père ne va jamais à l'église seul	**17** Leurs parents font souvent les magasins
	24 Nous n'allons nulle part avec lui	**25** Je ne vais plus au gymnase	**26** Notre sœur va aller en France en voiture	**27** Ma mère va toujours au bureau en bus	**28** Nous allons au ciné pour voir un film	**29** Cet après-midi je vais jouer au foot	**30** Mon meilleur ami fait toujours les magasins le samedi

DÉPART / **15** Je vais en vacances en France en juillet

16 Ma sœur va aux magasins pour acheter un CD / **17** (see above)

ARRIVÉE

THE LANGUAGE GYM

112

PYRAMID TRANSLATION

ALLER

Translate each part of the pyramid out loud with your partner, then write it into the spaces provided below.

a. I go to the sports centre

b. I go to the sports centre every weekend with our friends

c. I go to the sports centre every weekend with our friends, but I never go either to the swimming pool or the gym.

d. I go to the sports centre every weekend with our friends, but I never go either to the swimming pool or the gym. Tomorrow my sister and I are going to watch an action film at home

e. I go to the sports centre every weekend with our friends, but I never go either to the swimming pool or the gym. Tomorrow my sister and I are going to watch an action film at home. My parents are going to have a coffee with their friends.

Write your translation here

SOLUTION: Je vais au centre sportif tous les week-ends avec nos amis, mais je ne vais jamais ni à la piscine ni au gymnase. Demain ma sœur et moi allons regarder un film d'action à la maison. Mes parents vont prendre un café avec leurs amis.

THE LANGUAGE GYM

UNIT 4 – FAIRE

Je	fais
Tu	fais
Il / Elle / On	fait
Nous	faisons
Vous	faites
Ils / Elles	font

DOING & MAKING THINGS

Je fais les devoirs

Je fais la cuisine

DOING SPORTS

Quel sport fais-tu?

Je fais de l'escalade

WEATHER

Aujourd'hui, il fait beau mais il fait froid

4.1 TIME MARKER + JE FAIS + NOUN PHRASE
(SAYING WHAT I DO AND WHEN/HOW OFTEN)

Quand je sors	*When I go out*				***de l'exercice***	
					physical exercise	
De temps en temps					***des recherches*** *research*	
From time to time					***du sport*** *sport*	
En SVT	*in science*		**fais**		**la vaisselle**	*the washing-up*
En français	*In French*		*do*		**les courses**	*the shopping*
En espagnol	*In Spanish*				**les devoirs**	*homework*
					les tâches ménagères	
Le lundi	*On Mondays*	**je**		**souvent**	*house chores*	
Le mardi	*On Tuesdays*	*I*		*often*	**un voyage** *a trip*	
Le mercredi	*On Wednesdays*				**une balade** *a walk*	
Le jeudi	*On Thursdays*	**tu**	**fais**	**toujours**	**la cuisine**	*the cooking*
Le vendredi	*On Fridays*	*you*	*make*	*always*	**mon/le lit**	*my/the bed*
Le samedi	*On Saturdays*					
Le dimanche	*On Sundays*		**fais**			
			pay		**attention**	*attention*
Le week-end	*At the weekend*					
Tous les jours	*Every day*		**fais**		**la grasse matinée**	
			have		*a lie in*	
Une fois par semaine	*Once a week*					
Je ne fais jamais	*I never do / make / pay / have*					
***Je ne fais pas d'exercice**	*I don't do physical exercises*					
***Je ne fais pas de recherche**	*I don't do research*					
***Je ne fais pas de sport**	*I don't do sport*					
Je ne fais rien	*I don't do anything*					

LANGUAGE AWARENESS

FAIRE: to do, to make, and more!

In French, the verb *faire* can generally be translated, as either **"to do"** or **"to make"**. However, when combined with certain words, it can also be translated as **"to go"** or even **"to pay attention"**:

- Je fais **les devoirs**   *I do my homework*
- Je fais **de la voile**   *I go sailing*
- Je fais **la cuisine**   *I make food/I cook*
- Je fais **la queue**   *I line up*

DOUBLE NEGATIVES

JE NE FAIS RIEN

Do you remember how to use negatives in French? In French we sometimes negate twice! So, when we want to say, *I don't do anything*, we say:

Je ne fais rien   *I don't do **anything***

Literally: *I **don't** do **nothing***

Or: **Je ne fais jamais rien**   *I never do **anything***

THE LANGUAGE GYM

1. Match

Je fais toujours attention	*I have a lie in*
Je fais un voyage	*I always pay attention*
Je fais la grasse matinée	*I do nothing*
Je ne fais rien	*I do the house chores*
Je ne fais jamais le lit	*I do a trip*
Je fais mes devoirs	*I never do the shopping*
Je fais les tâches ménagères	*I never make the bed*
Je ne fais jamais les courses	*I do the cooking*
Je fais souvent du sport	*I often do sport*
Je fais la cuisine	*I do my homework*

2. Broken words

a. Je ne fais ja__ __ __ __ rien.

b. Je fais la cuis__ __ __

c. Je fais les tâ__ __ __ __ ménagères

d. Je fais toujours atten__ __ __ __

e. Le samedi je fais les cour __ __ __

f. En SVT, je fais des recher__ __ __ __

g. Je fais souvent la grasse ma__ __née

h. Le dimanche je fais du sp__ __ __

i. Le soir je fais mes de__ __ __ __

3. Listen and complete 🔊

a. Je fais souvent la _____

b. Je ne fais jamais les _____

c. Je fais toujours les _____ avec ma _____

d. Je ne fais jamais mes _____

e. Je fais toujours la _____

f. Je ne fais pas d'_____

g. Je fais une _____ tous les jours

h. Je fais la _____ une fois par semaine

i. En SVT je fais beaucoup de _____

4. Complete with a suitable word, then listen 🔊 and note down the differences

a. Je fais la _____ tous les jours.

b. Je ne fais jamais les _____ ménagères.

c. Je fais souvent la _____ _____.

d. Je fais la _____ tous les samedis.

e. Le week-end je ne fais pas d'_____. Je me repose.

f. Je suis sportive. Je fais beaucoup de _____.

g. Je fais toujours mes _____ de français.

h. Le dimanche je fais un _____ avec mon père.

5. Anagrams

a. el tli	*the bed*	g. ijamsa	*never*
b. misa	*friends*	h. joutruso	*always*
c. esl soiderv	*the homework*	i. al nciusie	*the cooking*
d. ed mptes ne mptes	*from time to time*	j. el uejid	*on Thursdays*
e. posrt	*sport*	k. sle sesruoc	*the shopping*
f. ienr	*nothing*	l. el disame	*on Saturdays*

THE LANGUAGE GYM

6. Sentence Puzzle

a. toujours Je fais quand je sors une balade — *I always go for a walk when I go out*

b. fais Je ne mes devoirs jamais de SVT — *I never do my science homework*

c. mes devoirs Le samedi je fais — *On Saturdays, I do my homework*

d. Je les les jours tâches ménagères fais tous — *I do the house chores every day*

e. Je fais ne les jamais courses — *I never go shopping*

f. fais Je la cuisine toujours le week-end — *I always make the food at the weekends*

g. Je tous fais les jours mon lit — *I make my bed every day*

7. Break the flow

a. Jefaissouventlagrassematinée

b. Jenefaisjamaislesdevoirs

c. Jefaislelittouslesjours

d. Jenefaisrienleweek-end

e. Jefaisattentionenfrançais

f. Jefaisrarementdusport

g. Lelundijefaislestâchesménagères

h. JenefaispasderechercheenSVT

8. Gapped translation: complete the translation

a. Je fais la _____ — *I do the washing-up*

b. Je ne fais _____ de sport — *I never do sport*

c. Je fais toujours les _____ — *I always go shopping*

d. Je ne fais pas mes _____ — *I don't do my homework*

e. Je fais souvent mon _____ — *I often make my bed*

f. Je fais de l'_____ — *I do physical exercise*

g. Je fais un _____ — *I go on a trip*

h. Je fais rarement _____ — *I rarely pay attention*

9. Spot and correct the errors

a. Je fais la grasse matine de temps en temps.

b. Je ne jamais fais la cuisine.

c. Le samedi je fais toujours les taches ménagères.

d. Je fais du sport de temp en temp.

e. Je fais les course avec ma mère le jeudi.

f. En maths, je fais mes devoirs tout les jours.

g. Quand je sors, je fais une balade avec mes amis.

h. Le dimanche je fais ne rien. Je me repose.

10. Listen and translate into French

a. I go for a walk

b. I do the house chores

c. I do sport

d. I make my bed

e. I do nothing

f. I do the cooking

g. I do my homework

THE LANGUAGE GYM

11. Complete with the words in the box

a. Tous les jours, je fais mon _____ dans ma chambre.

b. Quand je sors le samedi, je fais toujours une _____ avec mes amis.

c. Le jeudi, en général, je fais les _____ avec ma mère.

d. En SVT, je fais toujours des _____ si je ne comprends pas.

e. Pour aider ma mère, je fais les _____ ménagères presque tous les jours.

f. Tous les jours, je fais mon lit, et le soir je fais la _____ pour le dîner.

g. En français je travaille dur. Je fais toujours les _____.

h. Je suis très paresseux. Je ne fais jamais d'_____.

i. De temps en temps je fais un _____ à Paris pour rendre visite à mon cousin.

j. Je suis très sportive. Je fais du _____, surtout de la natation, tous les jours.

tâches	devoirs	sport	courses	exercice
recherches	cuisine	balade	voyage	lit

12. Complete the translation

a. *A lie in*

L__ g__ __ __ __ __   m__ __ __ __ __ __

b. *A trip*

U__ v__ __ __ __ __

c. *The shopping*

L__ __ c__ __ __ __ __ __ __

d. *Physical exercise*

D__ l'e__ __ __ __ __ __ __

e. *House chores*

L__ __ t__ __ __ __ __

m__ __ __ __ __ __ __ __

f. *The cooking*

L__ c__ __ __ __ __ __

g. *Sport*

D__ s__ __ __ __ __

h. *I don't do anything*

J__ n__ f__ __ __ r__ __ __

13. Tangled translation: translate into French

a. *I* fais *always* la *cooking*

b. Je ne fais *never* d'*exercise*

c. Je fais *the bed* de temps en temps

d. Une fois par *week* je fais les *shopping*

e. Je fais *always* les *house chores*

f. En anglais, *I do* toujours les *homework*

g. Le week-end je fais souvent *a lie in*

14. Translate into French

a. I go for a walk

b. I do the house chores

c. I do my homework

d. I do sport

e. I make my bed

f. I do the cooking

g. I do the shopping

h. I do physical exercise

i. I do research

THE LANGUAGE GYM

4.2 JE FAIS + NOUN + TIME MARKER + J'AIME + REASON
(SAYING WHAT LEISURE ACTIVITY YOU DO AND WHY YOU LIKE/DISLIKE IT)

Je fais *I "do"*	**souvent** *often* **toujours** *always*	**de l'**	**athlétisme** **équitation** **escalade** **exercice**	*athletics* *horse riding* *rock climbing* *physical exercise*	**de temps en temps** *from time to time* **le lundi** *on Mondays*	
		de la	**boxe** **musculation** **natation** **plongée** **voile**	*boxing* *weights* *swimming* *scuba diving* *sailing*	**le mardi** *on Tuesdays* **le mercredi** *on Wednesdays* **le jeudi** *on Thursdays* **le vendredi** *on Fridays* **le samedi** *on Saturdays*	
		du	**jogging** **sport** **vélo**	*jogging* *sport* *cycling*	**le dimanche** *on Sundays* **le week-end** *at the weekend*	
		des	**randonnées**	*hiking*	**tous les jours** *every day*	
Je ne fais pas *I don't do* **Je ne fais jamais** *I never do*		**de/d'**	**athlétisme / équitation / escalade /** **exercice / boxe / musculation / natation** **/ plongée / voile / jogging / sport / vélo /** **randonnées**		**une fois par semaine** *once a week*	

J'adore ça	*I love it*		**amusant**	*fun*
J'aime beaucoup ça	*I like it a lot*		**barbant**	*boring*
J'aime ça	*I like it*	**parce que c'est**	**difficile**	*difficult*
Je n'aime pas ça	*I don't like it*	*because it is*	**épuisant**	*exhausting*
Je n'aime pas du tout ça			**fatigant**	*tiring*
I don't like it at all			**passionnant**	*exciting*
			relaxant	*relaxing*

LANGUAGE AWARENESS:
FAIRE DU SPORT – I DO or I GO?

In French we use *faire (to do)* to talk about the sports/activities we practise. *Jouer (to play)* is used with sports we "play", such as ball sports: football, rugby, golf etc.

For other sports, we use *faire.* It can be translated with either an **"I do"** or an **"I go"** structure in English:

Je fais de l'athlétisme   *I **do** athletics*

(Faire + noun)   (I do + noun)

Je fais de la natation   *I **do/go** swimming*

(Faire + noun)   (I do/go + gerund)

JE FAIS DE LA VOILE – I GO SAILING
Verb + NOUN / Verb + GERUND

As shown, the verb *faire* can be translated using different verbs, but there is also an important structural difference to be aware of.

Not only does *je fais* mutate from **"I do"** to **"I go"**, but the phrase structure also often changes from **"*faire* + noun"** to **"to do/go + gerund"**.

Je fais des randonnées   *I **do/go** hiking*

(Faire + noun)   (To do/go + gerund)

 **THE LANGUAGE GYM**

1. Match

Je fais des randonnées	*I don't do anything*
Je fais du vélo	*I do boxing*
Je fais de la boxe	*I "do" cycling*
Je fais de l'athlétisme	*I do sport*
Je fais du sport	*I "do" hiking*
Je fais de la voile	*I "do" jogging*
Je fais du jogging	*I "do" sailing*
Je fais de l'équitation	*I do athletics*
Je ne fais rien	*I "do" horse riding*

2. Faulty translation: fix the English translation

a. Je fais souvent de la voile	*I always do weights*
b. Je fais du jogging	*I do hiking*
c. Je ne fais pas de natation	*I don't do anything*
d. Je fais de l'équitation	*I do jogging*
e. Je ne fais pas de musculation	*I don't do climbing*
f. Je fais des randonnées	*I do sailing*
g. Je ne fais jamais d'athlétisme	*I always do athletics*
h. Je fais du sport	*I do scuba diving*

3. Break the flow

a. Jefaissouventdesrandonnéesetdel'équitation

b. Jenefaisjamaisdevoilenideplongée

c. Jefaisdelaboxetroisfoisparsemaine

d. Jenefaisrien

e. Jefaisdelamusculationetdel'escaladetouslesjours

f. Jefaisdujoggingetduyogaledimanche

g. Jefaisrarementdusport

h. Jenefaisjamaisdesport

4. Cross out all the phrases which do not refer to sports

a. Je fais le lit

b. Je fais la cuisine

c. Je fais du jogging

d. Je fais les courses

e. Je fais de la boxe

f. Je fais de la natation

g. Je fais les tâches ménagères

h. Je fais les devoirs

5. Likely or unlikely? Rewrite any unlikely statement into a plausible one

a. J'aime ça parce que c'est barbant

b. Je n'aime pas ça parce que c'est passionnant

c. J'aime ça parce que c'est relaxant

d. J'aime ça parce que c'est très amusant

e. Je n'aime pas ça parce que c'est très fatigant et difficile

f. J'aime beaucoup ça parce que c'est épuisant

g. Je n'aime pas du tout ça parce que c'est amusant

6. Translate into English

a. Épuisant

b. Passionnant

c. Le vendredi

d. L'équitation

e. Le jogging

f. Amusant

g. Les devoirs

h. Les tâches ménagères

i. Le lit

j. Les courses

k. Barbant

l. Difficile

 THE LANGUAGE GYM

7. Categories

intéressant	je n'aime pas ça	mardi	natation
jeudi	dimanche	la plongée	mercredi
j'adore ça	barbant	j'aime ça	des randonnées
la boxe	lundi	amusant	samedi

Adjectives	Days of the week	Sports	Phrases to express likes and dislikes

8. Positive or Negative?

a. J'aime ça

b. Passionnant

c. Intéressant

d. C'est fatigant

e. J'adore ça

f. C'est difficile

g. Relaxant

h. Je n'aime pas ça

i. Je déteste ça

9. Sentence Puzzle

a. après le collège Je fais tous les jours de la boxe — *I do boxing every day after school*

b. du Je jogging fais tous le matin les jours — *I do jogging every day in the morning*

c. Je semaine de fais trois la musculation fois par — *I do weights three times a week*

d. fais Je ne jamais mais natation je de plongée fais de la — *I never do diving but I do swimming*

e. parce que Je ne jamais barbant de fais randonnée c'est — *I never do hiking because it is boring*

f. Tous fais je fais les je mon lit et du jours yoga — *Every day, I make my bed and I do yoga*

g. fais dimanche de du l'escalade Je et vélo le — *I do climbing and cycling on Sundays*

10. Tangled translation: translate into French

a. Je fais de la **boxing** tous les **days**. J'adore ça, mais c'est **tiring**.

b. Je ne fais **never** de **weights**. **I don't like it** parce que c'est **boring**.

c. Tous les jours **I make** le **bed and** puis **I do sport**. **I** ne fais **never the house chores.**

d. Après avoir fait **my homework** je fais du **jogging**. J'aime ça, **but it is** fatigant.

e. Je fais de l'**athletics** trois **times** par **week with** ma copine. C'est **exciting**!

f. **I do** de l'équitation **three** fois par semaine à la **countryside**. C'est très **relaxing.**

g. **Every** jours je fais de l'**physical exercise** avec **my brother** aîné. C'est très **difficult**!

h. Je ne fais **never** de plongée **because** c'est **boring**. Je préfère la **swimming.**

i. **I** ne fais **never nothing** parce que **I am** paresseux et le sport est **tiring** et **boring.**

j. Je fais les **chores** ménagères et puis **I do horse riding** avec mes **friends**. **I love it**!

11. Listen, complete, then translate into English

a. J'aime beaucoup le vélo parce que c'est _____.

b. J'aime beaucoup le jogging parce que c'est _____.

c. Je fais du _____. J'aime ça parce que c'est _____.

d. J'adore l'_____ parce que c'est _____.

e. Je déteste la _____ parce que c'est _____.

f. J'aime beaucoup le _____ parce que c'est _____.

g. Je n'aime pas du tout la _____ parce que c'est _____.

---

12. Listen and correct the errors 🔊

a. Je fais du sport de temps de temps

b. J'adore ça parce que barbant

c. J'aime ça parce que c'est fatigant

d. Je fais de la plongée tous jours

e. Je fais ne jamais de randonnée

f. Je fais voile le dimanche

g. Je fais de la musculation un fois par semaine

h. Je ne fais jamais de l'exercise

---

13. Gapped translation: complete the translation

a. J'adore __ __	*I love it*
b. Je fais de la voi __ __	*I do sailing*
c. Je n'aime pas __ __ tout ça	*I don't like it at all*
d. Je fais de la __ __ __ __ gée	*I go diving*
e. J'aime l'athlét __ __ __ __	*I like athletics*
f. Tous les j__ __ __ __	*Every day*
g. Je ne fais __ __ mais __ __ sport	*I never do sport*
h. Je fais de la mus__ __ lation	*I do weights*
i. De t__ __ ps en t__ __ ps	*From time to time*
j. C'est tr__ __ fati__ __ __ __	*It is very tiring*

---

14. Translate into French

a. I go jogging and swimming every day

b. I never do athletics because it is boring

c. I do the shopping from time to time

d. I never make my bed

e. I do sport nearly every day

f. I never go hiking because it is boring

g. I do boxing every day

h. I rarely do weights

i. I do sailing from time to time

j. First, I do the house chores and then I do sport

 THE LANGUAGE GYM

4.3 FULL PRESENT CONJUGATION OF FAIRE + NOUN + FREQUENCY ADVERB
(SAYING WHAT LEISURE ACTIVITIES ONE DOES AND HOW OFTEN)

Je fais *I do*	**souvent** *often* **toujours** *always*	**de l'**	**athlétisme** *athletics* **equitation** *horse riding* **escalade** *rock climbing* **exercice** *physical exercise*	**de temps en temps** *from time to time*
Tu fais *You do*		**de la**	**boxe** *boxing* **musculation** *weights* **natation** *swimming* **plongée** *diving* **voile** *sailing*	**le lundi** *on Mondays* **le mardi** *on Tuesdays* **le mercredi** *on Wednesdays* **le jeudi** *on Thursdays*
Il / Elle fait *He / She does*				
On fait *We do*		**du**	**jogging** *jogging* **sport** *sport* **vélo** *cycling*	**le vendredi** *on Fridays* **le samedi** *on Saturdays* **le dimanche** *on Sundays*
Nous faisons *We do*		**des**	**arts martiaux** *martial arts* **randonnées** *hiking*	**le week-end** *at the weekend*
Vous faites *You guys/girls do*	**la cuisine** *(do) the cooking* **le lit** *(make) the bed*			**tous les jours** *every day* **une fois par semaine** *once a week*
Ils / Elles font *They do*	**les courses** *the shopping* **les devoirs** *homework* **les tâches ménagères** *the chores*			

Je ne fais pas de boxe / d'équitation	*I don't do boxing / horse riding*
Je ne fais jamais de voile / d'escalade	*I never do sailing / rock climbing*
Je ne fais pas le lit / les devoirs	*I don't make the bed / do homework*
Je ne fais jamais la cuisine / les courses	*I never make the food / do the shopping*

Je ne fais rien	*I don't do anything*
Je ne fais jamais rien	*I never do anything*

LANGUAGE AWARENESS

NEGATIVE FORM

When you use a partitive (**du, de la, de l', des**) before a sport, it needs to change into **de** or **d'** in the negative form.

Affirmative:	Je fais **du** sport
Negative:	Je ne fais pas **de** sport
Affirmative:	Je fais **de l'**escalade
Negative:	Je ne fais pas **d'**escalade
Affirmative:	Je fais **de la** boxe
Negative:	Je ne fais pas **de** boxe

The many translations of *faire*

As you know, there are other ways to translate the verb *faire*, apart from *"to do"* and *"to make"*…

- To **do**:

Je fais du sport	*I do sport*

- To **make**:

Ils font le lit	*They **make** the bed*

- To **go**:

Il/Elle fait des randonnées	*He/She **goes** hiking*

- To **pay**:

Tu fais attention en classe	*You **pay** attention in class*

1. Faulty translation: fix the English translation

a. Nous faisons des randonnées — *They go hiking*

b. Tu fais quels sports? — *What sports does he do?*

c. Il ne fait pas de musculation — *He doesn't do swimming*

d. Ils font toujours de l'escalade — *We always go rock climbing*

e. Où faites-vous de la voile? — *Where do I go horse riding?*

f. Je fais des arts martiaux — *He does martial arts*

g. Elles ne font jamais de sport — *We never do sport*

h. Ils font les courses — *You do the shopping*

2. Broken words

a. Nous faisons de la voi__ __

b. Elles ne font ri__ __

c. Tu fais du s__ __ __ __?

d. Je fais de la nata__ __ __ __

e. Vous faites les cour__ __ __?

f. Mon frère fait de la plon__ __ __

g. Elle fait des arts mar__ia__ __?

3. Gapped (English) translation

a. Je fais des randonnées — _____ *hiking*

b. Ils font du sport — _____ *sport*

c. Qu'est-ce que tu fais? — *What do_____?*

d. Nous faisons de la voile — _____ *sailing*

e. Quel sport fais-tu? — *What sport do_____?*

f. Ils ne font pas de vélo — _____ *don't do cycling*

g. Vous faites du karaté? — *Do _____ karate?*

h. Elles ne font rien — _____ *nothing*

i. Faites-vous de la boxe? — *Do _____ boxing?*

j. Il fait attention en classe — *He _____ attention in class*

4. Match

Escalade	*We do*
Sport	*On Thursdays*
Je fais	*Rock climbing*
Jogging	*Never*
Nous faisons	*Martial arts*
Le jeudi	*Nothing*
Jamais	*Sport*
Ils/Elles font	*Swimming*
Natation	*Jogging*
Rien	*They do*
Arts martiaux	*I do*

5. Word hunt

a. A day of the week starting with J:
Le j__ __ __ __ __

b. A sport starting with E:
E__ __ __ __ __ __ __ __

c. A time adverb starting with J:
J__ __ __ __ __ __

d. A sport starting with É:
É__ __ __ __ __ __ __ __ __ __

e. A time adverb starting with S:
S__ __ __ __ __ __

f. Opposite of *barbant*:
A__ __ __ __ __ __

g. Opposite of *tout*: R__ __ __ __

Salut pingouin

6. Listen and complete with the missing vowels 🔊

a. I__s f__nt d__ l'__sc__l__ d__ t__ __ __s l__s j__ __ __rs

b. Q__ __nd __l f__ __t b__ __ __ __, __n f__ __ __t d__ l__
v__ __l

c. M__ s s__ __ __ __rs n__ f__nt r__ __ __n

d. __ll__n__ f__ __t j__m__ __s d__ j__gg__ng

e. T__ __n f__ __ __s p__ __s d__ sp__rt?

f. __ __ __ f__ __t __s-v__ __s d__ l__ m__ sc__l__t__ __n?

g. J__ n__ f__ __s j__m__ __s d__ v__l__ p__rc__
q__ __ __ c'__st b__ __rb__nt

THE LANGUAGE GYM

124

7. Translate into English

a. Je ne fais pas de sport

b. Ils ne font jamais d'exercice

c. Nous faisons de l'escalade tous les jours

d. On fait du jogging trois fois par semaine

e. Que faites-vous aujourd'hui?

f. Ce matin nous ne faisons rien

g. Où fais-tu de la natation?

h. Généralement, je fais de l'escalade seul

i. Je ne fais pas d'athlétisme: c'est barbant

j. Quel sport font-ils?

8. Tangled translation: translate into French

a. Il ne *does never* de sport parce que c'est *tiring*

b. Nous ne *do nothing*

c. Je ne *do never* de jogging parce que c'est *boring*

d. Le *Thursdays* mes parents *do* de l'équitation

e. Houda *does* de l'exercice *every day*

f. *What* sport *do* vous?

g. *You* ne fais jamais d'*physical exercise*!

h. Mon père *does* de la natation et ma *mother does* des randonnées

i. Mon cousin et moi *do weights* deux fois par semaine

9. Listen and choose the correct verb form

a. Je ne **faites/fais/faisons** pas d'athlétisme

b. Nous ne **font/faites/faisons** jamais nos devoirs

c. Il ne **font/fait/faites** presque jamais de voile

d. Quel sport **faites/fais/fait** -vous?

e. Est-ce qu'ils **faisons/fait/font** de l'équitation?

f. **Je fais/Tu fais/On fait** des randonnées

g. **Elle fait/Je fais/On fait** toujours mon lit

10. Complete the verbs

a. Je ne fa__ __ jamais de randonnée

b. Nous fais__ __ __ de la boxe

c. Mes parents ne f__ __ __ pas de sport

d. Quel sport f__ __ __ -tu?

e. Ma mère et moi fais__ __ __ les tâches ménagères tous les jours

f. On ne fa__ __ rien

11. Complete the table with the correct forms of *FAIRE*

Je	fais
Tu	
Elle	
Il	
Nous	
Vous	
Ils	
Elles	
Mon père	
On	

12. Complete with the correct forms of *FAIRE*

a. Mes parents ne _____ jamais de sport

b. Ma mère _____ du yoga tous les jours

c. Mon frère cadet ne _____ jamais rien

d. Mes frères _____ souvent de la musculation

e. Mes grands-parents _____ toujours le lit

f. Ma sœur _____ la cuisine aujourd'hui

g. Je ne _____ jamais d'escalade parce que j'ai peur

h. Nous _____ beaucoup de sport

i. Quel sport _____-vous?

j. Mon père et moi _____ de la natation

k. On ne _____ jamais rien

THE LANGUAGE GYM

13. Translate into French

a. I do rock climbing

b. We do sailing

c. You do weights

d. She does athletics

e. What sport do you do?

f. They make the bed

g. They pay attention

h. He does nothing

i. We never do sport

j. She doesn't do the house chores

k. Every day

l. Rarely

m. Often

n. This morning

o. I like it a lot

14. Guided translation

a. *We do boxing every day*   O_ f_ _ _ d_ l_ b_ _ _ _ t_ _ _ _ l_ _ j_ _ _ _ _

b. *They never do sport*   I_ _ n_ f_ _ _ j_ _ _ _ _ _ d_ s_ _ _ _ _

c. *What sport do you guys do?*   Q_ _ _ s_ _ _ _ _ f_ _ _ _ _ _ -v_ _ _ _?

d. *I don't do anything*   J_ n_ f_ _ _ _ r_ _ _ _

e. *My girlfriend and I...*   M_ c_ _ _ _ _ _ e_ m_ _ _...

f. *(we) never do cycling*   n_ _ _ n_ f_ _ _ _ _ _ _ j_ _ _ _ _ _ d_ v_ _ _ _

g. *My father does sailing*   M_ _ p_ _ _ _ f_ _ _ _ d_ l_ v_ _ _ _ _

h. *My brother does climbing*   M_ _ f_ _ _ _ _ f_ _ _ _ d_ l'e_ _ _ _ _ _ _ _

15. Find the French translation and write it next to the English prompts

a	v	o	u	s	n	e	f	a	i	t	e	s	p	a	s	d	e	v	o	i	l	e	b	c	d	t
j	e	n	e	f	a	i	s	r	i	e	n	q	w	e	i	l	n	e	f	a	i	t	r	i	e	n
o	n	n	e	f	a	i	t	p	a	s	d	é	q	u	i	t	a	t	i	o	n	r	t	y	u	i
o	p	n	o	u	s	n	e	f	a	i	s	o	n	s	r	i	e	n	a	s	d	f	g	h	j	k
l	z	x	c	v	i	l	f	a	i	t	d	e	l	a	n	a	t	a	t	i	o	n	b	n	m	q
w	e	j	e	n	e	f	a	i	s	j	a	m	a	i	s	l	e	l	i	t	r	t	y	u	i	o
p	a	s	d	f	e	l	l	e	s	n	e	f	o	n	t	p	a	s	d	e	s	p	o	r	t	g
h	j	k	l	m	n	b	v	c	o	n	n	e	f	a	i	t	p	a	s	d	e	s	p	o	r	t
x	z	q	u	e	f	a	i	s	t	u	l	p	o	j	u	y	g	r	f	d	s	e	t	g	c	d
i	l	s	n	e	f	o	n	t	j	a	m	a	i	s	d	e	s	c	a	l	a	d	e	e	d	c
v	h	u	i	n	d	a	i	l	s	f	o	n	t	d	e	l	a	p	l	o	n	g	é	e	e	r

a. I never make the bed

b. You guys don't go sailing

c. They never go rock climbing

d. We don't go horse riding

e. He does nothing

f. We don't do sport

g. I do nothing

h. What do you do?

i. They go scuba diving

j. We do nothing

k. They don't do sport

l. He goes swimming

THE LANGUAGE GYM

16. Staircase translation: translate each sentence from memory

a.	I do	sport						
b.	We do	rarely	horse riding					
c.	They do	often	swimming	with us				
d.	We do	sailing	once a week	with our parents.	I like it a lot			
e.	She does	jogging	alone	every day	because	it is relaxing		
f.	They do	sailing	alone	at the weekend.	We never	do sailing.	It's boring	

a. _____

b. _____

c. _____

d. _____

e. _____

f. _____

17. Complete with the correct form of *FAIRE* and possessive adjective

a. Je _____ de la musculation avec ____ meilleur ami

b. Elle _____ de la voile avec _____ parents

c. Nous _____ du karaté avec _____ oncle André

d. Elles _____ de l'escalade avec _____ cousins

e. Vous _____ de la boxe avec _____ père?

f. Nous _____ toujours les tâches ménagères avec _____ mère

g. Il _____ de la plongée avec _____ père

h. Tu ne _____ jamais d'équitation avec _____ amies

i. Elles _____ la grasse matinée avec _____ copines

18. Complete with the correct form of *FAIRE* and *AVOIR*

a. Quand j'_____ du temps libre, je _____ du jogging au parc

b. Quand il _____ du temps libre, il _____ de la musculation

c. Quand ils _____ du temps libre, ils _____ de l'équitation avec nous

d. Quand elle _____ du temps libre, elle _____ les tâches ménagères

e. Quand nous _____ du temps libre, nous _____ de la boxe avec notre oncle

f. Que _____ -tu quand tu _____ du temps libre?

THE LANGUAGE GYM

4.4 QUAND + WEATHER EXPRESSIONS + PRESENT OF FAIRE
(SAYING WHAT ONE DOES IN DIFFERENT TYPES OF WEATHER)

Quand *When*	**il fait** *it is*		**beau**	*nice weather*
			chaud	*hot*
			froid	*cold*
			mauvais	*bad weather*

Quand il pleut	*When it rains*
Quand il neige	*When it snows*
Quand il y a du soleil	*When it is sunny*
Quand il y a du vent	*When it is windy*

Je fais *I do*		**de l'**	**athlétisme**	*athletics*
			équitation	*horse riding*
			escalade	*rock climbing*
Tu fais *You do*		**de la**	**musculation**	*weights*
			natation	*swimming*
Il / Elle fait *He / She does*	**souvent** *often*		**planche à voile**	*windsurf*
			plongée	*scuba diving*
			voile	*sailing*
On fait *We do*	**toujours** *always*	**du**	**ski**	*ski*
			sport	*sport*
Nous faisons *We do*			**vélo**	*cycling*
			yoga	*yoga*
Vous faites *You guys/girls do*		**des**	**arts martiaux**	*martial arts*
			randonnées	*hiking*
Ils / Elles font *They do*	**la cuisine**	*(do) the cooking*		
	les courses	*the shopping*		
	les devoirs	*homework*		
	les tâches ménagères	*the chores*		

Je ne fais pas de boxe / d'équitation	*I don't do boxing / horse riding*
Je ne fais pas le lit / les devoirs	*I don't make the bed / do homework*

Nous ne faisons jamais rien	*We never do anything*

LANGUAGE AWARENESS

FAIRE – THE WEATHER MAKER!

Salut!

There is one more important use of ***faire,*** apart from "to do", "to make" and the others seen in the previous units, it is also used for some common weather descriptions.

• **Il fait chaud**	*It **is** hot*	• **Il fait froid**	*It **is** cold*
Literally	It **makes** hot	Literally	It **makes** cold

Il y a du soleil et il fait beau

1. Gapped translation: complete the translation

a. Quand il y a du vent, je fais de la voile — *When it is _____, I go sailing*

b. Quand il fait très froid, je ne fais rien — *When it is very cold, I do _____*

c. Quand il fait beau, je fais du jogging — *When it is _____ weather, I go jogging*

d. Quand il neige, je fais du ski — *When it _____, I go skiing*

e. Quand il fait très chaud, je fais de la natation — *When it is very _____, I go swimming*

f. Quand il pleut, je reste chez moi et… — *When it _____, I stay at home and…*

g. …je fais les tâches ménagères — *…I do the _____*

h. Quand il fait mauvais, je fais les courses — *When it is _____ weather, I do the _____*

i. Quand il fait chaud, je fais de la planche à voile — *When it is _____, I go _____*

2. Complete with the correct present form of *FAIRE*

a. Quand il y a du vent, on _____ de la planche à voile

b. Quand il fait beau, ils ne _____ rien

c. Quand il pleut, je _____ les tâches ménagères

d. Quand il fait très chaud, elles _____ de la plongée

e. Qu'est-ce que tu _____ quand il fait très chaud?

f. Ma mère ne _____ jamais de sport quand il fait trop chaud.

g. Nous ne _____ pas d'escalade quand il fait mauvais

h. Mes oncles _____de la voile quand il ne fait pas froid

i. Mon frère _____ du yoga quand il fait mauvais

3. Listen and complete

a. Quand il fait _ _ _ _ _

b. Quand il y a du _ _ _ _ _

c. Quand il fait _ _ _ _ _ _ _ _

d. Quand il fait _ _ _ _ _ _

e. Quand il _ _ _ _ _ _

f. Quand il y a du _ _ _ _ _ _ _

g. Quand il fait _ _ _ _ _ _

h. Quand il _ _ _ _ _ _ _

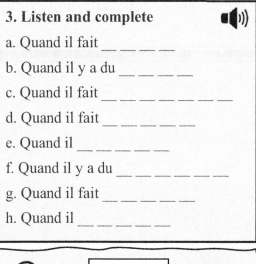

Quand il neige, je fais du ski

4. Sentence Puzzle

a. du vent, je fais il y a de la Quand planche à voile — *When it is windy, I go windsurfing*

b. de la natation il fait Quand elle fait chaud, — *When it is hot, she goes swimming*

c. Quand du soleil, il y a de la plongée on fait — *When it is sunny, we go diving*

d. il neige, Quand du ski ils font — *When it snows, they go skiing*

e. Quand je il fait ne fais froid,rien — *When it is cold, I don't do anything*

f. il Quand fait elle de l'escalade beau,fait — *When it is nice weather, she goes climbing*

g. mauvais, les devoirs Quand il fait ils font — *When it is bad weather, they do the homework*

h. tu fais mauvais quand Qu'est-ce que il fait? — *What do you do when the weather is bad?*

i. il fait vous faites quand chaud Qu'est-ce que? — *What do you guys do when it is hot?*

 THE LANGUAGE GYM

5. Translanagrams: unscramble the phrases and translate them into English

a. Il y a ud tvne   e. Il y a ud llosie

b. Il tiaf hdcua   f. Il ifta rodfi

c. Il gneie   g. Il ueptl

d. Il tiaf uabe   h. Il tiaf vmsiaua

6. Listen and translate into English. 🔊

a.

b.

c.

d.

e.

f.

g.

h.

i.

7. Find the French translation and write it next to the English prompts

a	d	t	y	h	i	d	r	m	n	b	v	c	x	z
a	s	d	f	m	g	h	a	j	k	c	h	a	u	d
l	q	w	e	a	r	t	n	y	u	i	o	p	q	a
z	w	s	x	u	e	d	d	c	r	f	v	t	s	g
v	b	y	h	v	n	u	o	j	m	i	k	o	o	l
o	p	l	m	a	n	k	n	o	i	b	j	b	l	v
i	g	y	u	i	h	f	n	e	d	e	c	v	e	g
l	q	w	e	s	f	g	é	h	j	a	t	y	i	v
e	d	f	y	h	v	d	e	w	s	u	x	f	l	k
a	u	r	e	v	o	i	s	r	s	a	l	u	t	d
f	f	r	o	i	d	y	i	o	m	n	r	i	e	n
g	t	y	v	e	n	t	b	o	n	j	o	u	r	e
v	f	y	u	i	k	j	g	d	e	w	s	x	c	f
v	b	n	e	s	c	a	l	a	d	e	g	f	d	s

a. Bad weather   f. Rock climbing

b. Good weather   g. Hiking

c. Hot   h. Nothing

d. Wind   i. Cold

e. Sailing   j. Sun

8. Complete

a. Il fait mau__ __ __ __   *It's bad weather*

b. Il fait __ __ __ __   *It's nice weather*

c. Il y a du __ __ __ __ __ __   *It's sunny*

d. Il fait __ __ __ __ __   *It's hot*

e. Il y a du __ __ __ __   *It's windy*

f. Il fait __ __ __ __ __   *It's cold*

g. Ils font de la __ __ __ __ __   *They go sailing*

h. Je fais les de__ __ __ __ __   *I do homework*

i. On fait du __ __ __   *We go skiing*

9. Translate into French

a. When it is hot, I go swimming

b. When it snows, I go skiing

c. When it is cold, I do my homework

d. When it is bad weather, I do the house chores

e. When it is nice weather, I go jogging

f. When it is hot, I do nothing

g. When it is cold, I do weights in the gym

h. When it is windy, I go windsurfing

i. When it rains, I go shopping

THE LANGUAGE GYM

Pendant les prochaines vacances *During the next holidays* **Pendant les vacances d'été** *During the summer holiday* **Pendant les vacances d'hiver** *During the winter holiday*	**je vais** *I am going* **tu vas** *you are going* **il/elle va** *he/she is going* **on va** *we are going* **nous allons** *we are going* **vous allez** *you guys/girls are going* **ils/elles vont** *they are going*	**souvent** *often* **toujours** *always*	**faire** *to do/make*	**de l'**	**athlétisme** **equitation** **escalade** **exercice**	*athletics* *horse riding* *rock climbing* *physical exercise*
				de la	**boxe** **musculation** **natation** **planche à voile** **plongée** **voile**	*boxing* *weights* *swimming* *windsurf* *diving/snorkelling* *sailing*
				du	**jogging** **ski** **sport** **vélo** **yoga**	*jogging* *ski* *sport* *cycling* *yoga*
				des	**arts martiaux** **randonnées**	*martial arts* *hiking*
					la cuisine **les courses** **les devoirs** **les tâches ménagères**	*(do) the cooking* *the shopping* *homework* *the chores*

je ne vais pas faire de boxe	*I am not going to do boxing*
je ne vais pas faire le lit	*I am not going to make the bed*
je ne vais rien faire	*I am not going to do anything*

LANGUAGE AWARENESS

NOUS or ON?

You use **nous (we)** when you want to be more formal. It is mostly used in written form.

Nous allons faire de la plongée demain.   *We are going to go diving tomorrow.*

You use **on (we)** mainly in speech or casual writing – it is the informal form of **we.**

On va faire les tâches ménagères.   *We are going to do the house chores.*

You can replace "**nous**" by "**on**" in everyday language but it must be the subject of a conjugated verb.

Nous allons faire le lit.   *We are going to make the bed.*

On va faire le lit.   *We are going to make the bed.*

 **THE LANGUAGE GYM**

1. Match

Il va faire de la boxe	I am going to make the bed
Je vais faire la cuisine	We are going to do yoga
On va faire du ski	They are going to go cycling
Je vais faire le lit	I am going to do the cooking
Nous allons faire du yoga	She is going to go sailing
Je ne vais rien faire	We are going to ski
Elle va faire de la voile	You are going to shop
Ils vont faire du vélo	He is going to do boxing
Vous allez faire les courses	I am not going to do anything

2. Write the correct pronoun

a. _____ va faire du sport

b. _____ allons faire de la voile

c. _____ vont faire le lit

d. _____ vais faire de l'escalade

e. _____ va faire de la musculation

f. _____ ne vais pas faire de ski

g. _____ vas faire la cuisine

h. _____ allez faire de la natation

i. _____ vont faire les courses

3. Listen: write the pronoun and the verb

a. _____ _____ faire de la musculation

b. _____ _____ faire le lit

c. _____ _____ faire les tâches ménagères

d. _____ _____ faire de l'équitation

e. _____ _____ faire des arts martiaux

f. _____ _____ faire de la planche à voile

g. _____ _____ faire la cuisine

h. _____ _____ faire du sport

i. _____ _____ faire de l'escalade

4. Choose the correct verb

a. Je **vas/vais/va** faire du yoga

b. Ils **vont/allons/va** faire de la natation

c. Mon frère **vas/va/vais** faire les courses

d. Ma mère et moi **va/vais/allons** faire de la boxe

e. Elle ne **va/vont/vas** pas faire de plongée

f. Vous **allons/allez/vont** faire les devoirs

g. Tu **vas/vais/allez** faire du karaté

h. Nous **allez/allons/vont** faire le lit

5. Faulty translation: fix the English translation

a. Pendant les prochaines vacances, je vais faire de l'escalade et aussi des randonnées

During the next holiday, I am going to go horse riding and also jogging

b. Pendant les vacances d'été, mon frère va souvent faire de la plongée

During the summer holiday, my brother is always going to go windsurfing

c. Il va aussi faire de la planche à voile à la mer

She is also going to go sailing at the sea

d. Ma copine et moi allons faire de la musculation au gymnase

My friend and I are going to do athletics at the gym

e. Je ne vais rien faire pendant les vacances

I am going to do loads during the holiday

THE LANGUAGE GYM

6. Break the flow

a. Pendantlesvacancesilvafaireduski

b. Qu'estcequetuvasfaire?

c. Pendantlesvacancesd'hiver,…

d. …jevaisfaireduskitouslesjours

e. Pendantlesvacancesd'été…

f. …monamietmoiallonsfaireduyoga

g. Monfrèrevafairedesartsmartiaux

h. Monpèrevatoujoursfairelescourses

7. Gapped translation: complete the translation

a. Pendant les _____ vacances, je vais faire de la _____

During the next holidays, I am going to go sailing

b. Pendant les _____ d'été, on va faire des _____

During the summer holiday, we are going to go hiking

c. Pendant les vacances _____, mes amies ____ faire du ski

During the winter holiday, my friends are going to ski

d. Je ___ vais _____ faire pendant les vacances

I am not going to do anything during the holiday

8. Listen, complete and translate

a. Pendant les vacances, mon frère…

b. Cet été, mes parents…

c. Pendant les vacances d'hiver, nous…

d. Pendant les vacances d'été, mes amis…

e. Tous les jours, tu…

f. Le week-end, ma grand-mère…

g. Mon grand-père va rarement…

h. Tes sœurs et toi…

9. Spot and correct the mistakes

a. Pendant les vacances d'ete, je vais faire de l'équitation

b. Elle vas souvent faire des arts martiaux en vacances

c. Est-ce que tu va faire des randonnée?

d. Pendant les vacances d'hiver, je ne pas vais faire d'athlétisme.

e. Pendant les vacances, mon père va toojours faire du vélo

f. Pendant les prochaine vacance, mon ami va fait de la musculation et aussi de la natation

10. Tangled translation: translate into French

a. Pendant les *holidays,* je vais faire du *cycling*

b. Pendant les vacances d'*summer,* ma mère *is going* faire des arts martiaux *every day*

c. Pendant les vacances d'*winter,* je ne vais pas *do sport*

d. Mes amis vont *often* faire des *hiking* à la montagne

e. Le week-end, tu *are not going* faire les tâches ménagères – tu vas te reposer!

f. Mon frère est sportif – il *is going* faire de l'*athletics* tous les jours *on holiday*

11. Translate into French

a. I am not going to do scuba diving on holiday

b. My brother is going to do the shopping

c. My father is not going to make the bed

d. Are you going to do the homework?

e. My brother and my father are not going to do the house chores

f. My grandparents are not going to go rock climbing

g. During the next holiday, I am not going to do anything

h. My sister and I are not going to do anything

THE LANGUAGE GYM

ORAL PING PONG

FAIRE

ENGLISH 1	FRENCH 1	ENGLISH 2	FRENCH 2
I often do physical exercise because I am sporty and I love it.	Je fais souvent de l'exercice parce que je suis sportif et j'adore ça.	I rarely make my bed at weekends because I am tired.	
I always do the house chores at the weekends, but I don't like it at all.	Je fais toujours les tâches ménagères le week-end, mais je n'aime pas du tout ça.	I go scuba diving from time to time when it is hot.	
My sister goes swimming from time to time.	Ma sœur fait de la natation de temps en temps.	My parents do nothing on Fridays.	
My friends and I go hiking when it is nice weather.	Mes amis et moi faisons des randonnées quand il fait beau.	My friends and I go cycling in the park when it doesn't rain.	
I go sailing every day when it is sunny.	Je fais de la voile tous les jours quand il fait beau.	Do you go sailing when it is windy?	
We never do anything at weekends.	On ne fait / Nous ne faisons jamais rien le week-end.	I never do anything when it is very hot.	
I am going to do sport when it is nice weather.	Je vais faire du sport quand il fait beau.	I am going to do the cooking every day on holiday.	
I am not going to do anything.	Je ne vais rien faire.	My brother is not going to do martial arts.	

INSTRUCTIONS - You are **PARTNER A.** Work in pairs. Each of you has two sets of sentences - one set has already been translated for you. You will ask your partner to translate these. The other set of sentences have not been translated. Your partner will ask you to translate these.

HOW TO PLAY - Partner A starts by reading out his/her/their first sentence <u>in English</u>. Partner B must translate. Partner A must check the answer and award the following points: **3 points** = perfect, **2 points** = 1 mistake, **1 point** = mistakes but the verb is accurate. If they cannot translate correctly, Partner A will read out the sentence so that Partner B can learn what the correct translation is.
Then Partner B reads out his/her/their first sentence, and so on.

OBJECTIVE - Try to win more points than your partner by translating correctly as many sentences as possible.

 **THE LANGUAGE GYM**

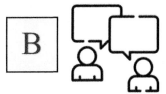

ORAL PING PONG

FAIRE

ENGLISH 1	FRENCH 1	ENGLISH 2	FRENCH 2
I often do physical exercise because I am sporty and I love it.		I rarely make my bed at weekends because I am tired.	Je fais rarement mon lit le week-end parce que je suis fatigué.
I always do the house chores at the weekends, but I don't like it at all.		I go scuba diving from time to time when it is hot.	Je fais de la plongée de temps en temps quand il fait chaud.
My sister goes swimming from time to time.		My parents do nothing on Fridays.	Mes parents ne font rien le vendredi.
My friends and I go hiking when it is nice weather.		My friends and I go cycling in the park when it doesn't rain.	Mes amis et moi faisons du vélo au parc quand il ne pleut pas.
I go sailing every day when it is sunny.		Do you go sailing when it is windy?	Tu fais de la voile quand il y a du vent?
We never do anything at weekends.		I never do anything when it is very hot.	Je ne fais jamais rien quand il fait très chaud.↕
I am going to do sport when it is nice weather.		I am going to do the cooking every day on holiday.	Je vais faire la cuisine tous les jours en vacances.
I am not going to do anything.		My brother is not going to do martial arts.	Mon frère ne va pas faire d'arts martiaux.

INSTRUCTIONS - You are **PARTNER B.** Work in pairs. Each of you has two sets of sentences - one set has already been translated for you. You will ask your partner to translate these. The other set of sentences have not been translated. Your partner will ask you to translate these.

HOW TO PLAY - Partner A starts by reading out his/her/their first sentence <u>in English</u>. Partner B must translate. Partner A must check the answer and award the following points: **3 points** = perfect, **2 points** = 1 mistake, **1 point** = mistakes but the verb is accurate. If they cannot translate correctly, Partner A will read out the sentence so that Partner B can learn what the correct translation is.

Then Partner B reads out his/her/their first sentence, and so on.

OBJECTIVE - Try to win more points than your partner by translating correctly as many sentences as possible.

 **THE LANGUAGE GYM**

135

FAIRE

No Snakes No Ladders

#	Sentence
DÉPART	
1	I go swimming when it is sunny
2	I do house chores at the weekend
3	I do the cooking on Saturdays
4	We are going to the beach
5	We go scuba diving when it rains
6	My friends go sailing in summer
7	I always do my homework
8	My friend always pays attention in Science
9	My sister does yoga because she likes it
10	My father does boxing on Mondays
11	My friend often does martial arts
12	My friend never does the cooking
13	Do you do boxing on Tuesdays?
14	I go hiking on Sundays with my sister
15	My friends and I do weights
16	My parents go scuba diving
17	He often does sport.
18	Do you often go sailing?
19	When I go out, I always do the shopping
20	They do not do anything on Mondays
21	I go swimming from time to time
22	Do you guys like going swimming?
23	I do the shopping from time to time
24	My brother does the cooking on Tuesdays
25	My mother goes jogging at weekends
26	When it rains, I do weights
27	I do not go cycling on Sundays in the evening
28	I never do anything on Fridays in the evening
29	I do not pay attention in French
30	My parents do the shopping
ARRIVÉE	

No Snakes No Ladders 2

	1	2	3	4	5	6	7
DÉPART	Je fais de la natation quand il y a du soleil	Je fais les tâches ménagères le week-end	Je fais la cuisine le samedi	Nous allons à la plage	On fait de la plongée quand il pleut	Mes amis font de la voile en été	Je fais toujours mes devoirs
15 — Mes amis et moi faisons de la musculation	14 — Je fais des randonnées le dimanche avec ma sœur	13 — Tu fais de la boxe le mardi?	12 — Mon ami ne fait jamais la cuisine	11 — Mon amie fait souvent des arts martiaux	10 — Mon père fait de la boxe le lundi	9 — Ma sœur fait du yoga car elle aime ça	8 — Mon ami fait toujours attention en SVT
16 — Mes parents font de la plongée	17 — Il fait souvent du sport	18 — Tu fais souvent de la voile?	19 — Quand je sors, je fais toujours les courses	20 — Ils ne font rien le lundi	21 — Je fais de la natation de temps en temps	22 — Vous aimez faire de la natation?	23 — Je fais les courses de temps en temps
ARRIVÉE	30 — Mes parents font les courses	29 — Je ne fais pas attention en français	28 — Je ne fais jamais rien le vendredi soir	27 — Je ne fais pas de vélo le dimanche soir	26 — Quand il pleut, je fais de la musculation	25 — Ma mère fait du jogging le week-end	24 — Mon frère fait la cuisine le mardi

THE LANGUAGE GYM

137

PYRAMID TRANSLATION

FAIRE

Translate each part of the pyramid out loud with your partner, then write it into the spaces provided below.

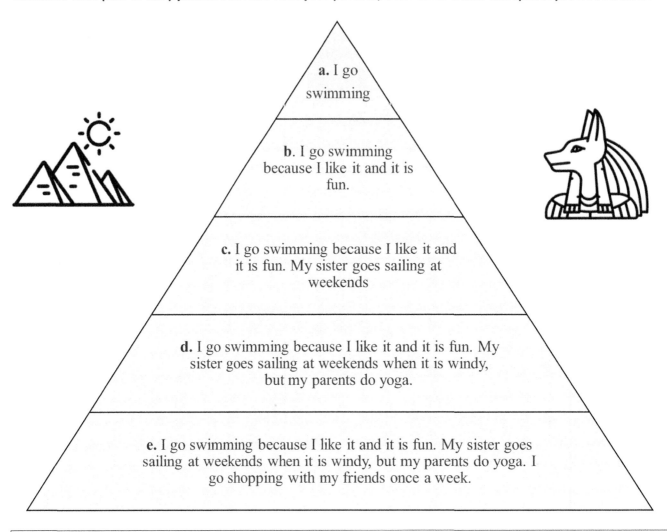

a. I go swimming

b. I go swimming because I like it and it is fun.

c. I go swimming because I like it and it is fun. My sister goes sailing at weekends

d. I go swimming because I like it and it is fun. My sister goes sailing at weekends when it is windy, but my parents do yoga.

e. I go swimming because I like it and it is fun. My sister goes sailing at weekends when it is windy, but my parents do yoga. I go shopping with my friends once a week.

Write your translation here

SOLUTION: Je fais de la natation parce que j'aime ça et c'est amusant. Ma soeur fait de la voile le week-end quand il y a du vent, mais mes parents font du yoga. Je fais les courses avec mes amis une fois par semaine.

THE LANGUAGE GYM

UNIT 5 – AIMER

J'	aime
Tu	aimes
Il / Elle / On	aime
Nous	aimons
Vous	aimez
Ils / Elles	aiment

AIMER + VERB

J'aime **aller** à la plage, **jouer** aux cartes et **faire** de la natation

AIMER + NOUN

J'aime **le chocolat**

MOI AUSSI: EMPHASIS

J'aime dormir

Moi aussi, **j'aime ça!**

5.1 AIMER + NOUN + PARCE QUE + C'EST + ADJECTIVE
(TALKING ABOUT FOOD LIKES AND DISLIKES)

J'aime *I like* **Tu aimes** *You like*	**le café** *coffee* **le lait** *milk* **le miel** *honey* **le poisson** *fish* **le poulet** *chicken* **le riz** *rice*	**parce que c'est** *because it is* **mais c'est** *but it is*	**amer** *bitter* **dégoûtant** *disgusting* **délicieux** *delicious*
	la confiture *jam* **la limonade** *lemonade* **la pizza** *pizza* **la viande** *meat*	**parce que ce n'est pas** *because it is not* **mais ce n'est pas** *but it is not*	**sain** *healthy* **savoureux** *tasty* **sucré** *sweet*
Je n'aime pas *I don't like* **Tu n'aimes pas** *You don't like*	**les bonbons** *sweets* **les burgers** *burgers* **les légumes** *vegetables* **les œufs** *eggs* **les sandwichs au fromage** *cheese sandwiches*	**parce qu'ils (ne) sont (pas)** *because they are (not)* **mais ils (ne) sont (pas)** *but they are (not)*	**amers** **dégoûtants** **délicieux** **sains** **savoureux** **sucrés**
	les frites *chips* **les glaces** *ice creams* **les tomates** *tomatoes*	**parce qu'elles (ne) sont (pas)** *because they are (not)* **mais elles (ne) sont (pas)** *but they are (not)*	**amères** **dégoûtantes** **délicieuses** **saines** **savoureuses** **sucrées**
Tu aimes les frites?	*Do you like chips?*		

1. Match

J'aime le lait	I like chicken
Je n'aime pas les frites	You don't like honey
Je n'aime pas les légumes	Do you like burgers?
J'aime le poulet	I like milk
J'aime le poisson	Do you like honey?
J'aime les glaces	I don't like meat
Tu aimes les burgers?	I like ice creams
Tu aimes le miel?	I like fish
J'aime les légumes	I don't like vegetables
Je n'aime pas la viande	I don't like chips
Tu n'aimes pas le miel	I like vegetables

2. Complete the table with the missing English or French word

Sain	
	Fish
Sucré	
	Tomatoes
Savoureux	
	Ice creams
Dégoûtant	
	Burgers
Les légumes	
	Milk
La viande	

3. Translate into English

a. J'aime le lait

b. Je n'aime pas les sandwichs

c. Je n'aime pas les tomates

d. J'aime les glaces

e. Tu n'aimes pas les frites?

f. J'aime beaucoup les œufs!

g. Tu aimes la pizza?

h. J'aime les pâtes

i. J'aime les bonbons

4. Choose the correct definite article then translate the sentence into English

a. J'aime **le / la** riz

b. J'aime **la / les** glaces

c. Je n'aime pas **le / la** lait

d. Tu aimes **les / le** burgers?

e. J'aime **les / le** sandwichs au fromage

f. Je n'aime pas **la / le** poisson

g. Je n'aime pas beaucoup **le / la** poulet

h. Tu aimes **la / les** tomates?

5. Break the flow

a. J'aimelecafémaisc'estunpeuamer

b. Jen'aimepaslaconfitureparcequec'estsucré

c. Tuaimesleslégumes?

d. Jen'aimepaslesglacesparcequ'ellessontdégoûtantes

e. Tun'aimespaslapizzaparcequecen'estpassain

f. J'aimelepoissonparcequec'estsain

g. J'aimelaviandeparcequec'estdélicieux

h. Tuaimeslesbonbons?

i. J'aimelesbonbonsmaisilssonttropsucrés

j. Tun'aimespaslestomates?

6. Listen and translate into English

a.

b.

c.

d.

e.

f.

g.

h.

i.

j.

7. Anagrams

a. amJ'ie el lita

b. uT asmie lse rbrgues?

c. eJ aen'mi spa el sopisno

d. uT iesn'am asp el izr?

e. amiJ'e al zpzai

f. aeiJ'm al evinad

g. aemiJ' el éfac

h. uT asmie lse scdaniwhs ua foreamg

i. uT asime lse usœf?

8. Faulty Translation: fix the English translation

a. J'aime les burgers, mais ils ne sont pas très sains

 I like burgers because they are very tasty

b. J'aime le riz parce que ce n'est pas amer

 You like fish because it is not sweet

c. J'aime les glaces, mais elles sont trop sucrées

 I like ice creams because they are quite sweet

d. J'aime les sandwichs au fromage parce qu'ils sont assez savoureux

 We love cheese sandwiches, but they are not very tasty

e. Tu aimes les œufs, mais à mon avis ils sont assez dégoûtants

 You like cheese sandwiches, but in my opinion they are very disgusting

f. Qu'est-ce que tu aimes le plus: les légumes ou les bonbons?

 What do you like more: vegetables or meat?

9. Listen and spot the intruder

a. J'aime la confiture parce que selon moi c'est vraiment délicieux.

b. Je n'aime pas la pizza parce que ce n'est pas sain et c'est trop dégoûtant.

c. Tu aimes les légumes et aussi le poulet?

d. Tu n'aimes pas les tomates parce qu'elles ne sont vraiment pas délicieuses.

e. J'aime un peu le miel mais tu aimes la confiture parce que c'est sucré.

f. Tu aimes le poulet mais j'aime beaucoup le poisson parce que c'est sain et vraiment savoureux.

THE LANGUAGE GYM

10. One of three

		1	2	3
a.	Sain	*tasty*	*healthy*	*sweet*
b.	Les œufs	*meat*	*eggs*	*sandwiches*
c.	Les glaces	*honey*	*ice creams*	*vegetables*
d.	Sucré	*sweet*	*salty*	*tasty*
e.	Le café	*milk*	*fish*	*coffee*
f.	Les frites	*ice creams*	*chips*	*milk*
g.	Dégoûtant	*salty*	*tasty*	*disgusting*
h.	Le miel	*honey*	*sandwich*	*milk*
i.	Le lait	*meat*	*milk*	*fish*
j.	Les bonbons	*tomatoes*	*sweets*	*sweet*
k.	Savoureux	*salty*	*disgusting*	*tasty*
l.	Le poisson	*meat*	*vegetables*	*fish*

11. Complete with the missing word

a. Je n'aime pas la p_ _ _ _ _

b. J'aime le m_ _ _ _

c. J'aime les t_ _ _ _ _ _ _

d. Tu aimes la v_ _ _ _ _ _

e. Je n'aime pas les f_ _ _ _ _ _

f. J'aime les l_ _ _ _ _ _

g. Tu aimes les g_ _ _ _ _ _?

h. Tu a_ _ _ _ le poisson?

i. J'_ _ _ _ _ le poulet

j. Je n'aime pas le c_ _ _

k. Tu n'aimes pas le l_ _ _

12. Sentence Puzzle

a. le poisson c'est J'aime que sain parce   *I like fish because it is healthy*

b. aime J' œufs les …   *I like eggs…*

c. … ne sont mais très pas ils sains   *…but they are not very healthy*

d. frites aimes Tu les …   *You like chips…*

e. … assez parce sont savoureuses qu'elles   *…because they are quite tasty*

f. riz aimes Tu le?   *Do you like rice?*

g. légumes aimes Tu les?   *Do you like vegetables?*

h. savoureux parce que la viande c'est J'aime très   *I like meat because it is very tasty*

i. sucré aime c'est le miel J' très parce que   *I like honey because it is very sweet*

13. Spot the mistakes in French, correct them, and then listen to check 🔊

a. Je n'aime pas le riz parce que c'est délicieux
   I like rice because it is delicious

b. J'aime le poulet parce que c'est sain
   My brother likes fish because it is healthy

c. J'aime le sucre, mais sucré
   I like sugar, but it is sweet

d. Tu aimes les sandwichs au fromage parce qu'ils sont savoureux
   I like cheese sandwiches because they are tasty

e. J'aime les burgers parce qu'ils ne sont pas sains
   I don't like burgers because they are not healthy

f. Tu aimes lait? *Do you like milk?*

14. Tangled translation: translate into French

a. Je n'*like* pas les frites *because they are not* savoureuses

b. J'*like* le lait *because* c'est délicieux

c. *I like* les glaces *because* elles sont *sweet*

d. *I like* les burgers parce qu'ils sont *tasty*

e. Je n' *like* pas les *vegetables* parce qu'ils sont *disgusting*

f. *I do not like* les œufs parce qu'*they are not* bons

g. *You do not like* le poisson *because* c'est *bitter*

h. *I like* la viande *and* le poulet parce que c'est *tasty*

i. *I do not like tomatoes*, mais *they are healthy*

15. Translate into French

a. I like honey

b. I like rice

c. You like ice creams

d. Do you like burgers?

e. I like tomatoes

f. I like eggs

g. I don't like chips

h. I don't like coffee

i. Do you like pizza?

16. Guided Translation

a. J'a_____ l____ t_____ p_____ q____ e_____ s_____ s_____

    I like tomatoes because they are tasty

b. J'a_____ l___ b_____, m____ i___ n___ s____ p____ t_____ s_____

    I like burgers, but they are not very healthy

c. J'a_____ l___ s_____ a___ f_____ p_____ q___ i____ s____

    a_____ s_____

    I like cheese sandwiches because they are quite tasty

d. J'a_____ b_____ l___ m_____ p_____ q____ c'____ s_____

    I like honey a lot because it is sweet

e. T____ n'a_____ p___ l___ o_____ p_____ q___ i___ n____ s____ p__ s_____

    You do not like eggs because they are not healthy

f. J___ n'a_____ p___ l___ p_____ p_____ q___ c___ n'____ p___ s_____

    I don't like chicken because it is not tasty

17. Translate into French.

a. I like tomatoes because they are healthy, but you don't like tomatoes because they are not very tasty.

b. I like burgers, but they are not healthy. You like burgers because they are tasty.

c. Do you like coffee?

d. Do you like chicken and chips?

e. You like cheese sandwiches because they are tasty, but I don't like sandwiches.

f. You like meat because it is not disgusting, but I don't like meat because it is not tasty.

g. I like chips because they are tasty, but they are not healthy.

h. I don't like fish because it is disgusting, but it is very healthy.

 **THE LANGUAGE GYM**

5.2 AIMER + NOUNS + ADJECTIVE *(SAYING HOW MUCH ONE LIKES PEOPLE AND WHY)*

J'aime *I like* **Tu aimes** *You like* **Il / Elle aime** *He / She likes* **On aime** *We like*	**mon meilleur ami** *my best friend (m)* **mon oncle** *my uncle* **mon petit ami** *my boyfriend* **mon prof de français** *my French teacher* **mon prof d'anglais** *my English teacher*	**parce qu'il est** *because he is* **parce qu'il n'est pas** *because he is not*	**énervant** *annoying* **intelligent** *clever* **joyeux** *joyful* **paresseux** *lazy* **patient** *patient* **réservé** *reserved* **sympa** *nice* **travailleur** *hard-working*
Nous aimons *We like* **Vous aimez** *You guys/girls like* **Ils / Elles aiment** *They like*	**ma meilleure amie** *my best friend (f)* **ma petite amie** *my girlfriend* **ma prof d'anglais** *my English teacher* **ma prof de dessin** *my art teacher* **ma tante** *my aunt*	**parce qu'elle est** *because she is* **parce qu'elle n'est pas** *because she is not*	**énervante** **intelligente** **joyeuse** **paresseuse** **patiente** **réservée** **sympa** **travailleuse**
Je n'aime pas *I don't like* **Tu n'aimes pas** *You don't like* **Il / Elle n'aime pas** *He / She doesn't like* **On n'aime pas** *We don't like*	**mes amis** *my friends (m or m+f)* **mes cousins** *my cousins (m or m+f)* **mes grands-parents** *my grandparents* **mes parents** *my parents* **mes profs** *my teachers*	**parce qu'ils sont** *because they are* **parce qu'ils ne sont pas** *because they are not*	**énervants** **intelligents** **joyeux** **paresseux** **patients** **réservés** **sympas** **travailleurs**
Nous n'aimons pas *We don't like* **Vous n'aimez pas** *You guys/girls don't like* **Ils / Elles n'aiment pas** *They don't like*	**mes amies** *my friends (f)* **mes cousines** *my cousins (f)* **mes sœurs** *my sisters*	**parce qu'elles sont** *because they are* **parce qu'elles ne sont pas** *because they are not*	**énervantes** **intelligentes** **joyeuses** **paresseuses** **patientes** **réservées** **sympas** **travailleuses**

LANGUAGE AWARENESS: PLURAL NOUNS

In French, when we use a **masculine plural noun**, it can refer to two or more male people/animals, but it can also refer to a mixture of male and female people/animals.

• **Mes parents**	*My parents*	**Mes grands-parents**	*My grandparents*

When we talk about a group of friends, if we say *mes amis*, we are referring to a group of friends that is either **all male** or a **mixture of male & female:**

• **Mes amis**	*My friends (masc. or mixed)*	Literally: My male friends

In fact, in French, if we have a group of friends containing several girls and one boy, we use the **masculine plural noun**: *amis*. This can be considered an example of a **neutral form** being used for **linguistic economy.** If we are talking about a group that is composed **entirely** of **females,** only then we do use the **female plural noun**:

• **Mes amies**	*My friends*	Literally: My female friends

LANGUAGE AWARENESS: POSSESSIVE ADJECTIVES

	Masculine Singular	Feminine Singular	Masculine & Feminine Plural
My	Mon	Ma	Mes
Your	Ton	Ta	Tes
His/Her/Its	Son	Sa	Ses
Our	Notre	Notre	Nos
Your	Votre	Votre	Vos
Their	Leur	Leur	Leurs

Remember that *ma famille/mon ami/mon cousin*/etc. will change to *ton, son, notre, votre* or *leur* depending on the person we are talking about. It agrees with the noun that follows:

• **Nous aimons faire de l'équitation avec <u>notre</u> ami**   We like to go horse riding with ***our*** *friend*

1. Match

J'aime mon ami	*Do you guys/girls like your French teacher?*
Tu aimes ton ami	*He likes his friend*
Nous n'aimons pas notre tante	*Do you like your aunt?*
Elle aime son frère	*I like my friend*
Tu aimes ta tante?	*I like my French teacher*
Il aime son ami	*We don't like our aunt*
J'aime ma prof de français	*You like your friend*
Vous aimez votre prof de français?	*She likes her brother*

2. Complete the sentence with the correct pronoun and possessive adjective

a. ___ aime _____ prof de maths

   I like my maths teacher (m)

b. En général, _____ aimons ____ profs

   Generally we like our teachers

c. ____ aime parfois _____ frères

   She sometimes likes her brothers

d. ___ aimes ____ prof de SVT?

   Do you like your science teacher (f)?

e. _____ aimez _____ profs?

   Do you guys/girls like your teachers?

3. Translate into English

a. Ma sœur est paresseuse

b. J'aime mes frères

c. Ma tante est assez réservée

d. Mes parents sont sympas

e. Elle aime sa tante

f. Sa mère est assez énervante

g. Nous aimons nos profs

h. Ils aiment leurs profs

4. Break the flow and translate the sentences into English

a. J'aimemonprofd'anglaisparcequ'ilestintelligent

b. Monamiaimesesgrandsparentsparcequ'ilssontamusants

c. Ilaimesonpèreparcequ'ilestsympaetilsfontdelanatationensemble

d. Jen'aimepasmonfrèreparcequ'ilestparesseuxetilnefaitjamaislelit

e. Nousaimonsnotreprofdefrançaisparcequ'elleesttravailleuse

f. Tuaimestesprofs?Ouimaisdetempsentempsilssonténervants

g. Elleaimesatanteparcequ'elleestjoyeuseetsympa

5. Sentence Puzzle

a. n'est son prof Elle de maths aime paresseux parce qu'il pas

   She likes her Maths teacher because he is not lazy

b. aimons amusantes Nous parce qu'ils sont ils font patients et des activités nos parents très

   We like our parents because they are patient and do very fun activities

c. est joyeuse Ma sœur notre tante très sympa aime parce qu'elle et

   My sister likes our aunt because she is joyful and very nice

d. intelligents Ils parce qu'ils aiment leurs profs sont

   They like their teachers because they are clever

e. ton aimes frère Tu? Non, qu'il est je ne pas l'aime parce paresseux

   Do you like your brother? No, I don't like him because he is lazy

6. Listen and translate into English

a.

b.

c.

d.

e.

f.

g.

h.

i.

7. Gapped Translation: complete the translation

a. ____ aime mon _____, mais ___ ____ paresseux parce qu'il ___ fait _____ le _____ .

   I like my brother, but he is lazy because he never makes the bed.

b. _____ amis aiment _____ prof d'_____ parce qu'___ ____ intelligent.

   Our friends like their English teacher because he is clever

c. _____ père aime ____ ami parce qu'_____ n'est _____ paresseux et ils _____ toujours de l'escalade le _____-_____.

   My father likes his friend because he is not lazy and they always do rock climbing at the weekends.

d. ____ grands-parents _____ jouer aux _____. ____ aime mes _____-_____ parce qu'ils sont _____.

   My grandparents like to play cards. I like my grandparents because they are fun.

 THE LANGUAGE GYM

8. Listen and fill in the gaps

a. Nous aimons _____ profs parce qu'ils sont
_____

b. Ma _____ aime son petit ami parce qu'il est
_____

c. Nous _____ nos _____

d. _____ aimes tes frères?

e. Mon _____ n'aime pas son prof de _____

f. Mes parents sont assez _____ et bavards

g. _____ n'aime pas ton frère parce qu'il est _____
arrogant

h. Mon frère n'_____ pas sa prof d'anglais parce
qu'elle est très _____ et un peu _____

9. Anagrams

a. rpaesusex

b. xjyeou

c. asmyp

d. uVso azmie otvre peèr?

e. amiJ'e omn etpit aim

f. uT mieas otn ropf and'gisla?

g. ll iaem nso gndra-èper

h. oNus maiosn entor csouin

i. Isl anmiet lreu iam

j. uVso azmie otvre meèr?

k. lEle n'aeim psa sme aemis

10. Spot the mistakes in the French sentences.

a. J'aime mon ami meilleur parce qu'elle est patient et vraiment sympa.

I like my best friend because he is patient and really nice.

b. Je n'aime pas tes amis parce qu'il est très énervant et ils ne sont pas travailleurs.

I don't like your friends because they are very annoying and they are not hard-working.

c. Nous aimons votre prof de français parce qu'elle est un peu joyeux et patiente.

We like our French teacher because she is very joyful and patient.

d. Vous aimez notre mère parce qu'il fait les courses au centre commercial avec vous.

You like your mother because she does the shopping in the shopping centre with you.

e. Elles n'aime pas leur cousin parce qu'elle ne fait pas de yoga tous les jours.

They don't like their cousin (f) because she does not do yoga every day.

f. J'aime beaucoup mes grands-parents parce qu'ils sont réservés et ils font toujours des arts martiaux.

I like my grandparents a lot because they are not reserved and they often do martial arts.

g. Je n'aime pas ma sœur parce qu'il est paresseux et il ne fait rien jamais.

I don't like my brother because he is lazy and he never does anything.

11. Staircase translation – Translate each sentence from memory

a.	I like	my boyfriend				
b.	Our parents	are	patient			
c.	We like	our teachers	because they are	clever		
d.	They like	their teachers	because they are	nice and	fun	
e.	She doesn't like	her sister	because she is	lazy	and she doesn't do	chores

a. _____

b. _____

c. _____

d. _____

e. _____

12. Translate into French

a. Do you guys like your teachers? Generally, we like our teachers, but sometimes they are annoying.

b. I like my maths teacher because he is not lazy and he is quite nice.

c. My brother doesn't like his English teacher because she is too reserved and boring.

d. We like our friends because they are not lazy. We like going rock climbing at weekends.

e. I like my father because we like to play cards together (*ensemble*).

f. Do you guys like your parents? We like our parents, but they are annoying from time to time.

g. My sister likes her boyfriend, but he is too reserved. They like to go to the cinema.

h. My friend likes his teachers because they are nice and patient.

i. My brothers like to go to the cinema at weekends with my grandfather.

j. We don't like our science teacher because she is annoying.

k. Do you like your Maths teacher? Yes, because he is joyful and hard-working.

THE LANGUAGE GYM

5.3 PRESENT OF AIMER + INFINITIVES+ NOUN
OBJECT PRONOUN + Y/EN + PRESENT + TIME ADVERBIALS
(SAYING WHAT ONE LIKES/DISLIKES DOING AND HOW OFTEN THEY DO IT)

J'aime / Je n'aime pas *I like / I don't like* **Tu (n') aimes (pas)** *You (don't) like* **Il/Elle/Mon frère (n') aime (pas)** *He/She/My brother likes (doesn't like)* **Nous (n') aimons (pas)** *We (don't) like* **Vous (n') aimez (pas)** *You guys/girls (don't) like* **Ils/Elles (n') aiment (pas)** *They (don't) like* **Mes parents (n') aiment (pas)** *My parents (don't) like*	**faire** *to do* *(to go)*	**de l'équitation** **de l'escalade** **de la natation** **des randonnées** **du sport** **du vélo** **du yoga**	*horse riding* *rock climbing* *swimming* *hiking* *sport* *cycling* *yoga*
	jouer *to play*	**au basket** **au foot** **au tennis** **aux cartes** **aux jeux vidéo**	*basketball* *football* *tennis* *cards* *videogames*
	aller *to go*	**au centre commercial** **au ciné** **au stade** **à la piscine** **à la plage**	*to the shopping centre* *to the cinema* *to the stadium* *to the swimming pool* *to the beach*

J'en fais	*I do it*	**souvent**	*often*
Tu en fais	*You do it*	**de temps en temps**	*from time to time*
Il/Elle en fait	*He/She does it*	**le lundi**	*on Mondays*
Nous en faisons	*We do it*	**le mardi**	*on Tuesdays*
Vous en faites	*You guys/girls do it*	**le mercredi**	*on Wednesdays*
Ils/Elles en font	*They do it*	**le jeudi**	*on Thursdays*
		le vendredi	*on Fridays*
Je <u>n</u>'en fais <u>pas/jamais</u>	*I **don't/never** do it*	**le samedi**	*on Saturdays*
Tu <u>n</u>'en fais <u>pas/jamais</u>	*You **don't/never** do it*	**le dimanche**	*on Sundays*
Il/Elle <u>n</u>'en fait <u>pas/jamais</u>	*He/She **doesn't** do/**never** does it*	**le week-end**	*at the weekends*
Nous n'en faisons pas/jamais	*We **don't/never** do it*	**toujours**	*always*
Vous <u>n</u>'en faites <u>pas/jamais</u>	*You guys/girls **don't/never** do it*	**tous les jours**	*every day*
Ils/Elles <u>n</u>'en font <u>pas/jamais</u>	*They **don't/never** do it*	**une fois par semaine**	*once a week*

Je n'aime rien faire	*I don't like to do anything*

THE LANGUAGE GYM

LANGUAGE AWARENESS

RIEN, JAMAIS & PERSONNE

When we use **rien, jamais** or **personne** with a verb, we must use **ne** in front of such verb.

Remember that in French we negate twice!

• **Je ne fais rien**   *I don't do nothing/anything*

• **Je n'en fais jamais** *I never do it*

And sometimes even three times!

• **Je ne fais jamais rien avec personne**

I never do anything with anyone

Literally: *I never do nothing with no-one*

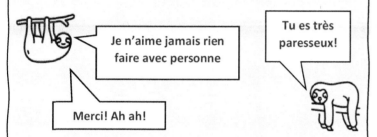

Je n'aime jamais rien faire avec personne

Tu es très paresseux!

Merci! Ah ah!

EXTRA EMPHASIS

You can add the extra pronoun ***"Moi/Toi/Lui/Elle/Nous/Vous/Eux/Elles aussi"*** if you want to make your sentence more emphatic:

• **Moi aussi,** j'aime faire du vélo
I like to do/go cycling

• **Elle aussi,** elle aime jouer au tennis
She likes to play tennis

This would be the equivalent of raising the pitch & volume of "I" / "She" in the above sentences to make it really clear who it is that likes either cycling or tennis.

Moi aussi, j'aime y aller!

Nous aimons aller à la plage

LANGUAGE AWARENESS

PRONOUNS "Y" AND "EN"

"**Y**" is a pronoun that is used to replace something such as objects, ideas or places (but not someone) when using the structure <u>à + noun</u>.

Je joue **au** basket le lundi   J'**y** joue le lundi

I play basketball on Mondays   *I play it on Mondays*

Je vais souvent **au** parc   J'**y** vais souvent

I often go to the park   *I often go there*

J'y joue	J'y vais
Tu y joues	Tu y vas
Il/Elle y joue	Il/Elle y va
Nous y jouons	Nous y allons
Vous y jouez	Vous y allez
Ils/Elles y jouent	Ils/Elles y vont

"**En**" is also a pronoun that is used to replace the structure <u>partitive article + noun</u> or <u>de + noun</u>.

Je fais **du** vélo tous les jours   J'**en** fais tous les jours

I go cycling every day   *I do it every day*

Je fais **de** la natation de temps en temps   J'**en** fais de temps en temps

I go swimming from time to time   *I do it from time to time*

THE LANGUAGE GYM

1. Match

J'aime	Do you guys like?
Mon frère aime	Our teachers like
Nous aimons	They (m) like
Ma grand-mère aime	My parents like
Tu aimes?	You guys like
Vous aimez	I like
Ils aiment	My brother likes
Mes parents aiment	Do you like?
Vous aimez?	We like
Nos profs aiment	My grandmother likes

2. Complete the table

Français	Anglais
	We do it
Il y va	
Vous y jouez	
	I play it
	I go there
Ma grand-mère en fait	
	My uncles do it
Mes grands-parents en font	
	You guys do it

3. Anagrams

a. eJ'mia — *I like*

b. uT semia? — *Do you like?*

c. lI ne tfia — *He does it*

d. osuN mnasio — *We like*

e. yJ' svia — *I go there*

f. yJ' oeuj — *I play it*

g. lI iema — *He likes*

h. slI ne ntof — *They do it*

i. sVuo zimea? — *Do you guys like?*

j. uT ne sfia — *You do it*

k. aM roeus miae — *My sister likes*

l. uT y sva — *You go there*

4. Gapped translation: complete the translation

a. _____ jouer à l'ordinateur. J'_____ joue souvent.

   I like to play on the computer. I play it often.

b. Nous n'_____ pas aller à la piscine. Nous _____ allons rarement.

   We don't like to go to the swimming pool. We go there rarely.

c. Mes parents n'_____ pas aller au ciné. Ils n'____ vont jamais.

   My parents don't like to go to the cinema. They never go there.

d. Qu'est-ce que ____ aimes faire le week-end? Je n'aime _____ faire.

   What do you like to do at the weekend? I don't like to do anything.

e. Hélène _____ faire de l'escalade. Elle _____ fait trois fois par semaine.

   Hélène likes to go rock climbing. She does it three times a week.

f. Où _____-vous aller le week-end? Nous _____ faire de la natation.

   Where do you guys like to go at the weekend? We like to go swimming.

g. Ma petite amie et moi _____ jouer au tennis. On _____ joue presque tous les jours.

   My girlfriend and I like to play tennis. We play it nearly every day.

 THE LANGUAGE GYM

5. Break the flow

a. Jen'aimepasalleràlaplageavecmesamisleweekendparcequec'estbarbant.

b. J'aimealleraucinéavecmafamilleleweekend.

c. Mesamisaimentfaireduyoga.Ilsenfontsouvent.

d. Mesparentsaimentsouventallerausupermarché.Ilsyvontlesamedi.

e. Tuaimesalleraucinéavectesamisleweekend?

f. Vousaimezfairedelanatationavecvotrefamilledetempsentemps?

g. Ilaimefairedesrandonnéesavecsonpère.Ilenfaitledimanche.

h. Nousaimonssouventalleraustade.Nousyallonslesamedi.

i. Mesgrandsparentsn'aimentrienfairelejeudi.

6. Listen, complete with Y or EN and translate

a. Vous ____ faites

b. Tu ____ joues

c. Elle ____ va

d. Ils ____ font

e. J'____ vais

f. On ____ fait

g. Vous ____ jouez

h. Nous ____ allons

i. Elles ____ jouent

7. Listen and complete the table

	Pronoun	Verb aimer	Infinitive	Verb	Time expression
Exemple	J'	aime	aller au ciné.	J'y vais	de temps en temps.
a.					
b.					
c.					
d.					
e.					
f.					
g.					

8. Sentence Puzzle

a. faire du aimons sport Nous et faisons nous en souvent — *We like to do sport and we do it often*

b. aux J'aime cartes jouer et les joue j'y tous jours — *I like to play cards and I play it every day*

c. la plage Elle aller aime à — *She likes to go to the beach*

d. va le y samedi Elle — *She goes there on Saturdays*

e. de la aiment Elles faire voile — *They like to go sailing*

f. le week-end tu aimes Qu'est-ce que faire? — *What do you like to do at the weekend?*

g. natation Où faire de la aimez-vous? — *Where do you guys like to go swimming?*

h. n'aime Je faire le rien week-end — *I don't like to do anything at the weekend*

i. basket aiment-ils au Avec qui jouer? — *Who do they like to play basketball with?*

j. aime jouer Ma maman avec moi au basket — *My mum likes to play basketball with me*

k. jouons le dimanche Nous le samedi y et — *We play it every Saturday and Sunday*

THE LANGUAGE GYM

9. Choose the correct pronoun

a. **J'/Tu/Nous** aime aller au ciné avec mes amis

b. **Ils/Vous/Nous** aimons faire de l'équitation avec notre père

c. **Tu/Vous/Ils** aiment aller au supermarché le vendredi

d. **Elles/Elle/Nous** aime faire du yoga le dimanche avec sa fille

e. **Tu/Il/Ils** aimes jouer au foot avec tes cousins?

f. **Elles/Nous/Vous** aimez jouer aux cartes avec vos frères?

g. **Tu/Ils/J'** aime jouer aux jeux vidéo avec mon grand-père

h. **Vous/Nous/Elle** aime jouer aux cartes avec sa mère

i. **Nous/Vous/Elle** aime aller au ciné de temps en temps

10. Translate into English

a. Nous aimons aller au ciné

b. Ils aiment beaucoup faire du sport

c. Elle aime jouer au basket

d. Qu'est-ce que tu aimes faire le week-end?

e. Vous aimez jouer au tennis?

f. Nous aimons beaucoup aller au parc

g. Nous y allons tous les jours

h. Ils en font rarement

11. Choose the correct word from the options given in the table below

a. J'aime aller au ciné avec mes amis. J'_____ de temps en temps.

b. _____ frère aime aller au stade et jouer au foot.

c. Mes frères et moi aimons jouer aux jeux vidéo. Nous y _____ le week-end.

d. Vous _____ faire de l'équitation avec votre famille?

e. Ils aiment aller à la plage avec leur père. Ils y _____ souvent.

f. Tu aimes aller au centre commercial avec ton ami. Tu y _____ le samedi.

g. _____ aimes aller à la piscine le mercredi?

h. Mes parents _____ faire la cuisine ensemble.

| vas | y vais | vont | aiment | mon | aimez | jouons | tu |

12. Correct the mistake in each sentence and then listen to check

a. Tu aimes aller au ciné avec mes amis. Tu y vas le week-end.

b. Nous n'aimez rien faire le week-end.

c. Mon frère aime jouer aux jeux vidéo. Ils y jouent le vendredi.

d. Tu aimez aller au ciné avec ton frère?

e. Vous aimons aller au supermarché qui est dans le centre?

f. Mon grand-père aime jouer aux cartes. Vous y jouez souvent.

g. Mes amis aimons jouer au foot. Ils y jouent le mardi.

h. Ma mère aime faire de la natation. J'en fais une fois par semaine.

13. Translate to French

a. I like

b. We like

c. I do it

d. They go there

e. She likes

f. They do it

g. Do you like it?

h. What do you like?

i. We play it

j. Do you guys like it?

THE LANGUAGE GYM

14. Guided translation

a. *I like to go to the cinema with my sister. We go there at the weekends.*

J'_____ a_____ a___ c_____ a____ m___ s_____ . N____ y a_____ l___ w____ -
____ .

b. *Do you guys like to go to the beach from time to time?*

V_____ a_____ a_____ à l___ p_____ d___ t_____ e___ t_____ ?

c. *My sister likes to play cards with my mother. They play it often.*

M___ s_____ a_____ j_____ a___ c_____ a____ m___ m_____ . E_____ y j_____
s_____ .

d. *My brothers like to play videogames because it is fun. They play it on Sundays.*

M___ f_____ a_____ j_____ a___ j_____ v_____ p_____ q___ c'___ a_____ . I___ y
j_____ l___ d_____ .

15. Listen. Spot the missing pronoun. Write it in and then translate into English 🔊

a. N'aime rien faire le vendredi soir.

b. Aimez faire du sport. Vous faites le week-end.

c. Mon père va au supermarché avec ma mère. Ils vont le vendredi.

d. Aime aller au ciné avec mes amis.

e. Aiment faire de la natation avec leurs amis. Ils font une fois par semaine.

f. Est-ce que aimez aller à la plage avec vos amis?

g. Oui, nous allons assez souvent quand il fait beau.

16. Translate the following words/phrases into French

a. Hiking

b. Beach

c. Chess

d. Never

e. To play cards

f. Nothing

g. My father

h. Weekends

i. My sister

j. We go there

k. Saturdays

l. Your friends

m. Often

n. Because

o. Fridays

p. I play it

q. Swimming

r. He does it

17. Translate the sentences into French

a. We like to go to the beach with our friends because it is fun. We go there often. Do you like it?

b. My brother likes to play chess with my father. They play it on Fridays and Saturdays.

c. I don't like to do anything at weekends because I am tired. What do you do?

d. Do you like to go to the cinema with your friends at weekends? I don't like it much. I rarely go there.

e. We don't like to do horse riding. We never do it. We like a lot to play videogames.

f. My sister doesn't like to do hiking. She never does it. She loves to do swimming and boxing.

g. My parents don't like to play videogames. They never play it. They love to play cards.

THE LANGUAGE GYM

155

5.4 PRESENT OF AIMER + NOUN + WHO WITH + Y/EN + TIME ADVERBIALS
(SAYING WHAT ACTIVITIES WE DO WITH PEOPLE)

J'aime / Je n'aime pas *I like / I don't like* **Tu (n') aimes (pas)** *You (don't) like* **Il/Elle (n') aime (pas)** *He/She likes (doesn't like)*	**faire** *to do* *(to go)*	**de l'équitation** *horse riding* **de l'escalade** *rock climbing* **de la natation** *swimming* **des randonnées** *hiking* **du sport** *sport* **du vélo** *cycling* **du yoga** *yoga*		***ma cousine** *my cousin (f)* ***ma famille** *my family* ***ma petite amie** *my girlfriend* ***mes amis** *my friends* ***mes amies** *my (girl) friends*
Nous (n') aimons (pas) *We (don't) like* **Vous (n') aimez (pas)** *You guys/girls (don't) like* **Ils/Elles (n') aiment (pas)** *They (don't) like*	**jouer** *to play*	**au basket** *basketball* **au tennis** *tennis* **aux cartes** *cards* **aux jeux vidéo** *videogames*	**avec** *with*	***mon cousin** *my cousin (m)* ***mon meilleur ami** *my best friend* ***mon petit ami** *my boyfriend*
Mes parents (n') aiment (pas) *My parents (don't) like*	**aller** *to go*	**au ciné** *to the cinema* **au stade** *to the stadium* **à la plage** *to the beach* **à la piscine** *to the pool*		***mon/ma partenaire** *my partner* **Possessive adjectives can be found in 5.2*
Je n'aime <u>rien</u> faire avec <u>personne</u>		*I don't like to do anything with anyone*		

J'en fais	*I do it*			
J'y joue	*I play it*	**après le collège**	*after school*	
		souvent	*often*	
J'y vais	*I go there*	**de temps en temps**	*from time to time*	
		le week-end	*at the weekends*	
Je <u>n'</u>en fais <u>pas</u> / jamais	*I don't / never do it*	**toujours**	*always*	
Je <u>n'</u>y joue <u>pas</u> / jamais	*I don't / never play it*	**tous les jours**	*every day*	
Je <u>n'</u>y vais <u>pas</u> / jamais	*I don't / never go there*	**une fois par semaine**	*once a week*	

THE LANGUAGE GYM

1. Match

Faire du vélo	To do rock climbing
Faire des randonnées	To do nothing
Jouer aux cartes	To do horse riding
Aller à la plage	To play videogames
Jouer aux jeux vidéo	To do cycling
Aller au stade	To go to the stadium
Faire de l'équitation	To go to the beach
Ne rien faire	To go hiking
Faire de l'escalade	To do swimming
Faire de la natation	To play cards

2. Anagrams

a. *I like* — iJ'mea

b. *I don't like* — eJ imn'ea sap

c. *To do yoga* — reiFa ud gyoa

d. *To do swimming* — reiFa ed al ttniaano

e. *Once a week* — neU isof rap imaesne

f. *To play cards* — rJoue uxa tecsra

g. *Videogames* — esL ujxe doéiv

h. *To go to the beach* — lelrA à al eplga

i. *From time to time* — eD mtpse ne mtpse

3. Break the flow

a. J'aimealleràlaplageavecmafamilleleweekendparcequec'estamusant.

b. J'aimealleraucinépourregarderunfilmparcequec'estrelaxant.

c. J'aimefairedel'équitationavecmonmeilleuramileweekend.

d. Elleaimejoueraufootavecsesamiesparcequec'estpassionnant

e. Tuaimesalleraustadeavectonmeilleuramidetempsentemps.

f. Ilaimejoueraubasketavecsoncousinlelundiparcequec'estrelaxant.

g. Vousaimezjouerauxcartesavecvosgrandsparentstouslesjours.

h. Jen'aimerienfairelesamedi.

i. Jen'aimepasfairedel'équitationavecmonpère.Jen'enfaisjamais.

4. Draw a circle around the time expressions and underline the hobbies

a. Souvent

b. Randonnées

c. Jeux vidéo

d. Toujours

e. Natation

f. Jamais

g. Sport

h. Escalade

i. De temps en temps

5. Listen and translate 🔊

a.

b.

c.

d.

e.

f.

g.

h.

i.

6. Gapped translation: complete the translation

a. Je n'aime rien faire — *I don't like to do _____*

b. J'aime aller à la piscine — *I like to go to the _____*

c. J'en fais souvent — *I do it _____*

d. J'aime faire du sport — *I like to do _____*

e. Il aime jouer aux cartes — *He _____ to play cards*

f. Il y joue de temps en temps — *He plays it _____*

g. Tu aimes faire de l'équitation — *You like to do _____*

h. Je n'en fais jamais — *I _____ do it*

 **THE LANGUAGE GYM**

7. Faulty translation: fix the French translation

a. *I like to do swimming* Je n'aime rien faire

b. *I like to go to the cinema* J'aime aller au stade

c. *I like to go to the park* Je n'aime pas aller au parc

d. *He likes to go to the pool* Il aime aller à la plage

e. *I do it every day* J'en fais le lundi

f. *With my boyfriend* Avec ma petite amie

g. *I never go there* J'y vais toujours

h. *I always play it* J'y joue tous les jours

8. Rearrange the words in the correct order

a. randonnées J'aime des faire

b. fais J'en de en temps temps

c. à la Je plage n'aime aller pas

d. en tous fait les Il jours

e. jouer Elle le lundi basket aime au

f. aller Mes parc n'aiment parents pas au

g. amie Mon n'aime piscine aller pas à la

9. Gapped translation: complete the translation

a. J'aime _____ ___ ___ natation. J'en fais _____. *I like to do swimming. I do it often.*

b. Je n' _____ pas jouer aux _____ _____. *I don't like to play videogames.*

c. Je n'en _____ jamais. *I never do it.*

d. Mon père _____ jouer aux _____. *My father likes to play cards.*

e. Il ___ _____ tous les _____-_____. *He plays it every weekend.*

f. Mon meilleur ami _____ _____ ___ ___ musculation. *My best friend likes to do weights.*

g. Il en fait le _____. *He does it on Tuesdays.*

h. Tu n' _____ pas faire du jogging. *You don't like to go jogging.*

i. Tu n'en fais _____. *You never do it.*

j. _____ n'aime _____ _____. *I don't like to do anything.*

k. Ma _____ _____ aime aller à la _____. *My girlfriend likes to go to the beach.*

10. Listen and complete the words with the missing vowels

a. J_ n'_ _m_ p_s _ll_r _ l_ pl_g_ _v_c m_ f_m_ll_ . J_ n'_ v__s j_m__s.

b. J'_ _m_ _ll_r __ c_ntr_-v_ _l_ _v_c m_s _m_s. J'_ v__s l_ d_m_nch_.

c. J'_ _m_ _ll_r __ c_ntr_ c_mm_rc__l _v_c n_ m__ll__r _m_.

d. J'_ _m_ f__r_ d_ l'_sc_l_d_ _v_c m_n p_r_. J'_n f__s d_ t_mps _n t_mps.

e. J'_ _m_ j___r __x c_rt_s _v_c m_ m_r_. J'_ j___ l_ l_nd_.

f. J'_ _m_ j___r __ t_nn_s, m__s c'_st d_ff_c_l_. J'_ j___ t__s l_s j__rs.

g. J_ n'_ _m_ r__n f__r_ _v_c m_ f_m_ll_ l_ v_ndr_d_.

h. J_ n'_ _m_ p_s _ll_r __ c_ntr_ c_mm_rc__l _v_c m_ m_r_ . J_ n'_ v__s j_m__s.

11. Listen and correct the mistakes

a. J'en fais un fois par semaine 🔊

b. Je n'aime pas faire aux cartes

c. Il n'y jamais va

d. Tous jours

e. Vous aimez aller à la natation

f. J'aime aller à le ciné avec mon ami

g. Elle aime jouer cartes avec sa mère ou son frère

h. Vous n'aimez pas aller plage

12. Translation

a. I like	j. I do it often
b. I like a lot	k. I like to go to the beach
c. I don't like	l. We like to do swimming
d. Much	m. You like a lot
e. Often	n. I never do it
f. On Fridays	o. He likes to go to the park
g. On weekends	p. With her brother
h. You guys like to do hiking	q. With my father
i. She likes to do weights	r. With his girlfriend

13. Guided translation

a. *I don't like to do homework with my friend. I never do it.*   J__ n'a__ __ __ p__ __ f__ __ __ __
l__ __ d__ __ __ __ __ __ a__ __ m__ a__ __ . J__ n'__ __ f__ __ __ j__ __ __ __ __ .

b. *I like to do swimming with my friends. I do it at weekends.*   J'__ __ __ __ f__ __ __ __ d__ l__
n__ __ __ __ __ __ __ a__ __ m__ __ a__ __ __ . J'__ f__ __ __ l__ w__ __ __ -__ __ __ .

c. *He likes to play cards with his grandfather. He always plays it.*   I__ a__ __ __ j__ __ __ __ a__ __
c__ __ __ __ __ a__ __ s__ __ g__ __ __ __ __ -__ __ __ __ . I__ y j__ __ __ t__ __ __ __ __ __ .

d. *She likes to go to the stadium and play football with her friends. She plays it once a week.*
E__ __ __ a__ __ __ a__ __ __ __ a__ s__ __ __ __ e__ j__ __ __ __ a__ f__ __ __ a__ __ __ s__ __
a__ __ __ __ . E__ __ __ __ y j__ __ u__ __ f__ __ __ p__ __ s__ __ __ __ __ __ .

e. *You like to do horse riding with your best friend (f). You do it on Saturdays.*   T__ a__ __ __ __
f__ __ __ __ d__ l'__ __ __ __ __ __ __ __ __ __ __ __ a__ __ t__ m__ __ __ __ __ __ __ __ __ a__ __ __ .
T__ e__ f__ __ __ l__ s__ __ __ __ __ __ .

14. Translate into French

a. I don't like to go swimming with my father. I do it once a week.

b. I like to go to the park with my friends. I go there nearly (*presque*) every day.

c. He likes to go to the beach with his girlfriend. He goes there every weekend.

d. I don't like to go horse riding with my mother. I do it every Sunday.

e. We don't like to play cards with our family.

f. You like a lot to go to the cinema with your boyfriend. You go there once a week.

g. I like to do rock climbing with my brother. I do it three times a week.

h. He likes to play basketball with his best friend. He plays it every day after school.

THE LANGUAGE GYM

5.5 CE QUE J'AIME + LE PLUS/LE MOINS + PARCE QUE + C'EST + ADJECTIVES
(SAYING HOW I FEEL ABOUT THINGS AND WHY)

Ce que j'aime *What I like*	le plus *the most*	c'est *is*	faire *to do (to go)*	de l'équitation *horse riding* de l'escalade *rock climbing* de la natation *swimming* des randonnées *hiking* du sport *sport* du vélo *cycling* du yoga *yoga*	parce que c'est *because it is* parce que ce n'est pas *because it is not*	amusant *fun* barbant *boring* dangereux *dangerous* difficile *difficult* énervant *annoying* ennuyeux *boring* facile *easy* fascinant *fascinating* fatigant *tiring* intéressant *interesting* passionnant *exciting* relaxant *relaxing* stupide *stupid*
	le moins *the least*		jouer *to play*	au basket *basketball* au tennis *tennis* aux cartes *cards* aux jeux vidéo *videogames*		
			aller *to go*	au ciné *to the cinema* au stade *to the stadium* à la plage *to the beach* à la piscine *to the pool*		

1. Match

Énervant	*The most*
Amusant	*Tiring*
Le plus	*The least*
Ce que j'aime	*Annoying*
Le moins	*Fascinating*
Fascinant	*Exciting*
Fatigant	*Fun*
Passionnant	*What I like*

2. Anagrams

a. eC uqe aeij'm el lpus

b. c'set rfiea ud ptosr

c. eprac uqe sec't acisnafnt

d. eC uqe eij'ma el lpus

e. c'set eriaf ud goya

f. repac euq ec'st lxaanret

g. eC ueq j'maie el mnois

h. sc'et llrea ua nicé

i. eacpr uqe sec't uxenuyne

j. te tsc'e dtispue

Ce que j'aime le plus
c'est faire du yoga !

3. Break the flow and translate the sentences into English

a. Cequej'aimelepluscestjouerautennisparcequec'estfascinant

b. Cequej'aimelemoinsc'estfairedesrandonnées:c'estfatigant

c. Cequej'aimeleplusc'estfairedelanatation:c'estamusant

d. Cequej'aimeleplusc'estfairedel'équitation:c'estrelaxant

e. Cequej'aimelemoinsc'estjoueraubasket:c'estennuyeux

f. Cequej'aimelemoinsc'estfairedusportparcequec'estdangereux

g. Cequej'aimeleplusc'estjouerauxjeuxvidéoparcequec'estfacile

4. Listen and fill in the gaps 🔊

a. Ce que j'aime _____

c'est _____ parce que

c'est _____

b. Ce que j'aime _____

c'est _____ parce que

c'est _____

c. Ce que j'aime _____

c'est _____ parce que

c'est _____

d. Ce que j'aime _____

c'est _____ parce que

c'est _____

5. Gapped Translation: please complete

a. Ce que j'aime _____ c'est aller à la piscine

What I like the most is to go to the pool

b. parce que _____ vraiment _____

because it is really fun

c. _____ le moins c'est faire de l'_____ avec mon frère

What I like the least is to go rock climbing with my brother

d. parce que ce n'est pas _____ et c'est _____

because it is not easy and it is dangerous

6. Translate into English

a. Ce que j'aime le plus c'est faire de l'escalade parce que c'est dangereux. J'en fais une fois par semaine.

b. Ce que j'aime le moins c'est faire du yoga parce que ce n'est pas passionnant. Je n'en fais jamais.

c. Ce que j'aime le plus c'est aller à la plage parce que c'est amusant. J'y vais tous les jours.

d. Ce que j'aime le moins c'est aller au stade parce que ce n'est pas fascinant. Je n'y vais jamais.

e. Ce que j'aime le plus c'est aller à la plage.

 THE LANGUAGE GYM

7. Faulty translation: fix the English translation

a. Ce que j'aime le plus c'est jouer aux cartes
What I like the least is to play cards

b. parce qu'à mon avis ce n'est pas ennuyeux
because in my opinion it is exciting

c. Ce que j'aime le moins c'est aller à la piscine et faire de la natation
What I like the least is to go to the beach and go swimming

d. parce que c'est assez dangereux. Je n'en fais jamais.
because it is very dangerous. I don't do it.

e. Ce que j'aime le plus c'est faire du vélo. C'est facile.
What I like the most is to go cycling. It is fun.

8. Tangled translation: into French

a. Ce que j'aime *the most* c'est faire des *hiking*

b. parce que *it is* relaxant et *fascinating*

c. Ce que j'aime *the least* c'est jouer aux *videogames*

d. *because* c'est *boring* et *stupid*

e. *What* j'aime le plus *is* aller à la *pool*

f. parce que c'est *very* relaxant et *fun*

g. *What I like the least* c'est faire de l'*horse riding*

h. parce que c'est *quite dangerous* et parfois *difficult*

9. Correct the mistakes and listen to check

a. Ce que j'aime le plus c'est faire l'équitation avec mon amie une fois par semaine.

b. Ce que j'aime le moins c'est jouer à le basket après le collège parce que c'est un peu barbant.

c. Ce que j'aime le plus c'est aller au ciné le week-end avec mes amis parce que amusant.

d. Ce j'aime le moins c'est faire de l'escalade parce que c'est vraiment dangereux difficile.

e. Ce que j'aime le plus jouer au tennis avec mon père parce que ce est pas ennuyeux.

f. Ce que j'aime le c'est faire les courses les samedi parce que ce n'est pas intéressant.

g. Ce que j'aime le plus c'est aller au souvent stade.

10. Choose the correct words

a. Ce que j'aime **le plus** / **le moins** c'est aller à la plage parce que c'est vraiment relaxant.

b. Ce que j'aime le plus c'est faire de la natation parce que c'est **barbant** / **amusant**.

c. Ce que j'aime le plus c'est jouer aux cartes parce que ce n'est pas **difficile** / **intéressant.**

d. Ce j'aime **le plus** / **le moins** c'est faire du sport parce que c'est un peu ennuyeux.

e. Ce que j'aime le moins c'est jouer aux jeux vidéo parce que c'est **fascinant** / **énervant.**

f. Ce que j'aime le moins c'est aller au stade parce que ce n'est pas **passionnant** / **fatigant**.

11. Translate into French

a. What I like the most is to do cycling with my brother once a week because it is very relaxing.

b. What I like the least is to play basketball after school because it is not interesting. I never play it.

c. What I like the most is to go to the beach. I go there every day after school with my friends.

d. What I like the least is to do horse riding. I never do it because it is too (*trop*) dangerous.

e. What I like the most is to play tennis and to do yoga because it is very relaxing and it is not difficult.

ORAL PING PONG

AIMER

ENGLISH 1	FRENCH 1	ENGLISH 2	FRENCH 2
I like to play basketball with my friends at the park.	J'aime jouer au basket avec mes amis au parc.	I like my friends because they are nice.	
My brother likes to go swimming. He does it on Fridays.	Mon frère aime faire de la natation. Il en fait le vendredi.	I like to go to the swimming pool with my cousin (m). I go there every day.	
We like to go to the cinema. We go there at the weekends.	Nous aimons aller au ciné. Nous y allons le week-end.	My friends like to play tennis. They play it from time to time.	
My parents don't like to play videogames. They never play it	Mes parents n'aiment pas jouer aux jeux vidéo. Ils n'y jouent jamais.	My sister doesn't like to play cards. She never plays it.	
Do you like to go to the beach in the summer?	Tu aimes aller à la plage en été?	Do you guys like to go cycling in the park at weekends?	
My friends and I like sweets, but they are not healthy.	Mes amis et moi aimons les bonbons, mais ils ne sont pas sains.	My mum likes vegetables because they are healthy.	
My dad doesn't like honey because it is too sweet.	Mon papa n'aime pas le miel parce que c'est trop sucré.	My sister doesn't like tomatoes because they are disgusting.	
I like my English teacher because she is joyful and hard-working.	J'aime ma prof d'anglais parce qu'elle est joyeuse et travailleuse.	My brothers and I like our grandparents, but they are annoying sometimes.	

INSTRUCTIONS - You are **PARTNER A.** Work in pairs. Each of you has two sets of sentences - one set has already been translated for you. You will ask your partner to translate these. The other set of sentences have not been translated. Your partner will ask you to translate these.

HOW TO PLAY - Partner A starts by reading out his/her/their first sentence <u>in English</u>. Partner B must translate. Partner A must check the answer and award the following points: **3 points** = perfect, **2 points** = 1 mistake, **1 point** = mistakes but the verb is accurate. If they cannot translate correctly, Partner A will read out the sentence so that Partner B can learn what the correct translation is.

Then Partner B reads out his/her/their first sentence, and so on.

OBJECTIVE - Try to win more points than your partner by translating correctly as many sentences as possible.

 **THE LANGUAGE GYM**

163

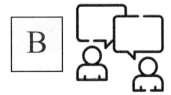

ORAL PING PONG

AIMER

B

ENGLISH 1	FRENCH 1	ENGLISH 2	FRENCH 2
I like to play basketball with my friends at the park.		I like my friends because they are nice.	J'aime mes amis parce qu'ils sont sympas.
My brother likes to go swimming. He does it on Fridays.		I like to go to the swimming pool with my cousin (m). I go there every day.	J'aime aller à la piscine avec mon cousin. J'y vais tous les jours.
We like to go to the cinema. We go there at the weekends.		My friends like to play tennis. They play it from time to time.	Mes amis aiment jouer au tennis. Ils y jouent de temps en temps.
My parents don't like to play videogames. They never play it		My sister doesn't like to play cards. She never plays it.	Ma sœur n'aime pas jouer aux cartes. Elle n'y joue jamais.
Do you like to go to the beach in the summer?		Do you guys like to go cycling at the park at weekends?	Vous aimez faire du vélo au parc le week-end?
My friends and I like sweets, but they are not healthy.		My mum likes vegetables because they are healthy.	Ma maman aime les légumes parce qu'ils sont sains.
My dad doesn't like honey because it is too sweet.		My sister doesn't like tomatoes because they are disgusting.	Ma sœur n'aime pas les tomates parce qu'elles sont dégoûtantes.
I like my English teacher because she is joyful and hard-working.		My brothers and I like our grandparents, but they are annoying sometimes.	Mes frères et moi aimons nos grands-parents, mais ils sont parfois énervants.

INSTRUCTIONS - You are **PARTNER B.** Work in pairs. Each of you has two sets of sentences - one set has already been translated for you. You will ask your partner to translate these. The other set of sentences have not been translated. Your partner will ask you to translate these.

HOW TO PLAY - Partner A starts by reading out his/her/their first sentence <u>in English</u>. Partner B must translate. Partner A must check the answer and award the following points: **3 points** = perfect, **2 points** = 1 mistake, **1 point** = mistakes but the verb is accurate. If they cannot translate correctly, Partner A will read out the sentence so that Partner B can learn what the correct translation is.
Then Partner B reads out his/her/their first sentence, and so on.

OBJECTIVE - Try to win more points than your partner by translating correctly as many sentences as possible.

AIMER

No Snakes No Ladders

	1 — We like chips	2 — I like to go to the beach in the summer	3 — She likes to go hiking	4 — Do you like to do rock climbing?	5 — I like to play tennis at weekends	6 — I like my English teacher	7 — My mum likes my sister
DÉPART	14 — My sister doesn't like ice creams	13 — Do you like to go to the cinema?	12 — We like to do rock climbing	11 — She likes to do rock climbing once a week	10 — They like to play football every day	9 — We like our friends, they are nice	8 — We like our father, he is patient
15 — I like my best friend, she is not lazy	17 — We like chicken, it is healthy	18 — Do you guys like to play videogames ?	19 — They like to do yoga	20 — We like to play tennis	21 — I like my aunt, she is nice	22 — They do not like to play cards	23 — My girlfriend likes her mother
16 — I like to go swimming. I do it often	30 — We do not like burgers	29 — I don't like to do anything at weekends	28 — She likes to play football on Fridays	27 — We like eggs and chips	26 — I do not like my cat, he is annoying	25 — We don't like to do anything at weekends	24 — I like chips, they are tasty
ARRIVÉE							

No Snakes No Ladders

AIMER

DÉPART	1 Nous aimons les frites	2 J'aime aller à la plage en été	3 Elle aime faire des randonnées	4 Tu aimes faire de l'escalade?	5 J'aime jouer au tennis le week-end	6 J'aime ma prof d'anglais	7 Ma maman aime ma sœur
15 J'aime ma meilleure amie, elle n'est pas paresseuse	14 Ma sœur n'aime pas les glaces	13 Tu aimes aller au ciné?	12 Nous aimons faire de l'escalade	11 Elle aime faire de l'escalade une fois par semaine	10 Ils aiment jouer au foot tous les jours	9 Nous aimons nos amis, ils sont sympas	8 Nous aimons notre père, il est patient
16 J'aime faire de la natation souvent	17 Nous aimons le poulet, c'est sain	18 Vous aimez jouer aux jeux vidéo?	19 Ils aiment faire du yoga	20 Nous aimons jouer au tennis	21 J'aime ma tante, elle est sympa	22 Ils n'aiment pas jouer aux cartes	23 Ma petite amie aime sa mère
ARRIVÉE	30 Nous n'aimons pas les burgers	29 Je n'aime rien faire le week-end	28 Elle aime jouer au foot le vendredi	27 Nous aimons les œufs et les frites	26 Je n'aime pas mon chat, il est énervant	25 Nous n'aimons rien faire le week-end	24 J'aime les frites, elles sont savoureuses

PYRAMID TRANSLATION

AIMER

Translate each part of the pyramid out loud with your partner, then write it into the spaces provided below.

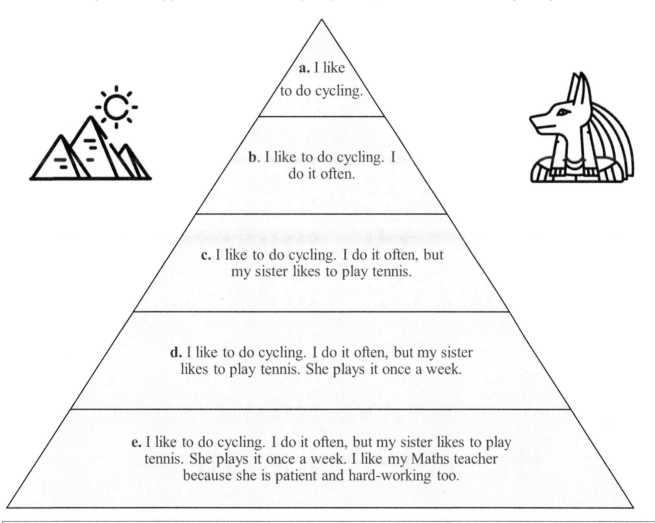

a. I like to do cycling.

b. I like to do cycling. I do it often.

c. I like to do cycling. I do it often, but my sister likes to play tennis.

d. I like to do cycling. I do it often, but my sister likes to play tennis. She plays it once a week.

e. I like to do cycling. I do it often, but my sister likes to play tennis. She plays it once a week. I like my Maths teacher because she is patient and hard-working too.

Write your translation here

✂ ✂ ✂

SOLUTION: J'aime faire du vélo. J'en fais souvent, mais ma sœur aime jouer au tennis. Elle y joue une fois par semaine. J'aime ma prof de maths parce qu'elle est patiente et aussi travailleuse.

THE LANGUAGE GYM

UNIT 6 – JOUER

Je	joue
Tu	joues
Il / Elle / On	joue
Nous	jouons
Vous	jouez
Ils / Elles	jouent

SPORTS & GAMES

Je joue au foot

Nous jouons aux jeux vidéo

INSTRUMENTS

Je joue de la guitare

COMPARING

Je joue mieux au tennis que mon ami

6.1 TIME MARKER + JE JOUE + À LA/AU/AUX/SUR + NOUN + AVEC + NOUN
AFFECTIVE VERB + PARCE QUE + C'EST + ADJECTIVE.
(SAYING WHAT GAMES I PLAY, WITH WHOM AND HOW I FEEL ABOUT THEM)

Quand j'ai le temps *When I have time* **Le week-end** *At the weekends* **Le lundi** *On Mondays*	**je joue** *I play*	**à la PlayStation** **au basket** **au foot** **au tennis** **aux cartes** **aux échecs** **aux jeux vidéo** **sur l'ordinateur** **sur mon portable**	*on the PlayStation* *basketball* *football* *tennis* *cards* *chess* *video games* *on the computer* *on my mobile phone*	**avec** *with*	**ma famille** **mon meilleur ami/ma meilleure amie** *my best friend* **mon petit ami/ma petite amie** *my boyfriend/girlfriend* **mon cousin/ma cousine** *my cousin* **mes amis** *my friends* **mes amies** *my (girl) friends*

Je n'aime pas ça	*I don't like it*	**parce que c'est** *because it is*	**amusant** **barbant** **drôle** **dur** **fatigant** **incroyable** **passionnant** **trop bien**	*fun* *boring* *funny* *hard* *tiring* *amazing* *exciting* *awesome*
J'aime ça	*I like it*			
J'adore ça	*I love it*			
Je déteste ça	*I hate it*			

J'y joue	*I play it*	**souvent** **de temps en temps** **le week-end** **(presque) tous les jours** **une fois par semaine**	*often* *from time to time* *at the weekends* *(almost) every day* *once a week*
On y joue	*We play it*		
Je n'y joue jamais	*I never play it*	**On n'y joue jamais**	*We never play it*

LANGUAGE AWARENESS: *JOUER À* + ARTICLE

When talking about what games (including sport games) we play, we need to say:

***je joue à* + article + activity**. Depending on whether the activity is masculine/feminine and singular/plural, the phrase is formed differently:

- Je joue **au** foot   *I play football*   (Masculine singular activity)
- Je joue **à la** PlayStation   *I play on the PlayStation*   (Feminine singular activity)
- Je joue **aux** jeux vidéo   *I play videogames*   (Masculine plural activity)
- Je joue **aux** cartes   *I play cards*   (Feminine plural activity)

This structure functions in the same way as ***aller* + *à* + place** that you saw earlier in the book (Unit 3):

- Je vais **au** musée et **à la** plage   *I go to the museum and to the beach*

1. Match

Je n'aime pas	*Once a week*
J'adore	*Tiring*
Je déteste	*Basketball*
Je joue	*I hate*
Échecs	*From time to time*
Basket	*I play*
Une fois par semaine	*Chess*
De temps en temps	*I don't like*
Fatigant	*I love*

2. Complete with a suitable word

a. __ __ lundi je joue aux échecs avec mon père

b. Je n'_____ pas ça parce que c'est barbant

c. J'__ joue souvent

d. J'__ __ __ __ __ ça parce que c'est amusant

e. Je joue au __ __ __ __ __ __ tous les jours

f. Je déteste le tennis parce que c'est __ __ __

g. On y __ __ __ __ de temps en temps

h. Je joue aux __ __ __ __ __ __ le week-end

3. Slalom translation: use one item from each column of the table to translate each sentence

Je joue aux échecs	tous les jours.	J'y joue	ça.	du temps libre.
Je joue aux cartes	avec mon père	On y joue	tous les jours	parce que c'est amusant.
Je joue aux jeux vidéo	avec mon meilleur ami	une fois par semaine.	Je n'aime pas ça	mais c'est fatigant.
Je joue au basket	avec ma famille.	de temps en temps.	j'ai	parce que c'est trop bien
Je joue à la PlayStation	avec mon cousin.	On y joue souvent.	J'adore ça	parce que c'est barbant.
Je joue sur mon portable.	avec mes camarades de classe.	J'aime beaucoup	J'aime beaucoup ça,	J'y joue avec mon frère.
Je joue au tennis	J'y joue	quand	presque tous les jours	parce que c'est incroyable

a. *I play chess with my father once a week. I don't like it because it is boring.*

b. *I play cards with my family. We play it often. I love it because it is fun.*

c. *I play videogames with my cousin. I play it every day because it is amazing.*

d. *I play basketball with my classmates. We play it nearly every day because it is awesome.*

e. *I play on the PlayStation every day. I like it a lot. I play it with my brother.*

f. *I play on my mobile phone. I play it when I have free time.*

g. *I play tennis with my best friend from time to time. I like it a lot, but it is tiring.*

LANGUAGE AWARENESS: *J'Y JOUE/ON Y JOUE*

To say that we play something we say:

- **J'y joue**   *I play it*
- **On y joue**   *We play it*

In this structure the *y (it)* is known as a **Pronoun.** It is called a **Pronoun** because it replaces the **noun** in the sentence. For example:

- Je joue **au foot**   *I play football*
- **J'y** joue souvent   *I play it often*
- On joue **aux cartes**   *We play cards*
- **On y** joue toujours   *We play it always*

ADVERBS OF FREQUENCY

We use adverbs of frequency, such as *toujours* (always) and *souvent* (often) to say how often we do an activity. They are placed **straight after the verb** in the sentence:

- Je joue **toujours** au tennis   *I always play tennis*

Other adverbs are placed either at the **start** or at the **end**:

- **Tous les jours** je joue au tennis   *I play tennis every day*

But when you use the pronoun **y,** the adverb needs to go after the verb

- J'y joue **une fois par semaine**   *I play it once a week*

NEGATIVE FORM

The negative structure goes around the verb:

- Je **ne** joue **jamais** au golf   *I never play golf*
- Je **n'y** joue **jamais**   *I never play it*

---

4. Complete with the missing letters

a. Je j__ __ __ sou__ __ __ __ à la PlayStation

b. Quand j'ai le te__ __ __, je joue aux éche__ __

c. Je n'aime p__ __ ça, c'est fatig__ __ __

d. On y j__ __ __ le lun__ __

e. J'aime ça par__ __ que c'est passionn__ __ __

f. Je dét__ __ __ __ ça parce que c'est d__ __

g. Je joue aux car__ __ __ avec ma fami__ __ __

h. Je ne jo__ __ pas __ __ __vent au basket

5. Tick the expressions in the list below which refer to time and cross the adjectives

a. Souvent   h. Amusant

b. Passionnant   i. Le lundi

c. Barbant   j. Rarement

d. De temps en temps k. Tous les jours

e. Le week-end   l. Dur

f. Jamais   m. Drôle

g. Fatigant   n. Une fois par semaine

6. Complete with *à, au, aux, avec, le,* or *les*

a. Je joue _____ ma famille

b. Je joue _____ basket

c. J'y joue tous _____ jours

d. Je joue ___ tennis ___ collège

e. J'y joue ____ samedi

f. Je joue _____ mon frère

g. Je joue ___ la PlayStation ___ soir

h. Je joue ____ cartes

7. Listen and complete with a suitable word

a. Le lundi je _____ au basket avec mes amis.

b. Généralement, je joue au _____ avec mon père.

c. Je joue à la PlayStation presque tous les _____.

d. Je joue aux cartes avec ma mère. On ____ joue souvent.

e. Je joue au tennis, mais je _____ joue pas souvent parce que c'est _____.

f. J'_____ beaucoup le foot parce que c'est amusant.

g. Je ne joue jamais aux _____.

h. Je_____ le golf parce que c'est super barbant!

THE LANGUAGE GYM

8. Guided translation; then listen and check your answers

a. J__ n'___ p__ l_ b_____. J__ n'__ j____ j____. *I don't like basketball. I never play it.*

b. O__ y j___ u____ f____ p___ s_____. *We play it once a week.*

c. J__ d_____ l_ g_____. C'___ t___ b_____. *I hate golf. It is very boring.*

d. J__ j____ a___ c_____ a__ m_ f_____. *I play cards with my family.*

e. J'__ j____ t_____ l__ j____. *I play it every day.*

f. J__ n__ j____ j_____ s__ m__ p_____. *I never play on my mobile phone.*

g. J__ n__ j___ p_____ j_____ a__ t_____. *I hardly ever play tennis.*

h. J__ j___ s_____ à l_ P_____. *I play often on the PlayStation.*

---

9. Translate into French

a. Once a week

b. Often

c. Basketball

d. Cards

e. Never

f. Boring

g. Tiring

h. Awesome

i. Computer

j. Mobile phone

---

10. Tangled translation: translate into French

a. *I don't* joue pas au *tennis*. Je n'*like* pas ça parce que *it is* barbant.

b. Je joue au *football*. J'*like it because* c'est *exciting*.

c. *I* ne *play* jamais aux *cards*. Je n'*like* pas *it* parce que ce n'est pas *fun*.

d. Je joue *on my* portable. J'*love it* parce que *it is awesome*.

e. *I don't* joue pas au *football*. *I don't like it* parce que *it is tiring*.

f. Je joue sur l'*computer*. *I like it* parce que *it is* drôle.

g. *I play* aux *chess* avec *my friends*. J'*like it* parce que *it is fun*.

---

11. Translate into French

a. I don't play tennis. I don't like it because it is boring.

b. I play often basketball. I love it because it is exciting.

c. I play on the PlayStation every day. I like it a lot because it is fun.

d. I play cards with my family. We play it every Saturday.

e. I play videogames with my best friend. We play it every day.

f. I love tennis because it is fun. However (*Cependant*), it is quite tiring.

g. I never play golf. I hate it because it is very boring.

h. I play on my mobile phone all the time. It is a lot of fun.

i. I play football every day after school. I love it. It is awesome.

6.2 PRESENT OF JOUER + À LA/AU/ AUX/SUR + NOUN + AU/À LA/DANS + NOUN + PRONOUN + JOUER + FREQUENCY ADVERBS
(SAYING WHERE ONE PLAYS GAMES AND HOW OFTEN ONE DOES IT)

Quand j'ai le temps	When I have time	Le week-end	At the weekends
Le lundi / mardi / mercredi / jeudi / vendredi / samedi / dimanche			

Je *I*	**joue** *play*	**à la PlayStation** *on the PlayStation*	**au** *at*	**collège**
				stade
Tu *You*	**joues** *play*			**parc**
		au basket *basketball*		**centre sportif**
Mon ami (e) *My friend* **Mon frère** *My brother* **Ma sœur** *My sister* **On** *We*	**joue** *play(s)*	**au billard** *pool* **au foot** *football* **au tennis** *tennis*	**à la** *at*	**bibliothèque** **piscine** **plage**
Mon ami(e) et moi *My friend and I* **Nous** *We*	**jouons** *play*	**aux cartes** *cards* **aux échecs** *chess* **aux jeux en ligne** *online games* **aux jeux vidéo** *video games*	**chez** *at*	**moi** *my home* **toi** *your home* **lui** *his home* **elle** *her home* **nous** *our home* **vous** *your home* **eux/elles** *their home (m/f)*
Vous *You guys/girls*	**jouez** *play*			
Mes ami(e)s *My friends* **Mes parents** *My parents*	**jouent** *play*	**sur l'ordinateur** *on the computer* **sur mon portable** *on my mobile phone*	**dans** *in*	**la chambre** *the bedroom* **le jardin** *the garden*

J'y joue	*I play it*	**de temps en temps**	*from time to time*	
Tu y joues	*You play it*	**le week-end**	*at the weekends*	
Il/Elle y joue	*He/She plays it*	**souvent**	*often*	
Nous y jouons	*We play it*	**tous les jours**	*every day*	
Vous y jouez	*You guys/girls play it*	**une fois par semaine**	*once a week*	
Ils/Elles y jouent	*They play it*			
Je n'y joue jamais	*I never play it*	**Nous n'y jouons jamais** **On n'y joue jamais**	*We never play it*	

THE LANGUAGE GYM

1. Choose the correct option

a. Je **joue/joues/jouent** au rugby le lundi

b. Nous ne **jouez/jouons/jouent** jamais au tennis

c. Elles **joue/joues/jouent** aux cartes

d. Le dimanche, ils **joues/jouent/jouez** au golf

e. A quoi **jouez/jouons/jouent**-vous aujourd'hui?

f. Tu **joues/joue/jouent** à la PlayStation!

g. Mes parents ne **jouons/jouez/jouent** jamais aux échecs

h. A quoi **joue/joues/jouent**-tu?

2. Complete

a. Je ne jou___ jamais au tennis

b. Nous ne jou___ ___ ___ pas au rugby

c. Il jou___ souvent à la PlayStation

d. Mes parents jou___ ___ ___ au golf

e. A quoi jou___ ___ -vous maintenant?

f. Mes frères jou___ ___ ___ aux échecs

g. Tu jou___ ___ toujours au foot

h. Nous jou___ ___ ___ au basket

3. Faulty translation: fix the English translation

a. Nous jouons au tennis au centre sportif   *They play tennis at school*

b. Elles jouent au golf le jeudi   *She plays tennis on Sundays*

c. Où joues-tu au basket? Au collège?   *Where do you guys play basketball? At home?*

d. Mon père et moi jouons au billard chez nous   *My father and I play videogames at home*

e. Le dimanche ils jouent au rugby au parc   *On Sundays we play rugby at the park*

f. Il joue toujours à la PlayStation dans sa chambre   *I always play on the PlayStation in my room*

g. Vous jouez aux jeux en ligne de temps en temps   *We play online games often*

h. Elles jouent toujours avec des poupées   *She still plays with dolls*

4. Broken translation

a. *They play football*   Ils jou___ ___ ___ a___ f___ ___ ___

b. *We never play rugby*   Nous ne jou___ ___ ___ ja___ ___ ___ ___ a___ rugby

c. *I don't play chess*   J___ n___ jou___ p___ ___ a___ ___ éch___ ___ ___

d. *My friend never play basketball*   M___ am___ n___ jo ___ ___ j___ ___ ___ ___ ___ a___ basket

e. *On Sundays I play cards*   L___ diman___ ___ ___ je j___ ___ ___ a___ ___ car___ ___ ___

f. *He plays tennis every day*   Il j___ ___ ___ a___ tennis to___ ___ l___ ___jo___ ___ ___

g. *We play rugby on Mondays*   N___ ___ ___ jou___ ___ ___ a___ r___ ___ ___ ___ ___ le lu___ ___ ___

h. *They play basketball...*   I___ ___ jou___ ___ ___ a___ b___ ___ ___ ___ ___

i. *...in the sports centre*   ...a___ c___ n___ ___ ___ sp___ ___ ___ i___

j. *Do you guys play on the PlayStation?*   V___ ___ ___ jou___ ___ à l___ PlayStation?

k. *You guys always play cards!*   V___ ___ ___ jou___ ___ tou___ ___ ___ ___ ___ aux cart___ ___!

THE LANGUAGE GYM

5. Match

À la campagne	*At the sports centre*
À la montagne	*At his/her house*
À la piscine	*In my room*
Au centre sportif	*At the swimming pool*
Chez moi	*At (my) home*
À la plage	*At the park*
Dans ma chambre	*In the mountain*
Chez lui / chez elle	*At the beach*
Au parc	*In the countryside*

6. Listen and Complete

a. Nous _____ au foot

b. Ils _____ au golf

c. Elle _____ au rugby

d. Je ne _____ jamais aux échecs

e. Elles _____ avec des poupées

f. Il _____ au basket

g. À quoi _____ -vous?

h. À quoi _____ -tu?

i. Mes parents _____ au tennis

7. Sentence Puzzle

a. lundi, à la Le et moi Pascal jouons PlayStation. chez Nous moi jouons y.

   On Mondays, Pascal and I play on the PlayStation. We play it at my home.

b. mes Le amis basket jouent vendredi, au. y Ils au jouent collège.

   On Fridays, my friends play basketball. They play it at school.

c. foot Le mon joue au frère week-end, joue y Il au sportif centre.

   At weekends, my brother plays football. He plays it at the sports centre.

d. ton Tu au golf samedi? joues avec le père joues Où -tu?

   Do you play golf with your father on Saturdays? Where do you play?

e. mon père Le week-end, échecs et aîné jouent mon frère aux. jouent Ils y le jardin dans.

   At weekends, my father and my older brother play chess. They play it in the garden.

8. Tangled translation: translate into French

a. Le week-end *he plays* aux *chess* avec mon *father* à *the* campagne.

b. Le *Thursdays* je joue au foot. *I play it* à la *countryside*.

c. De temps en temps *we play* aux *cards* avec nos *parents*. *We* y *play* chez nous.

d. *Do you guys play tennis* au club de tennis près de chez vous, *on* samedi?

e. *On Mondays* et le mercredi *they play* aux *games* en ligne. *They* y *play* chez Bertrand.

f. Fatima *plays* à la PlayStation *every day*. Elle y *plays* dans sa *room*.

g. Ma mère et ses *friends play* aux *cards* le *Tuesdays*. Elles y *play* chez Marine.

h. *On Fridays*, ma *sister* aînée *plays* au squash avec mon *father*. Elle y *plays* au *sports centre*.

9. Listen and fill in each gap with the correct word

a. Le _____ ma _____ et moi _____ au basket. On __ _____ au centre sportif.

b. Le _____-_____ , mes frères _____ au foot au _____ _____ .

c. ___ vendredi, après le collège, mes _____ de classe _____ au foot. Ils __ _____ au _____ .

d. Ma mère et ses _____ jouent aux cartes le _____ . Elles y _____ chez moi.

e. Pierre _____ aux jeux en ligne le _____ avec son _____ ami. Il y joue dans sa _____ .

f. Le _____ mes frères _____ au rugby pour leur collège. _____ ___ jouent au stade.

---

10. Guided translation

a. *I play tennis* J__ j___ ___ a__t___ ___ ___ ___

b. *We play cards* N___ ___ jou ___ ___ ___ a___ ___ cart___ ___

c. *With my father* A__ ___ ___ m___ ___ p___ ___ ___ ___

d. *In the countryside* À l__ c___ ___ ___ ___ ___ gne

e. *They play football* Ils jou___ ___ ___ a__ f___ ___

f. *At weekends* L__ w___ ___ ___ -___ ___ ___

g. *Do you play rugby?* T__ jou ___ ___ a__ r___ ___ ___ ___ ?

h. *I play it at my home* J'__ jou__ c___ ___ ___ m___ ___

---

11. Complete the table

Pronoun	Verb Jouer	Verb Y + jouer
Je / J'	Je joue	J'y joue
Tu	Tu joues	
Il		Il y joue
Elle	Elle joue	
Nous		Nous y jouons
Vous	Vous jouez	
Ils		Ils y jouent
Elles	Elles jouent	

---

12. Translate into French

a. In the countryside

b. We play it

c. They play cards

d. I play it

e. On the beach

f. They play pool

g. She plays football

h. At weekends

i. In the sports centre

j. She plays it

k. They play it

---

13. Translate into French

a. At weekends, she plays chess with my father at my home.

b. On Sundays, I play with my dog in the countryside.

c. On Saturdays, we play cards with our uncles. We play it at their home.

d. On Mondays, do you guys still play tennis at the tennis club near (*près de*) your home?

e. They play online games every day. They play it at Théo's home.

f. Pierre plays on the PlayStation all the time. He plays it in his room.

g. My father and his friends play cards on Tuesdays. They play it at the home of their friend Amadou.

h. On Fridays, my younger brother plays volleyball with my older brother. They play it at the sports centre near (*près de*) my home.

6.3 PRESENT OF JOUER + À LA/AU/ AUX + NOUN
+ MIEUX/PIRE QUE + NOUN/PRONOUN
(SAYING HOW WELL ONE PLAYS GAMES COMPARED TO OTHERS)

Je *I*	**joue** *play*		**à la PlayStation**		**moi** **me*
Tu *You*	**joues** *play*		**au basket**		**toi** **you*
Mon ami (e) *My friend* **Mon frère** *My brother* **Ma sœur** *My sister* **On** *We*	**joue** *play(s)*	**mieux** *better*	**au billard** *pool* **au foot** **au rugby** **au tennis** **au volley**	**que / qu'** *than*	**lui** **him* **elle** **her* **ma sœur** **mon ami/e** **mon frère**
Mon ami(e) et moi *My friend and I* **Nous** *We*	**jouons** *play*	**moins bien** *worse (literally "less well")*	**aux cartes** *cards* **aux échecs** *chess*		**nous** **us* **vous** **you guys* **eux/elles** **them*
Vous *You guys/girls*	**jouez** *play*		**aux jeux en ligne** *online games* **aux jeux vidéo** *video games*		**mes amis/es** *my friends*
Mes ami(e)s *My friends* **Mes parents** *My parents*	**jouent** *play*				**nos amis** *our friends*

LANGUAGE AWARENESS: COMPARATIVES

When we use comparatives in French *mieux que* (better than) or *moins bien que* ("less well" than), the structure used in French is almost the same as English.

- **Je joue mieux au tennis que _toi_**   *I play tennis better than _you_*

In the first half of the sentence, we use a **Subject Pronoun** (je, tu, il, elle, on, nous, vous, ils, elles) and in the second half, we use what we call a **Stressed Pronoun,** also called **Emphatic Pronoun** or **Disjunctive Pronoun.** They are used in addition to or in place of subject and object pronouns.

- **Tu joues mieux au tennis que _moi_**   *You play tennis better than _me_*

- **Il joue mieux qu'_elle_**   *He plays better than _her_*

- **On joue mieux au billard que _nos amis_**   *We play pool better than _our friends_*

- **Vous jouez mieux aux échecs que _nous_**   *You play chess better than _us_*

 **THE LANGUAGE GYM**

1. Match

Je joue au volley	*Better than them*
Mieux que lui	*They play volleyball*
On joue au volley	*Worse than me*
Mieux qu'eux	*Worse than her*
Mieux que moi	*I play volleyball*
Ils jouent au volley	*He/She plays volleyball*
Pire que moi	*Better than me*
Pire qu'elle	*Better than him*
Il/Elle joue au volley	*We play volleyball*

2. Listen and unjumble the words

a. moi que au billard frère Mon joue mieux

b. nous Ils moins bien jouent que rugby au

c. père que aux joue Mon échecs mieux moi

d. frères Mes au jouent foot moi mieux que

e. Tu aux cartes joues que mieux lui?

f. Ils jeux vidéo aux jouent qu' moins bien elle

g. mère mieux Ma tennis au mon joue que père

h. sœur Ma moins bien joue moi que tennis au

3. Faulty translation: fix the English translation

a. Mon frère joue mieux au foot que moi — *My sister plays rugby better than me*

b. Elle joue mieux au billard que son petit ami — *He plays pool better than his girlfriend*

c. Nous jouons mieux au tennis que toi — *They play tennis better than you*

d. Mes parents jouent moins bien aux cartes que moi — *My parents play videogames better than me*

e. Ma sœur joue mieux aux échecs que moi — *My brother plays chess worse than me*

f. Ils jouent mieux aux cartes que leur père — *We play cards better than our father*

g. Mon oncle joue mieux au foot que mon père — *My aunt plays football better than my uncle*

4. Listen and complete the table

	Person	Verb	Comparative	Activity	than	Possessive	Noun
e.g.	*Je*	*joue*	*mieux*	*au volley*	*que*	*notre*	*père*
a.		joues		au tennis		ma	
b.	Ils		moins bien		que		
c.				aux cartes			père
d.		joue		au basket			
e.	Mes parents		mieux			mes	
f.		joue	moins bien	aux cartes	que		
g.	Vous					ma	sœur
h.	Ils		moins bien		que		
i.		joue	moins bien	au foot			cousin

THE LANGUAGE GYM

5. Guided translation

a. *I play tennis better than my brother. I play it often.* J__ j_____ m_____ a__ t_____ q____
m___ f_____. J'___ j_____ s_____.

b. *We play cards worse than our grandfather. We play it rarely.* N_____ j_____ m____
b_____ a___ c_____ q____ n_____ g_____-p_____. N_____ y j_____ r_____.

c. *My parents play videogames worse than me. I play it every day.* M___ p_____ j_____
m_____ b_____ a____ j____ v_____ q____ m___. J'___ j_____ t____ l__ j____.

d. *My sister plays chess better than my father. She plays it often.* M____ s_____ j_____ m_____
a___ é_____ q___ m____ p_____. E____ y j_____ s_____.

e. *Do you play rugby better than her?* T___ j_____ m_____ a____ r_____ q____ e____?

6. Break the flow

a. Nousjouonsmieuxautennisqu'eux

b. Ilsjouentmieuxaurugbyquemesparents

c. Monfrèrejouemieuxauxjeuxvidéoquemoi

d. Mesamisjouentmoinsbienauxcartesquetoi

e. Masœurjouemieuxauxéchecsquemonpère

f. Mongrandpèrejouemieuxaurugbyquemonpère

g. Ellejouemieuxauvolleyquenous

h. Nousjouonsmieuxaurugbyquelui

i. Monfrèrejouemieuxauxjeuxenlignequemoi

7. Choose the correct word

a. Nous **jouons/jouent/joue** mieux aux cartes qu'eux

b. Je **joues/joue/jouent** mieux au billard qu'elle

c. Mes amis et moi **joues/jouons/jouent** mieux au foot que toi

d. Elle **jouons/joues/joue** mieux au tennis que moi

e. Mon grand-père **joue/jouez/joues** au billard

f. Mes oncles **joue/jouent/jouez** au rugby

g. Mon ami **joue/jouent/jouez** mieux au basket que moi

8. Translate into English

a. Ma mère joue mieux au foot que mon père

b. Mon frère joue mieux aux jeux vidéo que moi

c. Nous jouons mieux au foot qu'eux

d. Ma mère ne joue pas au basket

e. Elle joue mieux au volley que ses parents

f. Notre frère cadet joue mieux au foot que moi

g. Ma sœur joue mieux aux échecs que mon frère

h. Je joue moins bien aux cartes que mes amies

9. Translate into French

a. My sister plays football better than me

b. I play cards worse than my father

c. My grandparents play pool better than my parents

d. My sister plays online games better than us

e. I play chess worse than my grandfather

f. Do you play chess better than him?

g. My sister plays basketball better than her.

h. My parents play on the PlayStation better than me

THE LANGUAGE GYM

6.4 PRESENT OF JOUER + NOUN + À LA/AU/ AUX/ DE LA/DE L'/DU/ + NOUN + TIME MARKER *(SAYING WHAT INSTRUMENT AND GAMES ONE PLAYS)*

		de la basse	the bass		
		de la batterie	the drums		
		de la flûte	the recorder	de temps en temps	
Je joue	I play	de la guitare		*from time to time*	
Tu joues	You play	de la trompette		rarement	
Il/Elle joue	He/She plays	de l'orgue	the organ	*rarely*	
On joue	We play	du saxophone	the saxophone	souvent	
Nous jouons	We play	du violon		*often*	
Vous jouez	You guys/girls play	du violoncelle	the cello	tous les jours	
Ils/Elles jouent	They play			*every day*	
		à la PlayStation		une fois par semaine	
		au basket		*once a week*	
		au foot		deux fois par semaine	
		au rugby		*twice a week*	
		au tennis			
		aux cartes *cards*			
		aux jeux en ligne *online games*			
		aux jeux vidéo *video games*			

USING ADVERBS – *BIEN / MAL*

Je joue **bien** de la guitare	*I play the guitar well*	Je joue **mal** au foot	*I play football badly*

The adverbs ***bien*** (well) and ***mal*** (badly) go **after the verb**.

Je joue bien de la guitare   *I play the guitar well*

In French these adverbs are placed directly after the verb *(je joue bien)*, but in English it can **only** go after the noun.

LANGUAGE AWARENESS: *JOUER DE VS JOUER À*

In Fench, *jouer* means to play and can be used with games, sports or instruments.

If we are talking about playing a <u>sport</u> or a <u>game</u>, we use ***jouer à*** + **article**

• **Je joue <u>au</u> foot**   *I play football*

If we are talking about playing <u>music</u> or a <u>musical instrument</u>, we must use ***jouer de*** + **article**

• **Je joue <u>du</u> violon**   *I play the violin*

1. Match up

Je joue de la guitare	*I play tennis*
Je joue aux échecs	*I play online games*
Je joue au tennis	*I play the drums*
Je joue aux cartes	*I play the saxophone*
Je joue de la batterie	*I play the guitar*
Je joue au basket	*I play the piano*
Je joue aux jeux en ligne	*I play basketball*
Je joue du piano	*I play chess*
Je joue du saxophone	*I play the recorder*
Je joue de la flûte	*I play cards*

2. Faulty translation: fix the English translation

a. Nous jouons de la guitare — *They play the guitar*

b. De quel instrument joues-tu? — *What instrument do I play?*

c. Il joue bien aux échecs — *We play chess badly*

d. Ils jouent bien de la batterie — *He plays the piano very well*

e. Il ne joue jamais de la basse — *He never plays the recorder*

f. On joue très bien au foot — *I play football very well*

g. Ils jouent très mal au tennis — *He plays football very badly*

h. Tu joues du saxophone? — *Do we play the saxophone?*

i. Vous jouez souvent au basket — *We often play basketball*

j. Il ne joue ni du violon ni du violoncelle
   I neither play the saxophone nor the recorder

3. Listen and complete the words

a. On j__ __ __ de la guitare

b. Elle j__ __ __ du piano

c. Tu j__ __ __ __ du violon

d. Elles jou__ __ __ de la flûte

e. Ils jou__ __ __ du saxophone?

f. De quel instrument jou__ __ -tu?

g. Je j__ __ __ de la trompette

h. Nous jou__ __ __ de l'orgue

i. Elles jou__ __ __ du violoncelle

j. Vous jou__ __ de la batterie

4. Guided translation

a. *We play the guitar very well*
N_____ j_____ t_____ b_____ d__ l_ g_____

b. *They play football badly*
I___ j_____ m_____ a__ f_____

c. *I don't play the piano*
J___ n___ j_____ p____ d___ p_____

d. *They play the trumpet badly*
I___ j_____ m_____ d__ l__ t_____

e. *We play videogames*
O___ j_____ a___ j_____ v_____

f. *I don't play the drums well*
J___ n___ j_____ p____ b_____ d___ l__ b_____

g. *You always play on the PlayStation*
T__ j_____ t_____ à l____ P_____

h. *I never play the bass*
J___ n___ j_____ j_____ d__ l__ b_____

5. Tangled translation: translate into French

a. *I play* très *badly* de la trompette

b. *We play very* mal du piano

c. *They play* très *well* de la batterie

d. *I* ne *play* jamais de *the* basse

e. *My* frère *plays very badly* du violoncelle

f. *My* parents ne *play* pas d'*instruments* musicaux

g. De quel *instrument do you guys play*?

h. *Do you play* du violon?

6. Translate into French

a. We play the guitar very well

b. I never play the piano

c. We play football and play the saxophone

d. I play the trumpet and I play online games

e. She plays videogames and the drums

f. My father plays the violin very well

g. What instrument do you guys play?

h. My sister plays the bass and the guitar well

6.5 TIME MARKER + ALLER + JOUER + GAMES/INSTRUMENT + PLACE
(SAYING WHAT ONE IS GOING TO PLAY AND WHERE)

Ce matin *This morning*	**je vais** *I am going*		**de la basse** *the bass* **de la batterie** *the drums* **de la flûte** *the recorder*		**au** *at*	**collège** *school* **stade** *the stadium* **parc** *the park* **centre sportif** *sports centre*
Ce soir *This evening*	**tu vas** *you are going*		**de la guitare** **de la trompette** **de l'orgue** *the organ*		**à l'** *in*	**église** *church*
Cet après-midi *This afternoon*	**il/elle va** *he/she is going* **on va** *we are going*	**jouer** *to play*	**du saxophone** *the saxophone* **du violon** **du violoncelle** *the cello*		**à la** *in/on* *the*	**bibliothèque** *library* **plage** *beach*
La semaine prochaine *Next week*	**nous allons** *we are going*		**à la PlayStation** **au basket** **au foot** **au rugby** **au tennis** **aux cartes** **aux jeux en ligne** **aux jeux vidéo**		**dans** *in*	**la chambre** *the bedroom* **la salle de musique** *the music room* **le jardin** *the garden*
Pendant les prochaines vacances *During the next holidays*	**vous allez** *you guys/girls are going* **ils/elles vont** *they are going*					

LANGUAGE AWARENESS: IMMEDIATE FUTURE

The immediate future tense is used to talk about what is going to happen in the near future.

Ce soir, je vais jouer de la batterie   *This evening, I am going to play the drums*

To form it, you need a **Subject Pronoun + Aller in the Present Tense + any Infinitives**

La semaine prochaine,	**tu** (subject pronoun)	**vas** (aller)	**jouer** (infinitive)	**au rugby**
Next week,	*you*	*are going*	*to play*	*rugby*

Cet après-midi,	**elle** (subject pronoun)	**va** (aller)	**jouer** (infinitive)	**du piano**
This afternoon,	*she*	*is going*	*to play*	*the piano*

1. Match

Je vais jouer au foot	*This morning*
Nous allons jouer au tennis	*At school*
Vous allez jouer du piano	*This afternoon*
Ils vont jouer de la guitare	*In the bedroom*
Ce matin	*You guys are going to play the piano*
Je vais jouer du violoncelle	*She is going to play online games*
Cet après-midi	*I am going to play football*
La semaine prochaine	*This evening*
Au collège	*They are going to play the guitar*
Elle va jouer aux jeux en ligne	*Next week*
Ce soir	*We are going to play tennis*
Dans la chambre	*I am going to play the cello*

2. Listen and complete

a. _____ jouer au foot au parc.

b. _____ jouer du violon au collège.

c. _____ jouer de l'orgue à l'église.

d. _____ jouer aux cartes à la plage.

e. _____ jouer aux jeux en ligne à la bibliothèque.

f. _____ jouer de la trompette dans la salle de musique.

g. _____ jouer du saxophone dans le jardin.

h. _____ jouer à la PlayStation avec son frère dans la chambre.

i. _____ jouer de la flûte avec ses amies au parc.

j. _____ jouer de la basse avec ton père dans le garage.

3. Faulty translation: fix the English translation

a. Ce matin, je vais jouer de la guitare avec mon frère. J'en joue tous les jours.

This afternoon I am going to play the cello with my brother. I play it once a week.

b. Pendant les prochaines vacances, je vais jouer au tennis. J'aime ça parce que c'est amusant.

During the next holidays, he is going to play tennis. I don't like that because it is boring.

c. Pendant mon temps libre je vais jouer du piano et aux jeux vidéo. Cependant, c'est un peu barbant.

In our free time we play the piano and videogames. However, it's really boring.

d. Ce soir, mon papa va jouer au tennis avec ma maman parce qu'ils aiment souvent faire du sport.

This afternoon, my dad is going to play football with his mum because they always like to do sports.

e. Et toi, tu joues de quel instrument pendant ton temps libre?

And you guys? Do you guys play an instrument in your spare time?

 **THE LANGUAGE GYM**

4. Break the flow

a. Pendantmontempslibrejevaisjoueraurugbyavecmesamisaustade.J'yjouetrèssouvent.

b. Pendantlesprochainesvacancesmonfrèrevajoueurauxcartesavecmamère.Ilaimejoueravecelle.

c. Cematinmesgrandsparentsvontjouerdupianoàl'église.Ilsaimentçaparcequec'estrelaxant.

d. Cetaprèsmidimesamisvontjoueraufootaucollège.Ilsyjouenttoujourspendantlesvacances.

e. MonamivajoueràlaPlayStationdanssachambreparcequ'iladoreça.

f. Cesoirjevaisjouerdusaxophoneavecmonamieàlaplageparcequej'aimejoueravecelle.

g. Aujourd'huimamèrevajouerduviolondanslejardinavecsonpèreparcequ'elleaimejoueraveclui.

5. Choose the correct word, then listen and check

a. Mon frère **joue/jouons/jouez** au foot au stade.

b. Pendant mon temps libre, je vais aller à la **centre sportif/église/plage**.

c. Mes parents vont **jouons/jouer/jouent** du piano parce que c'est relaxant.

d. Mes amis vont aller au **centre sportif/église/plage** pour faire de la musculation.

e. Pendant son temps libre, mon grand-père va jouer **à/aux/à la** cartes. Il y joue à la bibliothèque.

f. Ce matin, je vais jouer **du/de la/des** violon dans la salle de musique avec mon ami.

6. Staircase translation – Translate each sentence from memory

a.	My father	plays the piano			
b.	Our parents	go to the swimming pool	and they play tennis		
c.	In my free time	I play the piano and the recorder,	but my mother	does jogging	
d.	This morning	I am going	to play	the drums	with my sister
e.	In her free time	my mother	is going	to play cards	in the garden	with my grandad

a. _____

b. _____

c. _____

d. _____

e. _____

7. Guided translation

a. *My father plays the guitar and goes to the swimming pool. He loves going to the swimming pool.*

M_____ p_____ j_____ d__ l__ g_____ et v___ à l__ p_____. I__

a_____ a_____ à la p_____.

b. *My friends are going to play the piano this morning at the church. They like it because it is very fascinating.*

M_____ a_____ v_____ j_____ d__ p_____ c__ m_____ à l'_____. I__

a_____ ç__ p_____ q__ c'___ t___ f_____.

c. *My grandfather is going to play cards with my mother. He plays it at weekends. He also goes to the shopping centre.*

M___ g_____-p___ v__ j_____ a___ c_____ a____ m___ m_____. I__ y j____ l___

w_____-e_____. I__ v__ a_____ a__ c_____ c_____.

d. *In our free time we are going to play tennis with our uncle at the sports centre. We like to go there because it is fun.*

P_____ n_____ t_____ l_____, o___ v__ j_____ a__ t_____ a____ n_____

o_____ a__ c_____ s_____. O__ a_____ y a_____ p_____ q__ c'__ a_____.

8. Translate into English

a. Ma mère joue au basket, joue du piano et va à la piscine tous les week-ends. Elle aime faire ces choses (*things*).

b. Mes amis vont à la plage quand il fait beau parce qu'ils aiment faire de la natation. Cependant, ils ne jouent pas d'un instrument et ils ne font pas de boxe.

c. Mes parents vont faire de l'escalade et vont jouer au tennis pendant les prochaines vacances. Ils font beaucoup de sport parce qu'ils adorent ça.

d. Pendant notre temps libre, mes frères et moi allons jouer du violoncelle et aussi de la batterie. On adore jouer de la musique parce que c'est vraiment relaxant.

e. Mes cousins ne vont pas jouer aux cartes parce que c'est trop barbant.

9. Translate into French

a. In my free time I do climbing, I play the guitar and I go to the swimming pool in order to swim. I love doing these things (*ces choses*).

b. My brother is very sporty. He plays tennis and does boxing, but he doesn't play the drums. He doesn't like it.

c. My grandparents are going to play chess this weekend with my brother. My grandfather plays better than my brother. My grandfather loves playing chess.

d. My sister is going to play the piano. She plays it (*en joue*) every day, but she never does sport and she doesn't play football.

THE LANGUAGE GYM

ORAL PING PONG

JOUER

ENGLISH 1	FRENCH 1	ENGLISH 2	FRENCH 2
When I have time, I play chess with my father. We play it at weekends.	Quand j'ai le temps, je joue aux échecs avec mon père. On y joue le week-end.	I play basketball with my friends. We do it often at weekends.	
My friend plays handball with his cousins. They play it often in the sports centre.	Mon ami joue au handball avec ses cousins. Ils y jouent souvent au centre sportif.	My sister plays football with our cousins. They do it from time to time.	
On Fridays my grandparents play cards with my older brother in my home.	Le vendredi, mes grands-parents jouent aux cartes avec mon frère aîné chez moi.	My parents play tennis better than my brother and me.	
My sister plays tennis better than me, but I play videogames better than her.	Ma sœur joue mieux au tennis que moi, mais je joue mieux aux jeux vidéo qu'elle.	I play cards worse than my grandfather, but I play chess better than him.	
Do you play the violin? I play the drums, and I play tennis better than my father.	Tu joues du violon? Je joue de la batterie et je joue mieux au tennis que mon père.	I play the recorder better than my sister.	
My family and I play the guitar very well, but we never play it.	Ma famille et moi jouons très bien de la guitare, mais on n'en joue jamais.	My cousins like playing the cello. They play it (en) every day.	
In my free time I play basketball, I do rock climbing and I play the bass.	Pendant mon temps libre, je joue au basket, je fais de l'escalade et je joue de la basse.	My mum goes to the cinema, does martial arts and plays the sax because she likes it.	
My dad plays golf and goes to the swimming pool because he likes going swimming.	Mon papa joue au golf et va à la piscine parce qu'il aime faire de la natation.	Do you play the drums? I play the piano, but I don't like it.	

INSTRUCTIONS - You are **PARTNER A.** Work in pairs. Each of you has two sets of sentences - one set has already been translated for you. You will ask your partner to translate these. The other set of sentences have not been translated. Your partner will ask you to translate these.

HOW TO PLAY - Partner A starts by reading out his/her/their first sentence <u>in English</u>. Partner B must translate. Partner A must check the answer and award the following points: **3 points** = perfect, **2 points** = 1 mistake, **1 point** = mistakes but the verb is accurate. If they cannot translate correctly, Partner A will read out the sentence so that Partner B can learn what the correct translation is.

Then Partner B reads out his/her/their first sentence, and so on.

OBJECTIVE - Try to win more points than your partner by translating correctly as many sentences as possible.

ORAL PING PONG

JOUER

ENGLISH 1	FRENCH 1	ENGLISH 2	FRENCH 2
When I have time, I play chess with my father. We play it at weekends.		I play basketball with my friends. We play it often at weekends.	Je joue au basket avec mes amis. On y joue souvent le week-end.
My friend plays handball with his cousins. They play it often in the sports centre.		My sister plays football with our cousins. They play it from time to time.	Ma sœur joue au football avec nos cousins. Ils y jouent de temps en temps.
On Fridays my grandparents play cards with my older brother in my home.		My parents play tennis better than my brother and me.	Mes parents jouent mieux au tennis que mon frère et moi.
My sister plays tennis better than me, but I play videogames better than her.		I play cards worse than my father, but I play chess better than him.	Je joue aux cartes moins bien que mon père, mais je joue mieux aux échecs que lui.
Do you play the violin? I play the drums, and I play tennis better than my father.		I play the recorder better than my sister.	Je joue mieux de la flûte que ma sœur.
My family and I play the guitar very well, but we never play it.		My cousins like playing the cello. They play it (en) every day.	Mes cousins aiment jouer du violoncelle. Ils en jouent tous les jours.
In my free time I play basketball, I do rock climbing and I play the bass.		My mum goes to the cinema, does martial arts and plays the sax because she likes it.	Ma maman va au ciné, fait des arts martiaux et joue du saxophone parce qu'elle aime ça.
My dad plays golf and goes to the swimming pool because he likes going swimming.		Do you play the drums? I play the piano, but I don't like it.	Tu joues de la batterie? Je joue du piano, mais je n'aime pas ça.

INSTRUCTIONS - You are **PARTNER B.** Work in pairs. Each of you has two sets of sentences - one set has already been translated for you. You will ask your partner to translate these. The other set of sentences have not been translated. Your partner will ask you to translate these.

HOW TO PLAY - Partner A starts by reading out his/her/their first sentence <u>in English</u>. Partner B must translate. Partner A must check the answer and award the following points: **3 points** = perfect, **2 points** = 1 mistake, **1 point** = mistakes but the verb is accurate. If they cannot translate correctly, Partner A will read out the sentence so that Partner B can learn what the correct translation is.
Then Partner B reads out his/her/their first sentence, and so on.

OBJECTIVE - Try to win more points than your partner by translating correctly as many sentences as possible.

THE LANGUAGE GYM

No Snakes No Ladders

DÉPART

1. At the weekends, I play the piano
2. On Fridays, I play cards with my friends
3. My cousins play the recorder
4. I play the guitar very well
5. When I have time I play it
6. My dad plays the violin. He likes it
7. We play tennis with my cousin (f)
8. I play the guitar better than you
9. Do you like to play football?
10. My brothers like to do weights
11. We play the bass and go to the cinema
12. I do hiking and I love it
13. Do you play often the sax?
14. In my free time, I do cycling
15. My sister plays tennis better than my mother
16. My parents do yoga
17. My granddad plays cards
18. Do you guys play the guitar?
19. My father does boxing on Tuesdays
20. You play football rarely
21. I play often cards. with my father
22. Do you like to go to the swimming pool?
23. I like to do sports on Saturdays
24. My mother likes to play chess with me
25. We do not play basketball, it is hard
26. I play chess and videogames
27. My sister plays the piano on Tuesdays
28. My mother does yoga with my sisters
29. You play basketball. You play it often
30. My aunt plays the violin

ARRIVÉE

THE LANGUAGE GYM

JOUER

No Snakes No Ladders

7 On joue au tennis avec ma cousine	**6** Mon papa joue du violon. Il aime ça.	**5** Quand j'ai le temps j'y joue	**4** Je joue très bien de la guitare,	**3** Mes cousins jouent de la flûte	**2** Le vendredi je joue aux cartes avec mes ami(e)s
8 Je joue mieux de la guitare que toi	**9** Tu aimes jouer au foot?	**10** Mes frères aiment faire de la musculation	**11** Nous jouons de la basse et nous allons au ciné	**12** Je fais des randonnées et j'adore ça	**13** Tu joues du saxophone souvent?
23 J'aime faire du sport le samedi	**22** Tu aimes aller à la piscine?	**21** Je joue souvent aux cartes avec mon père	**20** Tu joues au foot rarement	**19** Mon père fait de la boxe le mardi	**18** Vous jouez de la guitare?
24 Ma mère aime jouer aux échecs avec moi	**25** Nous ne jouons pas au basket, c'est dur	**26** Je joue aux échecs et aux jeux vidéo	**27** Ma sœur joue du piano le mardi	**28** Ma mère fait du yoga avec mes sœurs	**29** Tu joues au basket. Tu y joues souvent

1 Le week-end, je joue du piano	DÉPART
14 Pendant mon temps libre, je fais du vélo	**15** Ma sœur joue mieux au tennis que ma mère
17 Mon grand-père joue aux cartes	**16** Mes parents font du yoga
30 Ma tante joue du violon	ARRIVÉE

THE LANGUAGE GYM

189

PYRAMID TRANSLATION

JOUER

Translate each part of the pyramid out loud with your partner, then write it into the spaces provided below.

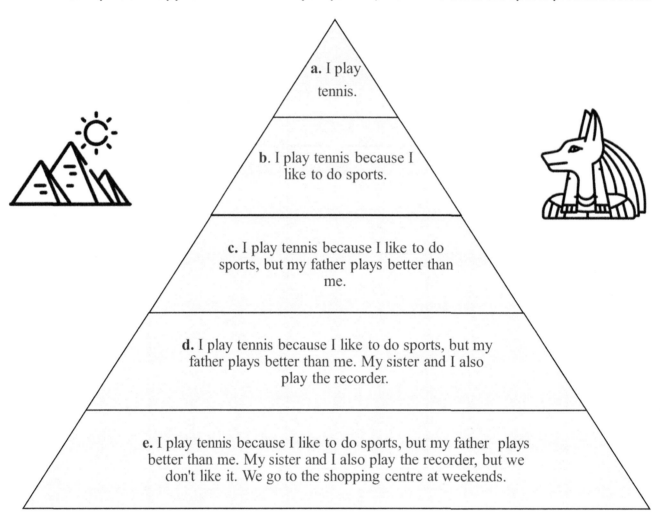

a. I play tennis.

b. I play tennis because I like to do sports.

c. I play tennis because I like to do sports, but my father plays better than me.

d. I play tennis because I like to do sports, but my father plays better than me. My sister and I also play the recorder.

e. I play tennis because I like to do sports, but my father plays better than me. My sister and I also play the recorder, but we don't like it. We go to the shopping centre at weekends.

Write your translation here

 **THE LANGUAGE GYM**

UNIT 7 – METTRE

Je	mets
Tu	mets
Il / Elle / On	met
Nous	mettons
Vous	mettez
Ils / Elles	mettent

WEARING CLOTHES

Qu'est-ce que tu mets aujourd'hui?

Aujourd'hui, je mets un pull.

PLACES & CLOTHES

Pour aller à la plage, je mets un maillot de bain.

OPINIONS

J'adore ton maillot de bain: il est joli!

7.1 TIME MARKER + JE METS + NOUN + COLOURS
(SAYING WHAT I PUT ON AND WHEN/HOW OFTEN)

Quand je sors *When I go out* **De temps en temps** *From time to time* **Le week-end** *At the weekend* **Tous les jours** *Every day* **Une fois par semaine** *Once a week*	**je mets** *I put on* **tu mets** *you put on*	**parfois** *sometimes* **souvent** *often* **toujours** *always*	**un blouson** *a jacket* **un jean** *jeans* **un pantalon** *trousers* **un pull** *a jumper*	**beige** *beige* **blanc** *white* **bleu** *blue* **bordeaux** *burgundy* **gris** *grey* **jaune** *yellow* **marron** *brown*	**noir** *black* **orange** *orange* **rose** *pink* **rouge** *red* **vert** *green* **violet** *purple*
			une chemise *a shirt* **une cravate** *a tie* **une jupe** *a skirt* **une robe** *a dress* **une veste** *a jacket*	beige blanche bleue bordeaux grise jaune marron	noire orange rose rouge verte violette
			des collants *tights*	beiges blancs bleus bordeaux gris jaunes marron	noirs orange roses rouges verts violets
			des baskets *trainers* **des chaussettes** *socks* **des chaussures** *shoes*	beiges blanches bleues bordeaux grises jaunes marron	noires orange roses rouges vertes violettes

LANGUAGE AWARENESS

ADJECTIVAL AGREEMENTS OF COLOURS (PART 1)

In French, the adjectives of colours agree with the noun they describe in **gender** (masculine/feminine) and **numbers** (singular/plural).

Je mets **un** pull **bleu**   *I put on a blue jumper*   Je mets **une** jupe **bleue**   *I put on a blue skirt*

Some adjectives are invariable, i.e., they don't change their spelling (bordeaux, marron, orange)

Je mets **un** pull **marron** *I put on a brown jumper*   Je mets **une** jupe **marron**   *I put on a brown skirt*

 **THE LANGUAGE GYM**

192

1. Match

Je mets un blouson beige	I put on socks
Je mets une jupe rose	I put on a purple dress
Je mets des chaussettes	I put on a grey jumper
Je mets un pull gris	I put on black jeans
Je mets des collants jaunes	I put on a green jacket
Je mets une robe violette	I put on a beige jacket
Je mets une veste verte	I put on blue shoes
Je mets un jean noir	I put on yellow tights
Je mets des chaussures bleues	I put on a pink skirt

2. Broken words

a. Je mets un panta__ __ __ rouge

b. Je mets des bas__ __ __ __ grises

c. Je mets un pull vio__ __ __

d. Tu mets des chauss__ __ __ __ __ ?

e. Je m__ __ __ des chaussures

f. Je mets une ro__ __ blan__ __ __

g. Tu mets une ju__ __ mar__ __ __ ?

h. Je mets des col__ __ __ __ __ gr__ __

i. Je mets un jean b__ __ __ __ __ __ __

3. Listen and complete 🔊

a. Je mets souvent un _____ bleu

b. De temps en _____ je mets une _____ rose

c. Quand je sors, je _____ une _____ jaune

d. Je mets toujours des chaussures _____

e. Le week-end, je mets _____ pantalon _____

f. Une fois par _____, je mets des _____ orange

4. Complete with a suitable word, then listen and note down the differences 🔊

a. Je mets parfois un _____ bleu

b. De temps en temps je mets des _____ grises

c. Quand je sors, je mets une _____ blanche

d. Je mets souvent des chaussettes _____

e. Le week-end, tu mets un _____ rose?

f. Une fois par mois, je mets des _____ noirs

g. Je mets une _____ violette

5. Anagrams

a. neu aaetcvr	*a tie*		g. gibee	*beige*
b. sde lltoancs	*tights*		h. inor	*black*
c. eJ stem	*I put on*		i. acbln	*blanc*
d. ed mptes ne mptes	*from time to time*		j. reboadxu	*burgundy*
e. nu ubonlos	*a jacket*		k. rspifao	*sometimes*
f. neu boer	*a dress*		l. sde cshseatstue	*socks*

6. Sentence Puzzle

a. bleue Je une toujours mets jupe — *I always put on a blue skirt*

b. noir Je rose parfois un mets pantalon et — *I sometimes put on pink and black trousers*

c. des De en temps vertes chaussures temps je mets — *From time to time I put on green shoes*

d. fois Une par pull je mets semaine un marron — *Once a week I put on a brown jumper*

e. mets Quand sors cravate je je une orange — *When I go out I put on an orange tie*

f. blanche? veste une souvent mets Tu — *Do you often put on a white jacket?*

g. jaunes Le chaussettes week-end mets je des — *At the weekend I put on yellow socks*

7. Break the flow

a. Jemetssouventunpullbeige

b. Jemetsparfoisunechemiseblanche

c. Jemetstoujoursdescollantsblancs

d. Quandjesorsjemetsdesbasketsgrises

e. Leweekendjemetsunpantalonnoir

f. Touslesjoursjemetsunerobegrise

g. Detempsentempsjemetsunecravate

h. Unefoisparsemainejemetsunjean

8. Gapped translation: complete the translation

a. Je mets un _____ bleu — *I put on a blue jumper*

b. Je mets une _____ rose — *I put on a pink skirt*

c. Je mets des _____ noires — *I put on black shoes*

d. Je mets une _____ blanche — *I put on a white shirt*

e. Je mets un _____ gris — *I put on a grey jacket*

f. Je mets des _____ vertes — *I put on green trainers*

g. Je mets des _____ orange — *I put on orange socks*

h. Je mets une _____ violette — *I put on a purple dress*

9. Spot and correct the errors

a. Quand je sors, je mets une cravatte verte.

b. Je mets toujours une veste marrone.

c. Tu mets parfois des chaussures noir?

d. De temps en temps je met des chaussettes blancs.

e. Une fois par semaine, je mets des chausures gris.

f. Le week-end, je mets des collants griss.

g. Tous les jours, je mets un robe rouge.

h. Je souvent mets un jean bleue.

10. Listen and translate into French

a. I put on a green skirt

b. I put on a blue dress

c. I put on brown trousers

d. I put on purple tights

e. I put on a pink shirt

f. I put on grey shoes

g. I put on a burgundy jumper

THE LANGUAGE GYM

11. Complete with the words in the box

a. Je mets souvent un _____ noir et une chemise blanche.

b. Quand je sors le samedi, je mets parfois _____ cravate orange.

c. Le week-end, je _____ toujours une jupe violette et blanche.

d. De temps en temps, je mets des _____ rouges avec des chaussures bordeaux.

e. Tous les jours, je mets une robe grise _____ une veste rose.

f. Je mets un blouson marron une _____ par semaine.

g. Quand je sors avec mes amis, je mets un jean _____ avec un pull jaune.

h. Je mets souvent une _____ orange et jaune.

i. Je mets parfois des baskets _____.

j. De temps en _____, je mets une veste beige.

mets	grises	avec	une	cravate
fois	pantalon	temps	bleu	chaussettes

12. Complete the translation

a. *A blue shirt*

U__ __ c__ __ __ __ __ __ b__ __ __ __

b. *Brown jeans*

U__ j__ __ __ m__ __ __ __ __

c. *Black trainers*

D__ __ b__ __ __ __ __ __ n__ __ __ __ __

d. *A grey jacket*

U__ __ v__ __ __ __ __ g__ __ __ __

e. *Green tights*

D__ __ c__ __ __ __ __ __ __ v__ __ __ __

f. *Pink shoes*

D__ __ c__ __ __ __ __ __ __ __ __

r__ __ __ __

g. *White socks*

D__ __ c__ __ __ __ __ __ __ __ __ __

b__ __ __ __ __ __ __

13. Tangled translation: translate into French

a. Je **put on** des chaussettes orange **every day**

b. Je **often** un pantalon **grey** avec une veste

c. **I** mets parfois des **tights** beiges **with** une jupe

d. De temps en temps, je mets une **dress purple**

e. **Once a week**, je mets un pull **grey** et **black**

f. Le week-end, **I put on** des baskets bordeaux

g. Quand je sors, je mets un **jacket brown**

14. Translate into French

a. I put on a dress

b. I put on a white shirt

c. Do you often put on a burgundy jacket?

d. I sometimes put on a black dress

e. I always put on red shoes when I go out

f. Once a week I put on a purple skirt

g. At the weekend I put on brown trousers with a yellow shirt

h. Every day I put on green socks with trainers

7.2 TIME MARKER + JE METS + CLOTHES + COLOURS + OPINIONS + REASONS
(SAYING WHAT I LIKE TO PUT ON)

Quand je sors *When I go out* **De temps en temps** *From time to time* **Le week-end** *At the weekend* **Tous les jours** *Every day* **Une fois par semaine** *Once a week*	**je mets** *I put on* **tu mets** *you put on*	**parfois** *sometimes* **souvent** *often* **toujours** *always*	**un blouson** *a jacket* **un jean** *jeans* **un pantalon** *trousers* **un pull** *a jumper* **une chemise** *a shirt* **une cravate** *a tie* **une jupe** *a skirt* **une robe** *a dress* **une veste** *a jacket* **des collants** *tights* **des baskets** *trainers* **des chaussettes** *socks* **des chaussures** *shoes*	**blanc cassé** *off-white* **bleu marine** *navy blue* **bleu vif** *bright blue* **jaune pâle** *pale yellow* **vert clair** *light green* **vert foncé** *dark green*

J'adore ça *I love it* **J'aime beaucoup ça** *I like it a lot* **J'aime ça** *I like it* **Je n'aime pas ça** *I don't like it* **Je n'aime pas du tout ça** *I don't like it at all*	**parce que c'est** *because it is* **parce que ce n'est pas** *because it is not*	**à la mode** *fashionable* **chic** *smart* **confortable** *comfortable* **démodé** *unfashionable*	**joli** *pretty* **moche** *ugly* **pratique** *practical*

1. Match

Je mets un pull vert clair	I put on bright blue trainers
Je mets une jupe blanc cassé	I put on pale yellow trousers
Je mets des baskets bleu vif	I put on a light green jumper
Je mets des chaussettes bleu marine	I put on a dark red shirt
Je mets un pantalon jaune pâle	I put on navy blue socks
Je mets une chemise rouge foncé	I put on an off-white skirt

2. Unjumble the colours

a. Je mets un blouson *ubel crali*

b. Je mets une robe *rsoe ocnfé*

c. Je mets des collants *etvr calri*

d. Je mets des baskets *clabn écsas*

e. Je mets un pantalon *lbue nfoéc*

f. Je mets une cravate *evrt aclri*

g. Tu mets un jean *lebu rmanie?*

h. Je mets des chaussures *rgis fnoéc*

i. Je mets une veste *ajuen eplâ*

3. Listen: write the missing word 🔊

a. Quand je sors, je mets une robe _____ _____

b. Je mets souvent un _____ bleu marine

c. Tu mets un pull _____ _____ ?

d. Tu mets parfois des _____ jaune _____

e. Tous les jours, je _____ une chemise _____ ____

f. Le week-end, je mets des baskets _____ _____

g. De temps en temps, je mets un jean _____ _____

h. Une fois par semaine, je mets des _____ vert foncé avec des chaussures _____ _____

4. Choose the correct adjective

a. J'adore ça parce que c'est *moche / à la mode*

b. J'aime beaucoup ça parce que c'est *chic / démodé*

c. Je n'aime pas ça parce que c'est *chic / démodé*

d. Je n'aime pas du tout ça parce que *ce n'est pas pratique / c'est joli*

e. J'aime ça mais ce n'est pas *moche / pratique*

f. J'adore ça mais c'est *démodé / chic*

5. Faulty translation: fix the English translation

a. De temps en temps, je mets une robe rose avec une veste blanc cassé.

From time to time I put on a red dress with a white jacket.

b. J'adore ça parce que c'est à la mode et c'est chic.

I like it because it is fashionable and it is practical.

c. Tu mets parfois un jean bleu marine avec un pull vert foncé.

You always wear blue jeans with a light green jumper.

d. Je n'aime pas du tout ça parce que ce n'est pas joli. C'est vraiment moche !

I don't like it at all because it is pretty. It is really smart!

e. Je mets souvent des chaussures rouges. J'aime beaucoup ça parce que ce n'est pas démodé.

I often put on red socks. I like it a lot because it is not ugly.

 **THE LANGUAGE GYM**

6. Break the flow

a. Touslesjoursjemetsunpullbleuclair

b. J'adoreçaparcequec'estjoli

c. Jcmetssouventdescollantsverts

d. J'aimeçaparcequec'estàlamode

e. Jemetsparfoisunpantalongrisfoncé

f. Jen'aimepasçaparcequec'estmoche

g. Jemetsunejuperoseetunechemise

h. J'aimebeaucoupça:c'esttrèschic

7. Gapped translation: complete the translation

a. Quand je _____, je mets un pantalon _____ foncé

When I go out, I put on dark burgundy trousers

b. J'_____ ça parce que ____ vraiment pratique et joli

I love it because it is really practical and pretty

c. Tu mets _____ des chaussures bleu _____?

Do you sometimes put on navy blue shoes?

d. Le week-end, je mets des baskets _____. J'adore ___!

At the weekend, I put on green trainers. I love it!

8. Listen, complete and translate

a. Une fois par semaine, je mets …

b. J'aime ça parce que c'est … et …

c. Quand je sors, je mets souvent …

d. J'adore ça parce que c'est vraiment …

e. Je mets parfois … pour aller au ciné

f. Mais c'est un peu … et ce n'est pas …

g. Tu mets … pour aller au collège?

h. Je déteste ça parce que c'est …

9. Spot and correct the mistakes

a. De temps en temps, je mets une robe blanc

b. J'adore ca parce que cest jolie et pratique

c. Je met parfois des chaussures rouges foncées

d. J'aime beaucoup ça parce que c'est a la mode et shic

e. Tu mets souvent des baskets vertes claires?

f. Tous les jours, je mets un pantaloon noire mais je n'aime pas ça parce que c'est demode

g. Tu mets parfois des collants griss?

10. Tangled translation: translate into French

a. Le week-end, je ***put on*** une robe ***off-white***

b. J'aime ***a lot*** ça parce que c'est très ***smart***

c. Tu mets ***often*** des chaussures ***white***?

d. De temps en temps, je mets une ***jacket*** grise

e. ***I like*** ça parce que c'est assez joli et ***fashionable***

f. Je mets ***always*** un pull jaune ***pale***

g. J'adore ça ***because*** c'est élégant et ***practical***

h. ***Do you put on*** des baskets ***black*** le week-end?

i. Je déteste ***it*** parce que ***it is*** vraiment démodé

j. Je mets une ***tie*** bleu ***navy*** tous les jours

11. Translate into French

a. When I go out, I put on a pale yellow dress and a white skirt. I love it because it is smart.

b. Once a week, I put on navy blue trousers and a light blue shirt. I like it a lot because it is pretty.

c. You often put on grey shoes but I don't like it because it is not fashionable.

d. Do you put on light green tights?

e. At the weekend, you sometimes put on red socks with black shoes but I don't like it because it is ugly and unfashionable.

7.3 QUAND + WEATHER + METTRE + CLOTHES + OPINION + REASONS
(SAYING WHAT ONE WEARS DEPENDING ON THE WEATHER)

Quand il fait beau *When it is nice weather* **Quand il fait chaud** *When it is hot* **Quand il fait frais** *When it is cool* **Quand il fait froid** *When it is cold* **Quand il fait humide** *When it is humid* **Quand il fait lourd** *When it is muggy* **Quand il fait mauvais** *When it is bad weather* **Quand il y a de l'orage** *When it is thundery* **Quand il y a des nuages** *When it is cloudy* **Quand il y a du brouillard** *When it is foggy* **Quand il y a du soleil** *When it is sunny* **Quand il y a du vent** *When it is windy* **Quand il gèle** *When it is freezing* **Quand il neige** *When it snows* **Quand il pleut** *When it rains* **Quand il pleut à verse** *When it pours down*	**je mets** *I put on* **tu mets** *you put on* **il/elle met** *he/she puts on* **on met** *we put on* **nous mettons** *we put on* **vous mettez** *you guys/girls put on* **ils/elles mettent** *they put on*	**un blouson** *a jacket* **un bonnet** *a woolly hat* **un imperméable** *a raincoat* **un maillot de bain** *a swimming suit* **un manteau** *a coat* **un pantalon** *trousers* **un pull** *a jumper* **un short** *shorts* **un tee-shirt** *a T-shirt*	**blanc cassé** *off-white* **bleu marine** *navy blue* **bleu vif** *bright blue*
		une casquette *a cap* **une écharpe** *a scarf* **une jupe** *a skirt* **une polaire** *a fleece* **une veste** *a jacket*	**jaune pâle** *pale yellow* **vert clair** *light green* **vert foncé** *dark green*
		des collants *tights*	
		des baskets **des chaussettes** **des chaussures** **des lunettes de soleil** *sunglasses*	

J'adore ça *I love it* **J'aime beaucoup ça** *I like it a lot* **J'aime ça** *I like it* **Je n'aime pas ça** *I don't like it* **Je n'aime pas du tout ça** *I don't like it at all*	**parce que c'est** *because it is* **parce que ce n'est** **pas** *because it is not*	**chaud** *warm* **chic** *smart* **confortable** *comfortable* **décontracté** *casual*	**joli** *pretty* **large** *large* **léger** *light* **pratique** *practical* **serré** *tight*

THE LANGUAGE GYM

1. Choose the correct option

a. Quand il fait froid, je **met/mets/mettons** un manteau

b. Quand il fait chaud, ils **mettez/met/mettent** un pull

c. Quand il neige, elle **met/mets/mettent** un bonnet

d. Quand il fait lourd, ils **met/mettent/mettez** un short

e. Qu'est-ce que tu **met/mets/mettez** quand il y a du vent?

f. Quand il pleut, vous **mettez/met/mets** un imperméable

g. Mes parents **met/mettent/mettez** un pull quand il fait frais

2. Complete

a. Je m__ __ __ __ une écharpe

b. Elle m__ __ des lunettes de soleil

c. Nous mett__ __ __ une casquette

d. Il m__ __ un maillot de bain

e. Elles mett__ __ __ une polaire

f. Tu m__ __ __ un tee-shirt

g. Vous mett__ __ un manteau

h. Mes amis mett__ __ __ un pull

3. Faulty translation: fix the English translation

a. Quand il fait frais, je mets un pull — *When it is warm, I put on a jumper*

b. Quand il fait mauvais, je mets un manteau — *When it is bad weather, I put on a hat*

c. Quand il gèle, mon père met un bonnet — *When it snows, my father put on a scarf*

d. Quand il pleut, mes amis mettent un imperméable — *When it rains, my friends put on a coat*

e. Quand il y a du soleil, ma mère met une casquette — *When it is hot, my mother puts on sunglasses*

f. Quand il y a du vent, je mets un pantalon — *When it is cold, I put on trousers*

g. Quand il fait chaud, tes frères mettent un short — *When it is muggy, your brothers put on shorts*

h. Quand il y a du brouillard, nous mettons un pull — *When it is windy, we put on a jumper*

4. Broken translation

a. *When it is sunny* — Qu__ __ __ il y a d__ so__ __ __ __

b. *I put on a light pink skirt* — je m__ __ __ u__ __ ju__ __ ro__ __ cl__ __ __

c. *I love it because it is fashionable* — J'ado__ __ ç__ parce que c'__ __ __ à la m__ __ __

d. *When it is thundery* — Qu__ __ __ i__ y a de l'ora__ __ __

e. *My mother puts on a raincoat* — m__ mè__ __ m__ __ un imper__ __ __ __ __ __

f. *I don't like it because it is not smart* — Je n'ai__ __ pas ça parce q__ __ ce n'est pas c__ __ __

g. *When it is hot* — Q__ __ __ __ il f__ __ __ ch__ __ __

h. *my sister puts on shorts* — ma s__ __ __ __ __ m__ __ un s__ __ __ __

i. *I don't like it because it is tight* — J__ n'ai__ __ p__ __ ça parce que c'__ __ __ ser__ __

j. *Do you guys put on a fleece...* — V__ __ __ mett__ __ u__ __ po__ __ __ __ __ ...

k. *...when it is freezing?* — ... q__ __ __ __ il g__ __ __ ?

5. Match

Quand il fait mauvais	*When it is cool*
Quand il y a des nuages	*When it pours down*
Quand il gèle	*When it is thundery*
Quand il fait frais	*When it is bad weather*
Quand il y a du brouillard	*When it is muggy*
Quand il pleut à verse	*When it is freezing*
Quand il fait lourd	*When it is foggy*
Quand il y a de l'orage	*When it snows*
Quand il neige	*When it is cloudy*

6. Listen and complete 🔊

a. Quand il fait _____

b. je mets une robe _____ _____

c. J'aime ça parce que c'est _____

d. Quand il y a _____ _____

e. mon frère met un _____ noir

f. Je déteste ça parce que c'est _____

g. Quand il _____

h. mes parents _____ un bonnet

i. J'aime ça parce que c'est _____

7. Sentence Puzzle

a. il verse pleut Quand à, mets jaune un je imperméable. ça pratique parce J'adore que c'est.

When it pours down, I put on a yellow raincoat. I love it because it is practical.

b. nuages Quand des il y a, pull grand-père mon un met. chaud Il ça parce que aime c'est.

When it is cloudy, my grandad puts on a jumper. He likes it because it is warm.

c. il Quand chaud fait, mère ma un met de maillot bain. aime Elle parce ça c'est que léger.

When it is hot, my mother puts on a swimming suit. She likes it because it is light.

d. mets Tu un quand fait manteau il froid?

Do you put on a coat when it is cold?

e. il Quand neige, mes mettent parents bonnet un et écharpe une mais n'est ce confortable pas.

When it snows, my parents put on a woolly hat and a scarf but it is not comfortable.

8. Tangled translation: translate into French

a. ***When*** il fait humide, je ***put on*** un short ***bright red***. J'adore ça parce que c'est ***casual***.

b. Quand il y a du ***foggy***, tu mets toujours un ***raincoat*** jaune pâle parce que ***it is*** léger.

c. Quand il ***freezing***, mon frère met ***often*** un bonnet ***because*** c'est vraiment ***warm***.

d. ***When it is muggy***, ma sœur met ***sometimes*** un short et un tee-shirt ***off-white***. Elle aime ça parce que ***it is not*** chaud et c'est ***comfortable***.

e. Quand il y a ***sunny***, je mets ***sunglasses***. J'aime ***a lot*** ça parce que c'est pratique et ***smart***.

f. Quand il ***rains***, mes grands-parents ***put on*** une casquette ***with a jacket***. Ils n'aiment pas ça parce que ce n'est pas ***practical*** et la veste est trop ***large***.

 **THE LANGUAGE GYM**

9. Listen and fill in each gap with the correct word

a. Quand il fait _____, je mets une _____ vert foncé parce que c'est _____ et très confortable.

b. Quand il y a du ____, mes frères et moi mettons un ____. Je n'aime pas ça parce que c'est trop serré!

c. Quand il _____, ma mère met un imperméable _____ _____ mais ce n'est pas très _____.

d. Quand il fait _____, je mets un pantalon et un blouson mais ce n'est pas très _____.

e. Quand il y a des nuages, ma grand-mère _____ une veste parce que c'est _____, _____ et _____.

f. Quand il neige, mon père met un _____, un manteau et une _____ parce que c'est vraiment chaud.

g. Quand il fait _____, je mets un short et un _____ parce que c'est léger et décontracté.

---

10. Guided translation

a. *I put on*   J__ m__ __ __

b. *We put on*   O__ m__ __

c. *A coat*   U__ m__ __ __ __ __ __

d. *A cap*   U__ __ c__ __ __ __ __ __ __

e. *Light green*   V__ __ __ c__ __ __ __

f. *Dark blue*   B__ __ __ f__ __ __ __

g. *Casual*   D__ __ __ __ __ __ __ __ __

h. *Too tight*   T__ __ __ s__ __ __ __

i. *Smart and pretty*   C__ __ __ e__ j__ __ __

---

11. Translate into French

a. She puts on

b. They put on

c. When it is cool

d. When it is foggy

e. When it rains

f. A raincoat

g. Sunglasses

h. Off-white

i. Warm

j. Large

---

12. Translate into French

a. When it pours down, I often put on a pale yellow raincoat with a cap because it is very casual and it is not too (*trop*) warm.

b. When I go out, I sometimes put on a black dress with a purple jacket (f). I love it because it is fashionable and it is not ugly.

c. When it is nice weather, my brother and I put on navy blue shorts with a white T-shirt because it is casual and it is not too tight.

d. Once a week, my mother puts on red shoes when she goes to the supermarket because it is comfortable and very smart.

e. When it snows, my grandparents put on a coat and a scarf. They love it because it is really warm and it is not light.

f. At the weekend, I put on grey trainers and white socks. My brother does not like it at all because it is ugly and it is not casual.

THE LANGUAGE GYM

7.4 NEGATIVES + PRESENT OF METTRE + CLOTHES + REASONS
(MAKING NEGATIVE SENTENCES WITH THE VERB METTTRE)

Quand il fait beau *When it is nice weather* **Quand il fait chaud** *When it is hot* **Quand il fait frais** *When it is cool* **Quand il fait froid** *When it is cold* **Quand il fait humide** *When it is humid* **Quand il fait lourd** *When it is muggy* **Quand il fait mauvais** *When it is bad weather* **Quand il y a de l'orage** *When it is thundery* **Quand il y a des nuages** *When it is cloudy* **Quand il y a du brouillard** *When it is foggy* **Quand il y a du soleil** *When it is sunny* **Quand il y a du vent** *When it is windy* **Quand il gèle** *When it is freezing* **Quand il neige** *When it snows* **Quand il pleut** *When it rains* **Quand il pleut à verse** *When it pours down*	**je ne mets pas** *I don't put on* **tu ne mets pas** *you don't put on* **il/elle ne met pas** *he/she doesn't put on* **on ne met pas** *we don't put on* **nous ne mettons pas** *we don't put on* **vous ne mettez pas** *you guys/girls don't put on* **ils/elles ne mettent pas** *they don't put on*	**de blouson** *a jacket* **de bonnet** *a woolly hat* **d'imperméable** *a raincoat* **de maillot de bain** *a swimming suit* **de manteau** *a coat* **de pantalon** *trousers* **de pull** *a jumper* **de short** *shorts* **de tee-shirt** *a T-shirt* **de casquette** *a cap* **d'écharpe** *a scarf* **de jupe** *a skirt* **de polaire** *a fleece* **de veste** *a jacket* **de collants** *tights* **de baskets** **de chaussettes** *socks* **de chaussures** *shoes*	**parce que c'est** *because it is* **parce que ce n'est pas** *because it is not*	**chaud** *warm* **confortable** *comfortable* **imperméable** *waterproof* **léger** *light* **pratique** *practical* **serré** *tight*

1. Match

Quand il fait chaud	*When it rains*
Quand il gèle	*Cap*
Manteau	*Casual*
Quand il pleut	*When it is freezing*
Je ne mets pas	*Socks*
Casquette	*When it is hot*
Chaussettes	*I don't put on*
Décontracté	*Warm*
Chaud	*Coat*

2. Missing letter challenge

a. Quand il pleut, je ne mets pas de bask__ __ __

b. parce que ce n'e__ __ pas imperméa__ __ __

c. Quand il f__ __ __ fr__ __ __, ma mère ne

m__ __ pas de sh__ __ __

d. parce q__ __ ce n'est p__ __ assez ch__ __ __

e. Quand il fait ch__ __ __, il n__ m__ __ p__ __
de chaussettes

f. parce que ce n'est __ __ __ confort__ __ __ __

3. Listening, gapped translation

a. Quand il fait __ __ __ __, je ne mets pas de polaire   *When it is nice weather, I don't put on a fleece*

b. parce que c'est trop __ __ __ __ __   *because it is too warm*

c. Quand il __ __ __ __ __, il ne met pas de short: *When it rains, he doesn't put on shorts:*

d. ce n'est pas __ __ __ __ __ __ __ __ __ __ __   *it is not waterproof*

e. Quand il __ __ __ __, on ne met pas de veste   *When it is freezing, we don't put on a jacket*

f. parce que __'est trop __ __ __ __ __   *because it is too light*

4. Faulty translation: fix the English translation

a. Quand il y a du vent, je ne mets pas de casquette   *When it is sunny, I don't put on a cap*

b. parce que c'est trop léger   *because it is really fashionable*

c. Quand il fait froid, elle ne met pas de short   *When it snows, she doesn't put on a skirt*

d. parce que ce n'est pas vraiment chaud   *because it is not really pretty*

e. Quand il fait chaud, on ne met pas de pantalon   *When it is hot, they put on trousers*

f. parce que c'est trop serré   *because it is too light*

5. Translate into English

a. Nous ne mettons pas

b. Ne…pas

c. Quand il neige

d. Parce que c'est

e. Jupe

f. Maillot de bain

g. Parce que ce n'est pas

h. Quand il pleut à verse

i. Je ne mets pas

j. Quand il fait beau

k. Elle ne met pas

l. Démodé

THE LANGUAGE GYM

6. Sentence Puzzle

a. pas Quand il je jupe ne neige, mets de   *When it snows, I don't put on a skirt*

b. fait froid Quand, il il ne met de chemise pas   *When it is cold, he doesn't put on a shirt*

c. des nuages, il y a tu mets pas de Quand ne robe   *When it is cloudy, you don't put on a dress*

d. pas de Quand lourd, on il manteau fait ne met   *When it is muggy, we don't put on a coat*

e. chaud il Quand fait, ils ne pas mettent bonnet de   *When it is hot, they don't put on a woolly hat*

7. Tangled translation: translate into French

a. Quand il y a du **wind**, je ne mets pas de

dress parce que c'est trop **light**.

b. **When** il fait **hot**, vous ne **put on** pas de

collants **because** ce n'est pas **practical**.

c. **When it is cold**, mon **brother** ne met pas

de **shirt** mais il met un **jumper**.

d. **When it rains**, mes parents **don't put on**

de baskets parce que ce n'est pas **waterproof**.

8. Listen and translate into English 🔊

a.

b.

c.

d.

e.

f.

g.

h.

9. Listen and correct the errors 🔊

a. Nous ne mettez pas de pull quand il fait beau parce que c'est chaud trop.

b. Je mets ne pas de chaussettes quand il y a du soleil parce que ce pas n'est pratique.

c. Hamadou met un veste quand il y a le vent mais il ne met pas de short.

d. Mon père met un pantaloon quand il pleut mais il ne mettent pas des baskets.

10. Guided translation

a. *When it snows, we don't put on a skirt because it is not warm.*

Q_ _ _ _ i_ n_ _ _ _, o_ n_ m_ _ p_ _ d_ j_ _ _ p_ _ _ _

q_ _ c_ n'_ _ _ p_ _ a_ _ _ _ c_ _ _ _.

b. *When it is sunny, I put on shorts and a T-shirt because it is light but I don't put on a jacket: it is too warm.*

Q_ _ _ _ i_ y a d_ s_ _ _ _ _ _,j_ m_ _ _ u_ s_ _ _ _ _ e_ u_

t_ _-s_ _ _ _ p_ _ _ _ q_ c'_ _ l_ _ _ m_ _ _ j_ n_

m_ _ _ p_ _ d_ v_ _ _ _ : c'_ _ _ t_ _ c_ _ _ _.

THE LANGUAGE GYM

7.5 POUR ALLER + PLACE + METTRE + CLOTHES + REASON
(SAYING WHAT ONE WEARS DEPENDING ON WHERE THEY GO)

Pour aller *To go to*	au centre commercial *the shopping centre* au centre sportif *the sports centre* au ciné *the cinema* au collège *school* au musée *the museum* au parc *the park* au supermarché *the supermarket*	je mets *I put on* tu mets *you put on* il/elle met *he/she puts on* on met *we put on*	un blouson *a jacket* un bonnet *a woolly hat* un imperméable *a raincoat* un maillot de bain *a swimming suit* un manteau *a coat* un pantalon *trousers* un pull *a jumper* un short *shorts* un tee-shirt *a T-shirt*	parce que c'est *because it is* parce que ce n'est pas *because it is not*	chaud *warm* chic *smart* confortable *comfortable* décontracté *casual* démodé *unfashionable* imperméable *waterproof* joli *pretty* large *large* léger *light* moche *ugly* pratique *practical* serré *tight*
	à la campagne *the countryside* à la montagne *the mountain* à la piscine *the pool* à la plage *the beach*	nous mettons *we put on* vous mettez *you guys/girls put on* ils/elles mettent *they put on*	une casquette *a cap* une écharpe *a scarf* une jupe *a skirt* une polaire *a fleece* une veste *a jacket*		
	aux magasins *the shops*		des collants *tights*		
			des baskets des chaussettes *socks* des chaussures *shoes*		

1. Match

À la plage	A swimming suit
Je mets	The shops
Un maillot de bain	To go to
Pour aller	Unfashionable
Décontracté	The beach
Dans les boutiques	A fleece
Une polaire	Casual
Démodé	I put on

2. Anagrams

a. oPur lalre ua écni

b. ej mtes nu lponatan te uen hcmiese

c. rcpae uqe ec'st tédtrénacoc

d. Prou alerl ua schurmpearé

e. am èmre emt nu ejna belu nmraie

f. arcpe ueq sec't abcfoonrtle

g. uPro ralel à al epalg

h. ems tspaern emettnt nu tsohr

i. crpae ueq tec's gleér

3. Break the flow

a. Pourallleràlacampagnejemetsunevestebleueparcequec'estjoli

b. Pourallleràlamontagnetumetsunmanteauparcequec'estchaud

c. Pouralllerauparconmetunshortparcequec'estdécontracté

d. Pourallleraucollègejenemetspasdepantalonparcequec'estserré

e. Pouralllerdanslesboutiquesellemetunejupeparcequec'estchic

f. Pourallleràlaplageonnemetpasdebonnetparcequec'estmoche

g. Pourallleraumuséejemetsunerobeparcequec'estconfortable

4. Listen and fill in the gaps 🔊

a. Pour aller à la _____, je mets un _____ parce que c'est _____

b. Pour aller au _____, mon frère met un _____ parce que c'est _____

c. Pour aller au _____, mes grands-parents mettent un _____ parce que c'est _____

5. Gapped Translation: please complete

a. Pour aller à la piscine, je mets un _____ ___ _____ jaune _____

To go to the pool, I put on a pale yellow swimming suit

b. parce que _____ vraiment _____

because it is really light

c. Pour aller dans les _____, mes parents mettent des _____

To go to the shops, my parents put on trainers

d. parce que c'est _____ _____

because it is very practical

6. Translate into English

a. Pour aller au centre commercial, je mets un pantalon bleu marine et un tee-shirt bleu clair parce que c'est joli.

b. Pour aller à la campagne, mes grands-parents mettent un manteau blanc cassé et une écharpe blanche parce que c'est chaud et confortable.

c. Pour aller au centre sportif, mon frère ne met pas de pantalon mais il met un short rouge parce que ce n'est pas très serré.

 **THE LANGUAGE GYM**

7. Faulty translation: fix the English translation

a. Pour aller au ciné, je mets un pantalon et un pull

To go to the cinema, I put on shorts and a shirt

b. parce qu'à mon avis c'est très décontracté

because in my opinion it is very comfortable

c. Pour aller au parc, tu mets un tee-shirt rouge foncé

To go to the park, you put on a light red T-shirt

d. parce que c'est vraiment joli mais un peu large

because it is really pretty but a bit tight

e. Pour aller à la montagne, elle met un bonnet vert

To go to the mountain, he wears a brown woolly hat

f. parce que c'est chaud mais un peu serré

because it is warm but a bit ugly

8. Tangled translation: into French

a. Pour aller au *sports centre*, je mets un jogging *black* et un tee-shirt *white* parce que c'est confortable et *practical*.

b. Pour aller à la *beach*, mes parents mettent un short *pale yellow* et un maillot de bain *light blue* parce que *it is not* chaud et c'est *light*.

c. Pour aller au collège, ma *sister* ne met pas de robe mais elle *puts on* une jupe *light green* parce que c'est chic.

d. Pour aller au centre commercial, *I put on* des baskets mais *I don't put on* chaussettes parce que c'est *ugly*.

9. Correct the mistakes and listen to check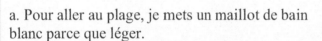

a. Pour aller au plage, je mets un maillot de bain blanc parce que léger.

b. Pour aller au commercial centre, mon père met une baskets parce que c'est confortable.

c. Pour aller à le parc, mes amies mettent un short foncé vert et un tee-shirt vert clair parce que c'est pas moche.

d. Pour aller aux magasins, ma mère met ne pas de baskets parce que ce n'est pas chic.

e. Pour aller la montagne, je mets une bonnet et un écharpe parce que c'est chaud.

f. Pour aller à la campagne, mes grands-parents met une polaire parce que c'est chaude.

10. Choose the correct words

a. Pour aller au *plage / ciné*, je mets un pull violet parce que c'est décontracté.

b. Pour aller au centre commercial, je mets une *jupe / blouson* marron clair parce que c'est joli.

c. Pour aller dans les boutiques, ma mère *mets / met* des chaussures mais elle ne met pas de baskets parce que c'est *joli / moche*.

d. Pour aller au collège, mon *sœur / frère* met un *pantalon / robe* bleu clair mais c'est trop *serré / joli*.

e. Pour aller à la montagne, mes parents *mettent / met* un *manteau / polaire* parce que *ce n'est pas / c'est* chaud.

11. Translate into French

a. To go to the supermarket, I put on trousers with trainers because it is practical and comfortable.

b. To go to school, my sister puts on a navy blue dress with a white jacket (f) because it is fashionable.

c. To go to the park, my friends put on shorts and a T-shirt because it is light and it is not tight.

d. To go to the countryside, my mother puts on a blue jacket (f) and a pink scarf because it is smart.

e. To go to the shops, my parents put on trousers because it is casual and practical.

ORAL PING PONG

METTRE

ENGLISH 1	FRENCH 1	ENGLISH 2	FRENCH 2
When I go out, I always put on a pink skirt with a white jacket (f)	Quand je sors, je mets toujours une jupe rose avec une veste blanche	From time to time I put on orange tights with yellow shoes	
Every day my brother puts on a blue shirt with a yellow tie	Tous les jours mon frère met une chemise bleue avec une cravate jaune	Once a week my father puts on a black jacket (m) with blue jeans	
At the weekend my sister sometimes puts on a bright red dress	Le week-end ma sœur met parfois une robe rouge vif	My brother often puts on a dark green jumper	
Once a week my parents put on navy blue jeans with an off-white jumper	Une fois par semaine mes parents mettent un jean bleu marine avec un pull blanc cassé	My grandparents sometimes put on yellow pale socks with dark yellow shoes	
I like it because it is fashionable	J'aime ça parce que c'est à la mode	I like it a lot because it is comfortable	
I don't like it at all because it is ugly and too tight	Je n'aime pas du tout ça parce que c'est moche et trop serré	I don't like it because it is unfashionable et too large	
When it is bad weather, I put on a woolly hat because it is warm	Quand il fait mauvais, je mets un bonnet parce que c'est chaud	When it is nice weather, I put on a jacket (f) because it is casual	
To go to school, when it is hot, I don't put on a coat because it is not light	Pour aller au collège, quand il fait chaud, je ne mets pas de manteau parce que ce n'est pas léger	To go to the cinema, when it is rainy, I put on a raincoat because it is waterproof	

INSTRUCTIONS - You are **PARTNER A.** Work in pairs. Each of you has two sets of sentences - one set has already been translated for you. You will ask your partner to translate these. The other set of sentences have not been translated. Your partner will ask you to translate these.

HOW TO PLAY - Partner A starts by reading out his/her/their first sentence <u>in English</u>. Partner B must translate. Partner A must check the answer and award the following points: **3 points** = perfect, **2 points** = 1 mistake, **1 point** = mistakes but the verb is accurate. If they cannot translate correctly, Partner A will read out the sentence so that Partner B can learn what the correct translation is.

Then Partner B reads out his/her/their first sentence, and so on.

OBJECTIVE - Try to win more points than your partner by translating correctly as many sentences as possible.

ORAL PING PONG

METTRE

ENGLISH 1	FRENCH 1	ENGLISH 2	FRENCH 2
When I go out, I always put on a pink skirt with a white jacket (f)		From time to time I put on orange tights with yellow shoes	De temps en temps je mets des collants orange avec des chaussures jaunes
Every day my brother puts on a blue shirt with a yellow tie		Once a week my father puts on a black jacket (m) with blue jeans	Une fois par semaine mon père met un blouson noir avec un jean bleu
At the weekend my sister sometimes puts on a bright red dress		My brother often puts on a dark green jumper	Mon frère met souvent un pull vert foncé
Once a week my parents put on navy blue jeans with an off-white jumper		My grandparents sometimes put on yellow pale socks with dark yellow shoes	Mes grands-parents mettent parfois des chaussettes jaune pâle avec des chaussures jaune foncé
I like it because it is fashionable		I like it a lot because it is comfortable	J'aime beaucoup ça parce que c'est confortable
I don't like it at all because it is ugly and too tight		I don't like it because it is unfashionable and too large	Je n'aime pas ça parce que c'est démodé et trop large
When it is bad weather, I put on a woolly hat because it is warm		When it is nice weather, I put on a jacket (f) because it is casual	Quand il fait beau, je mets une veste parce que c'est décontracté
To go to school, when it is hot, I don't put on a coat because it is not light		To go to the cinema, when it is rainy, I put on a raincoat because it is waterproof	Pour aller au ciné, quand il pleut, je mets un imperméable parce que c'est imperméable

INSTRUCTIONS - You are **PARTNER B.** Work in pairs. Each of you has two sets of sentences - one set has already been translated for you. You will ask your partner to translate these. The other set of sentences have not been translated. Your partner will ask you to translate these.

HOW TO PLAY - Partner A starts by reading out his/her/their first sentence <u>in English</u>. Partner B must translate. Partner A must check the answer and award the following points: **3 points** = perfect, **2 points** = 1 mistake, **1 point** = mistakes but the verb is accurate. If they cannot translate correctly, Partner A will read out the sentence so that Partner B can learn what the correct translation is.

Then Partner B reads out his/her/their first sentence, and so on.

OBJECTIVE - Try to win more points than your partner by translating correctly as many sentences as possible.

 **THE LANGUAGE GYM**

No Snakes No Ladders

METTRE

DÉPART	1	2	3	4	5	6	7
	I put on a purple jumper every day	My dad puts on black trousers	My cousins often put on a blue jumper	I put on a pink skirt, I love it	To go to the beach, you put on a T-shirt	My dad plays the piano. He likes it	We play tennis because we like it
15	14	13	12	11	10	9	8
My sister puts on shorts when it is sunny	To go to the sports centre, he puts on a T-shirt	Do you put on jeans when it is cold?	I don' t like it because it is too tight	I like it a lot because it is fashionable	They (f) put on shorts to go to the gym	Do you like to play football?	I play the guitar better than you
16	17	18	19	20	21	22	23
I put on a coat when it snows	She often puts on a skirt, she loves it	Do you guys put on a black jacket (m)?	My dad loves going to the museum	Do you like it?	When it snows, we put on a scarf	Do you like to go to the swimming pool?	I don' t put on a bright red dress
ARRIVÉE	30	29	28	27	26	25	24
	My aunt does not put on sunglasses	When I go out, I don' t put on a skirt	My mother never does yoga.	I don' t like it, it is ugly	I love it because it is smart	We play basketball from time to time	My mother puts on a light blue fleece

THE LANGUAGE GYM

211

No Snakes No Ladders

METTRE

7 On joue au tennis parce qu'on aime ça	**6** Mon père joue du piano. Il aime ça	**5** Pour aller à la plage, tu mets un T-shirt	**4** Je mets une jupe rose, j'adore ça	**3** Mes cousins mettent souvent un pull bleu	**2** Mon papa met un pantalon noir
8 Je joue de la guitare mieux que toi	**9** Tu aimes jouer au football?	**10** Elles mettent un short pour aller au gymnase	**11** J'aime beaucoup ça parce que c'est à la mode	**12** Je n'aime pas ça parce que c'est trop serré	**13** Tu mets un jean quand il fait froid?
23 Je ne mets pas de robe rouge vif	**22** Tu aimes aller à la piscine?	**21** Quand il neige, on met une écharpe	**20** Tu aimes ça?	**19** Mon père adore aller au musée	**18** Vous mettez un blouson noir ?
24 Ma mère met une polaire bleu clair	**25** Nous jouons au basket de temps en temps	**26** J'adore ça parce que c'est chic	**27** Je n'aime pas ça, c'est moche	**28** Ma mère ne fait jamais de yoga.	**29** Quand je sors, je ne mets pas de jupe

1 Je mets un pull violet tous les jours	**14** Pour aller au centre sportif, il met un tee-shirt	**17** Elle met souvent une jupe, elle adore ça	**30** Ma tante ne met pas de lunettes de soleil
DÉPART	**15** Ma sœur met un short quand il y a du soleil	**16** Je mets un manteau quand il neige	**ARRIVÉE**

Translate each part of the pyramid out loud with your partner, then write it into the spaces provided below.

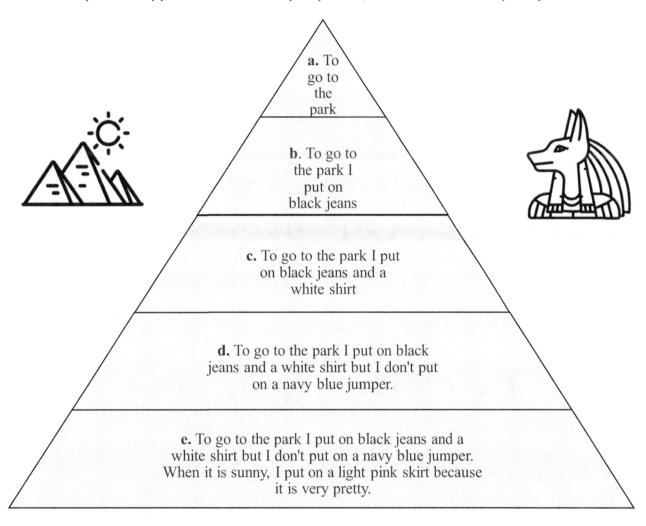

a. To go to the park

b. To go to the park I put on black jeans

c. To go to the park I put on black jeans and a white shirt

d. To go to the park I put on black jeans and a white shirt but I don't put on a navy blue jumper.

e. To go to the park I put on black jeans and a white shirt but I don't put on a navy blue jumper. When it is sunny, I put on a light pink skirt because it is very pretty.

Write your translation here

------- ✂ ------------ --------------- ✂ ------------- ----------------- ✂ --------

SOLUTION: Pour aller au parc, je mets un jean noir et une chemise blanche mais je ne mets pas de pull bleu marine. Quand il y a du soleil, je mets une jupe rose clair parce que c'est très joli.

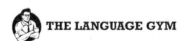

UNIT 8 – PRENDRE

Je	prends
Tu	prends
Il / Elle / On	prend
Nous	prenons
Vous	prenez
Ils / Elles	prennent

TO TAKE & TO HAVE (MEALS)

Tu prends le petit déjeuner?

Oui s'il te plaît!

TRANSPORT

Je prends le bus pour aller au collège! Et toi?

Moi, je prends mon vélo!

FOOD & DRINKS

Il fait chaud! Je prends une glace!

Moi, je prends une limonade!

8.1 PRENDRE + TRANSPORT + POUR ALLER + PLACE
(HOW ONE TRAVELS TO GO PLACES)

Je *I*	**prends** *take*	**l'avion** *the plane* **l'Eurostar** *the Eurostar*		**à la bibliothèque**	*to the library*
				à la gare	*to the train station*
				à la piscine	*to the swimming pool*
				à la plage	*to the beach*
				à la poste	*to the post office*
Tu *You*	**prends** *take*	**la voiture** *the car* **le bateau** *the boat* **la moto** *the motorbike* **le bus** **le car** *the coach* **le ferry** **le métro** *the tube*	**pour aller** *to go*	**au centre commercial**	*to the shopping centre*
				au centre sportif	*to the sports centre*
				au ciné	*to the cinema*
				au collège	*to school*
				au gymnase	*to the gym*
				au(x) magasin(s)	*to the shop(s)*
				au parc	*to the park*
				au supermarché	*to the supermarket*
Il *He* **Elle** *She*	**prend** *takes*	**le train** **le tram** *the tramway* **mon / son vélo** *my/his/her bicycle* **un taxi**		**au travail**	*to work*
				chez des amis	*to friends' house*
				en ville	*into town*
				en France	*to France*
				en Angleterre	*to England*
				en Espagne	*to Spain*

LANGUAGE AWARENESS

PRENDRE – Irregular Verb

Prendre is an **irregular verb**, and literally means **TO TAKE**. It is one of the most frequently used irregular -*RE* verbs.

There is a pattern to follow for each subject pronoun for irregular French -*re* verbs, and **prendre** is a reference point to know. In fact, and as you will see at the end of this unit, all verbs ending in the root word *prendre* (such as *apprendre, comprendre*) are conjugated the same way.

The two translations of *PRENDRE*

In this sub-unit, **prendre** is going to be used with its primary translation being **to take**.

However, and as you will see in sub-unit 8.3, **prendre** can also be translated as **to have** in some cases. Here are two examples:

• To **take**:

| Je **prends** le bus | *I **take** the bus* |
| Il **prend** l'avion | *He **takes** the plane* |

• To **have**:

| Je **prends** le petit déjeuner | *I **have** breakfast* |
| Elle **prend** un café | *She **has** a coffee* |

 **THE LANGUAGE GYM**

1. Match

Je prends le bus	I take the Eurostar
Il prend le ferry	She takes the plane
Je prends le tram	He takes the car
Elle prend le car	I take the tram
Il prend la voiture	He takes a taxi
Je prends l'Eurostar	She takes the coach
Elle prend l'avion	I take the bus
Il prend un taxi	I take the boat
Je prends le bateau	He takes the ferry

2. Faulty translation: fix the English translation

a. Je prends le métro   *I take the car*

b. Il prend le bateau   *He takes the plane*

c. Elle prend le tram   *He takes the tram*

d. Il prend le train   *He takes the bus*

e. Je prends l'avion   *She takes a taxi*

f. Elle prend le car   *She takes the car*

g. Je prends mon vélo   *I take my boat*

h. Il prend la voiture   *She takes the car*

3. Break the flow

a. Jeprendsl'avionpourallerenFrance

b. Ilprendlavoiturepouralleràlaposte

c. Elleprendl'avionpourallerenEspagne

d. Ilprenduntaxipouralleràlapiscine

e. Jeprendslemétropouralleraucentrecommercial

f. Elleprendl'EurostarpourallerenAngleterre

g. Jeprendsletrampourallerenvillelesweek-ends

h. Ilprendlebuspouralleraucollègetouslesmatins

4. Anagrams

a. eJ npreds el ubs

b. oPur alrle ne lvile

c. Il pnred al oitvure

d. orPu ealrl ua ctrene comrcimeal

e. lEle eprdn ln'avio

f. ourP leral ne raeFnc

g. eJ respnd el émotr

h. oPru llaer à al ibltuehioèbq

5. Likely or unlikely? Rewrite any unlikely statement into a plausible one

a. Je prends le métro pour aller en France

b. Il prend le ferry pour aller au centre commercial

c. Elle prend le bus pour aller au collège tous les matins

d. Il prend l'Eurostar pour aller à la piscine tous les week-ends

e. Je prends le train pour aller en ville ou chez des amis

f. Elle prend le tram pour aller en Angleterre de temps en temps

g. Je prends la voiture pour aller au ciné les samedis

6. Translate into English

a. Je prends la voiture

b. Il prend le ferry

c. Pour aller à la piscine

d. Elle prend le car

e. Il prend le bus

f. Pour aller à la gare

g. Elle prend l'Eurostar

h. Pour aller à la poste

i. Je prends l'avion

j. Pour aller en ville

k. Je prends mon vélo

l. Il prend un taxi

7. Listen, complete, then translate into English

a. Je prends _____ pour aller _____ de temps en temps

b. Il prend l'avion _____ en France _____

c. _____ le tram pour aller _____ tous les jours

d. Elle prend _____ pour aller _____ avec des amis

e. _____ le bus _____ au centre sportif _____

f. Il prend _____ pour aller _____ quelquefois

g. Je ne prends _____ mon vélo _____ au parc

8. Listen and correct the errors

a. Je prends la voiture pour aller au parc

b. Il prend le bus pour aller à la poste

c. Elle prend le car pour aller au collège

d. Je prends le train pour aller à la plage

e. Elle ne prend pas le tram

f. Quelquefois, je prends la moto

g. Je prends le bateau pour aller en ville

h. Il prend l'avion pour aller en France

i. Je ne prends jamais le métro le lundi

9. Gapped translation: complete the translation

a. Pour a_ _ _ _ à la p_ _ _g_ _   *To go to the beach*

b. P_ _ _ _ aller en v_ _ _ _ _   *To go into town*

c. Pour aller à la p_ _ _ _ _ _   *To go to the pool*

d. Pour a_ _ _ _ au c_ _n_ _m_ _   *To go to the cinema*

e. P_ _ _ aller au col_ _ _ _   *To go to school*

f. Je p_ _ _ _ _ _ l'_v_ _ _   *I take the plane*

g. J_ p_ _ _ _ _ _ l_ b_ _   *I take the bus*

h. Il p_ _ _ _ le b_ _ _ _ _   *He takes the boat*

i. E_ _ _ p_ _ _ _ _ le tram   *She takes the tram*

j. Je prends la v_ _ _ _ _ _   *I take the car*

10. Translate into French

a. I take the car to go into town every day with my brother.

b. He takes the train to go to the shopping centre every weekend with friends.

c. My sister takes the bus to go to school every morning.

d. She sometimes takes the car to go to the swimming pool or to the beach.

e. From time to time, I take the tube to go to the library, because I like it.

f. Every Friday, I take the tram to go to the sports centre with my brother.

g. I never take the Eurostar to go to France; I always take the plane.

h. He often takes a taxi to go to the shops.

i. She always takes the plane to go to England or to France.

j. I never take the motorbike to go to the supermarket; I always take my bicycle.

8.2 FULL CONJUGATION + PRENDRE + TRANSPORT + POUR ALLER + PLACE
(HOW ONE TRAVELS TO GO PLACES

Je *I*	**prends** *take*			**à la bibliothèque**	*to the library*
				à la gare	*to the train station*
				à la piscine	*to the swimming pool*
Tu *You*	**prends** *take*	**l'avion** *the plane* **l'Eurostar** **la voiture** *the car*		**à la plage**	*to the beach*
				à la poste	*to the post office*
				au centre commercial *to the shopping centre*	
Il *He* **Elle** *She*	**prend** *takes*	**le bateau** *the boat* **la moto** **le bus**		**au centre sportif**	*to the sports centre*
				au ciné	*to the cinema*
				au collège	*to school*
		le car *the coach*	**pour aller** *to go*	**au gymnase**	*to the gym*
Nous *We*	**prenons** *take*	**le ferry** **le métro** *the tube*		**au(x) magasin(s)**	*to the shop(s)*
				au parc	*to the park*
		le train		**au supermarché**	*to the supermarket*
		le tram		**au travail**	*to work*
Vous *You guys/girls*	**prenez** *take*	**le vélo** *the bicycle* **un taxi**		**chez des amis**	*to friends' house*
				en ville	*into town*
				en France	*to France*
Ils/Elles *They*	**prennent** *take*			**en Angleterre**	*to England*
				en Espagne	*to Spain*

Oh non... tu prends la mouche?*

Non, tout va bien! Je prends quatre mouches pour mon déjeuner!

*Prendre la mouche (idiom): To get angry, vexed, irritated

Prendre: Irregular -*RE* Verb

Je pren**ds**	Nous pre**nons**
I take	*We take*
Tu pren**ds**	Vous pren**ez**
You take	*You guys take*
Il/Elle pren**d**	Ils/Elles pren**nent**
He/She takes	*They take*

1. Match

Ils prennent l'avion	*We take the bus*
Je prends le ferry	*He takes the train*
Nous prenons le bus	*You take the car*
Vous prenez le tram	*They take the plane*
Pour aller à la gare	*They take the coach*
Il prend le train	*To go to work*
Tu prends la voiture	*I take my bicycle*
Elle prend le bateau	*I take the ferry*
Pour aller au travail	*She takes the boat*
Elles prennent le car	*To go to the station*
Je prends mon vélo	*You guys take the tram*

2. Complete the table

English	French
	Ils prennent
	La voiture
You guys take	
The tube	
	Au centre sportif
	Tu prends
We take	
The plane	
	Pour aller en France

3. Listen and complete the sentences 🔊

a. Pour aller au parc, elles _____ le _____

b. Nous _____ la voiture pour aller au _____

c. Je ne _____ _____ le train

d. Vous _____ un taxi pour _____ en ville?

e. ____ prend ___ _____ pour aller au _____

f. Tu _____ le _____ de temps en temps?

g. Ils ne _____ jamais le _____ ?

h. Pour _____ au ciné, je _____ mon vélo

4. Listen, complete and translate 🔊

a. Je pr__ __ __ __ souvent le bus

b. Pour a__ __e__ au c__ __l__ __ __

c. Ils pr__n__e__ __ toujours la voiture

d. P__ __ __ aller au c__n __ __ __ __

e. Tu pr__ __ __ __ le c__ __ quelquefois?

f. Vous pr__n__ __ l'avion ou l'Eurostar?

g. Il ne pr__ __ __ ja__ __ __ le bus

5. Broken words

a. No__s n_ pr__n__ __ __ j_m_i__ la vo__ __u_ e p_u__ al_e__ au c__l__ __ __ __
We never take the car to go to school

b. I__s pr__ __ __e_t le b_s p__ __r a__ __e__ au c__n_r_ co__m_r__ __ __ __
They take the bus to go to the shopping centre

c. V__u__ p__e__ e le t_a__ __ p__ __r _l e__ e v_l__ __l s_n_i__
You guys take the train to go into town on Mondays

d. J_n_ pr__d_ j_m__ __ l'__i__ p_u_ a__ __ __ __ e_ A__ __l_t_r_e
I never take the plane to go to England

e. E_ _l_ p__ __ __ __ le m_t__ p__ __r a__ __e__ à l_ p_s__ __
She takes the tube to go to the post office

f. I__ p_e__ __ le c__r p__ __ __ a__ __ __ __ à l_ p__ __ __ __ les s__m__ __i__
He takes the coach to go to the beach on Saturdays

THE LANGUAGE GYM

6. Faulty translation: fix the English translation

a. Il prend la voiture pour aller à la piscine *He takes the coach to go to the swimming pool*

b. Nous prenons le train pour aller en ville *You guys take the train to go into town*

c. Elles prennent le métro pour aller au collège *She takes the tube to go to school*

d. Je ne prends jamais le bus pour aller à la gare *I always take the bus to go to the train station*

e. Vous prenez souvent le tram pour aller au parc? *Does she often take the train to go to the park?*

f. Mon père prend la moto pour aller au travail *My mother takes the motorbike to go to work*

g. Elle prend le métro pour aller au ciné *They take the tube to go to the cinema*

h. Tu prends la voiture pour aller au gymnase? *Do you take the coach to go to the gym?*

7. Sentence Puzzle

a. prends ne aller jamais le Je collège bus pour au

b. poste Il voiture aller toujours la pour prend à la

c. Espagne l'avion Elle pour en prend aller

d. souvent le ville train pour prends Tu aller en?

e. prenons aux métro Nous pour le aller magasins

f. tram en le Ils temps de prennent temps

g. Vous l'Eurostar France pour en prenez aller?

h. ne le Elles mardis prennent jamais car les

8. Listen and write the ONE missing word in each sentence

a. Mon père prend voiture pour aller au travail

b. Je le bus pour aller au collège tous les matins

c. Ma sœur prend jamais le métro le soir

d. Prenons le train pour aller au centre sportif

e. Ils prennent toujours le pour aller en ville

f. Vous le bus pour aller au centre commercial?

g. Elles prennent pour aller en Espagne.

h. Je ne jamais l'Eurostar pour aller en France

9. Translate into English

a. De temps en temps, je prends le métro pour aller au centre commercial avec mes amis.

b. Quelquefois, ma sœur prend le train pour aller au gymnase ou au centre sportif.

c. Mon frère prend la voiture pour aller en ville le week-end, mais il ne prend jamais le train.

d. Nous prenons toujours l'avion pour aller en Angleterre, car nous n'aimons pas l'Eurostar.

e. Vous prenez souvent le tram pour aller aux magasins les lundis? Vous aimez le prendre?

f. Ils prennent toujours le car pour aller à la plage pendant les vacances.

g. Tous les week-ends, je prends mon vélo pour aller chez des amis.

h. Elles prennent le bus tous les jours pour aller au collège. Elles n'ont pas de voiture.

10. Translate the following phrases into French

a. My parents take

b. We sometimes take

c. I never take the plane

d. From time to time

e. She never takes the tram

f. They never take the boat

g. To go to the beach

h. I take my bicycle

i. They take the bus

j. You guys take the coach

k. You guys often take the car

l. We sometimes take a taxi

m. He always takes

n. You take the motorbike

o. To go to school every day

p. To go to the beach

q. To go into town with friends

r. They never take the Eurostar

11. Guided translation

a. M_____ p_____ n__ p_____ j_____ la v_____ *My parents never take the car*

b. J__ p_____ m___ v_____ p_____ a_____ au g_____ *I take my bike to go to the gym*

c. N_____ p_____ l__ b___ p_____ a_____ au c_____ *We take the bus to go to school*

d. I__ p_____ l__ t_____ p_____ a_____ e__ v_____ *He takes the tram to go to town*

e. J__ p_____ l'_____ p_____ a_____ e__ F_____ *I take the plane to go to France*

f. I__ p_____ l__ t_____ p_____ s_____ *He takes the train to go out*

12. Translate the following sentences into French

a. I never take the Eurostar to go to France. I always take the plane.

b. They never take the coach to go to the beach. They always take the car.

c. Usually, you guys take the bus to go to school every day.

d. Sometimes, we take the tube to go to the park or to the library.

e. I often take the tram to go to the gym or to the shopping centre with my friends.

f. From time to time, she takes the train to go to the shopping centre.

g. Sometimes, my parents take a taxi to go into town. I don't like to take taxis.

h. Do you often take the motorbike to go to work? Usually, I take the car.

THE LANGUAGE GYM

8.3 PRENDRE + DAILY ACTIVITIES + BUS/PETIT DEJ/DÎNER/MEALS + À + TIME
(AT WHAT TIME ONE DOES AN ACTIVITY)

PRENDRE – *TO TAKE*

Je *I*	**prends** *take*			**à la bibliothèque** *to the library*	
Tu *You*	**prends** *take*	**la voiture** *the car* **le bus** **le car** *the coach*		**à la gare** *to the train station*	
				à la piscine *to the swimming pool*	
				à la plage *to the beach*	
Il *He* **Elle** *She*	**prend** *takes*	**le métro** *the tube*	**pour aller** *to go*	**au centre commercial** *to the shopping centre*	
				au centre sportif *to the sports centre*	
Nous *We*	**prenons** *take*	**le train** **le tram**		**au ciné** *to the cinema*	
				au collège *to school*	
Vous *You guys/girls*	**prenez** *take*	**le vélo** *the bicycle* **un taxi**		**au gymnase** *to the gym*	
				au parc *to the park*	
				au supermarché *to the supermarket*	
Ils/Elles *They*	**prennent** *take*			**au travail** *to work*	
				chez des amis *to friends' house*	
				en ville *into town*	

PRENDRE - *TO HAVE*

Je *I*	**prends** *have*	**le petit déjeuner** *breakfast*		**cinq heures** *five o'clock*	
				six heures *six o'clock*	
Tu *You*	**prends** *have*	**le déjeuner** *lunch*		**sept heures** *seven o'clock*	
				huit heures *eight o'clock*	
				neuf heures *nine o'clock*	**du matin** *in the morning*
Il *He* **Elle** *She*	**prend** *has*	**le goûter** *snack*		**dix heures** *ten o'clock*	
			à *at*	**onze heures** *eleven o'clock*	**de l'après-midi** *in the afternoon*
Nous *We*	**prenons** *have*	**le dîner** *dinner*		**une heure** *one o'clock*	
				deux heures *two o'clock*	**du soir** *in the evening*
Vous *You guys/girls*	**prenez** *have*	**un bain** *a bath*		**trois heures** *three o'clock*	
				quatre heures *four o'clock*	
Ils/Elles *They*	**prennent** *have*	**une douche** *a shower*		**midi** *twelve o'clock/midday*	

1. Match

Je prends le petit déjeuner	We have dinner
À sept heures	At four o'clock
Nous prenons le dîner	At midday
Ils prennent le goûter	You guys have lunch
À quatre heures	You have a bath
Vous prenez le déjeuner	He has a shower
À midi	At seven o'clock
Tu prends un bain	At 9 in the evening
Il prend une douche	They have a snack
À neuf heures du soir	I have breakfast

2. Complete the table

English	Français
I have	
You guys have	
Breakfast	
We have lunch	
You guys have dinner	
At five in the morning	
She has a snack	
At four in the afternoon	
They have	

3. One of three

a. Je prends le **petit déjeuner/goûter/dîner** à six heures

   I have breakfast at six o'clock

b. Elle prend le dîner à **sept/huit/neuf** heures du soir

   She has dinner at eight o'clock in the evening

c. **Je/Tu/Il** prend le goûter à cinq heures de l'après-midi

   He has a snack at five o'clock in the afternoon

d. **Il prend/Tu prends/Elle prend** le bus pour aller en ville

   You take the bus to go into town

e. Ils prennent **un bain/une douche/le dîner** le soir

   They have a bath in the evening

f. Vous prenez le **déjeuner/dîner/goûter** au collège?

   Do you guys have lunch in school?

g. Je prends une douche tous les **matins/soirs/après-midis**

   I have a shower every morning

h. Nous prenons **la voiture/le car/le bus** pour aller en ville

   We take the car to go into town

4. Listen, complete and translate into English 🔊

a. Elle prend le _____ à sept heures _____

b. Il prend _____ pour aller au _____

c. Nous _____ le dîner à _____ heures du _____

d. Tu prends le _____ à _____?

e. _____ prenez le _____ à quatre heures de _____

f. Ils _____ une douche à _____ du soir

g. Nous ne _____ jamais le _____ à neuf heures du soir

h. Je prends _____ à six heures _____.

i. Tu prends le _____ pour aller _____?

THE LANGUAGE GYM

5. Correct the mistakes

a. Tu prend souvent le petit déjeuner à onze heures de le matin?

b. Nous prennons toujours le dîner chez moi le neuf heures du soir

c. Je prends le goûter avec mes amis à le collège à trois heures de le après-midi

d. De temps en temps, elles prendent le train pour vais au restaurant en ville

e. Quelquefois, il prend un bain à cinq heure du matin, et une douche à sept heure du soir

f. Vous prenez souvent le déjeuner petit au collège? Pour quoi?

g. Ils prennent la train pour aller au ciné tous le week-ends

h. Je ne prends le petit déjeuner avec ma sœur pendant la semaine

6. Guided translation

a. *I have breakfast at five o'clock*   J__ p_____ l_ p_____ _____ à c_____ _____

b. *He has dinner at seven o'clock*   I__ p_____ l_ d_____ à s_____ h_____

c. *They have lunch at school*   E___ p_____ l_ d_____ a_ c_____

d. *You have a snack at four o'clock*   T_ p_____ l__ g_____ à q____ _____

e. *At nine in the evening*   À n_____ h_____ d__ s_____

f. *We have a shower in the afternoon*   N__ p_____ u__ d_____ l'_____-_____

g. *You guys never have dinner*   V_____ n__ p_____ j_____ l_ d_____

h. *She takes the tram to go into town*   E___ p_____ l_ t_____ p____ a____ e_ v_____

i. *I have a bath at eight in the evening*   J__ p_____ u__ b_____ à h_____ h_____ d__ s_____

7. Gapped translation: complete the translation

a. Nous pr__ __ __ __ __ le petit déjeuner à neuf heures   *We have breakfast at nine o'clock*

b. Elle pr__ __ __ le dîner à huit he__ __ __ __   *She has dinner at eight o'clock*

c. Je pr__ __ __ __ toujours le dî__ __ __ chez moi   *I always have dinner at home*

d. Vous pr__ __ __ __ le go__ __ __ quelquefois?   *Do you guys have a snack sometimes?*

e. Elle pr__ __ __ souvent une do__ __ __ __ le matin   *She often has a shower in the morning*

f. Il ne pr__ __ __ jamais le d__ __ __ __ le soir   *He never has dinner in the evening*

g. Tu pr__ __ __ __ souvent le déj __ __ __ __ __ au travail?   *Do you often have lunch at work?*

h. Il pr__ __ __ le train pour al__ __ __ à la piscine   *He takes the train to go to the pool*

8. Sentence Puzzle

a. prenons heures matin toujours le petit déjeuner Nous à huit du

We always have breakfast at eight o'clock in the morning

b. moi D'habitude je soir le dîner chez à prends neuf du heures

Usually I have dinner at home at nine o'clock in the evening

c. temps je collège prends le De déjeuner au avec en mes temps amis

From time to time I have lunch at school with my friends

d. trois elle le goûter l'après-midi prend à Quelquefois heures de

Sometimes she has a snack at three o'clock in the afternoon

e. sept Pascal une matin douche prend à heures du, il et soir un heures bain à neuf prend du

Pascal has a shower at seven in the morning, and he has a bath at nine in the evening

f. travail prennent déjeuner elles à heures Aujourd'hui deux au le

Today they have lunch at two o'clock at work

g. prenez Vous le tram amis ou le train pour souvent au centre commercial aller avec des

You guys often take the tram or the train to go to the shopping centre with friends

9. Translate into English

a. D'habitude, je prends le petit déjeuner à huit heures du matin.

b. Mon frère prend toujours le déjeuner à midi avec des amis au collège.

c. Vous prenez un bain ou une douche de temps en temps?

d. Mes parents prennent le dîner à neuf heures du soir.

e. Nous ne prenons jamais le déjeuner ou le goûter au collège.

f. Tu prends le petit déjeuner avec ton frère ou ta sœur? Les deux?

g. Je prends toujours mon vélo pour aller au centre sportif car je n'ai pas de voiture.

h. Il prend toujours une douche à quatre heures de l'après-midi.

10. Translate into French

a. I always have breakfast with my family at six o'clock in the morning.

b. My brother has dinner at nine o'clock in the evening.

c. We always have lunch and snack at school with friends.

d. Do you guys have a bath at seven or eight o'clock in the evening?

e. I always have dinner with my parents at seven o'clock in the evening.

f. We always have snack at five o'clock in the afternoon.

g. They often have a shower at seven o'clock in the morning.

THE LANGUAGE GYM

8.4 AU + MEALS + PRENDRE + FOOD/DRINKS
(WHAT ONE EATS/DRINKS AT DIFFERENT MEALS)

Au petit déjeuner *At breakfast* **Au déjeuner** *At lunch* **Au goûter** *At snack time* **Au dîner** *At dinner*	**je prends** *I have* **tu prends** *you have* **il/elle prend** *he/she has* **nous prenons** *we have* **vous prenez** *you guys/girls have* **ils/elles prennent** *they have*	**de la pizza** *pizza* **de la salade verte** *green salad* **de la viande** *meat* **des biscuits** *biscuits* **des céréales** *cereals* **des frites** *fries* **des fruits** *fruits* **des légumes** *vegetables* **des œufs** *eggs* **des pâtes** *pasta* **du chocolat** *chocolate* **du fromage** *cheese* **du miel** *honey* **du pain** *bread* **du pain grillé** *toast* **du poisson** *fish* **du poulet rôti** *roast chicken* **du riz** *rice* **un burger** *a burger* **un sandwich** *a sandwich* **une omelette** *an omelette*	**avec** *with*	**du café** *coffee* **du chocolat chaud** *hot chocolate* **du jus de fruits** *fruit juice* **du lait** *milk* **du thé** *tea* **de l'eau** *water* **de la limonade** *lemonade*	
	je ne prends pas *I don't have* **nous ne prenons pas** *we don't have*	<u>d</u>'œufs <u>de</u> fromage <u>de</u> fruits <u>de</u> poulet rôti <u>de</u> salade <u>de</u> viande	**ou** *or*	<u>de</u> café <u>de</u> chocolat chaud <u>de</u> jus de fruits <u>de</u> lait	

LANGUAGE AWARENESS - PRENDRE

As mentioned previously in sub-unit 8.1, the verb *prendre* (to take) can also be used as (to have) when discussing food and different meals. By now, you will have had plenty of practice!

It is important to know that when we apply *prendre* to talk about transports, we use:

- **a definite article**: *le, la, les, l'*:
    → Je prends <u>le</u> bus, il prend <u>la</u> voiture, nous prenons <u>l'</u>avion, etc…
    → vous ne prenez pas <u>le</u> train, tu ne prends jamais <u>le</u> métro

However, when we use *prendre* to talk about food, we use **partitive articles.**

Partitive articles **(du, de la, des, de l')** are generally used to talk about food that cannot be quantified or counted. Partitive articles can be translated as *some*. For instance:

- Je prends **du** chocolat: *I have some chocolate.* In this example, I am having/eating a certain amount of chocolate that I cannot quantify. You could of course specify how many chocolates you are having/eating by using a specific number.
- Je bois **de l'**eau / **du** coca / **du** jus d'orange / **du** lait. In this example, liquid cannot be quantified, unless it is specified through a certain number (je bois **un** coca / je bois **deux** jus d'orange, etc…).

To understand which **partitive article** to use, remember the following:

- **Du**: **du** is used in front of a masculine noun
- **De la**: **de la** is used in front of a feminine noun
- **Des**: **des** is used in front of a plural noun
- **De l'**: **de l'** is the contraction of **de le**. It is used when two vowels encounter one another. We would say: je prends **de l'**eau and not je prends **de le** eau.

PARTIVE ARTICLES IN NEGATIVE SENTENCES

Partitive articles change to **de** in negative sentences:

Affirmative sentence: Je prends **de la** viande
Negative form: Je ne prends pas **de** viande

Affirmative sentence: Il prend **du miel**
Negative form: Il ne prend pas **de** miel

Affirmative sentence: Tu prends **de l'**eau
Negative form: Tu ne prends pas **d'**eau

Affirmative sentence: Ils prennent **des** légumes
Negative form: Ils ne prennent pas **de** légumes

Prendre le melon : to become arrogant

THE LANGUAGE GYM

1. Match up

De la viande	Honey
Du pain grillé	Fish
Du poulet rôti	Vegetables
Du miel	An omelette
De la salade	Pasta
Du poisson	Rice
Une omelette	Meat
Des légumes	Roast chicken
Des pâtes	Salad
Du riz	Toast

2. Faulty translation: fix the English translation

a. Je prends du fromage — *He has cheese*

b. Nous prenons de la viande — *We have roast chicken*

c. Ils prennent des œufs — *They have toast*

d. Il ne prend pas de salade — *She doesn't have salad*

e. Tu prends du poisson — *You have meat*

f. Vous prenez des frites — *You guys have fruits*

g. Je prends du jus de fruits — *I have orange juice*

h. Elles prennent du lait — *They have water*

i. Il prend un chocolat chaud — *He has a hot tea*

3. Break the flow

a. Jeprendsdespâtes

b. Tuprendsduthéavecdulait

c. Nousprenonsunsandwich

d. Ilsprennentdesbiscuits

e. Vousprenezdesfruits

f. Elleneprendpasdemiel

g. Jeprendsdupaingrillé

h. Tuprendsdescéréales

4. Gapped translation: complete the translation

a. Je prends du pain grillé — *I have _____*

b. Tu prends du poulet rôti — *You have _____*

c. Il prend du thé avec du lait — *He has_____ with _____*

d. Elle ne prend jamais de café — *She never has _____*

e. Nous prenons des œufs — *We have _____*

f. Vous prenez du poisson — *You guys have _____*

g. Ils prennent du fromage — *They have _____*

h. Elles prennent de la viande — *They have _____*

5. Choose the correct option

	1	2	3
Bread	Du pain	De la pain	Des pains
Meat	Du viande	De la viande	De l'viande
Water	Du l'eau	De la eau	De l'eau
Coffee	Du café	De la café	De l'café
Milk	Du lait	De la lait	De l'lait
Salad	Du salade	De la salade	De l'salade
Pizza	Du pizza	De la pizza	De l'pizza

6. Broken words

a. Pe_____ dé_____ — *Breakfast*

b. Dé_____ — *Lunch*

c. G_____ — *Snack time*

d. D_____ — *Dinner*

e. D___ lé_____ — *Vegetables*

f. D__ ch_____ — *Chocolate*

g. D__ l'_____ — *Water*

 THE LANGUAGE GYM

228

7. Dicto-translation: listen, transcribe and translate into English

French	English
a.	
b.	
c.	
d.	
e.	
f.	
g.	
h.	

8. Tangled translation: into French

a. Au *breakfast*, je prends *cereals*

b. Au *lunch*, il prend *roast chicken*

c. Au *dinner,* nous prenons *fish*

d. Au *snack time,* ils prennent *biscuits*

e. *At breakfast*, vous prenez *fruits*

f. *At dinner*, tu prends *pasta*

g. *At lunch,* elle prend *eggs*

h. *At snack time*, je prends *chocolate*

9. Guided translation

a. J__ p_____ d__ f_____   *I have cheese*

b. N____ p_____ d__ p_____   *We have fish*

c. I___ p_____ d___ o_____   *They have eggs*

d. T__ p_____ d__ l__ v_____   *You have meat*

e. I__ p_____ d__ l_____   *He has milk*

f. E____ p_____ d__ t_____   *She has tea*

g. J__ p_____ d___ f_____   *I have fruits*

10. Listen and spot the mistakes

a. Au déjeuner, il prend du l'eau

b. Au dîner, elles prennent du pâtes

c. Au petit déjeuner, tu prends de la pain

d. Au goûter, nous prenons de la biscuits

e. Au dîner, vous prenez de l'poisson

f. Au déjeuner, elle prend du œufs

g. Je ne prends jamais du fromage

h. Ils ne prennent pas du café

11. Translate into French

a. At lunch, I have roast chicken with water

b. At breakfast, my father has toast with coffee

c. At snack time, my sister has biscuits with milk

d. At dinner, we have fish with fries, and tea

e. At lunch, they have a burger with fries

f. I never have fruit juice at breakfast

g. Do you guys often have lemonade at snack time?

h. My sister does not have cereals at breakfast

8.5 AU + MEALS + PRENDRE + FOOD/DRINKS + WHY
(WHAT ONE EATS/DRINKS AT DIFFERENT MEALS AND WHY)

Au petit déjeuner *At breakfast* **Au déjeuner** *At lunch* **Au goûter** *At snack time* **Au dîner** *At dinner*	**je prends** *I have* **tu prends** *you have* **il/elle prend** *he/she has* **nous prenons** *we have* **vous prenez** *you guys/girls have* **ils/elles prennent** *they have*	**de l'eau** *water* **de la limonade** *lemonade* **de la salade verte** *green salad* **de la viande** *meat* **des biscuits** *biscuits* **des boissons gazeuses** *fizzy drinks* **des céréales** *cereals* **des frites** *fries* **des fruits** *fruits* **des légumes** *vegetables* **des œufs** *eggs* **des pâtes** *pasta* **du chocolat** *chocolate* **du café** *coffee* **du fromage** *cheese* **du jus de fruits** *fruit juice* **du lait** *milk* **du miel** *honey* **du pain** *bread* **du pain grillé** *toast* **du poisson** *fish* **du poulet rôti** *roast chicken* **du riz** *rice* **du thé** *tea*		**car c'est** *because it is* **mais c'est** *but it is*	**amer** *bitter* **bon** *good* **dégoûtant** *disgusting* **délicieux** *delicious* **dur** *hard* **épicé** *spicy* **fade** *bland* **gras** *greasy* **juteux** *juicy* **léger** *light* **malsain** *unhealthy* **rafraîchissant** *refreshing* **riche en protéines** *rich in protein* **riche en vitamines** *rich in vitamins* **sain** *healthy* **savoureux** *tasty* **sucré** *sweet* **trop sucré** *too sweet*
	je ne prends pas *I don't have* **nous ne prenons pas** *we don't have*	**d'**œufs **de** fromage **de** fruits **de** poulet rôti **de** salade **de** viande	**de** café **de** chocolat chaud **de** jus de fruits **de** boissons gazeuses		

THE LANGUAGE GYM

1. Match

C'est délicieux	It's juicy
C'est léger	It's good
C'est amer	It's sweet
C'est savoureux	It's unhealthy
C'est juteux	It's delicious
C'est bon	It's healthy
C'est dégoûtant	It's bland
C'est sucré	It's light
C'est fade	It's disgusting
C'est malsain	It's tasty
C'est sain	It's bitter

2. Faulty translation: fix the English translation

a. Car c'est épicé — *Because it's bitter*

b. Car c'est amer — *Because it's salty*

c. Car c'est trop sucré — *Because it's too salty*

d. Car c'est malsain — *Because it's healthy*

e. Car c'est savoureux — *Because it's sweet*

f. Car c'est dégoûtant — *Because it's delicious*

g. Car c'est juteux — *Because it's light*

h. Car c'est bon — *Because it's bad*

3. Break the flow

a. Audéjeunerjeprendsdelaviandecarc'estbon

b. Audînerilprenddupoissoncarc'estsain

c. Ilneprendpasdechocolataugoûtercarc'estmalsain

d. Nousprenonsdujusdefruitscarc'estrafraîchissant

e. Vousneprenezpasdecaféaupetitdéjeuner?

f. Ilsneprennentpasdeviandeaudînercarc'estdur

g. Jeneprendspasdefritesaudéjeunercarc'estmalsain

h. Tuneprendspasdemielcarc'esttropsucré?

4. Cross out all the phrases which refer to negative opinions

a. Car c'est dur et dégoûtant

b. Car c'est savoureux et juteux

c. Car c'est sain et rafraîchissant

d. Car c'est amer et gras

e. Car c'est malsain et trop sucré

f. Car c'est léger et délicieux

g. Car c'est fade et dur

h. Car c'est délicieux et savoureux

5. Likely or unlikely? Rewrite any unlikely statement into a plausible one

a. Au petit déjeuner, je prends des fruits car c'est malsain

b. Au goûter, il prend du chocolat car c'est épicé

c. Nous ne prenons jamais de miel car c'est trop sucré

d. Elles prennent du jus de fruits au déjeuner car c'est dur

e. Vous ne prenez pas de poulet rôti car c'est savoureux

f. Tu prends de la salade verte car c'est sain et léger

g. Au déjeuner je prends du poisson car c'est gras

6. Translate into English

a. Délicieux

b. Savoureux

c. Au petit déjeuner

d. Au goûter

e. Malsain

f. Au dîner

g. Sain

h. Rafraîchissant

i. Dégoûtant

j. Gras

k. Épicé

l. Au déjeuner

7. Listen, complete, then translate into French

a. Au _____ je prends _____ car c'est _____

b. Au _____ ma sœur prend _____ car c'est _____

c. Au _____ nous prenons _____ car c'est _____

d. Au dîner, mes parents _____ du poisson _____ très sain

e. Vous prenez _____ au goûter car c'est _____ et _____

f. Je ne prends _____ de _____ car c'est _____ et _____

g. _____ du jus de fruits _____ au petit déjeuner?

h. Elles ne prennent pas _____ au déjeuner car _____

i. Tous les _____, au _____, je prends _____ car c'est _____

8. Slalom translation: use one item from each column of the table to translate each sentence

De temps en temps,	ma sœur ne prend jamais	une omelette	c'est savoureux	amer et dégoûtant.
Au petit déjeuner,	mon frère prend	au déjeuner car	car c'est délicieux	car c'est sain.
Au déjeuner,	nous prenons	de café car	c'est	c'est rafraîchissant
Au petit déjeuner,	elles prennent	thé avec	mais c'est	et sain.
Au dîner,	je prends du	du poisson avec des frites	avec du riz car	trop sucré et malsain.
Vous prenez	je prends	des biscuits	du lait au dîner car	et savoureux.
Au goûter,	de la viande et des légumes	du poulet rôti	avec ma sœur	c'est bon et épicé.

a. *At breakfast, I have an omelette with my sister because it is healthy.*

b. *At dinner, we have fish and chips because it is delicious and tasty*

c. *At snack time, my brother has biscuits but it's too sweet and unhealthy.*

d. *At lunch, they have roast chicken with rice because it is good and spicy.*

e. *You guys have meat and vegetables at lunch because it is tasty and healthy.*

f. *At breakfast, my sister never has coffee because it is bitter and disgusting.*

g. *From time to time, I have tea with milk at dinner because it is refreshing.*

9. Sentence Puzzle

a. fromage prenons c'est du pain grillé avec Nous au délicieux du petit déjeuner car toujours

We always have toast with cheese at breakfast because it's delicious

b. prends goûter quelquefois je des avec savoureux du lait Au car c'est biscuits très

At snack time, I sometimes have biscuits with milk because it is very tasty

c. elle malsain prend dîner jamais de frites car c'est ne Au

At dinner, she never has fries because it is unhealthy

d. Au de temps déjeuner tu prends épicé du rôti avec du car en riz c'est temps poulet bon et

At lunch, from time to time, you have roast chicken with rice because it is good and spicy

e. ne déjeuner Vous légumes ? jamais Pourquoi de fruits prenez ou de au.

You guys never have fruits or vegetables at lunch. Why?

f. prennent vendredis du poisson les Mes riche car c'est en toujours protéines parents

My parents always have fish on Fridays because it is rich in proteins

g. Ma ne prend tante jamais malsain de gazeuses car dégoûtant c'est et boissons

My aunt never has fizzy drinks because it is disgusting and unhealthy

10. Translate into English

a. Au déjeuner, je prends toujours du poulet rôti avec du riz car c'est délicieux.

b. Mes parents prennent du jus de fruits au petit déjeuner car c'est rafraîchissant.

c. Ma sœur prend souvent des fruits au goûter car c'est sain et savoureux.

d. Tu ne prends jamais de chocolat au petit déjeuner car c'est trop sucré.

e. Au dîner, mon frère prend du thé avec du miel car c'est bon et sucré.

f. Vous prenez toujours de la salade au déjeuner car c'est sain et léger.

g. Elles ne prennent jamais de boissons gazeuses car c'est malsain.

h. De temps en temps, au petit déjeuner, je prends des œufs car c'est riche en protéines.

11. Translate into French

a. At breakfast, I always have fruit juice or fruits because it is refreshing.

b. My parents never have fizzy drinks because it is unhealthy and disgusting.

c. Jérôme always has pasta or roast chicken at lunch because it is very tasty.

d. From time to time, you guys have fish at dinner because it is healthy.

e. Aurélie always has green salad at dinner because it is light and delicious.

f. You often have eggs and cheese at breakfast because it is rich in proteins.

g. Dylan never has anything at breakfast, at lunch, at snack time, or at dinner.

 THE LANGUAGE GYM

8.6 VERBS LIKE PRENDRE – APPRENDRE / COMPRENDRE

Apprendre	Comprendre			J'aime ça car c'est…
J'apprends	**Je comprends**	**l'anglais**	*English*	*I like it because it's*
I learn	*I understand*	**l'éducation civique**	*PSHE*	
Tu apprends	**Tu comprends**	**l'EPS**	*PE*	**Je n'aime pas ça car c'est…**
You learn	*You understand*	**l'espagnol**	*Spanish*	*I don't like it because it's*
Il/Elle apprend	**Il/Elle comprend**	**l'histoire**	*history*	
He/She learns	*He/She understands*	**l'informatique**	*ICT*	
Nous apprenons	**Nous comprenons**			**barbant**
We learn	*We understand*	**la géographie**	*geography*	*boring*
Vous apprenez	**Vous comprenez**	**la musique**	*music*	**compliqué**
You guys/girls learn	*You guys/girls understand*	**la technologie**	*DT*	*complicated*
				créatif
Ils/Elles apprennent	**Ils/Elles comprennent**	**le français**	*French*	*creative*
				difficile
They learn	*They understand*	**les arts plastiques**	*art*	*difficult*
Je n'apprends pas…		**les maths**	*maths*	**éducatif**
I don't learn		**les sciences**	*science*	*educational*
Je ne comprends pas…				**ennuyeux**
I don't understand				*boring*
J'apprends aussi…				**facile**
I also learn…		**à faire de la natation**	*to do swimming*	*easy*
		à faire du judo	*to do judo*	**intéressant**
		à faire du karaté	*to do karate*	*interesting*
la cuisine	*cooking*	**à faire la cuisine**	*to do the cooking*	**inutile**
la danse	*dancing*	**à jouer au basket**	*to play basketball*	*useless*
la guitare	*the guitar*	**à jouer au foot**	*to play football*	**marrant**
la lutte	*wrestling*	**à jouer au golf**	*to play golf*	*fun*
la musculation	*weight training*	**à jouer au tennis**	*to play tennis*	**utile**
la natation	*swimming*	**à jouer de la guitare**	*to play the guitar*	*useful*
le judo	*judo*	**à jouer du piano**	*to play the piano*	**passionnant**
le karaté	*karate*	**à jouer du violon**	*to play de violin*	*exciting*
le piano	*the piano*			**stimulant**
				stimulating

1. Choose the correct option

a. **J'apprends/Je comprends** la guitare

b. **Il apprend/Il comprend** la cuisine

c. **Tu comprends/Tu apprends** le golf

d. **J'apprends/Tu comprends** à faire du judo

e. Il comprend **le français/la natation/à jouer au foot**

f. **Elle apprend/Elle comprend** à jouer au foot

g. **Nous n'apprenons/Nous ne comprenons** pas le piano

h. **J'apprends/Je comprends** à jouer du violon

2. Complete

a. Je comprend__ le français

b. Il appren__ à faire de la boxe

c. Nous comprenon__ l'histoire

d. Vous apprene__ le judo?

e. Ils ne comprennen__ pas les maths

f. Tu apprend__ le karaté?

g. Je n'apprend__ pas la danse

h. Elle compren__ l'anglais

3. Faulty translation: fix the English translation

a. Il apprend le français car c'est utile! *He understands French because it is useful*

b. Nous comprenons les maths car c'est facile *We learn maths because it is easy*

c. Tu apprends à faire de la natation? Où? *You learn to do karate? When?*

d. Mes parents apprennent à danser tous les lundis *My parents learn how to sing every Monday*

e. Elle ne comprend pas les maths car c'est difficile *She doesn't learn maths because it's difficult*

f. J'apprends à jouer de la guitare car j'aime ça! *I learn to play the guitar but I don't like it!*

g. Vous apprenez l'histoire car c'est éducatif? *You understand history because it's educational?*

h. Il apprend à faire la cuisine tous les dimanches *He learns how to clean the kitchen every Sunday*

4. Broken translation

a. *They learn how to play the piano* Il__ appre __ __ __ __ __ à jou__ __ du pia__ __

b. *We don't understand ICT* No__ s ne compr__ __ __ __ __ pas l'inform__ __ __ __ __ __

c. *She learns French...* El__ __ app__ __ __ __ le fr__ __ __ __ __ __...

d. *...because it's very stimulating* ...ca__ c'__ __ __ tr__ __ stim__ __ __ __ __

e. *I learn to do swimming...* J'ap__ __ __ __ __ à faire de la na__ __ __ __ __ __...

f. *...because it is very useful* ...c__ __ c'__ __ __ __ t__ __ __ ut__ __ __

g. *You guys understand Spanish...* Vo__ __ com__ __ __ __ __ __ l'esp__ __ __ __ __...

h. *...because it's quite exciting* ...c__ __ c'__ __ __ ass__ __ passi__ __ __ __ __

i. *We don't understand maths* No__ __ n__ com__ __ __ __ __ __ pa__ le__ m__ __ __ __

j. *He doesn't learn to play the violin* Il n'app__ __ __ __ p__ s à jo__ __ __ du vi__ __ __ __

k. *I don't understand geography!* J__ __ n__ com__ __ __ __ __ pas la géo__ __ __ __ __ __!

THE LANGUAGE GYM

5. Match

C'est passionnant	We learn
J'apprends à jouer	She learns to dance
Nous comprenons	It's stimulating
Nous apprenons	We understand
Il apprend la danse	You guys learn judo
Elle apprend à danser	It's exciting
C'est stimulant	It's useful
Vous apprenez le judo	I learn to play
C'est utile	He learns dance

6. Listen and Complete

a. Nous _____ la guitare

b. Ils _____ le français

c. Elle _____ la lutte

d. Je _____ pas la danse

e. Vous _____ les maths?

f. Tu _____ la cuisine?

g. Elles _____ le karaté

h. Je _____ l'espagnol

i. Il _____ pas le piano

7. Sentence Puzzle

a. j'apprends intéressant le français lundis et car c'est l'espagnol utile Les et

   On Mondays I learn French and Spanish because it is useful and interesting

b. ma apprend sœur danser le mercredis karaté et mon Les frère apprend à

   On Wednesdays my sister learns karate and my brother learns how to dance

c. Tu car facile l'histoire ? ennuyeux c'est je n'aime ça pas comprends car Moi c'est

   You understand history because it is easy? Me, I don't like it because it's boring

d. ne difficile pas Je les car c'est compliqué maths comprends et

   I don't understand maths because it is complicated and difficult

e. du nous apprenez golf apprenons à week-end jouer piano jouer et vous Le à au

   On the weekend we learn to play the piano and you guys learn to play golf

8. Tangled translation: translate into French

a. Tous les week-ends, ma sœur **learns to play tennis** car c'est **exciting**.

b. Les mardis, **we learn French** car c'est **useful** et très **stimulating.**

c. Mes amis **don't understand** les maths car c'est assez **complicated.**

d. Vous **don't learn to cook** car c'est **useless** et **boring?**

e. **I understand** l'espagnol **because it's** stimulant et **educational**.

f. **On Sundays,** mes parents **learn to dance** car c'est vraiment **creative**.

g. **He learns** la musculation. **He likes it** car c'est **stimulating** et **difficult**.

h. Tous les soirs, **I learn to play the guitar**. J'adore ça car c'est **exciting**.

 THE LANGUAGE GYM

9. Listen and Fill in each gap with the correct word

a. Tous les_____, mon frère et moi _____ à faire de la _____ au centre sportif.

b. Les mercredis, ma sœur _____ car c'est utile et_____.

c. _____ les maths car c'est_____, difficile et _____.

d. Ils _____ les arts _____ car c'est _____ et créatif.

e. Vous ne _____ pas l'histoire car c'est trop _____.

f. Tu apprends _____ avec ton père? C'est _____?

g. _____ à faire de la _____ car c'est _____ et barbant.

---

10. Guided translation

a. *I learn tennis*

J'_ _ _ _ _ _ _ _ l_ t_ _ _ _ _ _

b. *You understand French*

T_ _ c_ _ _ _ _ _ _ _ _ le f_ _ _ _ _ _ _

c. *She learns karate*

E_ _ _ a_ _ _ _ _ _ l_ k_ _ _ _ _

d. *We learn wrestling*

N_ _ _ a_ _ _ _ _ _ _ _ _ l_ l_ _ _ _

e. *They understand maths*

I_ _ _ c_ _ _ _ _ _ _ _ _ _ _ _ les m_ _ _ _

---

11. Complete the table

Pronoun	Verb Apprendre	Verb Comprendre
J'/Je		comprends
Tu	apprends	
Il		comprend
Elle	apprend	
Nous		comprenons
Vous	apprenez	
Ils		comprennent
Elles	apprennent	

---

12. Translate into French

a. I learn French and Spanish

b. He understands maths

c. We learn to do the cooking

d. You guys learn cooking

e. She understands science

f. They learn to play golf

g. You understand geography

h. I don't learn to dance

i. She doesn't understand

j. Do you understand?

k. She learns the piano

---

13. Translate into French

a. At weekends, she learns to play rugby because it's exciting.

b. He doesn't understand maths because it is complicated, but he understands French because it is easy and stimulating.

c. In the evening, my sister and I learn to play the piano because it is interesting and creative.

d. On Fridays, my father learns to swim because it is useful and very important.

e. You guys understand Spanish? Me, I understand French. I like it because it's very stimulating.

f. My cousin Léa learns to dance and to play football every Sunday.

g. We don't understand science because it is boring and difficult.

h. You guys learn to play the guitar and I learn the violin.

 **THE LANGUAGE GYM**

ORAL PING PONG

PRENDRE

A

ENGLISH 1	FRENCH 1	ENGLISH 2	FRENCH 2
I take the bus or the car to go to school every morning.	Je prends le bus ou la voiture pour aller au collège tous les matins.	He often takes the Eurostar to go to France or to England.	
At dinner, she has fish with salad because it is healthy.	Au dîner, elle prend du poisson avec de la salade parce que c'est sain.	On Saturday, they learn to play golf because it is fun.	
We learn French in school every day. I like it!	Nous apprenons le français au collège tous les jours. J'aime ça!	Sometimes, I have eggs and toast at breakfast because it is healthy.	
You guys never have roast chicken at lunch? Why?	Vous ne prenez jamais de poulet rôti au déjeuner? Pourquoi?	You guys learn how to play the piano and the guitar? I like it!	
They don't understand maths because it is difficult.	Ils ne comprennent pas les maths parce que c'est difficile.	We understand French and Spanish because it's easy.	
From time to time, you have biscuits with milk at snack time.	De temps en temps, tu prends des biscuits avec du lait au goûter.	Do you often have fizzy drinks at lunch? It's quite unhealthy…	
I never take the train to go to the sports centre on Monday.	Je ne prends jamais le train pour aller au centre sportif le lundi.	I always have tea with honey at dinner because it is sweet and tasty.	
My brother learns to cook because it is useful and important.	Mon frère apprend à cuisiner parce que c'est utile et important.	My sister learns weightlifting because it is stimulating.	

INSTRUCTIONS - You are **PARTNER A.** Work in pairs. Each of you has two sets of sentences - one set has already been translated for you. You will ask your partner to translate these. The other set of sentences have not been translated. Your partner will ask you to translate these.

HOW TO PLAY - Partner A starts by reading out his/her/their first sentence <u>in English</u>. Partner B must translate. Partner A must check the answer and award the following points: **3 points** = perfect, **2 points** = 1 mistake, **1 point** = mistakes but the verb is accurate. If they cannot translate correctly, Partner A will read out the sentence so that Partner B can learn what the correct translation is.

Then Partner B reads out his/her/their first sentence, and so on.

OBJECTIVE - Try to win more points than your partner by translating correctly as many sentences as possible.

 **THE LANGUAGE GYM**

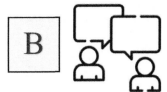

ORAL PING PONG

PRENDRE

ENGLISH 1	FRENCH 1	ENGLISH 2	FRENCH 2
I take the bus or the car to go to school every morning.		He often takes the Eurostar to go to France.	Il prend souvent l'Eurostar pour aller en France.
At dinner, she has fish with salad because it is healthy.		On Saturday, they learn to play golf because it is fun.	Le samedi, ils apprennent à jouer au golf parce que c'est marrant.
We learn French in school every day. I like it!		Sometimes, I have eggs and toast at breakfast because it is healthy.	Quelquefois, je prends des œufs et du pain grillé au petit déjeuner parce que c'est sain.
You guys never have roast chicken at lunch? Why?		You guys learn to play the piano and the guitar? I like it!	Vous apprenez à jouer du piano et de la guitare? J'aime ça!
They don't understand maths because it is difficult.		We understand French and Spanish because it's easy.	Nous comprenons le français et l'espagnol parce que c'est facile.
From time to time, you have biscuits with milk at snack time.		Do you often have fizzy drinks at lunch? It's quite unhealthy…	Tu prends souvent des boissons gazeuses au déjeuner? C'est assez malsain.
I never take the train to go sports centre on Monday.		I always have tea with honey at dinner because it is sweet and tasty.	Je prends toujours du thé avec du miel au dîner parce que c'est sucré et savoureux.
My brother learns to cook because it is useful and important.		My sister learns weight training because it is stimulating.	Ma sœur apprend la musculation parce que c'est stimulant.

INSTRUCTIONS - You are **PARTNER B.** Work in pairs. Each of you has two sets of sentences - one set has already been translated for you. You will ask your partner to translate these. The other set of sentences have not been translated. Your partner will ask you to translate these.

HOW TO PLAY - Partner A starts by reading out his/her/their first sentence <u>in English</u>. Partner B must translate. Partner A must check the answer and award the following points: **3 points** = perfect, **2 points** = 1 mistake, **1 point** = mistakes but the verb is accurate. If they cannot translate correctly, Partner A will read out the sentence so that Partner B can learn what the correct translation is.
Then Partner B reads out his/her/their first sentence, and so on.

OBJECTIVE - Try to win more points than your partner by translating correctly as many sentences as possible.

 **THE LANGUAGE GYM**

No Snakes No Ladders

7 At dinner, I have fish and chips.	**6** My mother learns the piano on Saturday	**5** You take the bus to go to school?	**4** We learn to play football in the evening	**3** I have cereals in the morning	**2** She takes the train to go in town	**1** He learns French in school
8 We take the car to on Sundays	**9** You learn to play the piano	**10** My brother learns cooking at home	**11** My parents often take the tram	**12** My brother learns to play the violin	**13** They learn to do judo	**14** At dinner, I always have fries
23	**22** My brother learns cooking. He likes it.	**21** Do you have fruit juice in the morning?	**20** She does not understand science	**19** My parents have coffee	**18** To go to the pool, I take my bicycle	**17** You often take a taxi to go out
24 I some-imes have a lemonade	**25** She often takes the motorbike	**26** He learns weight training	**27** He doesn't learn maths	**28** You guys understand science?	**29** My sister also learns the guitar	**30** They have rice at lunch

23 They never have chocolate

15 You guys never have coffee
START

16 She learns to play golf

FINISH

THE LANGUAGE GYM

No Snakes No Ladders

Prendre
Apprendre
Comprendre

7 Au dîner, je prends du poisson et des frites	**6** Ma mère apprend le piano le samedi	**5** Tu prends le bus pour aller au collège?	**4** Nous apprenons à jouer au foot le soir	**3** Je prends des céréales le matin	**2** Elle prend le train pour aller en ville	**1** Il apprend le français au collège
8 Nous prenons la voiture les dimanches	**9** Tu apprends à jouer du piano	**10** Mon frère apprend la cuisine à la maison	**11** Mes parents prennent souvent le tram	**12** Mon frère apprend à jouer du violon	**13** Elles apprennent à faire du judo	**14** Au dîner, je prends toujours des fruits
23 Ils ne prennent jamais de chocolat	**22** Mon frère apprend la cuisine. Il aime ça	**21** Tu prends du jus de fruits le matin?	**20** Elle ne comprend pas les sciences	**19** Mes parents prennent du café	**18** Pour aller à la piscine, je prends mon vélo	**17** Tu prends souvent un taxi pour sortir
24 Je prends quelquefois une limonade	**25** Elle prend souvent la moto	**26** Il apprend la musculation	**27** Il n'apprend pas les maths	**28** Vous comprenez les sciences?	**29** Ma sœur apprend aussi la guitare	**30** Ils prennent du riz au déjeuner
					15 Vous ne prenez jamais de café — **DÉPART**	**16** Elle apprend à jouer au golf — **ARRIVÉE**

 THE LANGUAGE GYM

241

PYRAMID TRANSLATION

PRENDRE-APPRENDRE-COMPRENDRE

Translate each part of the pyramid out loud with your partner, then write it into the spaces provided below.

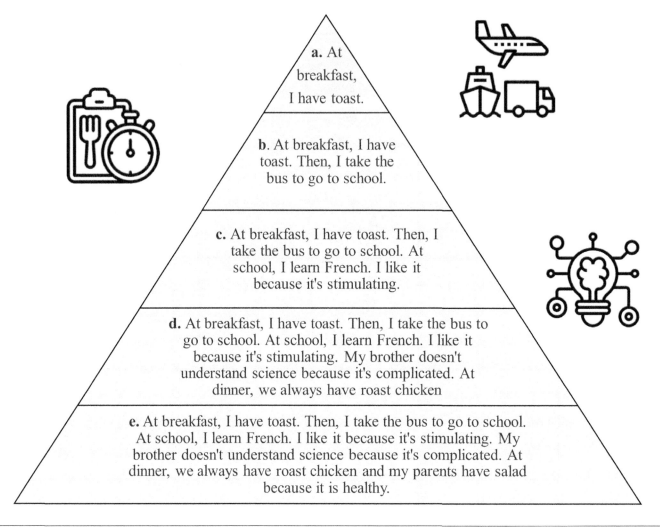

a. At breakfast, I have toast.

b. At breakfast, I have toast. Then, I take the bus to go to school.

c. At breakfast, I have toast. Then, I take the bus to go to school. At school, I learn French. I like it because it's stimulating.

d. At breakfast, I have toast. Then, I take the bus to go to school. At school, I learn French. I like it because it's stimulating. My brother doesn't understand science because it's complicated. At dinner, we always have roast chicken

e. At breakfast, I have toast. Then, I take the bus to go to school. At school, I learn French. I like it because it's stimulating. My brother doesn't understand science because it's complicated. At dinner, we always have roast chicken and my parents have salad because it is healthy.

Write your translation here

SOLUTION : Au petit déjeuner, je prends du pain grillé. Puis, je prends le bus pour aller au collège. Au collège, j'apprends le français. J'aime ça car c'est stimulant. Mon frère ne comprend pas les sciences car c'est compliqué. Au dîner, nous prenons toujours du poulet rôti et mes parents prennent de la salade car c'est sain.

UNIT 9 – MODAL VERBS
POUVOIR / VOULOIR / DEVOIR

Je	**peux**	**veux**	**dois**
Tu	**peux**	**veux**	**dois**
Il / Elle	**peut**	**veut**	**doit**
Nous	**pouvons**	**voulons**	**devons**
Vous	**pouvez**	**voulez**	**devez**
Ils / Elles	**peuvent**	**veulent**	**doivent**

WHAT I WANT + NOUN

Je veux une glace

WHAT I WANT + VERB

Je dois devenir chef!

Oui, chef!

WHAT ONE CAN & CAN'T DO

Dans mon collège, **on ne peut pas** mâcher de chewing-gum

9.1 DANS + MON / MA + NOUN + JE PEUX + FAIRE / ALLER / JOUER + NOUN / PREPOSITIONAL PHRASE + TIME MARKER
(SAYING WHAT I CAN DO AND PLAY AND WHERE I CAN GO)

Dans mon école	*In my school*			
Dans mon collège	*In my (secondary) school*			

Je peux *I can*	**faire** *(to) do*	**de l'athlétisme**	*athletics*	**après les cours** *after lessons* **de temps en temps** *from time to time* **les lundis** *on Mondays* **les mardis** **les mercredis** **les jeudis** **les vendredis** **les samedis** **les dimanches** **souvent** *often* **toujours** *always* **tous les jours** *every day* **une fois par semaine** *once a week*
		de la gymnastique	*gymnastics*	
		de la musculation	*weights*	
		de la natation	*swimming*	
		du théâtre	*drama*	
		les devoirs	*homework*	
	aller *(to) go*	**à l'atelier théâtre**	*to the drama workshop*	
		à la bibliothèque	*to the library*	
		au club d'échecs	*to the chess club*	
		au club d'espagnol	*to the Spanish club*	
		au club de sciences	*to the science club*	
		aux cours de danse	*to dance lessons*	
	jouer *(to) play*	**au football**		
		au rugby		
		au tennis		

Je ne peux pas *I can't*	**boire de boissons gazeuses**	*drink soft drinks*	
	boire d'alcool	*drink alcohol*	
	courir	*run*	**en classe** *in the classrooms*
	être impoli	*be rude*	
	fumer	*smoke*	**en cours** *in the lesson(s)*
	mâcher de chewing-gum	*chew gum*	
	porter de bijoux	*wear jewellery*	**dans les couloirs** *in the corridors*
	porter de maquillage	*wear make-up*	
	sécher les cours	*skip lessons*	
	utiliser mon portable	*use my mobile*	

Je ne peux jamais mâcher de chewing-gum	*I can never chew gum*

THE LANGUAGE GYM

1. Match

Aller à la bibliothèque	*To play rugby*
Aller au club d'échecs	*To wear make-up*
Faire du théâtre	*To run*
Porter du maquillage	*To skip lessons*
Porter des bijoux	*To go to the library*
Faire de la natation	*To chew gum*
Sécher les cours	*To do drama*
Utiliser mon portable	*To go to the chess club*
Courir	*To use my mobile*
Mâcher du chewing-gum	*To wear jewellery*
Jouer au rugby	*To do swimming*

3. Sentence Puzzle

a. bibliothèque peux à la Je une aller fois par semaine
I can go to the library once a week

b. peux ne école pas fumer mon dans Je
I can't smoke in my school

c. ne Je de porter jamais en maquillage peux cours
I can never wear make-up in lessons

d. cours ne sécher jamais Je peux les
I can never skip lessons

e. la peux devoirs après faire les bibliothèque Je à cours les
I can do homework in the library after lessons

f. faire mercredis les je Après peux de l'athlétisme cours les
After lessons I can do athletics on Wednesdays

2. Complete the words with the missing vowels, then listen and check

a. J__ n__ p__ __x p_ss __ch_r l_s c__ __rs
   I can't skip lessons

b. J__ n__ p__ __x p_s c__ __r__ d_ns l_s
   c__ _l__ rs *I can't run in the corridors*

c. J__ n__ p__ __x p_s p_rt_r d__
   m_q__ _ll_g_ *I can't wear make-up*

d. J__ p__ __x j__ __r ___ f__ __t
   I can play football

e. J__ p__ __x _ll_r ___ cl__b d'_ch_cs
   I can go to the chess club

f. J__ p__ __x f__ r_ d__ l__
   m_sc_l_t__ _n *I can do weights*

g. J__ n__ p__ __x p_s _t_l_s_r m_n
   p_rt_bl__ *I can't use my mobile*

h. J__ p__ __x f__ r__ d__ l__
   g_mn_st_q__ __ *I can do gymnastics*

i. J__ p__ __x _ll_r ___ x c__ r__ d__
   d_ns__ *I can go to dance lessons*

j. J__ p__ __x _ll_r __ l'_t_l__ r d__
   th__ __tr__ *I can go to the drama workshop*

k. J__ n__ p__ __x p_s f_m_r
   I can't smoke

4. Listen and underline the words you hear

a. Je peux aller au club **d'échecs/d'espagnol/de sciences** après les cours **tous les jours/les lundis/une fois par semaine**

b. Je ne peux jamais **fumer/porter de maquillage/porter de bijoux** dans mon école

c. Je peux faire **de la natation/de l'athlétisme/de la gymnastique** après les cours **de temps en temps/une fois par semaine/les lundis**

d. Je ne peux pas **utiliser mon portable/être impoli/courir** dans les couloirs

e. Je peux **jouer au foot/jouer au rugby/aller au club de sciences** après les cours **les lundis/une fois par semaine/les mardis**

THE LANGUAGE GYM

5. Faulty translation: fix the English translation

a. Je peux aller au club d'espagnol une fois par semaine après les cours

  I can go to the chess club twice a week after lessons

b. Dans mon école, je peux faire de la natation tous les jours après les cours

  In my school I can do weights once a week after lessons

c. Je ne peux pas porter de maquillage ni courir dans les couloirs

  I cannot wear jewellery nor run in the classrooms

d. Pendant les cours je ne peux jamais utiliser mon portable

  In lessons I can never chew gum

e. Dans mon collège, je peux aller à la bibliothèque pour faire les devoirs après les cours

  In my school, I can go to the drama workshop to do homework before lessons

f. Dans mon école, je peux faire du théâtre les lundis et de l'athlétisme les vendredis

  In my school I can do swimming on Thursdays and gymnastics on Mondays

6. Gapped translation: complete the translation

a. Dans mon école je _____ faire les _____ …   *In my school I can do homework…*

b. …à la bibliothèque _____ les _____   *…in the library after lessons*

c. Après les cours je _____ _____ à…   *After lessons I can go to…*

d. …__ _____ pour _____ les devoirs   *…the library in order to do homework*

e. Je _____ aller ___ _____ __ sciences…   *I can go to the science club….*

f. …de temps en temps____ _____   *…from time to time on Fridays*

g. Je ne peux _____ sécher les cours   *I can never skip lessons*

h. Je __ peux pas _____ ni _____ dans les couloirs   *I can't smoke or run in the corridors*

i. En _____ je ne _____ pas mâcher de _____ - _____   *In the classrooms I can't chew gum*

j. Dans mon école, je peux _____ au foot   *In my school I can play football*

7. Complete with the correct verb

a. Je ne peux pas _____ de chewing-gum

b. Je peux _____ à l'atelier de théâtre

c. Je peux _____ mes devoirs à la bibliothèque

d. Je ne peux pas _____ de cigarettes

e. Je ne peux pas _____ les cours

f. Je ne peux pas _____ mon portable

g. Je peux _____ aux cours de danse

h. Je peux _____ de l'eau en classe

i. Je ne peux pas _____ dans les couloirs

j. Je ne peux pas _____ de maquillage

k. Je peux _____ au club de sciences

l. Je ne peux pas _____ impoli

m. Je ne peux pas _____ de jus en classe

n. Je peux _____ de l'athlétisme

THE LANGUAGE GYM

8. Find the French translation and write it next to the English prompts

j	e	n	e	p	e	u	x	p	a	s	c	o	u	r	i	r	m	n	v	s	u	g	h	n
h	e	l	p	u	e	d	o	h	a	c	e	r	p	e	s	a	s	b	o	r	i	n	g	o
g	j	e	p	e	u	x	f	a	i	r	e	d	u	t	h	é	â	t	r	e	n	u	t	p
s	j	a	z	o	m	a	k	i	y	a	j	e	p	a	t	u	f	e	i	s	p	a	v	u
j	e	p	e	u	x	u	t	i	l	i	s	e	r	m	o	n	p	o	r	t	a	b	l	e
b	b	u	w	b	n	u	p	e	u	d	i	m	o	s	y	o	s	a	r	e	l	m	i	d
n	t	r	j	e	p	e	u	x	f	a	i	r	e	l	e	s	d	e	v	o	i	r	s	o
o	r	e	x	f	c	a	r	j	e	n	e	p	e	u	x	p	a	s	f	u	m	e	r	c
j	e	n	e	p	e	u	x	p	a	s	b	o	i	r	e	e	n	c	l	a	s	s	e	p
e	i	b	w	r	m	o	n	i	f	r	u	w	d	e	h	t	n	u	m	s	i	c	a	r
j	e	n	e	p	e	u	x	p	a	s	s	é	c	h	e	r	l	e	s	c	o	u	r	s
n	r	e	j	h	u	m	j	n	a	j	g	h	s	q	u	e	a	r	u	m	n	o	t	e
a	s	j	e	n	e	p	e	u	x	p	a	s	ê	t	r	e	i	m	p	o	l	i	s	r

a. I cannot be rude

b. I cannot skip lessons

c. I cannot run

d. I can do drama

e. I can use my mobile phone

f. I cannot drink in class

g. I cannot smoke

h. I can do the homework

9. Tangled translation: translate into French

a. Je ne peux pas *wear make-up*

b. Je peux aller *to the* club d'*chess*

c. Je ne *can* pas courir dans les *corridors*

d. Je ne peux pas *smoke*

e. Je peux faire de la *weights*

f. *I cannot* mâcher de *chewing gum*

g. Je peux *go* au club d'informatique

h. Je ne peux pas *wear* de bijoux

i. Je ne *can* pas *skip* les cours

j. Je ne peux pas *be impolite*

k. Je peux faire *my homework* à la *library*

l. Je peux faire de la *swimming*

10. Translate into English

a. Je ne peux pas courir dans les couloirs

b. Je peux aller au club de sciences tous les jours

c. Je peux aller à la bibliothèque et faire mes devoirs tous les jours

d. Je peux faire du théâtre les lundis

e. Je ne peux jamais sécher les cours

f. Je ne peux pas mâcher de chewing-gum

g. Je ne peux pas porter de maquillage

h. Je ne peux pas fumer ni boire d'alcool

11. Translate into French

a. I can't either smoke or drink alcohol

b. I can never wear jewellery

c. On Mondays I can go to the library to do the homework

d. In my school I can do swimming after lessons

e. I can never skip lessons

f. I can go to the Spanish club on Fridays

g. I cannot wear make-up

h. I can go to the chess club twice a week

9.2 FULL PRESENT CONJUGATION OF POUVOIR + FAIRE / JOUER / ALLER + NOUN/PREPOSITIONAL PHRASE + TIME MARKER
(SAYING WHAT ONE CAN DO AND PLAY AND WHERE ONE CAN GO)

Dans mon/ton/son/notre/votre/leur école	*in my/your/his/her/our/your/their school*
Dans mon/ton/son/notre/votre/leur collège	*in my/your/his/her/our/your/their (secondary)school*

On peut / *One can*		**faire** *(to) do*	de l'athlétisme de la gymnastique **de la musculation** *weights* **de la natation** **du théâtre** **les devoirs**	**après les cours** *after lessons* **de temps en temps** *from time to time* **les lundis** *on Mondays* **les mardis**
Je I	**peux** *can*			**les mercredis** **les jeudis**
Tu *You*	**peux** *can*	**aller** *(to) go*	**à la bibliothèque** **aller à l'atelier théâtre** *to the drama workshop* **au club d'échecs** **au club de français** *to the French club* **au club de sciences** **aux cours de danse** *to dance lessons*	**les vendredis** **les samedis** **les dimanches** **souvent** *often* **toujours**
Il / Elle *He / She*	**peut** *can*			
Nous *We*	**pouvons** *can*	**jouer** *(to) play*	**au foot** **au rugby** **au tennis**	*always* **tous les jours** *every day* **une fois par semaine** *once a week*
Vous *You guys/girls*	**pouvez** *can*			
Ils / Elles *They*	**peuvent** *can*	**boire de l'alcool** **courir** **être impoli(e)** **fumer** **mâcher du chewing-gum** **porter des bijoux** **porter du maquillage** **sécher les cours utiliser** **mon / son portable**	*drink alcohol* *run* *be rude* *smoke* *chew gum* *wear jewellery* *wear make-up* *skip lessons* *use my/his/her mobile*	**dans les couloirs** *in the corridors* **en classe** *in the classroom*
Je __ne__ peux __pas__ *I cannot* **On __ne__ peut __pas__** *One cannot*		**boire __d'__alcool** **mâcher __de__ chewing-gum** **porter __de__ bijoux** **porter __de__ maquillage**	*drink alcohol* *chew gum* *wear jewellery* *wear make-up*	

LANGUAGE AWARENESS
POUVOIR: A modal verb…

Pouvoir (to be able to) is a modal verb in French. Modal verbs are used to talk about what "we are able to do", what "we should do" or "must do". These verbs are always followed by an infinitive verb.

• **Je *peux* manger et boire en classe**
I can eat and drink in class

ON PEUT

On peut is a great expression to master, it means "One can" (as an **Indefinite Personal Pronoun**), but also "We can" (as a **Personal Pronoun** for WE).

It is used as an **Indefinite Personal Pronoun** when we are not specifying the person who does the action, hence the translation as "one".

• **Dans mon collège *on* ne peut pas fumer**
*In my school **one** cannot smoke*

… and a radical changing verb

Pouvoir is also a Radical Changing verb, like *Vouloir*. In this case the "*ou*" in *pouvoir* changes to "*eu*" in all present tense forms of the verb, **except** for the **we** (*nous*) and **you guys/girls** (*vous*) forms.

POUVOIR: Radical Changing Verb

Je p**eu**x	Nous p**ou**vons
I can	*We can*
Tu p**eu**x	Vous p**ou**vez
You can	*You (guys/girls) can*
Il / Elle p**eu**t	Ils / Elles p**eu**vent
He / She can	*They can*

Similar MODAL verb: VOULOIR

Je v**eu**x	Nous v**ou**lons
I want	*We want*
Tu v**eu**x	Vous v**ou**lez
You want	*You guys /girls want*
Il / Elle v**eu**t	Ils / Elles v**eu**lent
He / She wants	*They want*

1. Match

Je peux	*One can't smoke*
Nous pouvons	*I can't skip lessons*
Il / Elle peut	*Can you?*
Ils / Elles peuvent	*One can*
On peut	*They can*
Tu peux?	*We can*
Vous pouvez?	*He / She can*
Je ne peux pas sécher les cours	*Can you guys?*
On ne peut pas fumer	*We can play football*
Nous pouvons jouer au foot	*I can*

2. Gapped (English) translation

a. _____ *do homework after lessons in the*
  _____
  Je peux faire les devoirs après les cours à la bibliothèque

b. _____ *do drama on Mondays*
  Nous pouvons faire du théâtre les lundis

c. _____ *wear make-up in your school?*
  Tu peux porter du maquillage dans ton collège?

d. _____ *run in the corridors*
  Mes amis ne peuvent pas courir dans les couloirs

e. _____ *never skip lessons*
  On ne peut jamais sécher les cours

f. _____ *often play rugby in* _____ *school*
  Tu peux souvent jouer au rugby dans ton école

g. _____ *can play chess* _____
  Mon frère peut jouer aux échecs les lundis

3. Faulty translation: fix the English translation

a. Je peux aller à la bibliothèque et faire les devoirs après les cours

We can go to the library and read after lessons

b. Mon ami peut faire de l'athlétisme dans son école les mercredis

My sister can go swimming in our school on Wednesdays

c. Tu peux faire des activités extrascolaires dans ton école?

Can we do extracurricular activities in our school?

d. On peut aller aux cours de danse les jeudis après les cours

I can go to music lessons on Wednesdays after lessons

e. Dans notre école on peut jouer au foot tous les jours

In my school I can play rugby every day

f. Vous pouvez mâcher du chewing-gum en classe?

Can they chew gum in the classroom?

g. On ne peut ni sécher les cours ni fumer dans notre école

One can neither attend lessons nor wear make-up in my school

4. Listen and choose the correct option

a. Mon ami **peux/peut/pouvons** faire du théâtre dans son école.

b. On ne **peux/peuvent/peut** pas porter de maquillage.

c. Nous **pouvez/pouvons/peuvent** aller à la bibliothèque.

d. Tu **peux/pouvez/peut** utiliser ton portable en classe?

e. Vous **peuvent/peux/pouvez** porter du maquillage?

f. Je ne **peux/pouvons/peut** pas sécher les cours.

g. On **peuvent/peut/peux** aller au club de français.

h. Elle ne **peux/peut/peuvent** pas fumer. Elle ne le fait jamais.

5. Translate into English

a. Je peux faire beaucoup d'activités extrascolaires dans mon école.

b. Après les cours, mon frère peut faire les devoirs dans son collège. Il les fait souvent.

c. Vous pouvez porter du maquillage dans votre collège?

d. On ne peut jamais sécher les cours ou être impoli. Je ne le fais jamais.

e. On peut aller à l'atelier de théâtre et faire du théâtre les mardis. J'y vais de temps en temps.

f. Mes amis et moi pouvons jouer au rugby tous les jours après les cours.

g. On peut jouer au tennis dans ton école?

 **THE LANGUAGE GYM**

6. Spot the mistakes, make corrections; then listen and check

a. Je peuvent aller au club de sciences. J'y vas tous les jours.

b. Mon frère pouvez faire du théâtre les lundis. Il en fait toujours.

c. On ne pouvons pas sécher les cours. Je ne le faisons jamais.

d. On ne peuvent pas mâcher du chewing-gum en classe.

e. Mes amis peux être impolis quelquefois. Moi, je ne le suis jamais.

f. Ma sœur pouvez aller aux cours de danse. Elle y vais toujours.

g. Mes amis et moi peut jouer aux échecs. Nous y jouent les lundis soir.

h. Tu pouvez aller à la bibliothèque après les cours?

---

7. Tangled translation: translate into French

a. Mon frère *can play* au foot dans *his* école

b. Mon ami *can* aller au *science club* les *Thursdays*

c. *I can do drama* après les *lessons*

d. *One can* jouer au *football on* vendredis

e. Mes *friends* et *I can* aller *to the* bibliothèque l'*afternoon*

f. *One can't* fumer dans *my school*

g. On ne *can* jamais boire d'alcool dans *our school*

h. *Can you* porter des *jewellery* ou courir *in* les *corridors*?

Les bons pingouins ne fument pas et ne boivent pas.

---

8. Gapped translation: complete the translation

a. _____ aller à la bibliothèque de temps en _____. *I can go to the library from time to time.*

b. Mes amis _____ aller à l'atelier de _____. _____ car c'est marrant.

My friends can go to the drama workshop. They like it because it is fun.

c. Je _____ faire les devoirs à la _____ après les _____. J'aime ça car c'est _____ .

I can do homework in the library after lessons. I like it because it is useful.

d. _____ faire de l'athlétisme ou de la _____ les _____ . J'en _____ car _____ .

One can do athletics or gymnastics on Fridays. I do it because I like it.

e. Ma sœur _____ aller aux cours de _____ les jeudis après-midi. _____ car c'est _____ .

My sister can go to dance lessons on Thursdays in the afternoon. She likes it because it is exciting.

 THE LANGUAGE GYM

9. Listen and underline the words you hear

a. Mon ami peut faire **de la gymnastique/de la natation/de l'athlétisme** dans son collège. Il en **faites/fait/faisons** tous les vendredis.

b. Je **peuvent/pouvons/peux** aller **à la bibliothèque/au club de sciences/au club de français**. J'y **allons/vais/vas** les mardis.

c. On **peux/peut/peuvent** jouer au **foot/rugby/tennis** une fois par semaine **les mardis/les mercredis/les jeudis**.

d. On ne peut pas **fumer/utiliser son portable/courir** dans mon collège. C'est interdit.

e. On ne peut pas **fumer/porter de maquillage/courir** ou de bijoux.

---

10. Listen and fill in the gaps

a. Ma _____ peut faire du _____ dans son école. Elle en _____ les _____.

b. On ne peut pas _____ dans mon collège. Je ne _____ jamais ça.

c. Mon frère _____ faire les _____ après les cours à la _____.

d. Nous pouvons _____ de la gymnastique dans _____ école. J'____ fais les _____.

e. Tu peux _____ au club d' _____ dans ton collège?

f. Je ne peux ni _____ ni _____ de maquillage dans mon _____.

---

11. Staircase translation: translate each sentence from memory

a.	I can	do drama.				
b.	One can	do homework	after lessons.			
c.	We can	play rugby	every Thursday	after lessons.		
d.	One cannot	wear make-up	nor	jewellery	in our school.	
e.	My sister	can	play football	on Wednesdays	with her friends	from time to time.

a. _____

b. _____

c. _____

d. _____

e. _____

9.3 PRESENT OF VOULOIR (FIRST THREE PERSONS) + NOUN PHRASE
(SAYING WHAT FOOD ONE WANTS)

Je *I*	**veux** *want*	**de l'eau minérale** *mineral water* **des fruits** *fruit* **du café** *coffee* **du chocolat** *chocolate* **du riz** *rice* **du sucre** *sugar* **un burger** *a burger* **une glace** *an ice cream*			
Tu *You*	**veux** *want*	**une glace…** *a … flavoured ice cream*		**au chocolat** *chocolate* **à la fraise** *strawberry* **à la framboise** *raspberry* **à la vanille** *vanilla*	
		de la confiture *jam* **des frites** *fries* **des légumes** *vegetables* **du fromage** *cheese* **du gâteau** *cake* **du jus de fruits** *fruit juice*			
Il *He* **Elle** *She*	**veut** *wants*	**du jus d'orange** *orange juice* **du miel** *honey* **du pain** *bread* **du poisson** *fish* **du poulet rôti** *roast chicken* **du thé** *tea*			

LANGUAGE AWARENESS
THE VERB *VOULOIR*

Je veux literally means *"I want"*. However, in French, when we use this verb to ask for something to eat or to drink, for example in a restaurant or bar, we should use ***Je voudrais*** *"I would like"*

Serveur, je voudrais
du miel s'il vous plait!

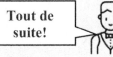

Tout de suite!

Je veux du poulet rôti / ***Je voudrais*** du poulet rôti

I want roast chicken / I would like roast chicken

THE LANGUAGE GYM

1. Match

Du fromage	Soup
Du pain	Water
Du jus de fruits	Rice
Du poulet rôti	Tea
Un burger	Fish
Du riz	Bread
De l'eau	Cakes
Du thé	A burger
Du poisson	Fruit juice
Des gâteaux	Vegetables
Des légumes	Roast chicken
De la soupe	Cheese

2. Faulty translation: fix the English translation

a. Je veux du fromage — *I want fish*

b. Tu veux de la glace? — *Does he want ice cream?*

c. Je veux des légumes — *I don't want vegetables*

d. Il veut du jus de fruit — *He wants fruit*

e. Ma sœur veut une soupe — *My brother wants a soup*

f. Tu ne veux pas de fruits — *You never want fruit*

g. Je veux de la confiture — *I want some honey*

h. Tu veux du chocolat? — *Does he want chocolate?*

i. Elle ne veut pas de thé — *She never wants coffee*

j. Ma mère veut du sucre — *My mother wants salt*

3. Choose the correct option

a. Ma mère ne **veux/veut/veulent** pas de pâtes

b. Je **veut/voulez/veux** de l'eau

c. Mon frère **veux/veulent/veut** une glace

d. Je ne **veut/veux/voulons** pas de gâteaux

e. Que **veux/veut/veulent**-tu?

f. Mon père ne **veux/veut/voulez** jamais de sucre

g. Je ne **voulons/voulez/veux** pas de chocolat.

h. Mon frère Jean **veux/veut/veulent** une poire

i. Ta sœur **veux/veut/veulent** un café

4. Translate into English

a. Je ne veux pas de glace

b. Il veut du poulet rôti

c. Tu veux du thé ou du café?

d. Je veux du jus d'orange

e. Elle veut un burger

f. Je ne veux rien

g. Il veut de l'eau minérale

h. Elle veut du riz ou des pâtes?

i. Il ne veut jamais de sucre dans son café

5. Listen and choose the correct word

a. **Il veut/Je veux/Tu veux** des frites et un hamburger

b. **Il veut/Je veux/Tu veux** du riz et du poulet, mais **je veux/tu veux/elle veut** un jus d'orange

c. **Elle veut/Je veux/Tu veux** du poisson et des frites

d. **Il veut/Je veux/Tu veux** du sucre avec le thé?

e. **Elle veut/Je veux/Tu veux** une glace au chocolat, mais ma mère **veux/veut/voulons** un gâteau

f. **Il veut/Je veux/Tu veux** de l'eau minérale et un café au lait

THE LANGUAGE GYM

254

6. Gapped translation: complete the translation

a. _____ du fromage   *I want cheese*

b. Elle ne _____ jamais de café   *She never wants coffee*

c. Je ne _____ pas de légumes   *I don't want vegetables*

d. Mon père _____ de l'eau   *My father wants water*

e. _____ des gâteaux   *He wants cakes*

f. Mon frère ne _____ pas de poisson   *My brother doesn't want fish*

g. Que _____-tu?   *What do you want?*

h. Que _____-il?   *What does he want?*

i. Je ne _____ rien   *I don't want anything*

7. Tangled translation: translate into French

a. Mon frère *wants* du riz avec du *chicken*

b. Je ne *want* rien, juste une *ice cream*

c. Elle ne *never wants* de sucre *in her coffee*

d. Que *do you want*?

e. Mon père ne veut *nothing*

f. Mon ami Jean *wants* un *fruit juice*

g. Ma mère *wants* un thé

h. Je *want* une *ice cream* à la fraise

i. Il *wants* du pain et de la *jam*

j. Je ne *want* pas de soupe, je *want bread*

> Nous voulons du poisson et des calamars!

> Aujourd'hui je veux du riz, de la salade et du canard!

8. Translate into French

a. I want bread and cheese

b. What do you want?

c. She never wants sugar in her coffee

d. My father wants nothing

e. Does she want pasta or rice?

f. I want a burger with salad

g. I don't want rice

h. Does he want tea or coffee?

i. Do you want a sandwich?

j. I want an ice cream

k. I don't want soup

l. She wants a fruit juice

9.4 FULL PRESENT CONJUGATION OF VOULOIR + NOUN PHRASE
(SAYING WHAT ONE WANTS)

Je *I*	**veux** *want*	de l'eau minérale	*mineral water*	
		des fruits	*fruit*	
		du café	*coffee*	
Tu *You*	**veux** *want*	du chocolat	*chocolate*	
		du riz	*rice*	
		du sucre	*sugar*	
		un burger	*a burger*	
		une glace	*ice cream*	
Il *He* **Elle** *She*	**veut** *wants*	une glace… *a … flavoured ice cream*	**au chocolat** *chocolate* **à la fraise** *strawberry* **à la framboise** *raspberry* **à la vanille** *vanilla*	
Nous *We* **Mon ami(e) et moi** *My friend and I / We*	**voulons** *want*	de la confiture	*jam*	
		des frites	*fries*	
		des légumes	*vegetables*	
		du fromage	*cheese*	
		du gâteau	*cake*	
Vous *You guys / You girls*	**voulez** *want*	du jus de fruits	*fruit juice*	
		du jus d'orange	*orange juice*	
		du miel	*honey*	
		du pain	*bread*	
Ils *They (m)* **Elles** *They (f)*	**veulent** *want*	du poisson	*fish*	
		du poulet rôti	*roast chicken*	
		du thé	*tea*	

LANGUAGE AWARENESS

Vouloir, *"to want"* is a modal verb in French. This modal is used to talk about what you want to do, as opposed to *pouvoir (what you are able to do)*. Like *pouvoir*, it is also a Radical Changing / Boot verb. See below to see what the **Radical Change** looks like for this boot verb.

JE T'AIME

Please note: if you say *"je t'aime"* to someone, it means *I love you*.

Je t'aime, mon pingouin!

Moi aussi, je t'aime!

Vouloir: Radical Changing Verb

Je v**eu**x	Nous v**ou**lons
I want	*We want*
Tu v**eu**x	Vous v**ou**lez
You want	*You guys/girls want*
Il / Elle v**eu**t	Ils / Elles v**eu**lent
He / She wants	*They want*

 **THE LANGUAGE GYM**

1. Match – Part A

Je veux	We want
Il/Elle veut	You guys want
Ils/Elles veulent	They want
Tu veux	He/She wants
Vous voulez	I want
Nous voulons	You want

2. Match – Part B

a.	Je veux du poisson avec des frites	1.	We want a chocolate cake
b.	Je veux du poulet rôti avec des frites	2.	I want fish and chips
c.	Il / Elle veut juste des frites	3.	We want a white coffee with sugar
d.	Nous voulons un café au lait avec du sucre	4.	I want roast chicken with chips
e.	Nous voulons un gâteau au chocolat	5.	He / She wants chips only

3. Sentence Puzzle

a. veut Elle du burgers deux, poulet je veux.   *She wants two burgers, I want chicken.*

b. ne Nous rien voulons. Que tu veux-?   *We don't want anything. What do you want?*

c. Que vous voulez-? du voulons Nous poisson.   *What do you guys want? We want fish.*

d. veut Il glace une. veux un Je gâteau.   *He wants an ice cream. I want a cake.*

e. Je ne rien veux. vous Qu'est-ce que voulez?   *I don't want anything. What do you guys want?*

f. Mon l'eau père de veut. veux un Je café.   *My father wants water. I want a coffee.*

g. fromage du veulent Ils. vous voulez- Que?   *They want cheese. What do you guys want?*

h. rien ne veut Elle. thé Nous du voulons.   *She doesn't want anything. We want tea.*

4. Faulty translation: fix the English translation

a. Je veux du poisson   *We want fish*

b. Vous voulez du poulet?   *Does he want chicken?*

c. Il veut du jus de fruits   *She wants fruit juice*

d. Elle veut du fromage   *You want cheese*

e. Que veut-il?   *What do you want?*

f. Tu veux de la glace?   *I want ice cream?*

g. Je veux du riz   *You want rice*

h. Qu'est-ce qu'ils veulent?   *What does he want?*

i. Ils veulent des frites   *We want fries*

5. Choose the correct option

a. Je **veux/veulent/veut** du poisson

b. Il **veux/veut/voulez** du chocolat

c. Nous **veux/veut/voulons** du café

d. Elle **veulent/veut/veux** une glace

e. Que **veut-/voulez-/veux-**tu?

f. Que **veux-/voulez-/veulent-** vous?

g. Mon frère Jean **veux/veut/voulez** du thé

h. Elles ne **veut/veulent/veux** rien

i. Je **veux/veut/voulons** du jus de fruit

THE LANGUAGE GYM

6. Spot and correct the mistakes

a. Ma mère veux du sucre dans son café.

b. Qu'est-ce que vous veut?

c. Je ne veux rien. Et toi, que voulez-vous?

d. Mon frère veut un café. Je veut une glace.

e. Que il-veut?

f. Nous veulent de la pizza.

g. Elles voulons un burger.

Il fait froid! Nous voulons un chocolat chaud et un café au lait

7. Guided translation

a. J__ v__ __ __ d__ p__ __ __ __
I want bread

b. T__ n__ v__ __ __ __ r__ __ __ __
You don't want anything

c. Q__ __ v__ __ __ __ - __ __?
What do you want?

d. I__ n__ v__ __ __ p__ __ d__ c__ __ __ __
He doesn't want coffee

e. Q__ __ v__ __ __ __ __ __ - __ __ __ __ __?
What do you guys want?

f. E__ __ __ __ v__ __ __ u__ bu __ __ __ __ __
She wants a burger

g. I__ v__ __ __ __ d__ p__ __ __ __ __ __ __ r__ __ __ __
He wants roast chicken

8. Listen and complete the broken words

a. J__ ve__ __ __ des fru__ __ __

b. Qu__ v__ __ __ __ -t__?

c. N__ __ __ __ vou__ __ __ __ du from__ __ __ __

d. El__ __ n__ ve__ __ __ rie__

e. Mo__ am__ __ __ ve__ __ __ un__ gl__ __ __ __

f. Qu__ vou__ __ __ __ -vo__ __ __?

g. Ma mè__ e v__ __ __ __ u__ g__ __ __ __ __ u

h. Il__ v__ __ __ __ __ __ __ __ u__ c__ __ __?

9. Listen and choose the correct word

a. Il veut du pain avec du **miel/fromage/beurre**

b. Elle ne veut pas de **poulet/poisson/sucre**

c. Nous voulons du **fromage/riz/poisson**

d. Tu veux du **miel/thé/café**?

e. Il veut un jus **d'orange/de tomate/de poire**

f. Je veux **un thé/un café/une glace**

g. Tu veux **du fromage/du pain/quelque chose**?

h. Elle veut du **poulet rôti/poisson/chocolat**

i. Ils veulent **des fruits/du riz/du beurre**

j. Nous voulons **de l'eau/du jus/du café**

10. Translate into French

a. I want pizza.

b. We want coffee.

c. She wants tea with sugar.

d. I don't want anything.

e. What do you want?

f. Do you guys want ice cream?

g. They (f) don't want sugar in the coffee.

h. We want water. They (m) want Coca-Cola.

i. I don't want beer. I want fruit juice.

j. My friend Jean wants cheese with wine.

k. She doesn't want chocolate. She wants fruit.

l. We don't want anything. Only water.

THE LANGUAGE GYM

9.5 PRESENT OF VOULOIR + INFINITIVE + NOUN PHRASE
(SAYING WHAT ONE WANTS TO EAT AND DRINK)

VOULOIR: To want					
Je *I*	**veux** *want*		**de l'eau minérale**	*water*	
			des frites	*fries*	
			des fruits	*fruit*	
Tu *You*	**veux** *want*		**du café**	*coffee*	
		boire *to drink*	**du chocolat**	*chocolate*	**pour le petit déjeuner** *for breakfast*
			du fromage	*cheese*	
Il *He* **Elle** *She*	**veut** *wants*		**du jus de fruits**	*fruit juice*	
		manger *to eat*	**du pain**	*bread*	**pour le déjeuner** *for lunch*
Nous *We* **Mon ami(e) et moi** *My friend and I*	**voulons** *want*		**du poisson**	*fish*	
		prendre *to have*	**du poulet rôti**	*roast chicken*	
			du riz	*rice*	**pour le dîner** *for dinner*
Vous *You guys / You girls*	**voulez** *want*		**du sucre**	*sugar*	
			du thé	*tea*	
			un burger	*a burger*	
Ils *They (m)* **Elles** *They (f)*	**veulent** *want*		**une glace**	*an ice cream*	
			une tartine	*toast*	

LANGUAGE AWARENESS (Reminder)

*The verb ***prendre*** works the same as the English 'to have' in the context of 'having something to eat or drink.' You can use it to replace ***boire*** and also ***manger*** in most contexts.

- **Je veux prendre de la glace**   *I want to have ice cream*
- **Mon amie veut prendre un café**   *My friend wants to have coffee*

1. Match

Je veux manger du riz	*You guys want to have tea for lunch?*
Je veux prendre du thé pour le petit déjeuner	*They want to have fish*
Il veut prendre du café pour le petit déjeuner	*We want to have rice*
Il / Elle veut boire de l'eau	*I want to eat rice*
Ils veulent manger du poisson pour le dîner	*You want to have tea for breakfast?*
Ils veulent prendre du poisson	*We want to eat rice for dinner*
Nous voulons manger du riz pour le dîner	*I want to have tea for breakfast*
Nous voulons prendre du riz	*He wants to have coffee for breakfast*
Tu veux prendre du thé pour le petit déjeuner?	*He / She wants to drink water*
Vous voulez boire du thé pour le déjeuner?	*They want to eat fish for dinner*

2. Categories

Vin – Tartine – Pain – Bière – Eau – Poisson – Jus de poire – Fromage – Riz – Poulet – Viande – Café – Thé – Frites   Glace   Burgers – Limonade – Chocolat chaud

Nourriture	Boissons

Qui te réveille le matin et qui sent le fromage?

La vache ki-kiri-ki!!

3. Complete with *BOIRE* or *MANGER* as appropriate

a. Je veux _____ du poisson et des frites

b. Nous voulons _____ de l'eau minérale

c. Je veux _____ un jus de fruits

d. Ils veulent _____ du poulet rôti

e. J'ai faim. Je veux _____

f. J'ai très soif. Je veux _____ un jus

g. Vous voulez _____ un burger?

h. Je n'ai pas faim. Je ne veux rien _____

i. Nous voulons _____ de la confiture

4. Listen and choose the words you hear 🔊

a. **Je veux/Nous prenons/Je mange** du poisson

b. **Nous voulons/Je veux/Je mange** du miel

c. **Il veut/Je veux manger/Il mange** un burger

d. **Vous voulez/Vous prenez/Tu veux** un café?

e. **Ils veulent/Il veut manger/Il veut prendre** une salade

f. **Je veux/Ils veulent prendre/Elle veut boire** un thé

g. **Je veux/ Je prends/ Il veut boire** une bière

 **THE LANGUAGE GYM**

5. Find the French translation and write it next to the English prompts

j	e	v	e	u	x	p	r	e	n	d	r	e	u	n	t	h	é	p	g	a	t	o	r	n
n	u	i	e	r	o	c	o	m	e	r	p	a	t	a	t	a	s	f	r	i	t	a	s	o
u	o	e	q	e	l	l	e	v	e	u	t	b	o	i	r	e	u	n	c	a	f	é	q	u
i	v	u	r	t	e	c	o	n	p	e	s	c	a	d	o	a	n	a	h	e	d	u	m	s
n	e	a	s	e	s	s	y	u	c	e	n	a	r	q	z	o	l	s	o	s	e	a	o	v
r	o	j	e	v	e	u	x	d	u	p	o	i	s	s	o	n	o	e	i	r	i	a	h	o
q	o	q	p	a	o	o	n	a	g	u	a	q	u	i	r	e	p	l	o	p	a	s	c	u
u	q	u	i	e	r	u	s	c	e	n	a	i	l	v	e	u	t	d	u	t	h	é	p	l
q	i	l	s	v	e	u	l	e	n	t	p	r	e	n	d	r	e	d	u	j	u	s	m	o
t	p	e	s	c	a	d	o	o	i	n	v	t	a	e	c	o	a	y	a	b	s	a	l	n
a	j	e	v	e	u	x	b	o	i	r	e	d	e	l'	e	a	u	u	s	e	r	i	u	s
n	e	f	j	e	v	e	u	x	m	a	n	g	e	r	d	e	s	f	r	i	t	e	s	d
i	q	u	i	e	r	o	b	e	b	e	r	a	g	u	a	c	r	a	d	y	l	a	n	o

a. I want to have a tea

b. She wants to drink a coffee

c. We want

d. I want fish

e. I want to eat chips

f. He wants tea

g. They want to have juice

h. I want to drink water

6. Tangled translation: translate into French

a. *I want* boire du *coffee*

b. Ils veulent *to have* du poisson *for lunch*

c. *Do you want* prendre quelque chose?

d. *We want* du *fruit juice* pour le déjeuner

e. Il veut *to eat a burger*

f. *They want to have* du poulet rôti *for dinner*

g. Non, *she doesn't want* boire de *coffee*

h. Je veux *to eat* des légumes *and fish*

i. Nous voulons *to have* une glace à la *strawberry*

j. *They want* du *fish* et des *chips* pour le dîner

k. Il veut *to have* du fromage

l. *We want* manger *bread* et *cheese*

7. Listen and complete the broken words 🔊

a. J__ v_____ m_____ un b_____

b. T__ v_____ p_____ un t____

c. I__ v_____ d__ p_____ a_____ d__ f_____

d. E___ v_____ d__ p_____ e__ d_ l__ v_____

e. T__ v_____ m_____ d___ f_____ ?

f. N____ v_____ b_____ d__ j__ d__ f_____

g. V____ v_____ p_____ d__ t__ p_____ l__ p_____ d_____

h. I___ v_____ m_____ d__ p_____ r_____

i. E___ v_____ p_____ u____ g_____

THE LANGUAGE GYM

8. Faulty translation: fix the French translation

a. *They want to have tea*   Nous voulons prendre du thé

b. *She wants to eat a burger*   Elles veulent manger un burger

c. *We want to drink coffee with sugar*   Je veux boire du café avec du sucre

d. *They want to have fish for lunch*   Il veut prendre du poisson pour le déjeuner

e. *We want to have fish with fries*   Vous voulez prendre du poisson avec des frites

f. *They want to drink fruit juice*   Tu veux boire du jus de fruits

9. Sentence Puzzle

a. pour déjeuner Je le riz prendre légumes et du veux des

   I want to have rice and vegetables for lunch

b. veux café boire Je un sucre de fruits avec du et un jus

   I want to drink a coffee with sugar and a fruit juice

c. vous Qu'est-ce que prendre voulez? voulons du Nous thé boire

   What do you guys want to have? We want to drink tea

d. voulons Nous chocolat une glace manger au

   We want to eat a chocolate ice cream

e. ne rien veut Elle mais veux burger manger je un

   She doesn't want anything, but I want to eat a burger

f. veut manger des frites légumes veux Ma mais sœur je des

   My sister wants to eat fries, but I want vegetables

g. Nous elle du frites fromage pain et du voulons manger mais veut des

   We want to eat bread and cheese, but she wants fries

10. Translate into English

a. Je veux prendre du thé avec du sucre et une tartine

b. Ma sœur veut manger un burger

c. Mes parents veulent du poisson avec des frites

d. Vous voulez prendre quelque chose? Je veux une glace

e. Mes amis et moi voulons prendre du riz pour le déjeuner

f. Ils veulent manger du pain avec du fromage et une tartine

11. Translate into French. Then listen and check

a. My parents want to drink tea with sugar   🔊

b. My sister wants to have a burger and fries

c. My brothers and I want to have fish for lunch

d. I want to have a burger for dinner

e. My mother wants a strawberry ice cream

f. We don't want to have sugar

g. My parents want to have fish with fries for dinner

9.6 PRESENT OF VOULOIR + INFINITIVE + NOUN / PREPOSITIONAL PHRASE
(SAYING WHAT ONE WANTS TO EAT AND DRINK, WHAT GAMES ONE WANTS TO DO AND WHAT CHORES ONE WANTS TO DO)

Je *I*	**veux** *want*	boire de l'eau		*to drink water*
		cuisiner		*to cook*
		faire mon lit		*to make my bed*
		laver la voiture		*to wash the car*
		manger un sandwich		*to eat a sandwich*
		tondre la pelouse		*to cut the grass*
Tu *You*	**veux** *want*	**aller** *to go*	**au ciné**	*to the cinema*
			au parc	*to the park*
			faire les magasins	*to do shopping*
		jouer *to play*	**au foot**	*football*
			avec tes amis	*with your friends*
			sur l'ordinateur	*on the computer*
Il *He* **Elle** *She*	**veut** *wants*	faire la lessive		*to do the laundry*
		faire la vaisselle		*to do the washing up*
		nettoyer le sol		*to clean the floor*
		passer l'aspirateur		*to do the vacuuming*
		prendre des photos		*to take photos*
		ranger sa chambre		*to tidy his/her bedroom*
		regarder un film		*to watch a film*
		sortir la poubelle		*to take the rubbish out*

LANGUAGE AWARENESS
VOULOIR + INFINITIVE/NOUN

When using the modal verb ***vouloir***, you can combine it in two ways:

Infinitive
• Je veux **aller** au parc   *I want <u>to go</u> to the park*

Noun
• Je veux **un café**   *I want <u>a coffee</u>*

A COMMON MISTAKE
ILLEGAL COMBINATION!

In French, we never place two conjugated verbs together. Verb structures usually work together with an infinitive:

• **Je veux ALLER**   *I want <u>to go</u>*
• **J'aime ALLER**   *I like <u>to go</u>*

If you use a present tense verb after **je veux (or je peux)**, you create an incorrect structure:

• **Je veux **JE VAIS*** *I want **I go***
*Please don't write this

 **THE LANGUAGE GYM**

1. Match

Nettoyer le sol	*To take the rubbish out*
Regarder un film	*To do the laundry*
Ranger la chambre	*To go to the park*
Cuisiner	*To take photos*
Boire de l'eau	*To cook*
Prendre des photos	*To make my bed*
Aller au parc	*To tidy up the room*
Faire la lessive	*To drink water*
Sortir la poubelle	*To watch a film*
Faire mon lit	*To clean the floor*

2. Complete with *VEUX* or *VEUT*

a. Je ne _____ pas nettoyer le sol

b. Il _____ boire un café

c. Ma mère ne _____ pas cuisiner

d. Qu'est-ce que tu _____ faire?

e. Aujourd'hui je _____ aller au parc

f. Mon frère _____ jouer au foot

g. Ma sœur _____ faire la lessive

h. Elle _____ ranger sa chambre

i. Aujourd'hui je ne _____ pas sortir

3. Complete with the missing verb and translate into English

a. Aujourd'hui je veux __ __ __ __ __ au parc

b. Ma sœur veut __ __ __ __ __ __ la poubelle

c. Mon frère veut __ __ __ __ __ son lit

d. Tu veux __ __ __ __ __ de l'eau?

e. Mon ami Jean veut __ __ __ __ __ au basket

f. Mon père veut __ __ __ __ __ la lessive

g. Aujourd'hui je ne veux pas __ __ __ __ __ la vaisselle

h. Qui veut __ __ __ __ __ au ciné avec moi?

4. Break the flow

a. Jeveuxrangermachambreetfairelavaisselle

b. Ilneveutnifairesonlitnifairelalessive

c. Jeveuxmangerunsandwichcarj'aimeça

d. Elleveutfairelesmagasinsavecmoi

e. Ilneveutpassortirlapoubellecariln'aimepasça

f. Jeveuxrangermachambresamedisoir

g. Tuneveuxpaspasserl'aspirateurtouslesjours

h. Detempsentempselleveutallerauciné

i. Ilneveutjamaisfairelavaisselleleslundis

j. Monfrèren'aimepasfairesonlitlematin

5. Faulty translation: fix the English translation

a. Je veux nettoyer ma chambre   *She wants to clean my room*

b. Tu ne veux pas cuisiner   *He doesn't want to cook*

c. Mon frère veut sortir la poubelle   *My sister wants to take out the rubbish*

d. Je veux jouer avec mes amis   *I want to go out with my friends*

e. Tu veux boire de l'eau?   *Does he want to drink water?*

f. Mon ami Jean veut jouer au basket   *My friend Jean wants to play on the computer*

g. Aujourd'hui je ne veux pas aller au parc   *Today I don't want to walk*

h. Mon père ne veut pas faire la vaisselle   *My father doesn't want to iron the shirts*

THE LANGUAGE GYM

264

6. Insert the missing vowels then listen and check

a. J__ v___ x b__ __r__ d__ l'__ __ __   *I want to drink water*

b. I__ n__ v___ t p_s a__ __ __ r ___ p__rc   *He doesn't want to go to the park*

c. M__ n p_r__ v__ __ t l_v__ r __a v__ __ t__ r__   *My father wants to wash the car*

d. __ __ j__ rd'h __ __, j__ n__ v__ __ x p_s s__rt__ r   *Today, I don't want to go out*

e. Q__ __ __ v___ x-t__ f__ __ r__ __ __ j__ __ rd'h __ __ __?   *What do you want to do today?*

f. __ l n__ v__ __ t p_s pr__ndr__ d__ ph__ t__ s   *He doesn't want to take photos*

7. Split sentences

Je veux sortir la	au cinéma
Mon frère ne veut	veux pas sortir
Tu ne veux jamais	de l'eau
Il ne veut pas aller	poubelle
Mon père veut jouer	le sol
Je ne	pas jouer
Elle veut boire	un film
Je veux regarder	faire ton lit
Tu ne veux pas nettoyer	au basket

8. Tick any sentence referring to a house chore

a. Mon père veut sortir la poubelle

b. Je ne veux pas jouer sur l'ordinateur

c. Tu ne veux pas aller au parc?

d. Ma mère veut cuisiner

e. Mon frère ne veut pas ranger sa chambre

f. Tu veux boire de l'eau?

g. Je ne veux jamais nettoyer la cuisine

h. Elle ne veut pas faire son lit

9. Translate the following verbs and nouns into French

a. To clean = N_____

b. To drink = B_____

c. To wash = L_____

d. To cook = C_____

e. To play = J_____

f. To make, do = F_____

g. To go = A_____

h. To tidy = R _____

i. To take out = S _____

j. To see, watch = R_____

k. Floor = S_____

l. Bed = L_____

m. Room = C_____

n. Film = F_____

o. Bin = P_____

10. Translate into French, and then listen to check:

a. My father wants to go to the cinema

b. My sister doesn't want to go to the park

c. She doesn't want to clean the floor

d. Do you want to eat?

e. He never wants to go out

f. I don't want to do the vacuuming

g. He never wants to take out the rubbish

h. She doesn't want to go out today

i. Today I don't want to go to school

j. My sister doesn't want to play with us

9.7 PRESENT OF VOULOIR + INFINITIVE + NOUN/PREPOSITIONAL PHRASE
(SAYING WHAT ONE WANTS TO EAT/DRINK OR WHAT ONE WANTS TO DO)

Je *I*	**veux** *want*	**boire de l'eau**	*to drink water*	
		cuisiner	*to cook*	
		faire mon lit	*to make my bed*	
Tu *You*	**veux** *want*	**laver la voiture**	*to wash the car*	
		manger un sandwich	*to eat a sandwich*	
		tondre la pelouse	*to cut the grass*	
Il *He* **Elle** *She*	**veut** *wants*	**aller** *to go*	**au cinéma**	*to the cinema*
			au parc	*to the park*
			faire les magasins	*to do shopping*
Nous *We* **Mon ami(e) et moi** *My friend and I*	**voulons** *want*	**jouer** *to play*	**au foot**	*football*
			avec des amis	*with some friends*
			sur l'ordinateur	*on the computer*
Vous *You guys* *You girls*	**voulez** *want*	**faire la lessive**	*to do the laundry*	
		faire la vaisselle	*to do the washing up*	
		nettoyer le sol	*to clean the floor*	
		passer l'aspirateur	*to do the hoovering*	
Ils *They (m)* **Elles** *They (f)*	**veulent** *want*	**prendre des photos**	*to take photos*	
		ranger la chambre	*to tidy the bedroom*	
		regarder un film	*to watch a film*	
		sortir la poubelle	*to take the rubbish out*	

1. Match

Je	veut
Tu	veulent
Il / Elle	voulez
Nous	veux
Vous	veux
Ils / Elles	voulons

2. Choose the correct form of *vouloir*

a. Mon père ne **veux/veulent/veut** jamais cuisiner

b. Ma sœur ne **veut/veux/voulez** pas nettoyer le sol

c. Je ne **veut/veux/veulent** pas aller au ciné

d. Mes parents ne **veux/veulent/voulons** pas jouer

e. Nous ne **voulons/veulent/veux** pas manger maintenant

f. Elles **veut/veulent/veux** faire les magasins

g. Vous **veux/voulez/veulent** sortir la poubelle?

h. Qu'est-ce que tu **veux/voulez/veut** faire maintenant?

i. Mes sœurs **veut/veulent/veux** aller au parc

j. Mon père et moi **voulez/voulons/veulent** jouer au tennis

 THE LANGUAGE GYM

3. Listen and write the verb you hear 🔊

a. Mon père _____ cuisiner

b. Mon frère ne _____ pas aller au parc

c. Vous ne _____ pas prendre de photos

d. Nous _____ ranger notre chambre

e. Tu ne _____ pas faire la lessive

f. Je ne _____ pas tondre la pelouse

g. Mes frères ne _____ pas jouer

h. Mes parents _____ regarder un film

i. Vous _____ faire la vaisselle?

j. Que _____-tu faire aujourd'hui?

4. Spot and correct the wrong forms of *vouloir*

a. Mon frère ne veux pas jouer au foot

b. Mes sœurs ne veut pas nettoyer le sol

c. Je ne veut pas faire mes devoirs

d. Ma sœur veulent aller au ciné

e. Mes parents voulons regarder un film

f. Qu'est-ce que tu voulez faire aujourd'hui?

g. Mon ami Jean et moi ne veut pas sortir

h. Vous ne veux jamais travailler!

i. Ma sœur voulons aller au parc

j. Mes amis voulez faire les magasins

5. Complete with *veux, veut, voulons, voulez* or *veulent* as appropriate

a. Ma mère ne _____ pas cuisiner

b. Mes frères _____ aller au parc

c. Jean et moi _____ manger de la pizza

d. Mon oncle _____ repasser ses chemises

e. Je ne _____ pas sortir avec toi

f. Mon petit frère _____ sortir la poubelle

g. Mon ami Jean ne _____ pas aller au collège

h. Tu _____ faire la vaisselle?

i. Elle ne _____ pas nettoyer le sol

j. Nous _____ jouer au foot

k. Il ne _____ pas faire ses devoirs

l. Vous _____ sortir avec moi?

m. Ma sœur _____ cuisiner aujourd'hui

n. Je _____ aussi cuisiner aujourd'hui

6. Complete the sentences, and then listen to check 🔊

a. Je n__ ve__ __ p__s al__ __ __ au c__ __ l__ e

b. Il n__ ve__ __ jam__ __ __ net__ __ __ __ __ le s__ __

c. Mon am__ Jean n__ ve__ __ jam__ __ __ sor__ __ __

d. Me__ par__ __ __ __ veu__ __ __ __ pre__ __ __ __ un t__ __

e. Me__ sœ__ __ __ n__ veu__ __ __ __ pa__ cuis__ __ __ __

f. Ma mère et moi voul__ __ __ reg__ __ __ __ __ un fi__ __

g. J__ n__ ve__ __ p__ __ jo__ __ __ __ a__ bas__ __ __

h. Tu n__ v__ __ __ p__ __ pre__ __ __ __ __ d__ pho__ __ __

i. I__ v__ __ __ jo__ __ __ sur l'ord__ __ __ __ __ __

7. Translate into French

a. I want

b. She wants

c. You don't want

d. They never want

e. He wants

f. I never want

g. We don't want

h. They want

i. Do you guys want?

j. My mum wants

k. My parents never want

THE LANGUAGE GYM

8. Faulty translation: fix the French translation

a. *My cousins do not want to do the vacuuming* — Mes frères ne veulent pas tondre la pelouse

b. *Do you guys want to go to the cinema today?* — Tu veux aller au ciné ce week-end?

c. *She wants to watch a film and have a tea* — Je veux regarder un film et manger un sandwich

d. *They don't want to do the washing up...* — Nous ne voulons pas ranger la vaisselle

e. *...on Friday evenings* — ...les vendredis matin

f. *My parents always want to take the rubbish out* — Mes parents veulent toujours sortir le chien

g. *We want to make the bed only at weekends* — Elle veut seulement faire le lit les week-ends

9. Gapped translation: please complete

a. Nous _____ aller au _____
aujourd'hui
We want to go to the cinema today

b. Mes _____ veulent _____ la
lessive demain
My brothers want to do the laundry tomorrow

c. Mon ami _____ manger _____
au fromage
My friend wants to eat a cheese sandwich

d. Je ne veux pas _____ la vaisselle les
_____
I don't want to do the washing up at weekends

e. Tu_____ tondre la pelouse
aujourd'hui?
Do you want to cut the grass today?

10. Translate into English

a. Nous ne voulons pas ranger notre chambre ni faire la lessive les week-ends.

b. Je veux aller au ciné avec mes amis tous les week-ends, mais je ne peux pas.

c. Ma sœur veut faire les magasins tous les jours, mais elle ne peut pas.

d. Mes amis ne veulent pas tondre la pelouse dans leur jardin.

e. Mes parents veulent aller à la piscine pour nager de temps en temps.

f. Je veux jouer sur l'ordinateur avec mes amis le soir, mais je ne peux pas.

g. Ma mère veut prendre des photos de ma sœur.

h. Ma sœur ne veut pas ranger ma chambre

i. Tu veux aller au ciné ce week-end?

11. Translate into French

a. I want to go to the cinema every day with my friends, but I cannot.

b. My sisters don't want to make the bed, they want to go shopping.

c. My mother doesn't want to cut the grass in the garden. She wants to go to the cinema.

d. My sister and I don't want to take the rubbish out every day.

e. Do you want to drink coffee?

f. I don't want to do the washing up in the evening.

g. My parents and I want to watch a film on Netflix.

THE LANGUAGE GYM

268

9.8 JE PEUX + INFINITIVE + NOUN PHRASE +TIME MARKER
(ASKING FOR PERMISSION TO DO THINGS)

Je peux *Can I* **Est-ce que je peux** *Can I*	**aller** *go*	**au cinéma**	*to the cinema*	**maintenant?** *now?* **demain?** *tomorrow?* **plus tard?** *later?* **ce week-end?** *this weekend?*
		au cours de musique	*to my music lesson*	
		aux toilettes	*to the toilet*	
		chez Anne	*to Anne's house*	
	sortir *go out*	**avec mon petit ami / ma petite amie** *with my boyfriend / girlfriend*		
		avec mes amis *with my friends*		
	jouer *play*	**aux jeux vidéo**	*videogames*	
		avec mes amis	*with my friends*	
	emprunter ce stylo		*borrow this pen*	
	emprunter cette gomme		*borrow this rubber*	
	manger plus de chocolat		*eat more chocolate*	
	utiliser mon portable		*use my mobile*	

1. Match

Utiliser mon portable	*To go to the toilet*
Emprunter ce stylo	*To go out this weekend*
Emprunter cette jupe	*To go to my boyfriend's house*
Aller au ciné	*To play videogames*
Jouer aux jeux vidéo	*To use my mobile*
Emprunter cette robe	*To borrow this pen*
Aller chez mon petit ami	*To borrow this skirt*
Sortir ce week-end	*To borrow this dress*
Aller aux toilettes	*To go to the cinema*

2. Split sentences

a. Je peux utiliser	1. gomme?
b. Je peux emprunter ce	2. chez Anne?
c. Je peux jouer	3. ciné demain?
d. Je peux sortir avec	4. du maquillage?
e. Je peux aller	5. stylo?
f. Je peux emprunter cette	6. mon portable?
g. Je peux aller à	7. avec mon portable?
h. Je peux aller au	8. mon petit ami?
i. Je peux emprunter	9. la piscine?
j. Je peux porter	10. ta robe?

THE LANGUAGE GYM

3. Break the flow

a. Jepeuxalleraucinéavec Marine?

b. Jepeuxsortirceweek-end?

c. JepeuxallerchezAnnecesoirpourdîner?

d. Jepeuxalleraucoursdemusique?

e. Jepeuxalleràuxtoilettes?

f. Jepeuxempruntertonlivredefrançais?

g. Jepeuxmangerplusderiz?

h. Jepeuxportercettejupedemain?

i. Jepeuxutilisermonportableenclasse?

4. Listen and fill in the blanks 🔊

a. Je peux _____ aux _____?

b. Je peux _____ avec ma _____ _____?

c. ___ _____ aller au _____ de _____?

d. Je peux _____ ta robe?

e. Je peux _____ cette chemise?

f. Je peux _____ plus de _____?

g. ___ _____ utiliser ____ _____ en classe?

h. Je peux _____ aux _____ _____?

i. ___ _____ sortir avec _____ _____?

j. Je peux _____ ton livre?

5. Faulty Translation: fix the English translation

a. Je peux sortir avec mes amis tous les jours? *Can I go to the cinema with my friends this evening?*

b. Je peux utiliser mon portable en classe? *Can I use my mobile now?*

c. Je peux emprunter ce stylo? *Can I borrow this dress?*

d. Je peux courir dans les couloirs? *Can I run in the school?*

e. Je peux aller chez ma petite amie demain? *Can I go to my boyfriend's house tomorrow?*

6. Complete the translation, then listen to check

a. Je peux _____ aux _____? 🔊

Can I go to the toilet?

b. ___ _____ sortir avec _____ _____?

Can I go out with my friends?

c. ___ _____ jouer aux _____ _____?

Can I play videogames?

d. Je peux _____ au cours de _____?

Can I go to my piano lesson?

e. Je peux _____ ton _____?

Can I borrow your mobile?

f. ___ _____ manger plus de riz?

Can I eat more rice?

g. ___ _____ aller _____ ma _____ _____?

Can I go to my girlfriend's house?

7. Translate into French

a. Can I go to the toilet?

b. Can I go to Marine's house this evening?

c. Can I go to the music lesson?

d. Can I go out with my friends this weekend?

e. Can I borrow this pen?

f. Can I borrow this book?

g Can I eat more ice cream?

h. Can I eat more vegetables?

i. Can I run in the corridors?

j. Can I play videogames tonight?

k. Can I wear make-up at school?

l. Can I use my mobile here?

m. Can I go to the cinema this weekend?

THE LANGUAGE GYM

9.9 CHEZ / AU + NOUN + JE DOIS + INFINITIVES
(WHAT ONE MUST DO IN DIFFERENT PLACES)

Chez moi *At home*	**je dois** *I must*	**faire la lessive**	*do the laundry*
		faire la vaisselle	*do the washing up*
		faire mes devoirs	*do my homework*
		manger sainement	*eat healthily*
		passer l'aspirateur	*do the vacuuming*
		ranger ma chambre	*tidy my bedroom*
		sortir la poubelle	*take the rubbish out*
Au collège *At school*		**écouter mes professeurs**	*listen to my teachers*
		être à l'heure	*be on time*
		être attentif / attentive	*be attentive*
		participer en classe	*participate in class*
		porter un uniforme scolaire	*wear a school uniform*
		respecter les élèves	*respect students*
		respecter les professeurs	*respect teachers*
		suivre le règlement intérieur	*follow the school policy*

Je ne dois pas *I mustn't*	**boire d'alcool**	*drink alcohol*	**chez moi** *at home*
	critiquer ma sœur	*criticise my sister*	
	être impoli(e)	*be rude*	
	fumer	*smoke*	
	manger dans ma chambre	*eat in my bedroom*	
Je ne dois jamais *I must never*	**courir dans les couloirs**	*run in the corridors*	**à l'école** *at school*
	mâcher de chewing-gum	*chew gum*	
	porter de bijoux	*wear jewellery*	
	porter de maquillage	*wear make-up*	
	sécher les cours	*skip lessons*	

LANGUAGE AWARENESS

Devoir, *"must"* or *"to have to"*, is a modal verb in French. This modal is used to talk about what you must do, as opposed to ***pouvoir** (what you are able to do)* and ***vouloir** (what you want to do)*. Like ***pouvoir*** and ***vouloir***, it is also a Radical Changing/Boot verb. Check the next box to see what the **Radical Change** looks like for this boot verb.

Devoir: Radical Changing Verb

Je d**oi**s	Nous d**e**vons
I must	*We must*
Tu d**oi**s	Vous d**e**vez
You must	*You guys/girls must*
Il / Elle d**oi**t	Ils / Elles d**oi**vent
He / She must	*They must*

 **THE LANGUAGE GYM**

1. Match

Être à l'heure	*To participate in class*
Manger sainement	*To be on time*
Suivre le règlement	*To wear a uniform*
Respecter les profs	*To do the laundry*
Participer en classe	*To criticise my sister*
Être attentif	*To be rude*
Critiquer ma sœur	*To eat healthily*
Porter un uniforme	*To respect teachers*
Être impoli(e)	*To be attentive*
Faire la lessive	*To follow the policy*

2. Gapped (English) translation

a. _____ *do my homework at home*

   Je dois faire mes devoirs chez moi

b. *I must _____ the school policy*

   Je dois suivre le règlement intérieur

c. _____ *wear make-up*

   Je ne dois jamais porter de maquillage

d. *I must eat _____ at home*

   Je dois manger sainement chez moi

e. *I must _____ the teachers*

   Je dois respecter les professeurs

f. *I must never _____ my sister*

   Je ne dois jamais critiquer ma sœur

3. Complete with the missing verb and translate into English

a. Ce soir, je dois _ _ _ _ _ mes devoirs

b. Chez moi je dois _ _ _ _ _ _ la poubelle

c. Je dois _ _ _ _ attentif au collège

d. Je dois _ _ _ _ _ _ un uniforme scolaire

e. Je ne dois jamais _ _ _ _ _ _ les cours

f. Je dois toujours _ _ _ _ à l'heure

g. Chez moi, je dois _ _ _ _ _ _ sainement

h. Je dois _ _ _ _ _ _ le règlement intérieur

i. Je dois _ _ _ _ _ _ _ mes professeurs

4. Break the flow

a. Jedoisrangermachambreetfairelavaisselle

b. Jedoisêtreaucollègeàl'heure

c. Aucollègejedoissuivrelerèglementintérieur

d. Chezmoijenedoispasmangerdanslachambre

e. Chezmoijenedoisjamaiscritiquermasœur

f. Aucollègejedoisrespectermesprofesseurs

g. Chezmoijedoistoujoursmangersainement

h. Jedoisporterununiformescolaireaucollège

i. Aucollègejedoisêtreattentifenclasse

j. Jenedoisjamaisfumerchezmoiouaucollège

5. Faulty translation: fix the English translation

a. Je dois être à l'heure au collège — *I must stay in school after lessons*

b. Je dois être attentive en cours — *I must be sleepy in lessons*

c. Je ne dois pas fumer chez moi ou au collège — *I shouldn't smoke at home or at school*

d. Je dois suivre le règlement intérieur — *I must respect the home policy*

e. Je dois participer en cours et être attentif — *I can chat in lessons and be talkative*

f. Au collège, je dois porter un uniforme scolaire — *At school, I must wear a uniform*

g. Chez moi, je dois manger sainement — *At home, I must eat junk food*

h. Chez moi, je ne dois jamais critiquer ma sœur — *At home, I should not criticise my sister*

6. Insert the missing letters then listen and check

a. J__ d_i_ ê_____ à l'__u_e *I must be on time*

b. J__ d_____ f_i__ l_ v____s_l__ *I must do the washing up*

c. J__ d_____ m_n___ s_n_e__ *I must eat healthily*

d. J__ d_____ p_t_i___e__ c__r_ *I must participate in lessons*

e. J__ d_____ r_s__c_e_l__ é_è____ *I must respect students*

f. J__ n_ d_____ j__a_s f_____ *I must never smoke*

7. Split sentences

Je ne dois pas sécher	sainement
Je dois respecter les	fumer
Au collège, je dois être	les cours
Chez moi, je dois manger	mon frère
Je dois faire	de bijoux
Je ne dois jamais	en classe
Je ne dois pas porter	élèves
Je ne dois pas critiquer	mes devoirs
Je dois participer	attentif

8. Translate into English

a. Chez moi, je dois faire la lessive et la vaisselle

b. Au collège, je dois respecter les professeurs

c. Je ne dois pas manger dans ma chambre

d. Je ne dois jamais critiquer mes parents

e. Au collège, je dois porter un uniforme scolaire

f. Chez moi, je dois manger sainement

g. Au collège, je dois participer en classe

h. Chez moi, je dois passer l'aspirateur le soir

9. Sentence puzzle

a. je professeurs dois collège écouter Au mes *At school I must listen to my teachers*

b. ne au jamais être Je collège impoli chez dois moi ou *I must never be rude at home or at school*

c. collège règlement je intérieur Au suivre dois le *At school I must follow the school policy*

d. dois en attentif classe participer et Je être *I must participate in class and be attentive*

e. sainement Je manger au dois petit déjeuner *I must eat healthily for breakfast*

10. Translate into French, and then listen to check:

a. At home, I must always do the washing-up

b. At school, I must always be on time

c. I must participate in class and be attentive

d. I must never smoke or drink alcohol

e. I must never criticise my cousins

f. I must respect my teachers and the students

g. At school, I must wear a school uniform

h. I must listen to my teachers and be attentive

i. At home, I must tidy my room and do my bed

j. I must never eat in my bedroom at home

 THE LANGUAGE GYM

DEVOIR: *MUST / TO HAVE TO*

Je *I*	**dois** *must*	**faire la lessive** **faire la vaisselle** **laver la voiture** **manger sainement** **nettoyer le sol** **passer l'aspirateur** **ranger la chambre** **sortir la poubelle** **tondre la pelouse**	*do the laundry* *do the washing up* *wash the car* *eat healthily* *clean the floor* *do the vacuuming* *tidy the bedroom* *take the rubbish out* *cut the grass*	**après les cours** *after lessons* **de temps en temps** *from time to time* **les lundis** *on Mondays* **les mardis** **les mercredis** **les jeudis**
Tu *You*	**dois** *must*	**écouter les professeurs** **être à l'heure** **être attentif / attentive** **faire mes devoirs** **participer en classe** **porter un uniforme scolaire** **respecter les élèves** **respecter les professeurs** **suivre le règlement intérieur**	*listen to the teachers* *be on time* *be attentive* *do my homework* *participate in class* *wear a school uniform* *respect students* *respect teachers* *follow the school policy*	**les vendredis** **les samedis** **les dimanches** **toujours** *always* **tous les jours** *every day* **une fois par semaine** *once a week*
Il *He* **Elle** *She*	**doit** *must*			

LANGUAGE AWARENESS
DEVOIR + INFINITIVE

When using the modal verb *devoir*, you can only combine it with a verb in the **infinitive.** Example:

- **Je dois <u>ÊTRE</u> à l'heure**
  I must <u>BE</u> on time

- **Tu dois <u>RESPECTER</u> les professeurs**
  You must <u>RESPECT</u> the teachers

- **Il doit <u>FAIRE</u> la lessive**
  He must <u>DO</u> the laundry

A COMMON MISTAKE
ILLEGAL COMBINATION!

In French, we never place two conjugated verbs together. Verb structures usually work together with an infinitive:

- **Je dois ALLER** *I must / I have to <u>go</u>*
- **J'aime ALLER** *I like <u>to go</u>*

If you use a present tense verb after **je dois (or je peux & je veux)**, you create an incorrect structure:

- ***Je dois <u>JE VAIS</u>** *I must <u>I go</u>*

*Please don't write this

1. Match

Respecter les professeurs	To go to the library
Porter un uniforme scolaire	To wear make-up
Être attentif/ve	To clean the floor
Porter du maquillage	To skip lessons
Écouter les professeurs	To listen to teachers
Être à l'heure	To be attentive
Sécher les cours	To cut the grass
Aller à la bibliothèque	To wear a school uniform
Nettoyer le sol	To be on time
Manger sainement	To respect the teachers
Tondre la pelouse	To eat healthily

3. Sentence Puzzle

a. bibliothèque dois à la Je une aller fois par semaine
I must go to the library once a week

b. doit ne collège pas fumer au Il
He mustn't smoke at school

c. ne Elle de porter jamais au maquillage doit collège
She must never wear make-up in school

d. cours ne sécher jamais Je dois les
I must never skip lessons

e. porter au doit un uniforme Il scolaire les jours tous collège
He must wear a school uniform every day at school

f. elle la mercredis faire Les doit la et vaisselle lessive
On Wednesdays she must do the washing-up and the laundry

2. Complete the words with the missing vowels, then listen and check

a. J__ n_ d____ s p_ s s_ ch_ r l_ s c___ rs
I must not skip lessons

b. J__ n_ d____ sp_ s c___ r r d_ ns l_ s
c__ __l __ rs *I mustn't run in the corridors*

c. E_ l_ n_ d____ t p_ s p_ rt_ r d__
m_ q___ ll_ g__ *She mustn't wear make-up*

d. J__ d___ s ê____ ___ a___ e___ i__
I must be attentive

e. I_ d__ t p_ r___ c___ e__ e__ c_ u__ __
He must participate in lessons

f. J__ d___ s f___ r_ m__ d_ __ o___ __
I must do my homework

g. T_ n_ d____ s p_ s __ t_ l_ s_ r t_ n
p__ rt__ bl__ *You mustn't use your mobile*

h. I_ d_ i_ r___ p_ c___ r l_ s é___ v___
He must respect the students

i. J__ d____ r____ g__ m_ c__ m__ e
I must tidy my bedroom

j. I__ d____ t l_ v___ l_ v___ t___ ___
He must wash the car

k. J__ n_ d____ s p_ s f_ m_ r
I must not smoke

4. Listen and underline the words you hear

a. Je dois **faire la vaisselle/laver la voiture/tondre la pelouse** après les cours **tous les jours/les lundis/une fois par semaine**

b. **Elle ne doit/Je ne dois/Il ne doit** jamais fumer au collège

c. Il doit **être attentif/être à l'heure/participer en classe** au collège **de temps en temps/une fois par semaine/tous les jours**

d. **Je dois/Il doit/Elle doit** porter un uniforme au collège **les lundis/les mercredis/tous les jours**

e. Elle doit **passer l'aspirateur/nettoyer le sol/tondre la pelouse** après les cours **les lundis/une fois par semaine/les mardis**

THE LANGUAGE GYM

5. Faulty translation: fix the English translation

a. Je dois respecter les professeurs et les élèves et être à l'heure tous les jours

I must respect teachers and students and be on time during the day

b. Au collège, il doit toujours participer en cours et porter un uniforme scolaire

At school, he must sometimes be attentive in lessons and wear a school uniform

c. Elle ne doit jamais porter de maquillage ni courir dans les couloirs au collège

She can never wear jewellery nor run in the classrooms at school

d. Les lundis et les mardis, je dois passer l'aspirateur et tondre la pelouse

On Tuesdays and Wednesdays, I must do the vacuuming and cut the grass

e. Il doit faire les devoirs tous les jours après les cours et nettoyer le sol le soir

He must do the homework from time to time after lessons and clean the floor in the morning

f. Au collège, elle doit toujours respecter les professeurs et suivre le règlement intérieur

At school, she must sometimes respect teachers and follow the students policy

6. Gapped translation: complete the translation

a. Au collège je _____ faire les _____ …   *At school I must do homework…*

b. à la bibliothèque _____ les _____   *in the library after lessons*

c. Après les cours je _____ _____ à…   *After lessons I must go to…*

d. __ _____ pour _____ les devoirs   *the library in order to do homework*

e. Chez moi, je _____ ranger ___ _____   *At home, I must tidy my room….*

f. et toujours _____ ____ _____   *and always take the rubbish out*

g. Mon frère ne doit pas _____ les cours…   *My brother must not skip lessons…*

h. au collège et il ne _____ jamais _____   *at school and he must never smoke*

i. Chez moi, ma sœur _____ manger _____   *At home my sister must eat healthily*

j. et _____ les devoirs _____ ___ _____   *and do the homework every day*

7. Complete with the correct verb

a. Je ne dois pas _____ de chewing-gum

b. Je dois _____ attentif en cours

c. Il doit _____ le règlement intérieur

d. Elle doit toujours _____ sainement

e. Je ne dois jamais _____ les cours

f. Les lundis, je dois _____ la pelouse

g. Je dois toujours _____ à l'heure en cours

h. Je dois souvent _____ la vaisselle

i. Il ne doit jamais _____ impoli

j. Elle doit toujours _____ en classe

k. Les jeudis je dois _____ l'aspirateur

l. Une fois par semaine je dois _____ le sol

m. Il doit _____ un uniforme scolaire

n. Elle ne doit jamais _____ de maquillage

THE LANGUAGE GYM

8. Find the French translation and write it next to the English prompts

j	e	n	e	d	o	i	s	p	a	s	ê	t	r	e	i	m	p	o	l	i	u	g	h	n
h	e	l	p	u	e	d	o	h	a	c	e	r	p	e	s	a	s	b	o	r	i	n	g	o
g	a	e	p	e	u	x	d	e	t	e	m	p	s	e	n	t	e	m	p	s	n	u	t	p
s	j	e	d	o	i	s	r	a	n	g	e	r	m	a	c	h	a	m	b	r	e	a	v	u
j	e	p	e	u	x	u	t	i	l	i	s	e	r	m	o	n	p	o	r	t	a	b	l	e
b	y	e	l	l	e	d	o	i	t	ê	t	r	e	a	t	t	e	n	t	i	v	e	i	d
n	t	r	i	l	d	o	i	t	ê	t	r	e	à	l'	h	e	u	r	e	o	i	r	s	o
o	r	e	x	f	c	a	r	j	e	n	e	p	e	u	x	p	a	s	f	u	m	e	r	c
j	e	n	e	d	o	i	s	p	a	s	s	é	c	h	e	r	l	e	s	c	o	u	r	s
e	i	b	w	r	m	o	n	i	f	r	u	w	d	e	h	t	n	u	m	s	i	c	a	r
i	l	n	e	d	o	i	t	p	a	s	f	u	m	e	r	a	u	c	o	l	l	è	g	e
n	r	e	j	h	i	l	d	o	i	t	ê	t	r	e	à	l	'	h	e	u	r	e	t	e
e	l	l	e	n	e	d	o	i	t	p	a	s	b	o	i	r	e	e	n	c	o	u	r	s

a. I mustn't be rude

b. I mustn't skip lessons

c. He must be on time

d. She must be attentive

e. I must tidy my bedroom

f. She mustn't drink in lessons

g. He mustn't smoke in school

h. From time to time

9. Tangled translation: translate into French

a. Je ne dois pas *wear make-up*

b. Elle doit toujours *listen* les *teachers*

c. Je ne *must* pas courir dans les *corridors*

d. Il ne doit *never smoke* au collège

e. Je dois *to wear* un *school uniform*

f. *He must not* être *rude*

g. *She must* participer en *lessons*

h. Je dois *be* à l'heure *every day*

i. Je ne *must* pas *skip* les cours

j. *On Mondays,* elle doit *cut the grass*

k. Il doit *clean* le sol *from time to time*

l. *I must* laver la voiture *once a week*

10. Translate into English

a. Je ne dois pas courir dans les couloirs

b. Il doit faire les devoirs tous les jours

c. Elle doit toujours écouter et respecter les professeurs et les élèves

d. Je dois ranger ma chambre de temps en temps

e. Les mercredis, il doit tondre la pelouse

f. Une fois par semaine, elle doit faire la lessive

g. Je ne dois pas porter de maquillage au collège

h. Je dois manger sainement tous les jours

11. Translate into French

a. I must not be rude at home or at school

b. He must be on time every day at school

c. He must always listen and respect teachers

d. She must do the vacuuming once a week

e. She must never use her mobile in school

f. I must be attentive and participate in lessons

g. On Sundays, I must often tidy my room

h. He mustn't skip lessons or smoke at school

9.11 – DEVOIR (ALL PERSONS) + INFINITIVE + NOUN PHRASE + TIME MARKER
(WHAT ONE MUST DO AND WHEN)

DEVOIR					
Je *I*	**dois** *must*	aller au cinéma	*go to the cinema*		**après les cours** *after lessons* **de temps en temps** *from time to time* **le matin** *in the morning* **le soir** *in the evening* **les lundis** *on Mondays* **les mardis** **les mercredis** **les jeudis** **les vendredis** **les samedis** **les dimanches** **toujours** *always* **tous les jours** *every day* **une fois par semaine** *once a week*
		aller au parc	*go to the park*		
		boire de l'eau	*drink water*		
		cuisiner	*cook*		
Tu *You*	**dois** *must*	déjeuner	*have lunch*		
		dîner	*have dinner*		
		jouer au foot	*play football*		
		prendre le petit déjeuner	*have breakfast*		
		sortir avec mes amis	*go out with my friends*		
Il *He* **Elle** *She*	**doit** *must*	faire la lessive	*do the laundry*		
		faire la vaisselle	*do the washing up*		
		laver la voiture	*wash the car*		
		manger sainement	*eat healthily*		
Nous *We*	**devons** *must*	nettoyer le sol	*clean the floor*		
		passer l'aspirateur	*do the vacuuming*		
		ranger ma chambre	*tidy my bedroom*		
		sortir la poubelle	*take the rubbish out*		
		tondre la pelouse	*cut the grass*		
Vous *You guys* *You girls*	**devez** *must*	écouter les professeurs	*listen to the teachers*		
		être à l'heure	*be on time*		
		être attentif(s) / attentive(s)	*be attentive*		
		faire les devoirs	*do the homework*		
Ils *They (m)* **Elles** *They (f)*	**doivent** *must*	participer en classe	*participate in class*		
		porter un uniforme scolaire	*wear a school uniform*		
		respecter les élèves	*respect students*		
		respecter les professeurs	*respect teachers*		
		suivre le règlement intérieur	*follow the school policy*		

THE LANGUAGE GYM

1. Match

Je dois	You guys must
Tu dois	They must
Il / Elle doit	I must
Nous devons	He/She must
Vous devez	We must
Ils / Elles doivent	You must

2. Choose the correct form of *devoir*

a. Mon père **dois/devons/doit** cuisiner le week-end

b. Ma sœur ne **doit/devez/doivent** jamais être impolie

c. Je ne **doivent/doit/dois** pas aller au ciné aujourd'hui

d. Mes parents ne **doit/doivent/devons** pas jouer au tennis

e. Nous ne **devez/devons/doivent** pas fumer au collège

f. Elles **doit/doivent/doit** participer en cours et être à l'heure

g. Les lundis, je **dois/doit/devons** faire mes devoirs le soir

h. Tu **doit/dois/devez** tondre la pelouse tous les jours?

i. Mes sœurs **devons/devez/doivent** aller au parc ce matin

j. Mon père et moi **devez/doivent/devons** laver la voiture

3. Listen and write the verb you hear

a. Mon père _____ cuisiner le soir

b. Mon frère ne _____ pas aller au parc

c. Vous ne _____ pas être impolis

d. Nous _____ aller au cinéma les lundis

e. Ils ne _____ pas fumer au collège

f. Je _____ nettoyer le sol le week-end

g. Mes frères _____ passer l'aspirateur

h. Mes parents _____ manger sainement

i. Vous _____ faire la vaisselle le soir

j. Que _____-tu faire aujourd'hui?

4. Spot and correct the wrong forms of *devoir*

a. Mon frère ne dois pas jouer au foot aujourd'hui

b. Mes sœurs ne doit pas fumer au collège

c. Je doit faire mes devoirs le week-end chez moi

d. Ma sœur doivent aller au ciné ce soir

e. Mes parents devons manger sainement

f. Qu'est-ce que tu devez faire aujourd'hui?

g. Mon ami Jean et moi doit être attentifs

h. Vous ne dois jamais sécher les cours ou fumer

i. Ma sœur devons suivre le règlement intérieur

j. Mon amie Juliette dois tondre la pelouse

5. Complete the sentences, and then listen to check

a. Je n__ do__ __ p__ssé__h___ l___ c_u__ __

b. Il n__ d_i__ jam_____ f_m___ a_c_l_____

c. M__ s___u__ do__ __ m__g___ s__n_m____

d. Me__ par_____ doi_____ d____u__e__

e. Me__ f___r__s doi_____ cuis_____ le s__i__

f. Vous dev___ t__j_u___ ê_r___ à l'___u____

g. J__ n__ do_____ p___ b___r d'__c__l

h. Tu d_____ r__p__t_r_l_s_p_o___s_e___

6. Translate into French

a. I must

b. She must

c. You must not

d. They must never

e. He must

f. I must never

g. We must not

h. They must

i. Do you guys must/have to?

THE LANGUAGE GYM

279

7. Insert the missing letters then listen and check

a. No___ d_v____ ê____ à l'__u__e   *We must be on time*

b. V_u_ d_v__f_i__ l_v_s__l   *You guys must do the washing up*

c. Il_ d_i____ m_n___ s_n_e__   *They must eat healthily*

d. El____ d____e_t al____ a__ c_n____   *They must go to the cinema*

e. No_s d___o_s r_s__c_e_ l__ é_è____   *We must respect students*

f. V____ n__d__e_ j__a_s f_____   *You guys must never smoke*

---

8. Split sentences

Je ne dois pas sécher	sainement
Elle doit respecter les	fumer
Au collège, il doit être	les cours
Chez moi, je dois manger	mon frère
Je dois toujours faire	de bijoux
Nous ne devons jamais	en classe
Vous ne devez pas porter	élèves
Je ne dois pas critiquer	mes devoirs
Elles doivent participer	attentif

9. Translate into English

a. Chez moi, je dois faire la lessive et la vaisselle

b. Au collège, il doit écouter les professeurs

c. Elle ne doit pas manger dans sa chambre

d. Nous ne devons jamais critiquer nos parents

e. Au collège, il doit porter un uniforme scolaire

f. Chez moi, nous devons manger sainement

g. Au collège, elles doivent participer en cours

h. Le week-end, vous devez tondre le gazon

---

10. Sentence puzzle

a. je professeurs dois collège écouter Au mes   *At school I have to listen to my teachers*

b. ne au jamais être Il collège impoli doit   *He must never be rude at school*

c. collège règlement nous intérieur Au suivre devons le   *At school we must follow the school policy*

d. doivent toujours attentifs participer et Ils être   *They must always participate and be attentive*

e. sainement Vous manger au devez dîner   *You guys must eat healthily for dinner*

---

11. Translate into French, and then listen to check

a. At home, I must always cut the grass

b. At school, he must always be on time

c. She must participate in class and be attentive

d. We must never smoke or drink alcohol

e. He must never criticise my cousins

f. They must respect the teachers and the students

g. At school, we must wear a school uniform

h. You must listen to the teachers and be attentive

i. You girls must wash the car every Monday

j. They must never eat and drink in the bedroom

POUVOIR – VOULOIR - DEVOIR			
Je *I*	**peux** *can* **dois** *must* **veux** *want*	**aller au cinéma** *go to the cinema* **aller au parc** *go to the park* **boire de l'eau** *to drink water* **cuisiner** *to cook* **déjeuner** *have lunch*	**après les cours** *after lessons* **de temps en temps** *from time to time*
Tu *You*	**peux** *can* **dois** *must* **veux** *want*	**dîner** *have dinner* **faire les magasins** *go shopping* **jouer au foot** *play football* **prendre le petit déjeuner** *have breakfast* **sortir avec mes amis** *go out with my friends*	**le matin** *in the morning* **le soir** *in the evening*
Il *He* **Elle** *She*	**peut** *can* **doit** *must* **veut** *wants*	**faire la lessive** *do the laundry* **faire la vaisselle** *do the washing up* **laver la voiture** *wash the car* **manger sainement** *eat healthily* **nettoyer le sol** *clean the floor*	**les lundis** *on Mondays* **les mardis** **les mercredis**
Nous *We*	**pouvons** *can* **devons** *must* **voulons** *want*	**passer l'aspirateur** *do the vacuuming* **ranger ma* chambre** *tidy my bedroom* **sortir la poubelle** *take the rubbish out* **tondre la pelouse** *cut the grass*	**les jeudis** **les vendredis** **les samedis**
Vous *You guys* *You girls*	**pouvez** *can* **devez** *must* **voulez** *want*	**écouter les professeurs** *listen to the teachers* **être à l'heure** *be on time* **être attentif(s) / attentive(s)** *be attentive* **faire les devoirs** *do the homework*	**les dimanches** **toujours** *always* **tous les jours** *every day*
Ils *They (m)* **Elles** *They (f)*	**peuvent** *can* **doivent** *must* **veulent** *want*	**participer en classe** *participate in class* **porter un uniforme scolaire** *wear a school uniform* **respecter les élèves** *respect students* **respecter les professeurs** *respect teachers* **suivre le règlement intérieur** *follow the school policy*	**une fois par semaine** *once a week*

THE LANGUAGE GYM

1. Conjugate the modal verbs *pouvoir, devoir, vouloir* for each subject pronoun

	Pouvoir	Vouloir	Devoir
Je			
Tu			
Il / Elle / On			
Nous			
Vous			
Ils / Elles			

2. Choose the correct pronoun

a. **Nous/Vous/Ils** devons respecter les professeurs

b. **Elles/Tu/Nous** veulent aller au ciné ce soir

c. **Tu/Nous/Vous** pouvez jouer au foot le week-end?

d. Ma tante, **elle/il/elles** ne veut jamais cuisiner

e. **Tu/Vous/Il** veux jouer au basket avec tes cousins?

f. **Nous/Vous/Ils** doivent être à l'heure tous les jours

g. **Je/Vous/Nous** pouvons souvent sortir le week-end

h. **Elle/Ils/Elles** ne veut pas ranger sa chambre

i. **Ils/Je/Vous** voulez aller au parc de temps en temps

3. Listen. Spot the missing pronoun. 🔊 Write it in and then translate into English

a. Le soir, devons toujours faire la vaisselle

b. De temps en temps, jouez au foot le soir

c. Tous les week-ends, veut aller au cinéma avec ses amis car il adore ça

d. Moi, dois manger sainement chez moi

e. Le matin, doivent prendre le petit déjeuner et manger sainement

f. Au collège, ne peut pas fumer car il faut suivre le règlement intérieur

g. Une fois par semaine, veux aller au parc

4. Sentence Puzzle

a. week-ends Nous faire du voulons tous sport les — *We want to do sport every weekend*

b. peux sortir amis souvent Je avec vendredi mes le — *I can often go out with my friends on Friday*

c. peut temps plage à de aller la Elle temps en — *She can go to the beach from time to time*

d. Vous professeurs respecter devez les toujours — *You guys must always respect teachers*

e. suivre Ils intérieur le collège règlement doivent au — *They must follow the school policy at school*

f. que week-end tu faire le veux Qu'est-ce? — *What do you want to do at the weekend?*

g. lessive la peux nettoyer Tu le sol et faire? — *Can you clean the floor and do the laundry?*

h. rien Je faire le veux week-end ne — *I don't want to do anything at the weekend*

i. Vous tous manger jours sainement devez les — *You guys must eat healthily every day*

5. Faulty translation: fix the French translation

a. *My cousins do not want to clean the floor* — Mes frères ne doivent pas nettoyer le sol

b. *Do you guys want to go to the cinema today?* — Vous devez aller au ciné ce week-end?

c. *She wants to watch a film and have a tea* — Elle peut regarder un film et manger un sandwich

d. *They don't want to do the washing up...* — Ils ne peuvent pas faire la lessive

e. *...on Friday evenings* — ...les jeudis soir

f. *My cousins must always take the rubbish out* — Mes parents veulent toujours sortir la poubelle

g. *We want to be on time every day* — Nous devons être à l'heure tous les jours

6. Listen and complete the table

	Person	**Modal**	**Infinitive + Action**		**Time expression**
Exemple	*Je*	*veux*	*aller*	*au parc*	*de temps en temps*
a.					
b.					
c.					
d.					
e.					
f.					
g.					

7. One of three

		1	2	3
a.	Tu dois	*You can*	*You must*	*You want*
b.	Nous pouvons	*We want*	*We can*	*We must*
c.	Il veut	*He can*	*He wants*	*He must*
d.	Elles doivent	*They can*	*They must*	*They want*
e.	Je peux	*I want*	*I must*	*I can*
f.	On doit	*One must*	*One can*	*One wants*
g.	Vous voulez	*You want*	*You must*	*You can*
h.	Ils peuvent	*They want*	*They can*	*They must*
i.	Tu veux	*You can*	*You must*	*You want*
j.	Nous devons	*We want*	*We can*	*We must*
k.	Vous pouvez	*You want*	*You must*	*You can*
l.	On peut	*One must*	*One can*	*One wants*

8. Anagrams

a. lEle evut laler ua incméa

b. uNos dveson rlvae al oituvre

c. eJ dosi fraie esm drveois

d. lI etuv orntde al elpeous

e. oVsu edevz êetr à hel'ure

f. sIl veulten alrle ua apcr

g. oNsu en oupnvos aps ortisr

h. nO en dtoi psa séhecr sle cosur

i. eJ uxpe rtsoir eavc ems aemis

j. uT osdi etêr atiftent ne orscu

9. Staircase translation – Translate each sentence from memory

a.	I want to go	to the cinema				
b.	My sisters must	be on time to lessons	every day			
c.	We must respect	the teachers	and we must also	be attentive in lessons		
d.	They can have lunch	at school	every day	but they must	eat healthily	
e.	You guys must never	smoke or drink alcohol.	You must follow the school policy	and you must always	do your homework	every day after lessons

a. _____

b. _____

c. _____

d. _____

e. _____

10. Translate this dialogue in French

a. Hi Jérôme. How are you? Do you want to go to the cinema with Nadim and I today?	_____ _____ _____
_____ _____ _____	b. Hi Aurélie. Yes I am fine and you? No, I can't. I must do the vacuuming and tidy my bedroom. Do you want to go out this weekend?
c. No I can't. I must do my homework this weekend. My brother and I must also cut the grass and clean the floor.	_____ _____ _____ _____
_____ _____ _____	d. Oh no, it's terrible! Do you want to skip lessons on Tuesday and play football with me? The Spanish teacher, Mr. Dylan, is boring!
e. No, one must not skip lessons. You must also be on time, and you must respect all the teachers, even Mr Dylan!	_____ _____ _____

THE LANGUAGE GYM

284

ORAL PING PONG

MODAL VERBS

ENGLISH 1	FRENCH 1	ENGLISH 2	FRENCH 2
I want to eat more vegetables and meat.	Je veux manger plus de légumes et de viande.	I want to eat a cheese sandwich and cake.	
I want to eat a burger and chips.	Je veux manger un burger et des frites.	My friends want to have roast chicken for dinner, but I want fish.	
She can never wear make-up or run in the corridors.	Elle ne peut jamais porter de maquillage ni courir dans les couloirs.	My friends want to play on the computer in the evening.	
We can't do athletics on Thursdays. We do it at weekends.	Nous ne pouvons pas faire de l'athlétisme les jeudis. Nous en faisons les week-ends.	Can I borrow your dress this evening?	
My sister must go to the library every day after school, but I mustn't.	Ma sœur doit aller à la bibliothèque tous les jours après les cours, mais je ne dois pas.	I mustn't chew gum or run in the classrooms.	
I would like to have fish and fries for lunch.	Je voudrais prendre du poisson et des frites pour le déjeuner.	One mustn't be rude in my school.	
My brother never wants to make the bed or cut the grass at home.	Mon frère ne veut jamais faire le lit ou tondre la pelouse à la maison.	Do you want to have a coffee?	
Can I go out tonight with my boyfriend? We want to go to the cinema.	Je peux sortir ce soir avec mon petit ami? Nous voulons aller au cinéma.	I don't want to tidy up my room at the weekends, but I do it.	

INSTRUCTIONS - You are **PARTNER A.** Work in pairs. Each of you has two sets of sentences - one set has already been translated for you. You will ask your partner to translate these. The other set of sentences have not been translated. Your partner will ask you to translate these.

HOW TO PLAY - Partner A starts by reading out his/her/their first sentence <u>in English</u>. Partner B must translate. Partner A must check the answer and award the following points: **3 points** = perfect, **2 points** = 1 mistake, **1 point** = mistakes but the verb is accurate. If they cannot translate correctly, Partner A will read out the sentence so that Partner B can learn what the correct translation is.

Then Partner B reads out his/her/their first sentence, and so on.

OBJECTIVE - Try to win more points than your partner by translating correctly as many sentences as possible.

 **THE LANGUAGE GYM**

ORAL PING PONG

MODAL VERBS

ENGLISH 1	FRENCH 1	ENGLISH 2	FRENCH 2
I want to eat more vegetables and meat.		I want to eat a cheese sandwich and cake.	Je veux manger un sandwich au fromage et du gâteau.
I want to eat a burger and chips.		My friends want to have roast chicken for dinner, but I want fish.	Mes amis veulent prendre du poulet rôti pour le dîner, mais je veux du poisson.
I can never wear make-up nor run in the corridors.		My friends want to play on the computer in the evening.	Mes amis veulent jouer sur l'ordinateur le soir.
We can't do athletics on Thursdays. We do it at weekends.		Can I borrow your dress this evening?	Je peux emprunter ta robe ce soir?
My sister can go to the library every day after school, but I can't.		I mustn't chew gum or run in the classrooms.	Je ne dois pas mâcher de chewing-gum ou courir dans les couloirs.
I would like to have fish and chips for lunch.		One mustn't be rude in my school.	On ne doit pas être impoli dans mon école.
My brother never wants to make the bed or cut the grass at home.		Do you want to have a coffee?	Tu veux prendre un café?
Can I go out tonight with my boyfriend? We want to go to the cinema.		I don't want to tidy up my room at the weekends, but I do it.	Je ne veux pas ranger ma chambre les week-ends, mais je le fais.

INSTRUCTIONS - You are **PARTNER B.** Work in pairs. Each of you has two sets of sentences - one set has already been translated for you. You will ask your partner to translate these. The other set of sentences have not been translated. Your partner will ask you to translate these.

HOW TO PLAY - Partner A starts by reading out his/her/their first sentence <u>in English</u>. Partner B must translate. Partner A must check the answer and award the following points: **3 points** = perfect, **2 points** = 1 mistake, **1 point** = mistakes but the verb is accurate. If they cannot translate correctly, Partner A will read out the sentence so that Partner B can learn what the correct translation is.
Then Partner B reads out his/her/their first sentence, and so on.

OBJECTIVE - Try to win more points than your partner by translating correctly as many sentences as possible.

 THE LANGUAGE GYM

No Snakes No Ladders

MODAL VERBS

7 Je ne dois pas être impoli(e)	**8** On ne peut pas courir dans les couloirs	**23** Ils doivent prendre une tartine ce matin	**24** Tu veux du thé avec du lait?			
6 Ma mère veut manger plus de légumes	**9** Je peux sortir avec mon petit ami	**22** Je peux aller aux toilettes?	**25** Nous ne pouvons pas manger en classe			
5 Je veux manger du gâteau	**10** Mon frère veut un café	**21** Je ne veux pas aller au cinéma à vélo	**26** Je peux faire la vaisselle ce soir			
4 Je peux aller au cinéma?	**11** Je veux manger du riz	**20** Nous voulons prendre un café au lait	**27** Mes amis peuvent faire les magasins			
3 Mes amis veulent jouer aux jeux vidéo	**12** Mon frère veut faire les magasins	**19** Mes parents doivent sortir	**28** Mon ami veut un sandwich au poulet			
2 Tu veux prendre un thé?	**13** Je veux sortir avec mes amis	**18** Il / Elle ne veut pas tondre la pelouse	**29** Ma sœur doit faire la lessive			
1 Je peux aller chez mon amie Anne	**14** Je veux des frites	**17** Nous voulons un burger	**30** Ils veulent du riz pour le déjeuner			
DÉPART	**15** Nous devons faire de la musculation	**16** Il ne doit pas mâcher de chewing-gum	**ARRIVÉE**			

THE LANGUAGE GYM

287

MODAL VERBS

No Snakes No Ladders

					7 I must not be rude	**8** We cannot run in the corridors
				6 My mother wants to eat more vegetables	**5** I want to eat cake	**9** I can go out with my boyfriend
			4 Can I go to the cinema?			**10** My brother wants a coffee
		3 My friends want to play videogames	**11** I want to eat rice	**12** My brother wants to go shopping	**13** I want to go out with my friends	
	2 Do you want to have a tea?					
1 I can go to my friend's Anne	**14** I want chips					

START

15 We must do weights

16 He must not chew gum

17 We want a burger

18 He/she doesn't want to cut the grass

19 My parents must go out

20 We want to have a coffee with milk

21 I don't want to go by bike to the cinema

22 Can I go to the toilet?

23 They must have toast this morning

24 Do you want tea with milk?

25 We cannot eat in the classroom.

26 I want to do the washing-up this evening

27 My friends can go shopping

28 My friend wants a chicken sandwich

29 My sister must do the laundry

30 They want rice for lunch

FINISH

PYRAMID TRANSLATION

MODAL VERBS

Translate each part of the pyramid out loud with your partner, then write it into the spaces provided below.

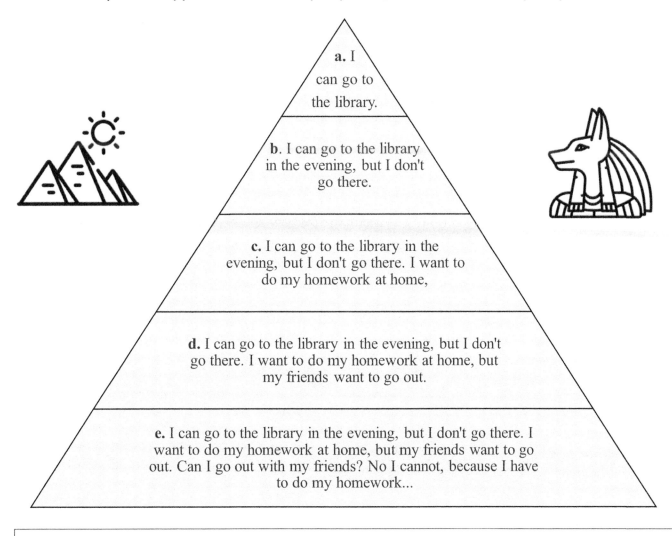

a. I can go to the library.

b. I can go to the library in the evening, but I don't go there.

c. I can go to the library in the evening, but I don't go there. I want to do my homework at home,

d. I can go to the library in the evening, but I don't go there. I want to do my homework at home, but my friends want to go out.

e. I can go to the library in the evening, but I don't go there. I want to do my homework at home, but my friends want to go out. Can I go out with my friends? No I cannot, because I have to do my homework...

Write your translation here

 **THE LANGUAGE GYM**